Hands-On Microsoft Windows Server 2003 Networking

Byron Wright

THOMSON

COURSE TECHNOLOGY

Australia • Canada • Mexico • Singapore • Spain • United Kingdom • United States

THOMSON

COURSE TECHNOLOGY

Hands-On Microsoft Windows Server 2003 Networking

is published by Course Technology

Senior Editor:
William Pitkin III

Manufacturing Coordinator:
Trevor Kallop

Editorial Assistant:
Nick Lombardi

Product Manager:
Charles G. Blum

MQA Technical Leader:
Nicole Ashton

Cover Design:
Julie Malone

Developmental Editor:
David George

Product Marketing Manager:
Jason Sakos

Text Designer:
GEX Publishing Services

Production Editor:
Anne Valsangiacomo

Associate Product Manager:
Tim Gleeson

Compositor:
GEX Publishing Services

Disclaimer
Course Technology reserves the right to revise this publication and make changes from time to time in its content without notice.

ISBN 0-619-18609-7

BRIEF
Contents

TABLE OF

Contents

CHAPTER THREE
TCP/IP Architecture   47

CHAPTER FOUR
Subnetting   69

Introduction

Welcome to *Hands-On Microsoft Windows Server 2003 Networking.* This book offers you real-world examples, interactive activities, and many hands-on projects that reinforce key concepts and help you prepare for a career in Microsoft network management. This book provides in-depth study of configuring, administering, and troubleshooting the services available within a network infrastructure. Throughout the book, we provide pointed review questions to reinforce the concepts introduced in each chapter. In addition to the review questions, we provide detailed hands-on projects that let you experience firsthand the processes involved in Windows Server 2003 configuration and management. Finally, to put a real-world slant on the concepts introduced in each chapter, we provide case studies to prepare you for situations that must be managed in a live networking environment.

Intended Audience

Hands-On Microsoft Windows Server 2003 Networking is intended for people who have some experience administering and supporting Windows Server 2003 network and directory services. To best understand the material in this book, you should have a background in basic computer concepts and have worked with the material presented in Course Technology's *Hands-On Microsoft Windows XP Professional* and *Hands-On Microsoft Windows Server 2003.*

Chapter Descriptions

Chapter 1, "Windows Server 2003 Networking Overview" provides an overview of new features, and introduces Windows Server 2003 networking services.

Chapter 2, "Networking Protocols" emphasizes the importance of proper TCP/IP configuration. It shows how to install and configure networking protocols including IPv4, IPv6, IPX/SPX, and AppleTalk.

Chapter 3, "TCP/IP Architecture" outlines how the different components of the TCP/IP protocol stack communicate. The purpose of each component is explored, including when each one is used.

Chapter 4, "Subnetting" introduces subnetting and explains how to divide a large IP network into smaller networks to implement routing. It also describes how supernetting is used to reduce routing complexity.

Chapter 5, "Dynamic Host Configuration Protocol", focuses on automating the configuration of network clients using TCP/IP. Service installation, scope creation, troubleshooting are explored.

Chapter 6, "Domain Name System" describes how to install and configure the Domain Name System service to support Active Directory and Internet services. It explains how to create primary, secondary, and Active Directory integrated zones.

Chapter 7, "Windows Internet Naming Service" explains how to support legacy Windows operating systems as clients with Windows Server 2003. Installation, configuration, and troubleshooting of Windows Internet Naming Service are covered.

Chapter 8, "Certificate Services" explains the role of cryptography in network services including how it relates to Public Key Infrastructure. The chapter also explains how to use Windows Server 2003 as a certification authority to create and distribute certificates perform authentication, encrypt data, and create digital signatures.

Chapter 9, "IP Security" outlines how the IPSec protocol can be used to provide data security on a network. It also describes how to enable and configure IPSec using IPSec policies.

Chapter 10, "Remote Access" describes how to configure Windows Server 2003 as both a dial-up server and virtual private network (VPN) server, as well as control user access. This chapter also outlines how to configure Windows Server 2003 to act as a Remote Authentication Dial-In User Service (RADIUS) server using Internet Authentication Service (IAS).

Chapter 11, "Routing" explains how to configure Windows Server 2003 as an IP router using standard network connections, and demand-dial connections. In addition, services that provide support for Internet connectivity are outlines, including Network Address Translation (NAT), Internet Connection Sharing (ICS), and Internet Connection Firewall (ICF).

Features and Approach

Hands-On Microsoft Windows Server 2003 Networking differs from other networking books in its unique hands-on approach and its orientation to real-world situations and problem solving. To help you comprehend how Microsoft Windows network management concepts and techniques are applied in real-world organizations, this book incorporates the following features:

- **Chapter Objectives**—Each chapter begins with a detailed list of the concepts to be mastered. This list gives you a quick reference to the chapter's contents and is a useful study aid.

- **Hands-on Activities**—Hands-on activities are incorporated throughout the text, giving you practice in setting up, managing, and troubleshooting a network system. The activities give you a strong foundation for carrying out network administration tasks in the real world. Because of the book's progressive nature, completing the hands-on activities in each chapter is essential before moving on to the end-of-chapter projects and subsequent chapters.

- **Chapter Summary**—Each chapter's text is followed by a summary of the concepts introduced in that chapter. These summaries provide a helpful way to recap and revisit the ideas covered in each chapter.

- **Key Terms**—All of the terms within the chapter that were introduced with boldfaced text are gathered together in the Key Terms list at the end of the chapter. This provides you with a method of checking your understanding of all the terms introduced.

- **Review Questions**—The end-of-chapter assessment begins with a set of review questions that reinforce the ideas introduced in each chapter. Answering these questions will ensure that you have mastered the important concepts.

- **Case Projects**—Finally, each chapter closes with a section that proposes certain situations. You are asked to evaluate the situations and decide upon the course of action to be taken to remedy the problems described. This valuable tool will help you sharpen your decision-making and troubleshooting skills, which are important aspects of network administration.

- **On the CD-ROM**—On the CD-ROM you will find a free 180-day evaluation copy of Windows Server 2003 Enterprise Edition.

Text and Graphic Conventions

Additional information and exercises have been added to this book to help you better understand what's being discussed in the chapter. Icons throughout the text alert you to these additional materials. The icons used in this book are described below.

 Tips offer extra information on resources, how to attack problems, and time-saving shortcuts.

 Notes present additional helpful material related to the subject being discussed.

 The Caution icon identifies important information about potential mistakes or hazards.

 Each Hands-on Activity in this book is preceded by the hands-on icon.

 Case project icons mark the end-of-chapter case projects, which are scenario-based assignments that ask you to independently apply what you have learned in the chapter.

Instructor's Resources

The following supplemental materials are available when this book is used in a classroom setting. All of the supplements available with this book are provided to the instructor on a single CD-ROM.

Electronic Instructor's Manual. The Instructor's Manual that accompanies this textbook includes Additional instructional material to assist in class preparation, including suggestions for classroom activities, discussion topics, and additional projects.

Solutions to all end-of-chapter material, including the Review Questions, and where applicable, Hands-on Activities and Discovery Exercises.

ExamView®. This textbook is accompanied by ExamView, a powerful testing software package that allows instructors to create and administer printed, computer (LAN-based), and Internet exams. ExamView includes hundreds of questions that correspond to the topics covered in this text, enabling students to generate detailed study guides that include page references for further review. The computer-based and Internet testing components allow students to take exams at their computers and also save the instructor time by grading each exam automatically.

PowerPoint presentations. This book comes with Microsoft PowerPoint slides for each chapter. These are included as a teaching aid for classroom presentation, to make available to students on the network for chapter review, or to be printed for classroom distribution. Instructors, please feel at liberty to add your own slides for additional topics you introduce to the class.

Figure files. All of the figures and tables in the book are reproduced on the Instructor's Resource CD, in bitmap format. Similar to the PowerPoint presentations, these are included as a teaching aid for classroom presentation, to make available to students for review, or to be printed for classroom distribution.

Minimum Lab Requirements

- **Hardware:**

Hardware Component	Requirement
CPU	Pentium III 533 or higher
Memory	256 MB RAM
Disk Space	Minimum 2GB (3GB if storing the installation files on local hard drive)
Drives	CD-ROM Floppy Disk
Networking	All labs assume a single instructor server acting as a domain controller. Two network cards are recommended to allow isolation from other networks. All student servers will be configured in pairs and must have two network cards to complete all of the exercises. The first network card is connected to the classroom network with the instructor server. The second network card is connected via crossover cable or hub to the other student server in the pair. Make sure to have Windows Server 2003-compatible network adapters. A connection to the Internet via some sort of NAT or Proxy server is assumed.

- **Software:**

  Windows Server 2003 Enterprise Edition for each computer

  The latest Windows Server 2003 Service Pack (if available)

- **Set Up Instructions:**

  To successfully complete the lab exercises, set up classroom computers as listed below:

  1. The instructor computer should initially be installed with default configuration options. The name of the server should be *Instructor*. The initial password should be *Password!*.

  2. After installation, rename one of the network connections as *Classroom* with an IP address of 192.168.1.10, a subnet mask of 255.255.255.0, and 192.168.1.10 as the DNS server. Rename the other connection as *External* and configure it with the appropriate IP address, subnet mask, and default gateway to allow access to the Internet. Configure routing and remote access and network address translation (if necessary) to allow access to the Internet. If network address translation is configured on this server then Classroom will be the internal interface, and External will be the external interface. For more information on how to configure network address translation please see Chapter 11.

  3. Configure the Instructor computer as a domain controller for the domain *Arctic.local*. When asked to create an Administrator password for the domain, use *Password!*. Allow the Active Directory installation wizard to automatically install DNS and create the domain. If the server does not detect Internet connectivity during the installation of Active Directory it will create a root domain on the instructor server. This will prevent the server from performing Internet DNS lookups. Delete the root domain if it is created.

  4. Install IIS on the Instructor computer and enable the processing of ASP scripts. This will be required for an exercise in Chapter 11. The final exercise in Chapter 11 contains step-by-step instructions on how to enable ASP scripts.

5. After IIS is installed, create the file **C:\inetpub\wwwroot\default.asp**. The contents of this file should be:

```
<html>
<body>

<p>Source IP address = <%=Request.ServerVariables("REMOTE_ADDR")%>
<p>Source TCP Port = <%=Request.ServerVariables("REMOTE_PORT")%>

<p>Server IP address = <%=Request.ServerVariables("LOCAL_ADDR")%>
<p>Server TCP Port = <%=Request.ServerVariables("SERVER_PORT")%>

</body>
</html>
```

6. Student servers should initially be installed with the default installation options. The name of each server should be *ServerXX*, where XX is a unique student number. The initial password should be *Password!*. This is the password of the Administrator account.

7. After installation, rename one of the network connections as *Classroom* with an IP address of 192.168.1.1XX, where XX is the same unique student number as used in the server name, a subnet mask of 255.255.255.0, a default gateway of 192.168.1.10, and a DNS Server of 192.168.1.10. Rename the second connection *Private*. The second connection can be left using default configuration.

8. Connect the Private connections between each pair of student computers with a crossover cable. Alternatively, they can be connected using straight cables and a hub or switch. During the course activities each pair of computers will be assigned a group number. Example, Server01 and Server02 will be group 1, Server03 and Server04 will be group 2.

9. On each student server, join the Arctic.local domain as a member server. Student servers should not be domain controllers.

10. To simplify the addition and removal of networking components during the course, copy the \I386 directory from the Windows Server 2003 CD-ROM to the root of the C: drive. Students can point to this directory when Windows Server 2003 requests the operating system CD-ROM. If this is done the minimum free hard drive space for the student computers rises to 3GB.

11. To make identification easier for students consider placing a paper label on the monitor of each server indicating the name of the server and the group number for that pair of computers.

12. It is important to remember that when performing the activities included in this book that the student logs in as the Administrator for the Arctic.local domain. The local Administrator accounts on the student member servers do not have enough privileges to complete some of the activities.

1

WINDOWS SERVER 2003
NETWORKING OVERVIEW

After reading this chapter and completing the exercises, you will be able to:

♦ Describe some of the new features of Windows Server 2003
♦ Understand the differences in the editions of Windows Server 2003
♦ Recognize the components in the Windows Server 2003 networking architecture
♦ List the networking services available in Windows Server 2003

To work with Windows Server 2003, you need to understand some basic concepts and acquire the skills that are needed, such as installing the operating system, adding users, and configuring services. This book focuses on networking features and services. The first section of this chapter introduces the Windows Server 2003 product family and Windows Server 2003 networking architecture, including the new features offered by both. More specific discussions of these topics are the subjects of later chapters. Networking protocols and services are outlined as well, and are covered in more depth later.

NEW FEATURES OF WINDOWS SERVER 2003

Windows Server 2003 is the latest **network operating system (NOS)** from Microsoft. It enhances many of the features found in Windows 2000 Server and adds new ones as well. Some of the features and services you will learn about in this book are outlined below:

- *Enhanced Active Directory*—**Active Directory** is now more flexible, manageable, and reliable. Flexibility has been enhanced with the addition of the ability to rename domains and deactivate **classes** and **attributes** in the **schema**. Manageability has been enhanced with the addition of cross-forest **trusts** and the ability to manage multiple user **objects** using Active Directory Users and Computers. Reliability has been enhanced through improvements to the **Intersite Topology Generator (ISTG)**, reduced **global catalog** synchronization, and the caching of global catalog information on **domain controllers** at remote offices.

- *.NET Framework*—Microsoft has introduced a new application development infrastructure with Windows Server 2003. Programmers can now develop applications in a variety of languages, such as C++, C#, or Visual Basic, which are then compiled and run by the **common language runtime (CLR)**. Using this framework, developers can create program components that can communicate with other components regardless of the language in which they were developed. In addition, the CLR monitors programs and safeguards the operating system from malicious or poorly designed code.

- *Web services*—Windows Server 2003 includes native support for XML Web services. Web services are a standardized way to develop application components that can be accessed across the Internet, and use Internet standards such as **Extensible Markup Language (XML)**, **Simple Object Access Protocol (SOAP)**, **Universal Description, Discovery, and Integration (UDDI)**, and **Web Services Description Language (WSDL)**.

- *Enhanced Clustering and Load Balancing*—The maximum **cluster** size has been increased from four nodes to eight nodes for the Enterprise and Datacenter versions of Windows Server 2003.

- *WebDAV support*—**Web Digital Authoring and Versioning (WebDAV)** allows documents to be shared and managed using **Hypertext Transfer Protocol (HTTP)**.

- *Automated System Recovery*—This allows a single step recovery of the operating system, system state, and hardware configuration.

- *Internet Information Server (IIS) 6.0*—The default configuration for IIS 6.0 is locked down to be more secure. In addition, it offers enhanced scalability and improved load balancing.

- *Internet Protocol version 6 (IPv6)*—IPv6 is the future of Internet connectivity and will replace the current **Internet Protocol version 4 (IPv4)** protocol over time. The implementation of IPv6 is designed to allow for backward compatibility with networks still running IPv4.

- *Point-to-Point Protocol Over Ethernet (PPPOE)*—PPPOE is used by many high-speed **Internet service providers (ISPs)** to control traffic on their networks. Windows Server 2003 can access these networks without installing third-party **client** software.

- *Network bridging*—Windows NT/2000 Server could be used as a **router** but not as a **bridge**. In smaller networks, Windows Server 2003 can be used as a bridge to allow multiple network segments to communicate without introducing the complexity of routing.

- *Wireless support*—Windows Server 2003 has built in support for wireless networks. This includes extensions to **Group Policy** that can push out wireless configuration information to clients and a **Microsoft Management Console (MMC) snap-in** to view wireless access statistics on clients or access points.

- *Enhanced IP Security (IPSec)*—IPSec has been enhanced to allow transmission of encrypted packets through **network address translation (NAT)**. Management of IPSec can now be accomplished through the command-line utility NETSH.

- *Internet Connection Firewall (ICF)*—ICF provides basic firewall protection for small businesses. It works with LAN, dial-up, **Virtual Private Network (VPN)**, and PPPOE connections.

- *Volume Shadow Copy*—This new feature is used by backup software to make a copy of files to be backed up. This system allows files to be backed up when they are open allowing an administrator to backup files while they are in use without errors.

- *Windows Media Services*—Windows Server 2003 includes the ability to provide streaming audio and video using Windows Media Services. This is used in combination with Windows Media Player on the client computers.

- *64-bit support*—The Enterprise and Datacenter versions of Windows Server 2003 support 64-bit processing on Intel **Itanium** Processors.

Activity 1-1: Comparing Windows 2000 Server and Windows Server 2003

Time Required: 10 minutes

Objective: Explain the new features of Windows Server 2003.

Description: As the new administrator of network services for Arctic University, you will be educating faculty members about the benefits and features of Windows Server 2003. Because each faculty controls its own purchases, it is essential that you be able to convince the faculties of the benefits of moving to Windows Server 2003. The best place to start learning about new features is in the Help and Support utility.

1. If necessary, start your server and log on as Administrator.

2. Click **Start,** and then click **Help and Support.**

3. Type **new features** in the Search box, and press **Enter**.

4. In the Search Results box, under the Help Topics heading, click the topic **Feature comparison: Windows NT, Windows 2000, and the Windows Server family: Getting Started**.

5. Click the **+** (plus symbol) beside the **Windows 2000 to the Windows Server family** option.

6. Browse through the features you are interested in and that you think may be relevant to Arctic University.

7. Close the Help and Support window.

THE WINDOWS SERVER 2003 FAMILY

As with Windows 2000, there are multiple versions (or editions) of Windows Server 2003. Each version is designed to meet the needs of certain market segments that Microsoft has targeted. The four versions are: Web Edition, Standard Edition, Enterprise Edition, and Datacenter Edition.

Web Edition

Windows Server 2003, Web Edition, is a lower-cost version of Windows Server 2003 that is optimized to be a dedicated Web server. This version is meant to counter **Linux** in the market for utility servers. Windows Server 2003, Web Edition, provides the easy manageability and performance of Windows without the complexity of Linux.

Some unique features of Web Edition are listed here:

- Must be a **member server** or **stand-alone server**.

- Load balancing is supported.

- Clustering is not supported.
- VPN support is limited.
- **Services for Macintosh** are not supported.
- Internet Authentication Service is not supported.
- Remote Installation Services is not supported.
- Windows Media Services are not supported.
- **Terminal Services** are not supported.

The hardware requirements for Windows Server 2003, Web Edition, are listed in the table below.

Table 1-1   Hardware requirements for Windows Server 2003, Web Edition

Hardware	Minimum System Requirements	Recommended System Requirements
CPU speed	133 MHz	550 MHz
RAM	128 MB	256 MB
Disk space for setup	1.5 GB	n/a
Maximum RAM	2GB	n/a
Maximum processors	2	n/a
Cluster nodes	n/a	n/a

Standard Edition

Windows Server 2003, Standard Edition, is the version most likely to be used as a departmental file and print server or application server. It has a wide variety of available services such as **Remote Installation Services (RIS)** and application deployment through Group Policy.

Some unique features of Standard Edition are listed here:

- Can be a domain controller, member server, or stand-alone server
- Load balancing is supported.
- Clustering is not supported.
- Full VPN support is available.
- Services for Macintosh are supported.
- Windows Media Server is supported.
- Terminal Services are supported.

The hardware requirements for Windows Server 2003, Standard Edition, are listed in the table below.

Table 1-2   Hardware requirements for Windows Server 2003, Standard Edition

Hardware	Minimum System Requirements	Recommended System Requirements
CPU speed	133 MHz	550 MHz
RAM	128 MB	256 MB
Disk space for setup	1.5 GB	n/a
Maximum RAM	4 GB	n/a
Maximum processors	2	n/a
Cluster nodes	n/a	n/a

Enterprise Edition

Windows Server 2003, Enterprise Edition, is designed to enable large enterprises to deliver highly available applications and Web services. It is available in 32-bit and 64-bit editions. This version of Windows Server 2003 is the logical upgrade from Windows 2000 Advanced Server for enterprises that are implementing Web services using the CLR.

Some unique features of Enterprise Edition are listed here:

- Can be a member server, domain controller, or stand-alone server.
- Load balancing is supported.
- Clustering is supported.
- **Metadirectory Services** are supported.
- 64-bit processing is supported.
- Hot add memory is supported.
- **Non-Uniform Memory Access (NUMA)** is supported.

The hardware requirements for Windows Server 2003, Enterprise Edition, are listed in the table below.

Table 1-3   Hardware requirements for Windows Server 2003, Enterprise Edition

Hardware	Minimum System Requirements	Recommended System Requirements
CPU speed	133 MHz for 32-bit processors 733 MHz Itanium	733 MHz for Itanium
RAM	128 MB	256 MB
Disk space for setup	1.5 GB for 32-bit processors 2.0 GB for Itanium	n/a
Maximum RAM	32 GB for 32-bit processors 64 GB for Itanium	n/a
Maximum processors	8	n/a
Cluster nodes	8	n/a

Datacenter Edition

Windows Server 2003, Datacenter Edition, is designed for mission-critical applications that require the highest levels of availability and scalability. It is available in 32-bit and 64-bit editions.

Unlike other versions of Windows Server 2003, Datacenter Edition cannot be bought as retail software. It can only be bought through qualified Microsoft partners. Most of the Microsoft partners are original equipment manufacturers (OEMs). Microsoft partners submit a server and drivers to Microsoft for testing. Only after Microsoft has approved the hardware and driver combination can it be sold to customers.

A team from Microsoft and the Microsoft partner provide support. Only this team is allowed to install and support Datacenter Edition. The customer can add users and make application adjustments, but cannot add, update, or remove drivers and hardware.

Some unique features of Datacenter Edition are listed here:

- Can be a member server, domain controller, or stand-alone server.
- Load balancing is supported.
- Clustering is supported.
- Metadirectory Services are not supported.
- 64-bit processing is supported.

- Hot add memory is supported.
- Non-Uniform Memory Access (NUMA) is supported.
- Datacenter program is required.
- Internet Connection Firewall (ICF) is not supported.

The hardware requirements for Windows Server 2003, Datacenter Edition, are listed in the table below.

Table 1-4   Hardware requirements for Windows Server 2003, Datacenter Edition

Hardware	Minimum System Requirements	Recommended System Requirements
CPU speed	400 MHz for 32-bit processors 733 MHz for Itanium	733 MHz Itanium
RAM	512 MB	1 GB
Disk space for setup	1.5 GB for 32-bit processors 2.0 GB for Itanium	
Maximum RAM	64 GB for 32-bit processors 128 GB for Itanium	n/a
Maximum processors	8 minimum, 32 maximum	n/a
Cluster nodes	8	n/a

Activity 1-2: View the Current Edition of Windows Server 2003

Time Required: Five minutes

Objective: Find the edition of Windows Server 2003 that is installed on a running server.

Description: You are getting settled in your new office. As you requested when you were hired, there are several servers in the office that you can use for testing software. One of them seems to have Windows Server 2003 installed, but you are not sure which edition it is. In this activity you will identify the edition of Windows Server 2003 that is running.

1. If necessary, start your server and log on as Administrator.
2. Click the **Start** button, and click **Manage Your Server**.
3. In the Tools and Updates box, click **Computer and Domain Name Information**.
4. Click the **General Tab**.
5. Observe the version of Windows Server 2003 that is installed.
6. Close all windows.

Activity 1-3: View the Features of Datacenter Edition

Time Required: 10 minutes

Objective: Identify the unique features of Windows Server 2003, Datacenter Edition.

Description: To evaluate whether Arctic University requires Windows Server 2003, Datacenter Edition, you decide to do some further research. In this activity you use the Microsoft Web site to find more information.

1. If necessary, start your server and log on as Administrator.
2. Click the **Start** button, point to **All Programs**, and click **Internet Explorer**. If this is the first time Internet Explorer has been started then a warning window will appear. In the warning window, click **In the future, do now show this message**, and click **OK**.

3. Type **www.microsoft.com/windowsserver2003** in the Address box, and press **Enter**. If this is the first web site you are visiting then you will receive a warning about blocked content. In the warning window, click **Continue to prompt when Web site content is blocked** to deselect it, and click **Close**.

4. Click the **Product Information** link.

5. Click the **Product Overviews** link.

6. Click the **Windows Server 2003, Datacenter Edition Overview** link.

7. Review the information and close Internet Explorer when you are finished.

WINDOWS SERVER 2003 NETWORK ARCHITECTURE

There are four major software components in networking: client, **service**, **protocol**, and **adapter**. Client software makes requests for resources on the network. Service software responds to requests from client software and provides access to resources. To communicate, the client and service software use a common protocol, which defines the language that the client and service use. The adapter is the driver for the network card. The operating system uses the network driver to communicate with the network card.

Windows Server 2003 has two interfaces to make it easier for developers to create clients, services, protocols, and adapter software. The **Network Device Interface Specification (NDIS)** resides between protocols and the adapter software. The **Transport Device Interface (TDI)** resides between clients and protocols as well as between services and protocols. Figure 1-1 shows how the networking components relate to NDIS and TDI.

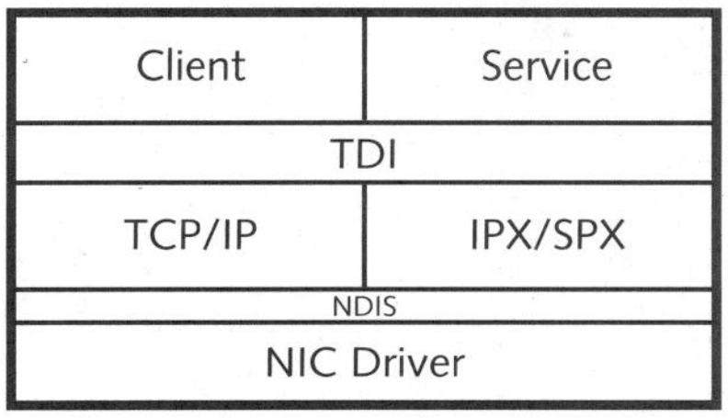

Client	Service
TDI	
TCP/IP	IPX/SPX
NDIS	
NIC Driver	

Figure 1-1   Windows Server 2003 networking architecture

NDIS

NDIS is a specification created by Microsoft and 3Com to speed the development of device drivers and enhance networking capabilities. Before a standard interface was defined, the developers of network card drivers had to write code to interact with each protocol being used by each hardware device to which the network card was attached.

Now with a standard specification in place, the developers of network card drivers write code that communicates with NDIS, and protocol developers also write code that communicates with NDIS. Neither the developers of network card drivers nor protocol developers need to be aware of what the other is doing. NDIS acts as an intermediary for all communication between the protocol and the network card driver.

Bindings between protocols and adapters are controlled by NDIS. A single adapter can be bound to multiple protocols. A single protocol can also be bound to multiple adapters. This is very important in a computer that is acting as a router or a server that communicates with clients using multiple protocols.

Windows Server 2003 uses NDIS version 5.1. Network drivers written for NDIS 4.0 or later are also supported. In Windows 9x operating systems, NDIS 4.0 was included, starting with Windows 95 OSR2. Windows NT 4.0 was the first NT-based operating system to support NDIS 4.0. Network drivers written for these operating systems or later versions should function properly in Windows Server 2003.

Windows Server 2003 does not support the use of ISA network cards.

TDI

The TDI layer provides clients and services with access to network resources. Applications talk to the TDI layer and the TDI layer passes on the requests to the protocols.

TDI emulates two network access mechanisms: **Network Basic Input Output System (NetBIOS)** and **Windows Sockets (WinSock)**. NetBIOS is an older network interface that is used by Windows 9x and Windows NT to access network resources. WinSock is used by Internet applications such as Internet Explorer and Outlook Express to access network resources. Starting with Windows 2000, WinSock can also be used by Windows to access Active Directory-based resources. **Windows Sockets Direct (WinSock Direct)** is a new enhancement to WinSock that is used to access resources on system area networks.

Developers write services and clients that communicate with NetBIOS or WinSock to access network resources. The applications communicate with the TDI layer, which emulates these interfaces. Developers creating protocols code them to communicate with the TDI layer. For a client and service to communicate, they must both be using the same network access mechanism and protocol.

Activity 1-4: Research Networking Architecture

Time Required: Five minutes

Objective: Find further information about NDIS and TDI.

Description: You would like to be sure you understand the difference between the TDI layer and NDIS. In this activity you will use the Help and Support utility to find more information.

1. If necessary, start your server and log in as Administrator.
2. Click **Start**, and then click **Help and Support**.
3. Click the **Index** button.
4. Type **glossary** in the **Type in the keyword to find** box.
5. Double-click the **main glossary** item.
6. Click the **N** button in the browse pane.
7. Scroll the browse pane to **Network Driver Interface Specification (NDIS)**, and read the description.
8. Click the **T** button in the browse pane.
9. Scroll the browse pane to **Transport Driver Interface (TDI)**, and read the description.
10. Close the Help and Support window.

NETWORK PROTOCOLS

Four major protocols are supported in Windows Server 2003: IPv4, IPv6, IPX/SPX, and AppleTalk.

IPv4 is the most common networking protocol used today. Most network components either require it or support using it, and it is also required for connecting to the Internet. IPv4 is normally referred to as TCP/IP without referencing a version number.

IPv6 is a newer version of TCP/IP and offers a number of enhancements. The most obvious enhancement is the expansion of the address space to alleviate a shortage of **IP addresses** on the Internet. It is not commonly in use yet, but will be in the next five to ten years.

1

Internetwork Packet eXchange/Sequenced Packet eXchange (IPX/SPX) is used primarily for backward compatibility with older networks running Novell Netware. Some older applications also require IPX/SPX. **AppleTalk** is used to communicate with Apple Macintosh computers.

Activity 1-5: Viewing Available Protocols

Time Required: 10 minutes

Objective: Verify the protocols available for installation.

Description: You need to verify the protocols that are available for Windows Server 2003 as part of the planning process for network services. In this activity you will view the list of available protocols in the properties of a network connection.

1. If necessary, turn on your server and log on as Administrator.

2. To open the properties of your local area network connection click **Start,** point to **Control Panel**, point to **Network Connections**, right-click **Classroom**, and then click **Properties**.

3. Notice that the TCP/IP protocol is already installed.

4. Click the **Install** button.

5. Click **Protocol** and click **Add**.

6. Notice that TCP/IP is not in the list because it is already installed.

7. Click **Cancel** to close the Select Network Protocol window.

8. Click **Cancel** to close the Select Network Component Type window.

9. Click **Cancel** to close the Classroom Properties window.

NETWORK SERVICES

There are a wide variety of network services available in Windows Server 2003. Most of these services are an updated version of what was available in Windows 2000 and Windows NT.

Dynamic Host Configuration Protocol (DHCP) is an automated mechanism used to assign IP addresses to client computers. Automating this process saves hours of work for a network administrator. In addition to assigning the IP address, DHCP can also provide IP configuration options such as **subnet masks**, the default gateway, and DNS servers.

Domain Name System (DNS) is a service that converts host names to IP addresses. Client computers require this to access resources through a host name. Active Directory uses DNS to store service location information.

Windows Internet Naming Service (WINS) converts NetBIOS names to IP addresses. Client computers require this to access resources through a NetBIOS name. Windows 9x and NT use WINS for service location.

Routing and Remote Access Service (RRAS) allows Windows Server 2003 to act as a router, VPN server, and dial-in server. Windows Server 2003 can route IPv4, IPv6, IPX/SPX, and AppleTalk packets. **Point-to-Point Tunneling Protocol (PPTP)** and **Layer-Two Tunneling Protocol/IP Security (L2TP/IPSec)** connections are supported for VPN access. The L2TP/IPSec VPN has been improved to allow connections through Network Address Translation (NAT). A dial-in server allows remote users to connect to office networks using a modem and phone line.

Network Address Translation allows an entire office of computers to share a single IP address when accessing the Internet. If Windows Server 2003 is used as a router to connect with an ISP, then only a single IP address is required. As packets are routed through the server running NAT, **packet headers** are modified to look as though the router created them. When response packets return, the router delivers them to the proper host on the internal network.

Internet Connection Sharing (ICS) is an automated way to set up DHCP, NAT, and a DNS proxy for small networks. DHCP automatically provides IP addresses and configuration options that define the ICS server as both the default gateway and the DNS server. The DNS proxy takes client DNS requests and forwards them to the DNS server it is configured to use. NAT allows all of the client computers to share a single IP address from an ISP.

Internet Authentication Service (IAS) allows a company to use Active Directory for centralized authentication of remote access clients on many different remote access servers. A company using IAS can have remote users dial in to an ISP and use the user ID and password of their Active Directory account for authentication. In addition, IAS can centralize the logging of internal dial-up servers.

IP Security (IPSec) is an enhancement to IPv4 that creates secure IP-based communications. In **Authentication Headers (AH) mode**, IPSec digitally signs packets to verify they were not modified in transit. In **Encapsulating Security Payload (ESP) mode**, IPSec digitally signs packets and encrypts the data to ensure that only the proper recipient can read the information.

Internet Connection Firewall (ICF) is a simple firewall that is suitable for small businesses using Windows Server 2003 as the router connecting to their ISP. ICF can be used in conjunction with ICS, RRAS, and NAT. If there is already a firewall between the office network and the Internet, then ICF is not required.

Public key infrastructure (PKI) is an increasingly important part of network and Internet security. **Certificates** can be used to secure e-mail and Web sites or to provide authentication using smart cards. Windows Server 2003 can generate and manage certificates for internal use.

Load balancing has been added as a standard feature to all versions of Windows Server 2003. In high-traffic environments a single server may not be able to keep up with the level of service that is required. This is particularly likely for Web-based applications that may be available to thousands of users. Load balancing transparently spreads the traffic between two or more servers. From the client perspective, it appears as if there is still only one server.

Activity 1-6: View Installed Services

Time Required: Five minutes

Objective: Identify installed network services.

Description: You are having trouble connecting to one of the test servers in your office. Because other staff have also been configuring the server, you think that Internet Connection Firewall may be installed and configured. In this activity you will verify that ICF is not running.

1. If necessary, start your server and log on as Administrator.

2. Click **Start**, point to **Administrative Tools**, and click **Services**.

3. Double-click the **Internet Connection Firewall (ICF)/Internet Connection Sharing (ICS)** service.

4. Verify that the status of the service is stopped and the Startup type is disabled. This means that the service is not currently running and will not start when the server is rebooted.

5. Click **Cancel** to close the properties window.

6. Close the Services window.

Activity 1-7: View Available Services

Time Required: Five minutes

Objective: Verify the network services that are available for installation.

Description: For your planning process, you need to verify the network services that are available for Windows Server 2003. In this activity you will go through the process of installing new Windows components to see which network services are available.

1. If necessary, start your server and log on as Administrator.

2. Click **Start**, point to **Control Panel**, and click **Add or Remove Programs**.

3. Click **Add/Remove Windows Components**.

4. Scroll through the list to see which services are available.

5. Click **Networking Services,** and click the **Details** button.

6. View the Networking Services, and then click **Cancel** to close the Networking Services window.

7. Click **Cancel** to close the Windows Components Wizard.

8. Close the Add or Remove Programs window.

CHAPTER SUMMARY

❏ Windows Server 2003 is the latest version of the Windows network operating system released by Microsoft. There are many new features, including enhanced Active Directory, the .NET Framework, Web Services, IPv6, network bridging, PPPOE support, built-in wireless support, Internet Connection Firewall, and 64-bit support.

❏ The Web Edition of Windows Server 2003 is designed to be a Web server only and cannot be a domain controller. Up to two processors and 2 GB of RAM are supported.

❏ The Standard Edition of Windows Server 2003 is designed to be a departmental server that provides file, print, and other services. Standard Edition can be configured as a domain controller, but does not support clustering and is not available in a 64-bit version. Up to two processors and 4 GB of RAM are supported.

❏ The Enterprise Edition of Windows Server 2003 is designed to be a highly available enterprise application server supporting up to eight node clusters. Up to eight processors are supported with 32 GB of RAM for 32-bit versions and 64 GB of RAM for 64-bit versions.

❏ The Datacenter Edition of Windows Server 2003 is designed for mission-critical applications supporting up to eight node clusters. A minimum of eight processors is required, and up to 32 processors are supported. In the 32-bit version, a maximum of 64 GB of RAM is supported and 128 GB of RAM are supported in the 64-bit version.

❏ The network architecture of Windows Server 2003 is composed of four main networking components: clients, services, protocols, and network adapters.

❏ The TDI layer resides between clients and protocols or between services and protocols. It emulates NetBIOS and WinSock.

❏ NDIS is responsible for binding protocols to network adapters. It also makes the development of protocols and network adapter drivers easier by providing a consistent interface.

❏ Four protocols are supported by Windows Server 2003: IPv4, IPv6, IPX/SPX, and AppleTalk.

❏ Many network services are available in Windows Server 2003, including: DHCP, DNS, WINS, RRAS, IAS, NAT, ICS, ICF, IPSec, and PKI.

KEY TERMS

Active Directory — A directory service for Windows 2000/2003 Servers that stores information about network resources.

adapter — The networking component that represents the network interface card and driver.

AppleTalk — A protocol that is used when communicating with Apple Macintosh computers.

attribute — A characteristic of an object in Active Directory

Authentication Headers (AH) mode — An IPSec operating mode that digitally signs packets but does not encrypt them.

binding — The process of configuring a network protocol to use a network adapter.

bridge — A network component that controls the movement of packets between network segments based on MAC addresses.

certificate — A combination of public key and private key that can be used to encrypt or digitally sign information.

class — A type of object in Active Directory. A class is defined by its attributes.

client — A networking component that is installed on computers requesting network services. Client software communicates with a corresponding service.

cluster — A group of computers that coordinate the provision of services. When one computer in a cluster fails, others take over its services.

common language runtime (CLR) — A common component that runs code developed for the .NET framework regardless of the language in which it is written.

Dynamic Host Configuration Protocol (DHCP) — A service used by the Windows operating system to automatically assign IP addressing information to clients.

domain controller — A Windows 2000/2003 server that holds a copy of the Active Directory information for a domain.

Domain Name System (DNS) — A service used by clients running TCP/IP to resolve host names to IP addresses. Active Directory uses DNS to store service location information.

Encapsulating Security Payload (ESP) mode — An IPSec operating mode that digitally signs packets and encrypts the contents.

Extensible Markup Language (XML) — A simple text-based mechanism to define content. It uses tags similar to HTML, but unlike HTML, developers can define their own tags.

global catalog — A subset of attributes of every object in an Active Directory forest. A global catalog holds universal group membership information.

Group Policy — An Active Directory-based mechanism to apply centrally defined configuration information out to client computers.

Hypertext Transport Protocol (HTTP) — The protocol used by Web browsers and Web servers. By default it uses TCP port 80.

Internet Authentication Service (IAS) — The Microsoft implementation of a RADIUS server. It allows distributed authentication for remote access clients.

Internet Connection Firewall (ICF) — A simple firewall suitable for home use or small offices when connecting to the Internet.

Internet Connection Sharing (ICS) — An automated way to configure DHCP, NAT, and DNS proxy to share a single IP address and configuration information from an ISP.

Internet Information Services (IIS) — A popular suite of Internet services that includes a Web server and FTP server.

Internet Protocol version 4 (IPv4) — This is the version of the Internet protocol (IP) that is used on the Internet. It is the IP part of TCP/IP.

Internet Protocol version 6 (IPv6) — An updated version of Internet protocol that uses 128-bit addresses and provides many new features.

Internet service provider (ISP) — A company that sells Internet access.

Internetwork Packet eXchange/Sequenced Packet eXchange (IPX/SPX) — The protocol required to communicate with servers running Novell NetWare 4 and earlier.

Intersite Topology Generator (ISTG) — The automatic mechanism that decides how domain information is replicated from one domain controller to others.

IP address — A unique address assigned to each computer with the TCP/IP protocol installed. It is 32-bits long and is composed of a network ID and a host ID.

IP Security (IPSec) — A service used with IPv4 to prevent eavesdropping on communication and to prevent data from being modified in transit.

1

Itanium — A 64-bit processor family manufactured by Intel.

Layer-Two Tunneling Protocol (L2TP) — A protocol that places packets inside an L2TP packet to move them across an IP-based network. This can be used to move IPX or AppleTalk packets through a network that is not configured to support them.

Linux — An open source operating system that is very similar to UNIX.

load balancing — When two or more computers share a single IP address to provide a service to clients. The load balanced computers share the responsibility of providing the service.

member server — A Windows server that is part of a domain but not a domain controller.

Metadirectory Services — A service in Windows that synchronizes Active Directory content with other directories and databases.

Microsoft Management Console (MMC) — The generic utility used to manage most features and components of Windows Server 2003. Snap-ins are required to give MMC the functionality to manage components.

.NET Framework — A new development system from Microsoft that uses a common language runtime. This makes programming objects language independent.

Network Address Translation (NAT) — A service that allows multiple computers to access the Internet by sharing a single public IP address.

network basic input/output system (NetBIOS) — An older interface used by programmers to access network resources.

Network Device Interface Specification (NDIS) — An interface for developers that resides between protocols and adapters. It controls the bindings between protocols and adapters.

network operating system (NOS) — An operating system that is optimized to act as a server rather than a client.

Non-Uniform Memory Access (NUMA) — A memory architecture for servers with multiple processors. It adds a third level of cache memory on motherboards.

object — An item within Active Directory. An example would be a user or a computer.

packet header — The first few bytes of a packet that contain the source address, destination address, and other information.

Point-to-Point Protocol over Ethernet (PPPoE) — A protocol used by some high-speed ISPs to authenticate and control IP traffic on their network.

Point-to-Point Tunneling Protocol (PPTP) — A protocol that can be used to provide VPN connectivity between a Windows client and VPN server. PPTP is supported by Windows 95 and later.

protocol — The language that two computers use to communicate on a network. Two computers must use the same protocol to communicate.

public key infrastructure (PKI) — A system to create and manage public keys, private keys, and certificates.

Remote Installation Services (RIS) — A service in Windows that automates the installation of Windows 2000 Professional or Windows XP Professional on client workstations.

router — A network device that forwards packets from one network to another. TCP/IP, IPX/SPX, and AppleTalk can be routed.

Routing and Remote Access Service (RRAS) — A service in Windows that controls routing, dial-in access, and VPN access on a Windows Server 2003.

schema — The list of definitions that defines classes and attributes supported by Active Directory.

service — A networking component that provides information to network clients. Each service communicates with corresponding client software.

Services for Macintosh — A service that allows Macintosh clients to access file and print services on Windows servers.

Simple Object Access Protocol (SOAP) — A standardized mechanism to access Web services using HTTP.

snap-in — A software component that is used with MMC to manage features and components of Windows Server 2003. Each snap-in manages a single component such as DHCP or DNS.

stand-alone server — A Windows server that is not a member of a domain.

subnet mask — A string of 32-bits that is used to define which portion of an IP address is the host ID and which part is the network ID.

Terminal Services — A service that lets users access Windows applications running on a remote server. The client software appears as a remote desktop.

Transport Device Interface (TDI) — A software layer that exists between client or service software and protocols. Clients and services use this layer to access network resources.

trust — The configuration of a domain to allow access to resources by users from a trusted domain.

Universal Description, Discovery, and Integration (UDDI) — A worldwide database of businesses and the Web services that they offer.

Virtual Private Network (VPN) — Encrypted communication across a public network.

Web Digital Authoring and Versioning (WebDAV) — A protocol that allows documents to be shared using HTTP.

Web service — A platform-independent service that is available across the Internet or an IP network.

Web Services Description Language (WSDL) — A standardized, XML-formatted mechanism to describe Web services. WSDL is used by UDDI to describe available services.

Windows Internet Naming Service (WINS) — A service used to resolve NetBIOS names to IP addresses as well as store NetBIOS service information.

Windows Media Services — A service that provides streaming audio and video to clients.

Windows Sockets (WinSock) — A programming interface used by developers to access TCP/IP based services.

Windows Sockets Direct (WinSock Direct) — An extension of the WinSock programming interface that allows developers to access resources on a system area network.

REVIEW QUESTIONS

1. Which of the following editions of Windows Server 2003 cannot be bought as retail software?

   a. Web Edition

   b. Standard Edition

   c. Enterprise Edition

   d. Datacenter Edition

2. Which of the following editions of Windows Server 2003 supports clustering? (Choose all that apply.)

   a. Web Edition

   b. Standard Edition

   c. Enterprise Edition

   d. Datacenter Edition

3. Which of the following features are available in Windows Server 2003, Standard Edition? (Choose all that apply.)

   a. IIS 6.0

   b. ICS

   c. load balancing

   d. 64-bit processing

1

4. Which of the following features of Windows Server 2003 lets developers create program components in different languages?

   a. NAT

   b. WebDAV

   c. .NET Framework

   d. IPv6

5. Which of the following new features of Windows Server 2003 allows servers to connect to high-speed Internet service providers without adding third-party software?

   a. wireless support

   b. PPPOE

   c. Internet Connection Firewall (ICF)

   d. Windows Media Services

6. The TDI layer allows multiple protocols to be bound to a network adapter. True or False?

7. Which of the following versions of Windows Server 2003 cannot be a domain controller?

   a. Web Edition

   b. Standard Edition

   c. Enterprise Edition

   d. Datacenter Edition

8. How many processors does Windows Server 2003 Enterprise Edition support?

   a. 2

   b. 4

   c. 8

   d. 16

   e. 32

9. What is the maximum amount of RAM that can be used in Windows Server 2003, Standard Edition?

   a. 2 GB

   b. 4 GB

   c. 32 GB

   d. 128 GB

10. How many cluster nodes are supported by Windows Server, Web Edition?

    a. 0

    b. 2

    c. 4

    d. 8

11. Which of the following network components requests services across the network?

    a. client

    b. service

    c. protocol

    d. NDIS

    e. TDI

12. Which of the following network components emulates NetBIOS?
    a. client
    b. service
    c. protocol
    d. NDIS
    e. TDI

13. Which of the following protocols is used to communicate on the Internet?
    a. TCP/IP
    b. IPv6
    c. IPX/SPX
    d. AppleTalk

14. Which of the following network services automatically assigns IP addresses and configuration information to client computers?
    a. NAT
    b. WINS
    c. DHCP
    d. PPTP

15. Which of the following is a VPN protocol? (Choose all that apply.)
    a. NAT
    b. PPTP
    c. L2TP/IPSec
    d. DNS

16. Which of the following network services is used for remote authentication?
    a. IAS
    b. DNS
    c. ICF
    d. ICS

17. Which of the following services allows an office of computers to connect to the Internet using a single IP address? (Choose all that apply.)
    a. DNS
    b. DHCP
    c. NAT
    d. ICS
    e. ICF

18. Routing and Remote Access Service controls VPN connections. True or False?

19. WINS is used by a client to convert host names to IP addresses. True or False?

20. Which of the following is a feature of NDIS? (Choose all that apply.)
    a. acts an intermediary for communications between protocols and network card drivers
    b. allows multiple protocols to be bound to a single adapter
    c. provides clients and services with access to network resources
    d. is the language clients and services use to communicate

CASE PROJECTS

Case Project 1-1: Choosing a Network Operating System

As the person in charge of implementing network services for Arctic University, you are responsible for ordering Windows Server 2003 for the faculties. To decide what software needs to be ordered, you are meeting with the head of each faculty. Create a document describing the benefits and drawbacks to each edition of Windows Server 2003 and when each is appropriate. You can distribute this document to each faculty head before the meetings.

Case Project 1-2: Choosing Network Services

As part of the planning process you are meeting with the rest of the IT Department to brainstorm on what services may be required on the network. Make a list of the network services that you think may be required and describe why.

Case Project 1-3: Choosing Network Drivers

A colleague is concerned that some network card drivers will not function after the existing Windows NT and Windows 2000 servers are upgraded to Windows Server 2003. What can you tell your colleague about network driver compatibility with previous versions of Windows and the role that NDIS plays in this?

2

NETWORKING PROTOCOLS

After reading this chapter and completing the exercises, you will be able to:

♦ Understand TCP/IP addressing
♦ Compare Internet Protocol version 6 with Internet Protocol version 4
♦ Understand the relevance of the IPX/SPX protocol
♦ Describe the purpose of the AppleTalk protocol
♦ Identify obsolete network protocols
♦ Use bindings to optimize network connectivity

Windows networking requires four components: a **client**, **service**, **protocol**, and **network** adapter. The client and service software are designed to talk to each other. In the case of Windows Server 2003, the server service is written to talk to the workstation (or client) service of Windows XP. For the client and service to be able to communicate with each other, they must speak the same language. From a computer's perspective this means that they must be using the same protocol. The most common protocol used today is TCP/IP; however, other protocols include IPX/SPX (NWlink), NetBEUI, AppleTalk, and DLC.

The **network adapter** must match the other networking hardware, such as hubs and switches. The most common standard for network adapters is **Ethernet**. There are many variations of Ethernet that include different types of cabling, many of which function at different speeds. In this chapter you will explore the different protocols that are available for Windows Server 2003.

TCP/IP

Transmission Control Protocol/Internet Protocol (TCP/IP) is the most commonly used network protocol suite in use today. There are several reasons why TCP/IP is so prevalent:

- *It has wide vendor support*—Vendors understand that their products will be more popular if their products can integrate with products from other vendors. Most vendors support TCP/IP, and therefore all new products are developed with TCP/IP support to make them interoperable.

- *It is an open protocol*—An open protocol is not controlled by any single company or individual; it is controlled by a standards process. This means that companies choosing to use TCP/IP do not need to be concerned that the owner of the protocol will charge expensive royalties or make changes that will affect their products.

- *It provides access to the Internet*—Internet access is required in business today and TCP/IP is the only protocol that is used on the Internet. Common Internet service protocols such as **Hypertext Transfer Protocol (HTTP)**, **File Transfer Protocol (FTP)**, and **Simple Mail Transfer Protocol (SMTP)** are part of the TCP/IP protocol suite, and the **Domain Name Service (DNS)**, which you will learn about later in this chapter, only functions with TCP/IP.

Although Windows Server 2003 has the ability to use several protocols, it has been designed so that many of its main features require the use of TCP/IP. For example, TCP/IP enables **Active Directory** to integrate with DNS for service location. TCP/IP also enables Windows XP Professional computers to use DNS to locate **domain controllers** for logging into the network.

Occasionally, when the TCP/IP protocol was installed on older versions of Windows, it would become corrupt in some way. The solution to this problem was to uninstall TCP/IP and reinstall it. This is no longer possible in Windows Server 2003, as TCP/IP is automatically installed and cannot be removed. If the configuration of TCP/IP becomes corrupt you must repair the connection.

Activity 2-1: Repairing a Network Connection

Time Required: Five minutes

Objective: Repair a connection that has a corrupt TCP/IP configuration.

Description: One of the servers you have installed in your test lab has mysteriously stopped communicating with the other servers. You have recently been installing and removing a number of services and you suspect that, as part of the process, the TCP/IP protocol has somehow become corrupt. To fix this, you need to repair the network connection.

The classroom connection on your server is not really corrupted, but these are the steps you would follow if it was.

1. If necessary, start your server and log on as Administrator.

2. Click **Start**, point to **Control Panel**, point to **Network Connections**, right-click **Classroom**, and click **Repair**.

3. Click **OK** to close the Repair Connection dialog box.

IP Addresses

An IP address is just like the mailing address for a house, in that it must be unique. If any two computers have the same **IP address**, it is impossible for information to be correctly delivered to them.

The most common format for IP addresses is four numbers called **octets** that are separated by periods. An example of an IP address is 192.168.5.66. Each octet can range in value between 0 and 255. These numbers

2

are normally displayed in dotted decimal notation because that is what most people are used to and find the easiest to use. However, you occasionally find some applications that allow the octets to be entered as hexadecimal numbers ranging between 0 and FF.

Each octet in an IP address represents eight bits of information. The prefix "oct" in "octet" means eight. If each octet is eight bits then a full IP address of four octets is 32 bits long. When a computer works with an IP address it is treated as a lump of 32 bits rather than four octets. The division into octets is just to make it easier for people to use the addresses.

 When the computer looks at an IP address, the numbers are converted to binary. It is only in binary that some of the more complex features of TCP/IP, such as subnetting and supernetting, are more understandable.

An IP address is composed of two parts: the network ID and the host ID. The **network ID** represents the network on which the computer is located. All movement of packets between **routers** is based on networks, and therefore movement of packets on the Internet is also based on networks. No two networks can have the same network ID or else routers cannot determine where to deliver packets that are addressed to that network ID. The **host ID** represents the individual computer on a network. No two computers on the same network can have the same host ID; however, two computers on different networks can have the same host ID.

 You can compare the network ID and the host ID to a postal mailing address. A postal mailing address is composed of two portions: the street name and the house number. The street name is similar to a network ID. No two streets can have the same name, just as no two networks can have the same network ID. The host ID is like the house number. Two houses can have the same house number as long as they are on different streets, just as two computers can have the same host ID as long as they are on different networks.

The IP addresses that can be used on the Internet are assigned by an **Internet service provider (ISP)**. When you sign up with an ISP, you are given at least one IP address. Generally, if you want more than one or two IP addresses, you have to pay a monthly fee for them. To minimize the use of IP addresses, most companies use **Network Address Translation (NAT)** or a **proxy server**. These two topics will be explored in Chapter 11.

The organization with overall authority for IP address assignments on the Internet is the Internet Corporation for Assigned Names and Numbers (ICANN). ICANN then works with regional authorities to manage addresses within a given region. Your ISP obtains IP addresses from these organizations. There are three regional authorities:

- American Registry for Internet Numbers (ARIN) is responsible for North America, Central America, South America, and sub-Saharan Africa.
- Asia Pacific Network Information Center (APNIC) is responsible for the Asia and Pacific region.
- Réseaux IP Européens (RIPE) is responsible for Europe and surrounding regions.

Subnet Masks

Each computer is configured with a **subnet mask** that defines which part of its IP address is the network ID and which part is the host ID. Subnet masks are composed of four octets just like an IP address. The simplest subnet masks use only the two values of 0 and 255. Wherever there is a 255 in the subnet mask, that octet is part of the network ID. Wherever there is a 0 in the subnet mask, that octet is part of the host ID. Table 2-1 shows two examples of how the network ID and host ID of an IP address can be calculated using the subnet mask.

Table 2-1   Examples of using a subnet mask to find network and host IDs

IP address	192.168.100. 33
Subnet mask	255.255.255. 0
Network ID	192.168.100. 0
Host ID	0 . 0 . 0 . 33
IP address	172. 16. 43.207
Subnet mask	255.255. 0 . 0
Network ID	172. 16. 0 . 0
Host ID	0 . 0 . 43.207

No matter how many octets are included in the network ID, they are always contiguous and start on the left. If the first and third octets are part of the network ID, then the second must be as well. Table 2-2 shows examples of valid and invalid subnet masks.

Table 2-2   Examples of valid and invalid subnet masks

Valid Subnet Masks	Invalid Subnet Masks
255.0.0.0	0.255.255.255
255.255.0.0	255.0.255.0
255.255.255.0	255.255.0.255

A computer uses its subnet mask to determine what network it is on and whether other computers with which it is communicating are on the same network or a different network. If two computers on the same network are communicating, then they can deliver packets directly to each other. If two computers are on different networks then they must use a router to communicate. An example of two computers that are on the same network is shown in Figure 2-1.

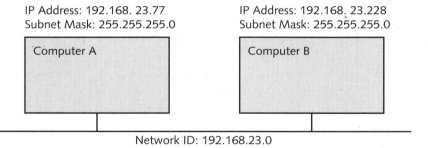

IP Address: 192.168. 23.77
Subnet Mask: 255.255.255.0

Computer A

IP Address: 192.168. 23.228
Subnet Mask: 255.255.255.0

Computer B

Network ID: 192.168.23.0

Figure 2-1   Two computers on the same network

In Figure 2-1, there are two computers. Computer A has an IP address of 192.168.23.77 and a subnet mask of 255.255.255.0. Computer B has an IP address of 192.168.23.228.

While you can look at the IP addresses of Computer A and Computer B and intuitively guess that they are on the same network, a computer cannot. Computers follow rules, and if Computer A is sending a message to Computer B, then Computer A must use its subnet mask to find out whether the two computers are on the same network or a different network.

Following are the steps that Computer A must follow before sending a message to Computer B:

1. Computer A compares its subnet mask and IP address to find its own network ID. Table 2-3 shows the calculation of the network ID for Computer A.

Table 2-3   Network ID calculation for Computer A

IP address of Computer A	192.168.23.77
Subnet mask of Computer A	255.255.255.0
Network ID of Computer A	192.168.23.0

2. Computer A compares its subnet mask and the IP address of Computer B to find out whether they are on the same network. Table 2-4 shows the calculation of the network ID for the IP address of Computer B using the subnet mask of Computer A.

Table 2-4   Network ID calculation for Computer B

IP address of Computer B	192.168.23.228
Subnet mask of Computer A	255.255.255.0
Network ID of Computer B	192.168.23.0

3. Both network IDs are the same, so Computer A delivers the packet directly to Computer B.

Default Gateway

In TCP/IP parlance, **default gateway** is another term for router. If a computer does not know how to deliver a packet, it gives the packet to the default gateway to deliver. This happens every time a computer needs to deliver a packet to a network other than its own.

A router is often a dedicated hardware device from a vendor such as Cisco, D-link, or Linksys. Other times, a router is actually a computer with multiple network cards. Operating systems such as Windows Server 2003, **Linux**, and **NetWare** have the ability to perform as routers.

The one consistent feature of routers, regardless of the manufacturer, is that they can distinguish multiple networks and how to move packets between them. Routers can also figure out the best path to use to move a packet between different networks.

It is important to note that routers keep track of networks, not computers.

A router has an IP address on every network to which it is attached. When a computer sends a packet to the default gateway for further delivery, the address of the router must be on the same network as the computer, as computers can only talk directly to devices on their own network. An example of a computer using a default gateway to communicate with another computer on a different network is shown in Figure 2-2.

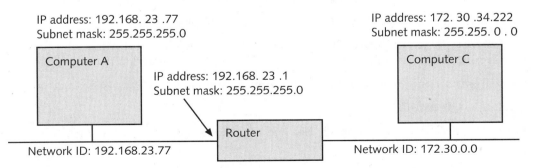

IP address: 192.168. 23 .77
Subnet mask: 255.255.255.0

IP address: 172. 30 .34.222
Subnet mask: 255.255. 0 . 0

Computer A

IP address: 192.168. 23 .1
Subnet mask: 255.255.255.0

Computer C

Router

Network ID: 192.168.23.77

Network ID: 172.30.0.0

Figure 2-2   Two computers on different networks

In Figure 2-2, Computer A is sending a packet to Computer C. Computer A uses its subnet mask to determine whether the default gateway is required.

1. Computer A compares its subnet mask and IP address to find its own network ID. Table 2-5 shows the calculation of the network ID for Computer A.

Table 2-5   Network ID calculation for Computer A

IP address of Computer A	192.168.23.77
Subnet mask of Computer A	255.255.255.0
Network ID of Computer A	192.168.23.0

2. Computer A compares its subnet mask and the IP address of Computer C to see if it is on the same network. This step does not calculate the network ID for Computer C. It only tests whether it is the same as Computer A. Computer A is not configured with the subnet mask of Computer C. So, it is impossible for Computer A to find the network ID for computer C. Table 2-6 shows testing the network ID for the IP address of Computer C using the subnet mask of Computer A.

Table 2-6   Network ID test for Computer C

IP address of Computer C	172.30.34.222
Subnet mask of Computer A	255.255.255.0
Network ID of Computer C	172.30.34.0

3. The two network IDs are different, so Computer A sends the packet to the router for delivery.

4. The router looks in its routing table to see if it knows where the network 172.30.0.0 is located.

5. Because the router is attached to network 172.30.0.0, it delivers the packet to Computer C. If the router were not attached to network 172.30.0.0, then it would forward it to another router.

Activity 2-2: View IP Address Configuration

Time Required: 10 minutes

Objective: View the current IP address settings on a server.

Description: The test lab in your office is also being used by other technical staff at Arctic University. You allow them access because you feel it is important for all staff to be familiar with Windows Server 2003 before you roll it out to the various faculties. One of the servers is no longer communicating with the others. You check the properties of the network card in device manager and it appears to be functioning properly. Now you need to verify that the IP addressing information is correct and document it for future reference.

1. If necessary, start your server and log on as Administrator.

2. Click **Start**, point to **Control Panel**, point to **Network Connections**, right-click **Classroom**, and click **Properties**.

3. Click the **Internet Protocol (TCP/IP)** option, and click the **Properties** button.

4. Click the **Advanced** button.

5. Document the IP address, subnet mask, and default gateway on a sheet of paper.

6. Click the **DNS** tab.

7. Document the DNS servers and any additional DNS suffixes on a sheet of paper.

8. Click the **WINS** tab.

9. Document the WINS addresses and NetBIOS setting on your sheet of paper. There will most likely not be any listed.

10. Click the **Options** tab, then click the **Properties** button.

11. Document the TCP/IP filtering settings on your sheet of paper.

12. Click the **Cancel** button in all windows to exit without saving any changes.

IP Address Classes

IP addresses are divided into classes. The class of an IP address defines the default subnet mask of the device using that address.

All of the IP address classes can be identified by the first octet of the address, as shown in Table 2-7.

Table 2-7   IP address classes

Class	Address Range	Subnet Mask
A	1-127. X . X . X	255.0.0.0
B	128-191. X . X . X	255.255.0.0
C	192-223. X . X . X	255.255.255.0
D	224-239. X . X . X	N/A
E	240-255. X . X . X	N/A

Class A addresses use eight bits for the network ID and 24 bits for the host ID. You can identify this from the subnet mask of 255.0.0.0. The value of the first octet will always be in a range from one to 127. This means there are only 127 potential class A networks available for the entire Internet, and even this small number of class A networks is reduced by reserved address ranges. Class A networks are only assigned to very large companies and Internet providers.

The number of hosts available on a class A network is 16,777,214, as shown in Table 2-8; however, it is not reasonable to have this many hosts on a single unmanaged network. In the rare cases where a class A network is in use, it is subnetted. **Subnetting** is the process in which a single large network is subdivided into smaller networks to control traffic flow. Chapter 4 will cover subnetting, as well as the process to find the number of available host IDs on a given network.

Table 2-8   Hosts and networks for IP address classes

Class	Subnet Mask	Number of Networks	Number of Hosts
A	255.0.0.0	127	16,777,214
B	255.255.0.0	16,384	65,534
C	255.255.255.0	2,097,152	254

Class B addresses use 16 bits for the network ID and 16 bits for the host ID. This is defined by the subnet mask of 255.255.0.0. The value of the first octet ranges from 128 to 191. There are 16,384 class B networks with 65,534 hosts on each network.

The number of class B networks is reduced slightly by reserved address ranges, but there are many more class B networks than class A networks. Class B networks are assigned to many larger organizations, such as governments, universities, and companies with several thousand users.

Class C addresses use 24 bits for the network ID and eight bits for the host ID. This is defined by the subnet mask 255.255.255.0. The value of the first octet ranges from 192 to 223. There are 2,097,152 class C networks with 254 hosts on each network. Although there are very many class C networks, they have a relatively small number of hosts, and thus are suited only to smaller organizations.

Class D addresses are not divided into networks and they cannot be assigned to computers as IP addresses. Class D addresses are used for multicasting. The value of the first octet ranges from 224 to 239.

Multicast addresses are used by groups of computers. A packet addressed to a multicast address is delivered to each computer in the multicast group. This is better than a **broadcast** message because routers can be configured to allow multicast traffic to move from one network to another. In addition, all computers on the network process broadcasts, while only computers that are part of that multicast group process multicasts.

Class E addresses are considered experimental and not used. The first octet of class E addresses ranges from 240 to 255.

Classless Inter-domain Routing

At one time, IP address classes were used by routers on the Internet to move packets. The routers used the network address and default subnet mask. This is called **classful routing**.

With classful routing each Internet backbone router would potentially need to keep 2,097,152 entries in its routing table for class C networks alone. As the number of class C networks assigned grew, this became unsustainable. Classful routing also wasted many IP addresses. If an organization needed 20 IP addresses, they required an entire class C address. Out of the 254 hosts on a class C network, 234 would be unused.

To make Internet routing and the assignment of IP addresses more efficient, **classless inter-domain routing (CIDR)** was introduced. CIDR does not use the default subnet masks for routing. Instead, the subnet mask must be defined for each network. A configurable subnet mask is more flexible and efficient because a single network can be subnetted and organizations can be assigned only a small part of a class C network. For example, a company that needs 20 IP addresses can be assigned a block of addresses as small as 32. This would waste only 12 addresses instead of 234 from the previous example. CIDR also reduces the number of routing table entries that Internet backbone routers must hold. A single routing table entry can replace hundreds or thousands of entries for class C networks.

CIDR notation is a common mechanism to indicate the number of bits in the network ID of an IP address. After the IP address, /XX is added, with XX being the number of bits in the host ID, as shown in Table 2-9.

Table 2-9   CIDR notation

CIDR Notation	Subnet Mask
192.168.1.0/24	255.255.255.0
172.16.0.0/16	255.255.0.0
10.0.0.0/8	255.0.0.0

Reserved Addresses

There are a number of IP addresses and IP networks that are reserved for special purposes and either cannot be assigned to hosts or cannot be used on the Internet.

Broadcasts are packets that are addressed to all computers on a network. There are two different types of broadcasts: local and directed. A local broadcast is delivered to all computers on a local network and is discarded by routers. The IP address 255.255.255.255 is a local broadcast; all bits in the address are set to 1.

A directed broadcast is a broadcast on a specific network. These packets can be routed to get to the network to which it is aimed. The IP address for a directed broadcast is composed of the network ID to which it is directed and then all host bits are set to 1. Routers can be configured to block directed broadcasts, but forward them by default. Table 2-10 shows some examples of IP networks and directed broadcasts for those networks.

Table 2-10   Directed broadcasts on specific networks

Network	Directed Broadcast
192.168.1.0/24	192.168.1.255
172.16.0.0/16	172.16.255.255
10.0.0.0/8	10.255.255.255

Any IP address with all host bits set to 0 refers to the network itself and cannot be assigned to a host. Table 2-11 shows some examples of IP addresses with all host bits set to 0.

Table 2-11   Host bits in IP addresses

IP Address	Network ID	Host ID
192.168.1.0/24	192.168.1.0	0.0.0.0
172.16.0.0/16	172.16.0.0	0.0.0.0
10.0.0.0/8	10.0.0.0	0.0.0.0

Any IP address with 127 as the first octet cannot be assigned to a host. These are referred to as **loopback** addresses. The most commonly used loopback address is 127.0.0.1. However, all of these addresses starting with 127 are actually the local host. If you **ping** 127.0.0.1, you are actually pinging the machine you are on. These addresses are used to test the IP stack software because this function works even if the network card is not functioning.

Several networks are reserved for internal use and are discarded by Internet routers. However, they can be routed internally within a corporate network. In order to provide Internet access to computers using these addresses, a proxy server or Network Address Translation is required. It is very common to use these addresses in a corporate environment. Table 2-12 shows the network addresses that are reserved for internal networks.

Table 2-12   Addresses for internal networks

CIDR Notation	IP Address Range
192.168.0.0/16	192.168.0.0-192.168.255.255
172.16.0.0/12	172.16.0.0-172.31.255.255
10.0.0.0/8	10.0.0.0-10.255.255.255

The network 169.254.0.0/16 is reserved for **Automatic Private IP Addressing (APIPA)**. Windows 2000/XP workstations automatically generate an address in this range if they are configured to lease an address from a Dynamic Host Configuration Protocol (DHCP) server and are unable to contact one. These addresses are not routable on the Internet. Windows Server 2003 also uses APIPA addresses if the server is configured to obtain a DHCP address and a DHCP server cannot be reached. However, most servers have static IP addresses.

DNS

Domain Name System (DNS) is essential to a Windows Server 2003 network. It is used to resolve host names to IP addresses, find domain controllers, and find e-mail servers. DNS is essential for Active Directory to work properly.

The most common use for DNS is resolving host names to IP addresses. When you access a Web site, you access a location such as *www.microsoft.com*. This is a **Fully Qualified Domain Name (FQDN)**, which is a combination of **host name** and **domain name**. Workstations cannot connect to a service on the Internet directly using a host name. Instead, they convert the host name to an IP address and then access the service via an IP address. Because it performs this critical service, DNS is essential for Internet connectivity.

Windows XP clients use DNS when finding a Windows Server 2003 domain controller to log into Active Directory. During login, a Windows XP client sends a query to the DNS server asking for a list of domain controllers. The DNS server responds with the IP address of a domain controller. Then the Windows XP client contacts the domain controller to log in.

E-mail servers on the Internet use DNS to deliver mail messages. When you send a message to someone@nowhere.com, a DNS server holds the record that indicates the name of the server responsible for e-mail addressed to the domain nowhere.com. Table 2-13 shows several DNS record types, including MX records, which are used to find e-mail servers.

Table 2-13   DNS record types

DNS Record Type	Description
A (host)	An A record is used to convert host names to IP addresses
SRV (Service)	Service records are used to hold information about services; Active Directory uses these to store the addresses of domain controllers
MX (Mail Exchange)	Mail Exchange records are used to indicate which server is responsible for handling the e-mail for a DNS domain

WINS

Windows Internet Naming Service (WINS) is used to resolve NetBIOS names to IP addresses. In addition, it stores information about services such as domain controllers.

WINS is used primarily for backward compatibility with Windows NT and Windows 9x. Windows NT and Windows 9x both use NetBIOS names as the primary mechanism for accessing network services. Joining a domain and browsing Network Neighborhood are just two examples of when NetBIOS names are required.

If WINS is configured, Windows Server 2003 registers its IP address and services with the WINS server during startup. When Windows Server 2003 is shut down, it contacts the WINS server and tells it to release the registration of its IP address and services.

DHCP

All IP configuration information can be manually entered on each workstation, but that is not very efficient. With each manual entry there is a risk of a typographical error. In addition, if the IP configuration changes, it is a very large task to visit each workstation to modify it.

Dynamic Host Configuration Protocol (DHCP) is an automated mechanism to assign IP addresses to clients. Automating this process avoids the problem of records being entered incorrectly. If a change needs to be made for the IP addressing information, you can simply change the DHCP server.

Take, for example, a 200-workstation network. If you were to manually change the IP addressing information on all of these workstations, it might take several days. With DHCP, the server can be updated and, on the next reboot, all workstations receive the new information.

Windows Servers 2003 can obtain its IP addressing information from DHCP, but it is not common to do so. Normally, network administrators prefer that servers have a consistent IP address so that it is easier to troubleshoot network connectivity problems. Newer clients, such as Windows XP, that attempt to contact a DHCP server and are unable to do so, generate an APIPA address in the 169.254.0.0/16 network.

As an alternative to APIPA addresses, Windows Server 2003 can be configured to use an alternate IP configuration. If a DHCP server cannot be contacted, then the alternative static IP settings are used.

Activity 2-3: Using IPCONFIG to View IP Configuration

Time Required: Five minutes

Objective: View the current IP settings using the IPCONFIG utility.

Description: As part of documenting the configuration of a test server you need to get the IP configuration from it. You are not sure whether the server is using DHCP or is configured with a static IP address. If the server is using DHCP you cannot view the current IP configuration in the properties of the network connection. The IPCONFIG utility can be used to view IP configuration information whether the IP address is assigned through DHCP or statically.

1. If necessary, start your server and log on as Administrator.

2. Click **Start**, and then click **Run**.

3. Type **cmd.exe** in the Open text box.

4. Click **OK**.

5. Type **ipconfig /all** and press **Enter** to view your IP configuration settings.

6. Close the command prompt window.

Activity 2-4: Test APIPA

Time Required: 15 minutes

Objective: Test the APIPA functionality in Windows .NET Server 2003.

Description: Some of your fellow technical staff have seen workstations on your network with IP addresses in the 169.254.X.X range. You have explained that this is an automatic function of Windows 2000/XP and Windows Server 2003 when they cannot contact a DHCP server. You are now going to demonstrate this for your colleagues.

1. Confirm that no DHCP servers are running on your network.

2. If necessary, start your server and log on as Administrator.

3. Click **Start**, point to **Control Panel**, point to **Network Connections**, right-click **Classroom**, and click **Properties**.

4. Click the **Internet Protocol (TCP/IP)** option, and click the **Properties** button.

5. Click the **Obtain an IP address automatically** option, and click **OK**.

6. Close the Classroom Properties window.

7. Click **Start**, click **Run**, type **cmd.exe**, and press **Enter**.

8. Type the following command to view your IP settings and then press **Enter**:

   ipconfig

9. If you do not see an address on the 169.254.X.X network, then wait for a few moments and repeat Step 7. Both the Classroom connection and the Private connection use APIPA addresses.

10. Close the command prompt and reopen the Classroom Properties window.

11. Click the **Internet Protocol (TCP/IP)** option, and click the **Properties** button.

12. Click the **Use the following IP address** option; type your IP address, subnet mask, and default gateway; and then click **OK**. You documented these settings in Activity 2-2.

13. Click **Close** to exit the Classroom properties window.

Activity 2-5: Alternative IP Configuration

Time Required: 10 minutes

Objective: Configure alternative IP address information to be used when a DHCP server is unavailable.

Description: Arctic University has a portable computer-based testing system that moves from location to location. Normally, the server for the testing system gets an address from a DHCP server at the remote site. However, the Iqualuit branch of the Arctic University campus does not use DHCP. You need to configure the server to use an IP address from the Iqualuit location when a DHCP-based address is not available.

1. Confirm that no DHCP servers are running on your network.
2. If necessary, start your server and log on as Administrator.
3. Open the Classroom Properties window (see Activity 2-4 if necessary).
4. Click the **Internet Protocol (TCP/IP)** option, and click the **Properties** button.
5. Click the **Obtain an IP address automatically** option.
6. Click the **Alternate Configuration** tab.
7. Click **User Configured**.
8. Enter the following IP configuration information:
   - IP address: 172.30.0.*x*, where *x* is your student number.
   - Subnet mask: 255.255.0.0
   - Default gateway: 172.30.0.254
   - Preferred DNS server: 172.30.0.253
9. Click **OK** to save the IP configuration changes, and click **Close** to exit the Classroom Properties window.
10. Open a command prompt (see Activity 2-4, if necessary).
11. Type **ipconfig** and press **Enter**.
12. If you do not see the address on the 172.30.0.*x* network, then wait a few moments and repeat Step 11.
13. Close the command prompt window.
14. Open the Classroom Properites window (see Activity 2-4, if necessary).
15. Click the **Internet Protocol (TCP/IP)** option, and click the **Properties** button.
16. Click the **Use the following IP address** option; type your IP address, subnet mask, and default gateway; and then click **OK**.
17. Click **Close** to exit the Classroom Properties window.

INTERNET PROTOCOL VERSION 6

Internet Protocol version 6 (IPv6) is the replacement for **Internet Protocol version 4 (IPv4)** which is currently used on the Internet and in networks. The creators of IPv4 could not have anticipated the expansion of the Internet and, as a result, IPv4 has some serious shortcomings when used for global networking. IPv6 addresses these shortcomings.

Improvements found in IPv6 include:

- Increased address space
- Hierarchical routing to reduce the load on Internet backbone routers
- Simpler configuration through automatic address assignment
- Inclusion of encryption services for data security
- Quality of service
- Extensibility to support new features

IPv6 is not currently in use on the Internet, but will eventually be phased in. Fortunately, the Microsoft implementation of IPv6 can be installed without affecting IPv4 communication. This means that IPv6 can be phased into the network, as required, without interfering with existing IPv4 services.

IPv6 Addressing

The address space for IPv4 is nearing depletion. The combination of class A, B, and C addresses results in about 3.6 billion addresses. However, because of inefficient assignment of addresses, the actual number of usable addresses is less than that. IPv6 has a significantly larger address space than IPv4. IPv6 addresses are 128 bits long, as compared to 32 bits for IPv4. The total number of IPv6 addresses is 3.4×10^{38}. This is millions of millions more addresses than are available in IPv4.

Obviously, this is many more addresses than would normally be required for computing devices, but IPv6 is designed for ease of use rather than efficiency of allocation. Many of these addresses will probably never be assigned to a host. In fact, only one-eighth of the total address space is allocated for Internet-accessible addresses.

While IPv4 addresses are represented in dotted decimal notation, IPv6 addresses are represented in hexadecimal with each four digits separated by colons. Each hexadecimal digit equals four bits. The total address length is a maximum of 32 digits. An example of an IPv6 address is: 222D:10B5:3355:00F3:8234:0000:32AC:099C.

To simplify the expression of IPv6 addresses, any group of four hexadecimal digits can drop leading zeros. The IPv6 address in the previous example can be simplified to: 222D:10B5:3355:F3:8234:0:32AC:99C.

When an IPv6 address contains a long set of zeros, the zeros can be compressed to a double colon "::". For example, the multicast address FF02:0:0:0:0:0:112A:CC87 could be shortened to FF02::112A:CC87. This type of zero compression can only be used once per address.

IPv6 Address Types

There are three IPv6 address types:

- Unicast
- Multicast
- Anycast

Unicast addresses are the equivalent to IPv4 addresses that can be assigned to hosts, but are divided into multiple categories. **Aggregatable global unicast addresses** are the equivalent of the Internet addressable class A, B, and C IPv4 addresses. **Link–local addresses** are the equivalent of APIPA IPv4 addresses. **Site–local addresses** are the equivalent of IPv4 internal network addresses. The IPv6 loopback address is ::1.

An individual interface is assigned at least three unicast addresses:

- A link–local address
- At least one global unicast address or site-local address
- Loopback

Multicast addresses are almost the same in IPv6 as they are in IPv4. However, 112 bits are allocated to the group ID in IPv6. This allows many more multicast addresses in IPv6 than in IPv4. The scope field is an additional option in IPv6 multicast addresses. The scope defines where routers should propagate the multicast address. Multicast addresses are used in place of broadcast addresses in IPv6.

An individual host in IPv6 has a minimum of three multicast addresses:

- FF01::1, node-local scope, all-nodes
- FF02::1, link-local scope, all-nodes
- A solicited node address for each unicast address (discussed further in Chapter 3)
- Joined multicast groups (optional)

The node-local scope is the local computer. The IPv6 address FF01::1 is the equivalent of an IPv4 loopback address. The link-local scope is the local subnet. The IPv6 address FF02::1 is the equivalent of an IPv4 local subnet broadcast.

Anycast addresses have no equivalent in IPv4. Anycast addresses are assigned to interfaces on multiple devices. When a packet is addressed to an anycast address, it is delivered only to the closest interface to which the anycast address is assigned. These are currently used only by routers.

Interface Identifiers

The first 64 bits of an IPv6 unicast address define the network number for routing. The second 64 bits define the **interface identifier**. The interface identifier is the IPv6 equivalent to a host ID in IPv4. Unlike an IPv4 host ID, an IPv6 interface identifier is always a consistent length of 64 bits.

There are three ways an interface identifier can be defined:

- Extended Unique Identifier (EUI)-64 address
- Randomly generated
- Assigned by DHCPv6

EUI-64 addresses are a new standard developed by the Institute of Electrical and Electronic Engineers (IEEE) to uniquely identify network interfaces. This will eventually replace MAC addresses, which are currently used to identify network interfaces.

An EUI-64 address is 64 bits long. The first 24 bits are used to uniquely identify vendors of networking devices. The last 40 bits are used to uniquely identify the interface produced by the manufacturer. A MAC address, by comparison, is a total of 48 bits with 24 bits used to identify vendors and 24 bits to identify the interface.

Many currently installed devices do not have EUI-64 addresses. To generate the interface identifier for IPv6, the MAC address can be converted to a EUI-64 address. The conversion process takes the first 24 bits of the MAC address, inserts 16 bits, and then adds the last 24 bits of the MAC address. When the first 24 bits of the MAC address are added, the seventh bit is complemented (one is converted to zero, and zero is converted to one). The 16 bits added to the middle of the address are all ones except for the final bit, which is zero (11111111 11111110), 0xFF 0xFE.

If the MAC address of a network card were AA:05:32:BD:19:61, then the converted EUI-64 address would be A8:05:32:FF:FE:BD:19:61. The AA in binary is 10101010; when the seventh bit is complemented this becomes A8, or 10101000 in binary.

Temporary address interface identifiers are randomly generated. This is done by organizations such as ISPs to provide anonymity to users accessing the Internet. If a EUI-64 address is used for the interface identifier, it is unique and may be tracked to an individual user over time. A temporary address interface identifier changes each time a computer connects to an ISP and therefore cannot be used to track an individual over time.

 DHCP can be used to assign an interface identifier the same way it can be used to assign an IPv4 address.

Configuring IPv6

The IPv6 protocol cannot be configured in the properties of a connection. Configuration must be done with the NETSH utility. This utility can also be used to view IPv4 configuration information.

Activity 2-6: Installing IPv6

Time Required: Five minutes

Objective: Install the IPv6 protocol.

Description: There is no current need to use IPv6 on the Arctic University network, but in the future it may be connected to an experimental backbone used by a consortium of universities for research. In preparation for this, you would like to install IPv6 on a server in your test lab.

1. If necessary, start your server and log on as Administrator.

2. Open the Classroom Properties window (see Activity 2-4, if necessary).

3. Click the **Install** button.

4. Click the **Protocol** option, and click **Add**.

5. Click the **Microsoft TCP/IP version 6** option, and click **OK**.

6. Click **Close** to close the Classroom Properties window. (You may be prompted to restart your computer.)

Activity 2-7: Viewing IPv6 Configuration

Time Required: Five minutes

Objective: View the automatically assigned IPv6 addresses.

Description: Now that you have installed IPv6, you would like to see which addresses have been automatically assigned. You need to run the utility NETSH to view the addresses.

1. If necessary, start your server and log on as Administrator.

2. Open a command prompt (see Activity 2-4, if necessary).

3. Type **netsh** and press **Enter**.

4. Type **interface** and press **Enter**.

5. Type **ipv6** and press **Enter**.

6. Type **show address** and press **Enter**. Note the addresses that have been assigned automatically.

7. Type **exit** and press **Enter**.

8. Close the command prompt window.

IPX/SPX

The most common protocol in use on **local area networks (LANs)** in the late 1980s and early 1990s was **Internetwork Packet eXchange/Sequenced Packet eXchange (IPX/SPX)**. It is much less common now because most companies have migrated their networks to TCP/IP instead.

The main reason companies started to move away from IPX/SPX was the development of the Internet. To use the Internet, companies had to implement TCP/IP. Rather than maintain two protocols, most companies chose to use TCP/IP only.

The primary reason IPX/SPX was so popular is that NetWare, a common network operating system (NOS), required it at the time. Even today, most companies that use IPX/SPX require it for connectivity with a NetWare server.

IPX/SPX is a routable protocol that is easy to configure. Because it is routable, it can be used on large networks. Easy configuration means there is very little maintenance of the client computers.

NWLink is the name Microsoft uses for the IPX/SPX-compatible protocol that it created. For Microsoft networks, the terms NWLink and IPX/SPX are often used interchangeably.

Activity 2-8: Installing NWLink

Time Required: Five minutes

Objective: Install the NWLink protocol.

Description: One of the servers on which you are installing Windows Server 2003 requires the NWLink protocol to support an older application. In this activity, you will install NWLink on the server before it is rolled out to the Arts faculty.

1. If necessary, start your server and log on as Administrator.
2. Open the Classroom Properties window (see Activity 2-4, if necessary).
3. Click the **Install** button.
4. Click the **Protocol** option, and click **Add**.
5. Click the **NWLink IPX/SPX/NetBIOS Compatible Transport Protocol** option, and click **OK**.
6. Click **Close** to close the Classroom Properties windows.

Service Location

When using TCP/IP, Windows Server 2003 with Active Directory uses DNS for service location. Older Windows servers and clients use WINS for service location. The primary disadvantage to both of these systems is that they require the clients to be configured with the IP address of the DNS or WINS server. However, the client configuration can be automated through DHCP.

IPX/SPX uses **Service Advertising Protocol (SAP)** to locate services. Each device that is providing IPX-based services sends a broadcast packet every 60 seconds to advertise its availability. Routers do not forward broadcasts, but IPX routers maintain a list of services of which they are aware and broadcast it out to all of the networks to which they are attached. In this way, service availability is eventually advertised throughout the entire network.

The broadcast of SAP packets every 60 seconds makes IPX/SPX very unpopular with **wide area network (WAN)** support staff. WAN support staff always wants to minimize the amount of traffic crossing the WAN links, and the SAP packets need to cross WAN links for services to be available across them. The constant advertising is considered unnecessary because the services being advertised do not change most of the time.

Addressing

Like a TCP/IP address, an IPX/SPX packet is composed of a network ID and a computer ID. The network ID is an eight-character hexadecimal number. The computer ID is a 12-character hexadecimal number. IPX/SPX does not require a subnet mask because the length of the network ID and the computer ID are always consistent. When written out, an IPX address includes the network ID and the computer ID, separated by a colon, as follows: A1A1A1A1:1234567890AB

The computer ID portion of the address is taken from the **MAC address** of the network card. Each network card has a unique 12-character hexadecimal address built into the card. IPX uses this as a convenient unique identifier on the network. This configuration is automatic.

The network ID portion of the address can be manually configured, but is normally automatically detected during the boot up of the server or workstation. It is detected from packets that are seen on the network.

Internal Network Address

When a Windows Server 2003 provides IPX/SPX-based services other than basic file and print, it must be configured with an **internal network address**. An internal network address is an eight-character hexadecimal number. This address must be different than any real IPX network address or the internal address of any other servers.

Applications running on Windows Server 2003 advertise their availability via SAP packets. In the SAP packets, services are advertised as available on the internal network address. The most common application that advertises via SAP is Microsoft SQL Server.

IPX routers must also be configured with an internal network address. This includes Windows Server 2003 when routing IPX.

 IPX/SPX is not available for the 64-bit version of Windows Server 2003—only 32-bit versions.

Frame Type

One unique characteristic of IPX/SPX is that it has multiple **frame types**. **Frame** is the term for a packet when it is fully built just before it is put onto the network cabling. Different frame types use slightly different formatting for the packet.

Two computers with IPX/SPX installed, but configured with different frame types, cannot communicate, even though the difference between the packet formats is small. This is similar to a system where information is placed in different colored envelopes. Each computer is configured to read one or more color of envelopes. If a computer receives an envelope color that it is not configured to read, it throws it away. Frame types are like the envelope colors in this example. Table 2-14 shows examples of different frame types and when they are used.

Table 2-14   Frame types

Frame Type	Common Use
Ethernet 802.3	NetWare 3.11 and earlier
Ethernet 802.2	NetWare 3.12 and above
Ethernet SNAP	Token Ring

A frame type can be manually configured, but is normally automatically detected during the initialization of network services. If multiple frame types are detected, Windows Server 2003 uses Ethernet 802.2. If Windows Server 2003 needs to be configured with multiple frame types, you must manually configure them. Figure 2-3 shows the window that can be used to configure frame types for NWLink.

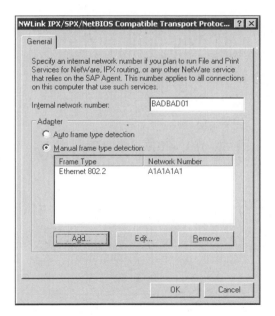

Figure 2-3   NWLink properties

If you would like to view the IPX configuration that your system is using, including the frame type, you can use the ipxroute config command. Figure 2-4 shows the results of running the ipxroute config command.

Figure 2-4   Results from the ipxroute command

Activity 2-9: Configuring NWLink

Time Required: 10 minutes

Objective: Configure NWLink to use a specific frame type, IPX network address, and internal network number.

Description: You are configuring a server with Windows Server 2003. The NWLink protocol is installed on the server, but there have been autoconfiguration problems where the server sometimes automatically detects an incorrect frame type. To fix this you need to configure the server with a specific frame type. In addition, this server will be hosting IPX services and requires an internal IPX number.

1. If necessary, start your server and log on as Administrator.

2. Open the Classroom Properties window (see Activity 2-4, if necessary).

3. Click the **NWLink IPX/SPX/NetBIOS Compatible Transport Protocol** option, and click the **Properties** button.

4. Type **BADBAD01** in the **Internal network number** box.

5. Click **Manual frame type detection**.

6. Click **Add**.

7. Verify that the **Ethernet 802.2** frame type is selected.

8. Type **A1A1A1A1** in the Network number box, and click **OK**.

9. Click **OK**, then **Close**.

10. Open a command prompt.

11. Type **ipxroute config** and press **Enter** to view your IPX settings.

12. Close the command prompt.

APPLETALK

The **AppleTalk** protocol is used for connectivity with Macintosh computers. When it is installed along with File Server for Macintosh or Print Server for Macintosh, Windows Server 2003 can emulate a Macintosh file or print server for Macintosh clients.

AppleTalk is a routable protocol and can be used on larger networks. However, there is no need for it if Macintosh clients are not supported.

Print Server for Macintosh is not available for the 64-bit versions of Windows Server 2003.

Activity 2-10: Installing AppleTalk

Time Required: Five minutes

Objective: Install the AppleTalk protocol.

Description: To support Macintosh computers in the Fine Arts faculty, you must install AppleTalk on Windows Server 2003.

1. If necessary, start your server and log on as Administrator.

2. Open the Classroom Properties window.

3. Click the **Install** button.

4. Click the **Protocol** option, and click **Add**.

5. Click the **AppleTalk Protocol** option, and click **OK**.

6. Click **Close** to exit the Classroom Properties window.

OBSOLETE PROTOCOLS

There are several protocols that were available in earlier versions of Windows that are not available in Windows Server 2003.

Data Link Control (DLC) is a nonroutable protocol that was used for connectivity to mainframe computers. It was also used for connectivity to Hewlett-Packard printers on a network.

NetBIOS Enhanced User Interface (NetBEUI) was one of the most common protocols used for early Windows networks. It is a fast, nonroutable, autoconfiguring protocol. The major advantage of this protocol was that all older Windows operating systems supported it. The lack of configuration options also made it very easy to use. As TCP/IP became more popular, the use of NetBEUI was phased out because it was not suited to larger routed networks and could not be used to access the Internet.

BINDINGS

Binding is the process where a network protocol is configured to use a network adapter. When a protocol is added to a network connection it is bound to the network adapter and the services that are part of that connection.

Windows Server 2003 allows you to optimize your network connectivity by adjusting the order in which protocols are used and defining the priority of network services. These settings are found in the Advanced Settings item of the Advanced menu in the Network Connections window, as shown in Figure 2-5.

The Adapters and Bindings tab, as shown in Figure 2-5, allows you to adjust the bindings for your adapters. For each adapter you can choose which clients and services are bound, and which network protocols are bound to each client or service. You can also choose the order of the bindings. The protocols used most often should be at the top of the list.

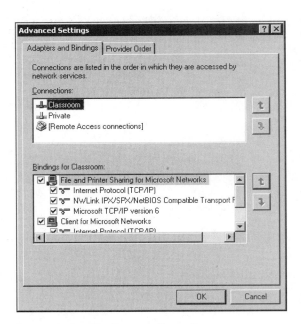

Figure 2-5   Binding configuration

For example, you could remove the NWLink protocol from File and Printer Sharing for Microsoft Networks if you decided that it was not required. This would mean that clients could access shared folders and printers on this server only if they were using TCP/IP. However, this server would still be able to access other NWLink-based resources on Microsoft networks because NWLink would still be bound to the Client for Microsoft Networks.

Activity 2-11: Optimizing Binding Order

Time Required: 10 minutes

Objective: Modify the binding order of protocols to optimize network communication.

Description: The server you are configuring for the Arts faculty has TCP/IP, NWLink, and TCP/IP version 6 installed. In this activity, you will configure NWLink to be the protocol with the highest priority for File and Printer Sharing for Microsoft Networks. TCP/IP will have the second highest priority and TCP/IP version 6 with the lowest priority. The Microsoft Client for Microsoft Networks will be configured with TCP/IP as the highest priority, NWLink as the second highest priority, and TCP/IP version 6 as the lowest priority.

1. If necessary, start your server and log on as Administrator.

2. To open the Network Connections window, click **Start**, point to **Control Panel**, right-click **Network Connections**, and click **Open**.

3. Click the **Advanced** menu, and click **Advanced Settings**.

4. If necessary, click **Classroom**, then in Bindings for Classroom under File and Printer Sharing for Microsoft Networks, click the **Internet Protocol (TCP/IP)** option, and click the **up arrow** button.

5. In Bindings for Classroom under Client for Microsoft Networks, click the **Internet Protocol (TCP/IP)** option, and click the **up arrow** button twice.

6. Click **OK** to exit the Advanced Settings window.

7. Leave the Network Connections window open for the next activity.

The Provider Order tab allows you to choose the order in which different providers are allowed access to network resources. In Figure 2-6, Microsoft Terminal Services has higher priority than Microsoft Windows network.

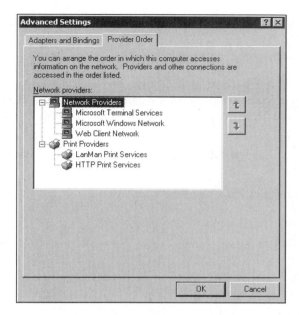

Figure 2-6   Provider order configuration

Activity 2-12 Removing Unnecessary Protocols

Time Required: Five minutes

Objective: Remove protocols that are no longer required.

Description: You would like to do a performance test on one of the servers in your test lab. To ensure peak performance, you need to remove all protocols except TCP/IP.

1. Open the Classroom Properties window.

2. Select the **AppleTalk Protocol** option, and click the **Uninstall** button.

3. Click **Yes** to confirm the removal.

4. Click the **NWLink IPX/SPX/NetBIOS Compatible Transport Protocol** option, and click the **Uninstall** button.

5. Click **Yes** to confirm the removal.

6. You will be requested to restart your computer. Click **No** to the request. You will restart your server after all unnecessary protocols are removed.

7. Click the **Microsoft TCP/IP version 6** option, and click the **Uninstall** button.

8. Click **Yes** to confirm the removal.

9. Close all open windows and restart your server.

CHAPTER SUMMARY

❑ Windows Server 2003 uses TCP/IP as its primary networking protocol. An IP address is comprised of both a network ID and a host ID. A subnet mask is used to define which part of the IP address is the network ID and which part is the host ID. A default gateway is required to deliver packets of information from one network to another.

❑ There are several ranges of IP addresses reserved for internal use that are not routable on the Internet. These address ranges are 10.$X.X.X$, 172.16.$X.X$-172.31.$X.X$ and 192.168.$X.X$.

- ❑ DHCP is used to automatically allocate IP addresses and other IP configuration information to clients.

- ❑ If a DHCP server cannot be contacted, then clients use APIPA, which randomly generates an IP address in the range 169.254.*X.X*.

- ❑ The IPX/SPX protocol can be used with the 32-bit version of Windows Server 2003. This protocol is primarily used in networks where Novell NetWare is present. The frame type is automatically detected when IPX/SPX is initialized during the boot process. If multiple frame types are present, then 802.2 is used.

- ❑ The AppleTalk protocol is available for Windows Server 2003. It is used for connectivity with Apple Macintosh computers.

- ❑ Bindings can be adjusted to optimize networking performance. The most used protocols should be listed first in the bindings.

KEY TERMS

Active Directory — A directory service for Windows 2000/2003 Servers that stores information about network resources.

aggregatable global unicast addresses — The IPv6 equivalent of IPv4 class A, B, and C addresses. They are designed for future use on the Internet.

anycast address — An IPv6 address that can be assigned to multiple hosts. A packet addressed to an anycast address is delivered to the single closest host that is assigned the anycast address.

AppleTalk — A protocol that is used when communicating with Apple Macintosh computers.

Automatic Private IP Addressing (APIPA) — A feature of newer Windows operating systems that automatically generates an IP address on the 169.254.*X.X* network when a DHCP server cannot be contacted.

binding — Configuring a network protocol to use a network adapter.

broadcast — A packet that is addressed to all computers on a network. A broadcast for the local network is addressed to 255.255.255.255.

classful routing — An older style of routing in which routing table entries would be based on class A, B, and C networks with default subnet masks.

classless inter-domain routing (CIDR) — An addressing scheme that uses a defined number of bits for the subnet mask rather than relying on default lengths based on address classes. The number of bits in the network ID is defined as /*XX* after the IP address. *XX* is the number of bits.

client — A networking component that is installed in computers requesting network services. Client software communicates with a corresponding service.

Data Link Control (DLC) — A nonroutable protocol originally developed for mainframe computers. It is not supported by Windows Server 2003.

default gateway — A dedicated hardware device or computer on a network that is responsible for moving packets from one IP network to another. This is another term for IP router.

domain controller — A Windows 2000/2003 Server that holds a copy of the Active Directory information for a domain.

domain name — The portion of DNS namespace that can be registered and controlled by an organization or individual.

Domain Name System (DNS) — A service used by clients running TCP/IP to resolve host names to IP addresses. Active Directory uses DNS to store service location information.

Dynamic Host Configuration Protocol (DHCP) — A protocol used to automatically assign IP addressing information to clients.

Ethernet — The most common networking standard for network cards, hubs, switches, and routers on local area networks. Variations exist for 10 Mbps, 100 Mbps, 1 Gbps, and 10 Gbps.

EUI-64 addresses — A new standard developed by the IEEE to uniquely identify network interfaces. These will eventually replace MAC addresses.

File Transfer Protocol (FTP) — The protocol used by FTP clients and servers to move files. By default, it uses TCP port 21 for control information and TCP port 20 for data transfer.

frame — A packet of information that is being transmitted on the network.

frame type — The format of IPX/SPX packets. Multiple frame types are available and two computers must be using the same frame type to communicate.

Fully Qualified Domain Name (FQDN) — The combination of a host name and domain name that completely describes the name of a computer within the global DNS system.

host ID — The portion of an IP address that uniquely identifies a computer on an IP network.

host name — The name of a computer using the TCP/IP protocol.

Hypertext Transfer Protocol (HTTP) — The protocol used by Web browsers and Web servers. By default, it uses TCP port 80.

interface identifier — The part of an IPv6 address that uniquely identifies the host on a network. It is equivalent to an IPv4 host ID.

internal network address — A unique eight-character hexadecimal identifier used by Windows computers that are providing IPX/SPX-based services. Services are advertised as available on this network.

Internet Protocol version 4 (IPv4) — The IP portion of the TCP/IP protocol suite. Version 4 uses 32-bit addresses expressed in dotted decimal notation. This is the version of IP that is currently used on the Internet.

Internet Protocol version 6 (IPv6) — The IP portion of the TCP/IP protocol suite. An update to IPv4, version 6 uses 128-bit addresses expressed in hexadecimal notation and adds many new features.

Internet service provider (ISP) — A company that sells Internet access.

Internetwork Packet eXchange/Sequenced Packet eXchange (IPX/SPX) — The protocol required to communicate with servers running Novell NetWare 4 and earlier.

IP address — A unique address assigned to each computer with the TCP/IP protocol installed. It is 32 bits long and is composed of a network ID and a host ID.

link-local address — The IPv6 equivalent of an IPv4 APIPA address.

Linux — An open source operating system that is very similar to UNIX.

local area network (LAN) — A group of computers and other devices networked together over a relatively short distance.

loopback — Any IP address that begins with 127.*X*.*X*.*X*. These addresses represent the local host.

MAC address — A number that uniquely identifies a network node. This address is hard-coded onto the NIC.

multicast — A packet that is addressed to a specific group of computers rather than a single computer. Multicast addresses range from 224.0.0.0 to 239.255.255.255.

NetBIOS Enhanced User Interface (NetBEUI) — A nonroutable protocol commonly used in smaller Windows networks. It is not supported by Windows Server 2003.

NetWare — A network operating system from Novell that traditionally uses the IPX/SPX protocol.

network adapter — In Windows networking this represents the network interface card and the driver that goes with it.

Network Address Translation (NAT) — A service that allows multiple computers to access the Internet by sharing a single IP address.

network ID — The portion of an IP address that designates the network on which a computer resides. This is defined by the subnet mask.

NWLink — An IPX/SPX-compatible protocol created by Microsoft for Windows operating systems.

octet — A group of eight bits. An IP address is composed of four octets, with each expressed as a decimal number.

ping — A utility used to test connectivity by sending an ICMP Reply Request packet.

protocol — The language that two computers use to communicate on a network. Two computers must use the same protocol to communicate.

proxy server — A server that can be used to control and speed up access to the Internet. It also allows multiple computers to access the Internet through a single IP address.

router — A network device that moves packets from one network to another. TCP/IP, IPX/SPX, and AppleTalk can be routed.

service — A networking component that provides resources to network clients. Each service communicates with corresponding client software.

Service Advertising Protocol (SAP) — A protocol used by IPX/SPX to advertise the availability of services by sending out a broadcast message every 60 seconds.

Simple Mail Transfer Protocol (SMTP) — A protocol used by e-mail clients to send messages to e-mail servers. It uses TCP port 25.

site-local address — The IPv6 equivalent of an IPv4 internal network address such as 10.0.0.0/8.

subnet mask — A string of 32 bits that is used to define which portion of an IP address is the host ID and which part is the network ID.

subnetting — A process where a single large network is subdivided into smaller networks to control traffic flow.

Transmission Control Protocol/Internet Protocol (TCP/IP) — A suite of protocols that allows interconnected networks to communicate with one another. It is the most common protocol in Windows networking and must be used to access the Internet.

unicast addresses — IP addresses that are assigned to a single host.

wide area network (WAN) — Geographically dispersed networks with more than one physical location. The links between each location are relatively slow compared to local area networks.

Windows Internet Naming Service (WINS) — A Windows service used to resolve NetBIOS names to IP addresses as well as store NetBIOS service information.

REVIEW QUESTIONS

1. The four components required for Windows networking are: _____.

2. For what type of protocol is the development process controlled by a standards committee rather than any single company or individual?

   a. open

   b. standard

   c. dynamic

   d. legacy

3. Which of the following protocols is required for access to the Internet?

   a. IPX/SPX

   b. NetBEUI

   c. IPv4

   d. IPv6

4. Which of the following network services is used by Active Directory for service location?

   a. DHCP

   b. DNS

   c. WINS

   d. TCP/IP

5. How many octets are in an IP address?

   a. 2

   b. 4

   c. 8

   d. 16

6. How many bits are in an octet?

    a. 2

    b. 4

    c. 8

    d. 16

7. Which of the following organizations is responsible for the management of IP addresses in North America?

    a. American Registry for Internet Numbers (ARIN)

    b. Asia Pacific Network Information Center (APNIC)

    c. Réseaux IP Européen (RIPE)

    d. Internet Corporation for Assigned Names and Numbers (ICANN)

8. Which of the following defines the part of an IP address that is the host ID and the part that is the network ID?

    a. default gateway

    b. DNS server

    c. WINS server

    d. subnet mask

9. What is the default subnet mask for a Class C IP address?

    a. 255.0.0.0

    b. 255.255.0.0

    c. 255.255.255.0

    d. 0.255.255.255

10. A computer will use a default gateway if the destination IP address is on a different network. True or False?

11. Which of the following is another name for default gateway?

    a. router

    b. switch

    c. hub

    d. host

12. IP address 227.43.76.109 is an example of which of the following classes of IP addresses?

    a. Class A

    b. Class B

    c. Class C

    d. Class D

    e. Class E

13. IP address 24.55.208.199 is an example of which of the following classes of IP addresses?

    a. Class A

    b. Class B

    c. Class C

    d. Class D

    e. Class E

14. The IP address 169.254.226.4 can be routed on the Internet. True or False?

15. The IP address 172.33.32.220 can be routed on the Internet. True or False?

16. What was introduced to make Internet routing and the assignment of IP addresses more efficient?

    a. subnet masks

    b. switches

    c. DHCP

    d. CIDR

17. How many octets are part of the network ID when using the subnet mask 255.255.255.0?

    a. 1

    b. 2

    c. 3

    d. 4

18. How many octets are part of the host ID for the IP address 176.167.98.3/24?

    a. 1

    b. 2

    c. 3

    d. 4

19. What type of server does a Windows client use to resolve NetBIOS names to IP addresses?

    a. DNS

    b. DHCP

    c. WINS

    d. Remote Access

20. What type of server does a Windows client use to resolve host names to IP addresses?

    a. DNS

    b. DHCP

    c. WINS

    d. Remote Access

21. Which of the following protocols is used to communicate with Apple Macintosh computers?

    a. TCP/IP

    b. IPX/SPX

    c. AppleTalk

    d. NetBEUI

22. Which of the following protocols was commonly used in small, older Windows networks, but is not available in Windows Server 2003?

    a. TCP/IP

    b. IPX/SPX

    c. AppleTalk

    d. NetBEUI

23. Which of the following features of IPX/SPX is automatically detected during boot up?

    a. frame type

    b. internal network address

    c. subnet mask

    d. default gateway

24. Which of the following terms is often used interchangeably with IPX/SPX when talking about Microsoft networks?

    a. NWLink

    b. IPv6

    c. default gateway

    d. DNS

25. Which of the following can you adjust to optimize networking performance on Windows .NET Server 2003?

    a. subnet mask

    b. bindings

    c. default gateway

    d. frame type

CASE PROJECTS

Because Arctic University is in a remote part of the north, Internet access has not been available. Now, thanks to a new satellite system, you will be able to receive Internet access from ZAP Internet Services, despite your location.

Most of the university network is made up of Windows-based computers. However, individual professors have independent funding for projects and can buy any equipment they want. As a result, some departments have Novell NetWare servers, the Engineering Department has Linux workstations, and the Fine Arts Department has Macintosh workstations.

Case Project 2-1: Documenting the Existing Network

In order to make sound decisions, your boss, Jerry, needs information about the protocols in use on your network. Write a short report for Jerry documenting all of the protocols that are required on your network, why they are required, and any configuration options that might be required.

Case Project 2-2: Choosing IP Addresses

Jerry is unsure whether you should use Internal IP addresses for your network or get Internet-accessible addresses from ZAP Internet Services. Write a short list of pros and cons for each option that you can use when discussing this matter in the weekly technical staff meeting.

Case Project 2-3: Solving an Upgrade Problem

On Monday morning you receive an e-mail asking for your help. Over the weekend one of your colleagues upgraded a departmental Windows NT server to Windows Server 2003. Now over half of the department can no longer log on to the server or access resources from it. What ideas do you have that may help your colleague?

3

TCP/IP ARCHITECTURE

After reading this chapter and completing the exercises, you will be able to:

♦ Describe the overall architecture of TCP/IP

♦ Describe application layer protocols

♦ Discuss transport layer protocols

♦ Understand the role of various network layer protocols including IP, ICMP, and ARP

♦ Understand network interface layer protocols

♦ Describe different physical layer protocols

♦ Discuss changes to IP introduced with IPv6

Each component of the TCP/IP protocol stack has its own tasks and responsibilities as part of the communication process. It is important to understand the overall architecture of TCP/IP and the roles of each component so that you have a starting point in troubleshooting connectivity issues. In this chapter, you will learn about the architecture of the TCP/IP protocol stack and the roles of each layer.

TCP/IP ARCHITECTURE OVERVIEW

The TCP/IP model can be broken down into four layers: application, transport, Internet, and network interface. Figure 3-1 shows the protocols that exist in each of the four layers in the TCP/IP model and how they relate to the OSI model. The **Open Systems Interconnection (OSI) reference model** is an industry standard that is used as a reference point to compare different networking technologies and protocols.

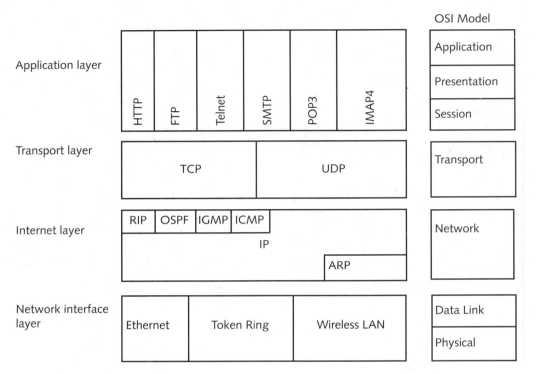

Figure 3-1   TCP/IP architecture

The **application layer** provides access to network resources. It defines the rules, commands, and procedures that client software uses to talk to a service running on a server. As an example, the HTTP protocol is an application layer protocol that defines how Web browsers and Web servers communicate.

The **transport layer** is responsible for preparing data to be transported across the network. This layer breaks large messages into smaller **packets** of information and tracks whether they arrived at their final destination.

The **Internet layer** is responsible for logical addressing and routing. IP addresses are logical addresses. Any protocol that is network-aware exists in this layer.

The **network interface layer** consists of the network card driver and the circuitry on the network card itself.

APPLICATION LAYER PROTOCOLS

There are many application layer protocols, each of which is associated with a client application and service. For example, FTP clients use the FTP protocol and telnet clients use the **Telnet** protocol. However, some client software is capable of using more than one protocol. For example, Web browsers are capable of using HTTP to communicate with Web servers, and FTP to communicate with FTP servers.

3

HTTP

Hypertext Transfer Protocol (HTTP) is the most common protocol used on the Internet today. This is the protocol used by Web browsers and Web servers. HTTP defines the commands that Web browsers can send and how Web servers are capable of responding. For example, when requesting a Web page, a Web browser sends a GET command. The server then responds by sending the requested Web page. Many commands are defined as part of the protocol.

Information can also be uploaded using the HTTP protocol. A survey form on a Web page is an example of information moving from a Web browser to a Web server. The capabilities of Web servers can also be extended using a variety of mechanisms that allow Web servers to pass data from forms to applications or scripts for processing. Some of the common mechanisms for passing data from a Web server to an application are:

- **Common Gateway Interface (CGI)**
- **Internet Server Application Programmer Interface (ISAPI)**
- **Netscape Server Application Programmer Interface (NSAPI)**

 The World Wide Web consortium (W3C) is the standards body responsible for defining the commands that are part of HTTP.

FTP

File Transfer Protocol (FTP) is a simple file-sharing protocol. It includes commands for uploading and downloading files, as well as requesting directory listings from remote servers. This protocol has been around the Internet for a long time and was originally implemented on UNIX during the 1980s. The first **Request for Comment (RFC)** describing FTP was created in 1985.

 Although there are still FTP servers running on the Internet, they number fewer than in previous years. This is because HTTP is capable of uploading and downloading files, which is slowly making FTP obsolete.

FTP is implemented in stand-alone FTP clients as well as in Web browsers. It is safe to say that most FTP users today are using Web browsers.

Activity 3-1: Using FTP to Download a File

Time Required: 10 minutes

Objective: Use FTP to download a utility.

Description: There is a utility that you wish to download from the Microsoft FTP server. Normally, you would use Internet Explorer to download this file, but Internet Explorer is not functioning properly on your workstation. As a result, you need to use the command-line FTP client to download the index of available files.

1. If necessary, start your server and log on as Administrator of the Artic domain.

   Note: For all activities, log on as the domain Administrator.

2. Click the **Start** button, and then click **Run**.

3. Type **FTP** and press **Enter**.

4. Type **open ftp.microsoft.com** and press **Enter**.

5. Type **anonymous** and press **Enter**.

6. Type your e-mail address, and press **Enter**.

7. Type **ls** and press **Enter**.

8. Type **cd softlib** and press **Enter**.

9. Type **dir** and press **Enter**.

10. Type **get index.txt** and press **Enter**. This command will retrieve the file index.txt from the remote server. All retrieved files are placed in the current directory on the local machine. In this instance the current directory is C:\Documents and Settings\Administrator.ARCTIC.

11. Type **bye** and press **Enter**.

Telnet

Telnet is a terminal emulation protocol that is primarily used to remotely connect to Unix and Linux Systems. The Telnet protocol specifies how a telnet server and telnet client communicate.

The most common reason to connect to a server via Telnet is to remotely manage Unix or Linux systems. All of the administration for these systems can be done through a character-based interface. This is important because Telnet does not support a **graphical user interface (GUI)**, only text.

Telnet is similar to the concept of a mainframe and dumb terminal. The telnet server controls the entire user environment, processes the keyboard input, and sends display commands back to the client. A telnet client is responsible only for displaying information on the screen and passing input to the server. There can be many telnet clients connected to a single server at one time. Each client that is connected receives its own operating environment; however, these clients are not aware that other users are logged into the system.

SMTP

Simple Mail Transfer Protocol (SMTP) is used to send and receive e-mail messages between e-mail servers that are communicating. It is also used by e-mail client software, such as Outlook Express, to send messages to the server. SMTP is never used to retrieve e-mail from a server when you are reading it. Other protocols control the reading of e-mail messages.

Activity 3-2 : Using Telnet to Verify SMTP

Time Required: 10 minutes

Objective: Use Telnet to verify the functionality of an SMTP server.

Description: A client is having a problem sending e-mail to a person at Microsoft. You want to verify that Microsoft's SMTP server is responding on the Internet. If you can Telnet to the mail server on port 25, that will indicate that the server is operational and accepting connections.

1. If necessary, start your server and log on as Administrator.

2. Click the **Start** button, and then click **Run**.

3. Type **cmd** and click **OK**.

4. Type **telnet** and press **Enter**.

5. Type **set localecho** and press **Enter**. This displays the commands that you type in the telnet window.

6. Type **open maila.microsoft.com 25** and press **Enter**.

7. Type **help** and press **Enter**. What commands does the mail server support?

8. Type **helo** and press **Enter**. What is the FQDN of the mail server?

9. Type **quit** and press **Enter**.

10. If you are prompted to press a key to continue then press **Enter** twice.

11. Type **quit** and press **Enter** to close the Telnet utility.

12. Close the command prompt.

POP3

Post Office Protocol version 3 (POP3) is the most common protocol used for reading e-mail messages. This protocol has commands to download messages and delete messages from the mail server. POP3 does not support sending messages. By default, most e-mail client software using POP3 copies all messages onto the local hard drive and erases them from the server. However, you can change the configuration so that messages can be left on the server. POP3 only supports a single inbox and does not support multiple folders for storage on the server.

IMAP4

Internet Message Access Protocol version 4 (IMAP4) is another common protocol used to read e-mail messages. The abilities of IMAP4 are beyond those of POP3. For example, IMAP can download message headers only, then allow you to choose which messages to download. In addition, IMAP4 allows for multiple folders on the server side to store messages.

TRANSPORT LAYER PROTOCOLS

Transport layer protocols are responsible for getting data ready to move across the network. The most common task performed by transport layer protocols is breaking entire messages down into packets. For instance, if an entire file is being moved across the network, then a transport layer protocol breaks it down into smaller pieces that can move more easily across the network.

One of the defining characteristics of transport layer protocols is the use of **port** numbers. Each service running on a server listens at a port number. Each transport layer protocol has its own set of ports. When a packet is addressed to a particular port, the transport layer protocol knows to which service to deliver the packet. The combination of an IP address and port number is referred to as a socket.

A port number is like an apartment number for the delivery of mail. The network ID of the IP address ensures that the packet is delivered to the correct street (network); the host ID ensures that the packet is delivered to the correct building (host); the transport layer protocol and port number ensure that the packet is delivered to the proper apartment (service).

The two transport layer protocols in the TCP/IP protocol suite are **Transmission Control Protocol (TCP)** and **User Datagram Protocol (UDP)**. Table 3-1 shows well-known services and the ports they use.

Table 3-1   Common services and ports

Service	Port
FTP	TCP 21,20
Telnet	TCP 23
SMTP	TCP 25
HTTP	TCP 80
DNS	TCP 53, UDP 53
Trivial FTP (TFTP)	UDP 69
POP3	TCP 110
NNTP	TCP 119
IMAP	TCP 143
Secure HTTP	TCP 443

Activity 3-3: Using Port Numbers

Time Required: Five minutes

Objective: Connect to resources using TCP and UDP port numbers.

Description: You have been explaining the concept of port numbers to a colleague. He is still unsure that he understands how they are used. You have explained that a Web browser automatically uses the default port for a protocol. In this hands-on exercise, you demonstrate for your colleague what happens when an incorrect port number is used.

1. If necessary, start your server and log on as Administrator.

2. Open Internet Explorer.

3. Type **http://www.microsoft.com** in the address bar, and press **Enter**. The Web browser will automatically connect you to port 80 on this server.

4. Type **http://www.microsoft.com:21** in the address bar, and press **Enter**. The Web browser will not be able to connect because port 21 is not used for HTTP.

5. Type **http://www.microsoft.com:80** in the address bar, and press **Enter**. The Web browser will connect and give you the same Web page as step 3.

6. Type **ftp://ftp.microsoft.com** in the address bar, and press **Enter**. The Web browser will automatically connect you to port 21 when using FTP.

7. Type **ftp://ftp.microsoft.com:80** in the address bar, and press **Enter**. The Web browser will not be able to connect because port 80 is not used for FTP.

8. Click **OK** to clear the error message window.

9. Type **ftp://ftp.microsoft.com:21** in the address bar, and press **Enter**. The Web browser will connect and give you the same information as step 6.

10. Close Internet Explorer

TCP

Transmission Control Protocol (TCP) is the most commonly used transport layer protocol. TCP is **connection-oriented** and reliable. Connection-oriented means that TCP creates and verifies a connection with a remote host before sending information. This verifies that the remote host exists and is willing to communicate before starting the conversation.

The establishment of a connection is a three-packet process between the source and destination host. It is often called a three-way handshake. Figure 3-2 shows the packets involved in the three-way handshake performed when a connection is established between Computer A and Computer B.

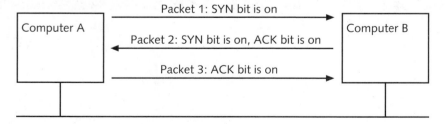

Figure 3-2   TCP three-way handshake

In Figure 3-2, you can see that the connection is initiated by Computer A. An option in the packet called the **SYN bit** is turned on. The SYN bit indicates that this packet is a request to negotiate a connection. This request includes parameters for the conversation such as the maximum packet size.

The response packet from Computer B to Computer A has the ACK and SYN bits turned on. The **ACK bit** is an option in a packet that indicates this packet is a response to the first packet. The SYN bit is on because this packet contains the parameters that Computer B would like to use when communicating with Computer A. If Computer B is able to use the parameters received in the first packet then those are the parameters sent in this packet. If Computer B cannot use a parameter from the first packet then it replaces that parameter with one that it can use in this packet.

The third packet is the final agreement from Computer A indicating that it has accepted the terms of the Computer B. This packet has the ACK bit turned on to indicate it is a response to the second packet.

TCP is considered reliable because it tracks each packet and makes sure that it arrives at its destination. If a packet is lost or damaged as part of the communication process, then the packet is transmitted again. The overall process is called a **sliding window**.

If a thousand packets are waiting to be sent as part of the communication process, not all of the packets are sent at once because it would be too difficult to track. Only a few packets are sent at a time. The number of packets is negotiated as part of the process of establishing the connection and is considered as being the size of the sliding window. For example, if the sliding window size is set to 10 packets, then only 10 packets are sent at a time. When the destination computer acknowledges receipt of the first 10 packets, then the window slides forward and another 10 packets are sent.

The sliding window cannot be moved past a packet that has not been received and acknowledged by the destination. If a packet goes missing it must be retransmitted and acknowledged before the sliding window can move past that point. A common reason why there is a pause in the middle of large downloads from the Internet is that a packet has been lost and must be retransmitted before the conversation can continue.

Being reliable and connection-oriented are generally desirable qualities. Consequently, TCP is the transport layer protocol used for most Internet services. HTTP, FTP, SMTP, POP3 and IMAP4 all use TCP.

Activity 3-4: Installing Network Monitor

Time Required: Five minutes

Objective: Install Network Monitor to enable packet capturing

Description: You would like to see exactly how some of the data packets on your network are addressed. To see packet details, you install the application Network Monitor that is included with Windows .NET Server 2003.

1. If necessary, start your server and log on as Administrator.
2. Click the **Start** button, point to **Control Panel**, and then click **Add or Remove Programs**.
3. Click **Add/Remove Windows Components**.
4. Scroll down in the Components section, then double-click **Management and Monitoring Tools**.
5. Click the check box beside **Network Monitor Tools** to select it, and click **OK**.
6. Click the **Next** button. If necessary, click **OK** in the Insert Disk dialog box, then browse to the C:\I386 folder, and click **OK** in the Files Needed dialog box.
7. Click the **Finish**, and close the Add or Remove Programs window.

Activity 3-5: Viewing a TCP Connection in Network Monitor

Time Required: 30 minutes

Objective: Capture and view TCP connection packets in Network Monitor.

Description: You are going to be configuring the Arctic University firewall in the next few weeks and would like to be familiar with the detailed packet information that is used when creating a TCP connection. In this exercise you capture and view the packets used when a TCP connection is created with HTTP.

1. If necessary, start your server and log on as Administrator.

2. Open Internet Explorer

3. Click the **Start** button, point to **Administrative Tools**, and click **Network Monitor**.

4. Click **OK**.

5. Click the **+** (plus sign) beside **Local Computer**, click **Classroom**, and click **OK**.

6. Press **F10** to start capturing packets.

7. In Internet Explorer, type **www.yahoo.com** in the address bar, and press **Enter**.

8. In Network Monitor, press **F11** to stop capturing packets.

9. Press **F12** to view the captured packets.

10. Filter the display to only show packets with a TCP source port or a TCP destination port of 80. This shows all packets addressed to the Web server or coming from the Web server.

    a. Click the **Display** menu, and click **Filter**.

    b. Double-click the green **And** to change it to **Or**.

    c. Double-click **Protocol==Any**.

    d. Click the **Property** tab.

    e. Double-click **TCP** in the Protocol: Property box, then, underneath TCP, click **Destination Port**, click the **Decimal** radio button, type **80** in the Value box, and click **OK**.

    f. In the Add box, click **Expression**.

    g. Under TCP, click **Source Port** and click **OK**.

    h. Click **ANY<--> ANY** and then click **Line** in the Delete box.

    i. Click **OK**.

11. View the first packet in a TCP handshake.

    a. Double-click the first packet in the Capture:/(Summary) window.

    b. Expand the **IP** section of the middle window to view the source and destination IP addresses. The source IP address is your computer. The destination IP address is the Web server.

    c. Expand the **TCP** section of the middle window to view the source and destination TCP ports. The source port varies, but the destination port is World Wide Web HTTP. Network Monitor substitutes the phrase World Wide Web HTTP for the number 80 to make it easier to read and understand.

    d. Expand the **TCP: Flags** section of the middle window to view the acknowledgement (ACK) and synchronize (SYN) flags. In this packet, the ACK flag is set to 0 and the SYN flag is set to 1.

    e. Expand the **TCP: Options** and **TCP: Maximum Segment Size Option** to view the packet size that is being requested.

12. View the second packet in a TCP handshake.

    a. Click the second packet in the top window.

    b. In the **IP** section of the middle window view the source and destination IP addresses. The source IP address is the Web server. The destination IP address is your server.

    c. In the **TCP** section of the middle window view the source and destination TCP ports. The destination port is the same as the source port in the first packet. The source port is World Wide Web HTTP.

d. In the **TCP: Flags** section of the middle windows view the acknowledgement (ACK) and synchronize (SYN) flags. In this packet, the ACK flag is set to 1 and the SYN flag is set to 1.

e. In the **TCP: Options** and **TCP: Maximum Segment Size Option** view the packet size that is being requested. This is the same as the first packet or smaller.

13. View the third packet in a TCP handshake.

a. Click the third packet in the top window.

b. In the **IP** section of the middle window view the source and destination IP addresses. The source IP address is your server. The destination IP address is the Web server.

c. In the **TCP** section of the middle window view the source and destination TCP ports. The source port is the same as the first packet and the destination port is World Wide Web HTTP.

d. In the **TCP: Flags** section of the middle windows view the acknowledgement (ACK) and synchronize (SYN) flags. In this packet, the ACK flag is set to 1 and the SYN flag is set to 0.

e. **TCP: Options** does not exist in this packet.

14. Click the fourth packet in the top window to view an HTTP GET request. This packet is the request for the Web page.

15. Click the fifth packet in the top window to view the response to the GET request. This is the information returned from the Web server based on the GET request.

16. Close Network Monitor (click **No** if prompted to save changes) and Internet Explorer.

UDP

User Datagram Protocol (UDP) is not as commonly used as TCP and is used for different services. UDP is **connectionless** and unreliable. Connectionless means that UDP does not attempt to negotiate terms with a remote host before sending information. UDP simply sends the information. If any terms need to be negotiated, the application layer protocol above has to do it. There is no handshake for UDP. Unreliable means that UDP does not track or guarantee delivery of packets between the source and destination. UDP just sends a stream of packets without waiting for acknowledgement. There is no sliding window for UDP.

UDP is the appropriate transport layer protocol to use when you are unconcerned about missing packets or would like to implement reliability in a special way. Streaming audio and video are in this category. If streaming audio were to pause and wait for missing packets to be sent again, then there could be long pauses in the sound. Most people prefer a small amount of static or silence be inserted for the missing packet and the rest of the audio track continue to play. UDP does this because it does not keep track of packets that are missing or needing to be sent again. In the case of streaming audio, re-sent packets are handled by the application layer protocol.

Connectionless communication also makes sense when the amount of data being exchanged is very small. Using three packets to set up a connection for a two-packet conversation is very inefficient. The resolution of a DNS name is a two-packet communication process and is done via UDP.

Activity 3-6: Capturing UDP Packets in Network Monitor

Time Required: 15 minutes

Objective: Capture and view UDP packets in Network Monitor.

Description: As preparation for configuring the Arctic University firewall in the next few weeks, you would like to be familiar with the detailed packet information that is used in UDP packets. In this activity you view DNS packets.

1. If necessary, start your server and log on as Administrator.

2. Open Internet Explorer.

3. Open Network Monitor (see Activity 3-5, if necessary).

4. Click the **Start** button, and click **Run**.

5. Type **ipconfig /flushdns** and press **Enter**. This removes any cached DNS lookup information. This ensures that, later in the activity, a DNS lookup will be required rather than getting DNS information from cache.

6. In Network Monitor, press **F10** to start capturing packets.

7. In Internet Explorer, type **www.yahoo.com** in the address bar, and press **Enter**.

8. In Network Monitor, press **F11** to stop capturing packets.

9. Press **F12** to view the captured packets.

10. Filter the display to only show packets with a TCP source port or a TCP destination port of 53. This shows all packets addressed to the DNS server or coming from the DNS server.

    a. Click the **Display** menu, and click **Filter**.

    b. Double-click the green **And** to change it to **Or**.

    c. Double-click **Protocol==Any**.

    d. Click the **Property** tab.

    e. Double-click **UDP** in the Protocol: Property box, and then, underneath UDP, click **Destination Port**, click the **Decimal** radio button, type **53** in the Value box, and click **OK**.

    f. In the Add box, click **Expression**.

    g. Under UDP, click **Source Port** and click **OK**.

    h. Click **ANY<--> ANY** and then click **Line** in the Delete box.

    i. Click **OK**.

11. View the first UDP DNS packet.

    a. Double-click the packet with the description **Std Qry for www.yahoo.com**.

    b. Expand the **IP** section of the middle window to view the source and destination IP addresses. The source IP address is your computer. The destination IP address is the DNS server.

    c. Expand the **UDP** section of the middle window to view the source and destination UDP ports. The source UDP port varies. The destination UDP port is Domain Name Server.

    d. Expand the **DNS** section of the middle window to view the DNS-specific information.

12. View the second UDP DNS packet.

    a. Click the packet with the description **Std Qry Resp. for www.yahoo.com**.

    b. In the **IP** section of the middle window view the source and destination IP addresses. The source IP address is the DNS server. The destination IP address is your server.

    c. In the **UDP** section of the middle window view the source and destination UDP ports. The source UDP is the Domain Name Server. The destination UDP port is the same as the source UDP port in the previous packet.

    d. In the **DNS** section of the middle window view the DNS-specific information.

13. Close Network Monitor (click **No** if prompted to save changes) and Internet Explorer.

TCP versus UDP

TCP is connection-oriented and reliable. This is similar to delivering a letter by registered mail. Inside the letter each page is numbered so that it can be read in the proper order. When the message is received the sender receives notice that it arrived properly at its destination.

UDP is connectionless and unreliable. If you were to take the same message as in the previous example and place it on several postcards, take all of the postcards and dump them in the mail box separately, then the likelihood is that the recipient would be able to put them in the proper order and understand the message. However, if one postcard was missing it would be very difficult for the recipient to understand the complete message.

INTERNET LAYER PROTOCOLS

Internet layer protocols are responsible for all tasks related to logical addressing. An IP address is a logical address. Any protocol that is aware of other networks, as in how to find them and how to reach them, exists at this layer. Each Internet layer protocol is very specialized. They include: IP, RIP, OSPF, ICMP, IGMP, and ARP.

IP

Internet Protocol (IP) is responsible for the logical addressing of each packet created by the transport layer. As each packet is built, IP adds the source and destination IP address to the packet.

When a packet is received from the network, IP verifies that it is addressed to this computer. IP looks at the destination IP address of the packet to verify that it is the same as the IP address of the receiving computer, or a broadcast address of which this computer is a part. For example, if a computer has an IP address of 192.168.1.50/24, then IP would accept packets addressed to 192.168.1.50, 192.168.1.255, and 255.255.255.255.

RIP and OSPF

Routing Information Protocol (RIP) and **Open Shortest Path First (OSPF)** are both routing protocols. They are responsible for defining how paths are chosen through the internetwork from one computer to another. They also define how routers can share information about the networks of which they are aware.

RIP and OSPF will be covered in more detail later in this book.

ICMP

Internet Control Messaging Protocol (ICMP) is used to send IP error and control messages between routers and hosts. The most common use of ICMP is the ping utility.

The ping utility uses ICMP packets to test connectivity between hosts. When you use ping to communicate with a host, your computer sends an ICMP Echo Request packet. The host that you are pinging sends an ICMP Echo Response packet back. If there is a response, you can be sure that the host you have pinged is up and functional. However, if a host does not respond, that does not guarantee it is nonfunctional. Many firewalls are configured to block ICMP packets.

The Internet Assigned Numbers Authority (IANA) maintains a complete list of ICMP packet types at *www.iana.org/assignments/icmp-parameters*. Table 3-2 lists the most common ICMP packet types.

Table 3-2 Common ICMP packet types

Packet Type	Packet Name	Description
0	Echo Reply	Used in response to an Echo Request packet from a host
3	Destination Unreachable	Used by routers to indicate that the intended destination IP address cannot be reached
4	Source Quench	Used by routers to indicate that packets are being sent too fast and should be slowed down; this is seldom used
8	Echo	Used to generate an Echo Reply packet from a host
11	Time Exceeded	Used by routers to indicate that the Time To Live (TTL) of a packet has expired

The Time Exceeded ICMP packet type indicates that a packet could not reach its destination because delivery took too long. The **Time To Live (TTL)** of a packet is a combination of router hops and seconds. Each router that forwards a packet reduces the TTL of the packet by one. If it takes longer than one second to forward the packet, then the TTL is also reduced by one for each second that it is delayed.

The default TTL of Windows .NET Server 2003 is 128. The default TTL used by other operating systems varies widely, but 64 is recommended by IANA.

Activity 3-7: Testing Host Functionality

Time Required: Five minutes

Objective: Test the functionality of a host using the ping command.

Description: One of your users has called with a problem. He is unable to connect to *www.microsoft.com* with his Web browser. In this activity you will use the ping utility to test Internet connectivity by connecting to *www.microsoft.com*.

1. If necessary, start your server and log on as Administrator.

2. Open a command prompt (see Activity 3-2, if necessary).

3. Type **ping www.microsoft.com** and press **Enter**. There is no response because Microsoft has configured their firewall to block ping packets by default. A non-response may also mean that the server is not functioning or Internet connectivity is down.

4. Type **ping www.yahoo.com** and press **Enter**. This server responds. This confirms that the server is definitely functional and Internet connectivity is working.

5. Close the command prompt.

6. Open Internet Explorer.

7. Type **www.microsoft.com** in the address bar, and press **Enter**. The Microsoft Web site appears. This confirms that the Web site is functional.

8. Close Internet Explorer.

Activity 3-8: Viewing TTL

Time Required: Five minutes

Objective: View the TTL of a ping packet.

Description: One of your users is complaining of slow Internet connectivity. To test the distance from Arctic University to the site, you use the ping utility. The ping utility shows the TTL of the packet, giving an approximation of how fast the connection is. Since the TTL is reduced by one for each router that is crossed, a smaller TTL means that there are more routers between you and the remote host.

1. If necessary, start your server and log on as Administrator.

2. Open a command prompt (see Activity 3-2, if necessary).

3. Type **ping 192.168.1.10** and press **Enter**. The TTL in the response is the TTL when no routers are passed through.

4. Type **ping www.yahoo.com** and press **Enter**. You can figure out the number of routers between you and *www.yahoo.com* by calculating the TTL from pinging the default gateway minus the TTL from pinging *www.yahoo.com*. For example, if you received a TTL of 128 when pinging your default gateway and a TTL of 113 when pinging *www.yahoo.com,* then the number of routers between your computer and *www.yahoo.com* is 128-113=15.

5. Type **ping –i 1 www.yahoo.com** and press **Enter**. This forces a TTL of 1. This results in an ICMP error message indicating that the TTL expired in transit.

6. Close the command prompt.

IGMP

Internet Group Management Protocol (IGMP) is used for the management of multicast groups. Hosts use IGMP to inform routers of their membership in multicast groups. Routers use IGMP to announce that their networks have members in particular multicast groups. The use of IGMP allows multicast packets to be distributed only to routers that have interested hosts connected.

ARP

Address Resolution Protocol (ARP) is used to convert logical IP addresses to physical MAC addresses. This is an essential part of the packet delivery process.

Network cards use a MAC address to filter irrelevant packets. When a packet is received, the network card verifies that the destination MAC address matches the MAC address of the network card or is a broadcast MAC address. For example, if the receiving computer has a MAC address of A1:B2:C3:D4:E5:F6, then the network card of the receiving computer passes the packet up to IP if the destination MAC address of the packet is A1:B2:C3:D4:E5:F6 or FF:FF:FF:FF:FF:FF (broadcast MAC address). This process offloads the responsibility for analyzing all the network packets from IP to the network card. This reduces CPU utilization on the computer.

Data packets have four addresses: source IP address, destination IP address, source MAC address, and destination MAC address. When a packet is created, the source computer must find the MAC address of the destination computer based on the destination IP address.

ARP uses a two-packet process to find the MAC address of the destination computer. The first packet is an ARP Request that is broadcast to all computers on the local network asking for the MAC address of the computer with the destination IP address. The destination computer sees this packet and sends an ARP Reply containing its MAC address. The sending computer can then create data packets using the destination MAC address. Figure 3-3 shows an example of a small computer network. Computer A needs to find the MAC address of Computer B before data packets can be delivered.

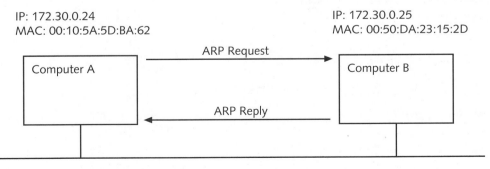

Figure 3-3   Computer A communicates with Computer B

Figure 3-4 shows the structure of an ARP Request packet sent as the first step of the resolution process. The ETHERNET section of the packet contains the MAC address information used by network cards when analyzing whether the packet should be passed up to IP. In this packet, the source MAC address is the MAC address of computer A, and the destination MAC address is the broadcast MAC address of FF:FF:FF:FF:FF:FF. All computers on the local segment process this packet and pass it up to ARP because the broadcast MAC address is the destination MAC address.

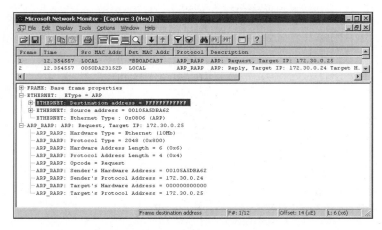

Figure 3-4   ARP Request packet

The ARP_RARP section of the packet shown in Figure 3-4 is the ARP information that is processed by ARP on the receiving computer. The most important information in this part of the packet is the Target's Protocol Address. This is the IP address of the destination computer. If the Target's Protocol Address matches the IP address of computer B, then an ARP Reply packet is created. If the Target's Protocol Address does not match the IP address of computer B, then the packet is discarded.

Figure 3-5 shows the structure of an ARP Reply packet sent as the second step of the resolution process. The ETHERNET section of the packet contains the MAC address information used by network cards when analyzing whether the packet should be passed up to IP. In this packet, the source MAC address is the MAC address of computer B and the destination MAC address is the MAC address of computer A. The ARP_RARP section of the packet has the ARP information required by computer A to create proper data packets. The Sender's Hardware Address is the MAC address that is required by computer A.

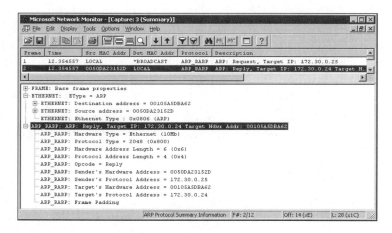

Figure 3-5   ARP Reply packet

If routers are forwarding packets, then the ARP process is modified. The first ARP Request is for the default gateway, then the ARP Response includes the MAC address of the router. The data packet is then built and sent to the router. The router removes and then replaces the source MAC address with its own and uses ARP to find the MAC address of the next router, if required, or the final destination host.

In Figure 3-6, Computer A is sending a data packet to Computer B. The data packet is addressed to Computer B at the IP layer, but must be given to the router for delivery. The MAC address is used to deliver the packet to the router.

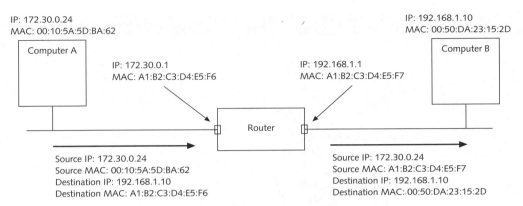

IP: 172.30.0.24
MAC: 00:10:5A:5D:BA:62

Computer A

IP: 172.30.0.1
MAC: A1:B2:C3:D4:E5:F6

IP: 192.168.1.10
MAC: 00:50:DA:23:15:2D

Computer B

IP: 192.168.1.1
MAC: A1:B2:C3:D4:E5:F7

Router

Source IP: 172.30.0.24
Source MAC: 00:10:5A:5D:BA:62
Destination IP: 192.168.1.10
Destination MAC: A1:B2:C3:D4:E5:F6

Source IP: 172.30.0.24
Source MAC: A1:B2:C3:D4:E5:F7
Destination IP: 192.168.1.10
Destination MAC: 00:50:DA:23:15:2D

Figure 3-6   Computer A communicates with Computer B across a router

The router removes the MAC address information from the data packet and replaces it with the MAC addresses required to deliver it to computer B. The source and destination IP addresses of the packet do not change.

Activity 3-9: Viewing the ARP Cache

Time Required: Five minutes

Objective: View the contents of the ARP cache.

Description: You are concerned that a user connectivity issue is being caused by incorrect MAC address information in the ARP. In this exercise, you view the contents of the ARP cache and clear the cache to force the rebuilding of the cache information. In this activity your instructor assigns you a partner.

1. If necessary, start your server and log on as Administrator.

2. Open a command prompt (see Activity 3-2, if necessary).

3. Type **arp –d** and press **Enter**. This clears the contents of the ARP cache.

4. Type **ping *partnercomputer*** and press **Enter** (where *partnercomputer* is the IP address of your partner's computer). Note: Be sure that your partner's computer is on the same network as your computer.

5. Type **arp –g** and press **Enter**. This shows the contents of the ARP cache. Right now it shows the IP address and MAC address of your partner's computer.

6. Type **ping www.yahoo.com** and press **Enter**.

7. Type **arp –g** and press **Enter**. Notice that the cache does not have an entry for *www.yahoo.com*. The cache has a new entry for your default gateway.

8. Close the command prompt.

NETWORK INTERFACE LAYER PROTOCOLS

Most of the common network interface layer protocols are defined by the **Institute of Electrical and Electronics Engineers (IEEE)**. The IEEE has a system of numbered committees that each defines a different network interface layer protocol. Table 3-3 lists some of the IEEE network interface layer protocols for which they are responsible.

Table 3-3   IEEE protocols

Protocol	Description
802.3	Ethernet
802.5	Token Ring
802.11	Wireless LAN
802.15	Wireless personal area network

Ethernet is the most common network interface layer protocol used in corporate networks today. There are many different varieties of Ethernet, all of which use Carrier Sense Multiple Access/Collision Detection (CSMA/CD) for access control. The most common version of Ethernet is implemented with twisted-pair cabling at 100 Mbps. Table 3-4 shows the different speeds of Ethernet for different cabling types.

Table 3-4   Ethernet cabling types and speeds

Cabling	Speed
Coaxial	10 Mbps
Twisted-pair (Cat 5e)	10 Mbps to 1 Gbps
Fiber-optic	10 Mbps to 10 Gbps

Token Ring is an older technology created by IBM that was implemented in the late 1980s and early 1990s. It was commonly implemented with mainframe computers. This standard uses twisted-pair cabling and operates at 4 Mbps or 16 Mbps. The access method used is token passing.

Wireless LAN is one of the fastest growing network types. The 802.11b standard defines the most common wireless standard. It uses radio signals to send data at 11 Mbps. The maximum distance of 802.11b is approximately 300 feet indoors and up to 1000 feet outdoors.

 Microsoft has added a number of features for wireless networks to Windows Server 2003. A wireless snap-in allows you to monitor and manage wireless access points and wireless clients. Group Policy has been extended to allow the management of wireless clients, including encryption settings. Some wireless functionality for network cards is also available in the operating system to make driver development easier for hardware developers and more reliable for users.

The IEEE standard 802.15 defines the physical layer portion of the **Bluetooth** standard. Bluetooth is a short-range wireless communication system with a maximum distance of approximately 30 feet and maximum speed of 720 Kbps. This is a much shorter range and much slower data transfer rate than 802.11b. The IEEE 802.15 committee intends to increase this speed. Support for Bluetooth is built into many smaller devices that need to minimize energy consumption, such as Palm and Windows CE devices.

Infrared communication is built into many devices for wireless connectivity. It is very common on laptops, Palm devices, and Windows CE devices. The official protocol implementation for infrared communication is **Infrared Data Association (IrDA)**. This is also the name of the group responsible for defining the protocol implementation. IrDA has a maximum range of three feet and maximum speed of 4 Mbps. The use of IrDA is being reduced as Bluetooth becomes more popular.

IPv6 CHANGES

The overall architecture of TCP/IP will experience only minor changes when IPv6 is introduced. At the transport layer, TCP and UDP will remain unchanged. However, when the Microsoft implementation of IPv6 is installed, additional versions of TCP and UDP will be installed with it. This is done to ensure that the introduction of IPv6 does not affect IPv4.

IPv6 is a replacement for IPv4 at the Internet layer. In order for application developers to start using IPv6, they must modify IPv4 applications to replace IPv4 function calls with ones that are supported by IPv6. Microsoft provides a utility named CHECKv4.EXE to help developers find code that must be modified to work with IPv6.

ARP is not used by IPv6. Instead a **Neighbor Solicitation** multicast packet is used to find the MAC address of an IPv6 host. The multicast addresses used for Neighbor Solicitation are generated in such a way that they are unique on a network segment. Using multicast addresses is more efficient than the broadcast addresses used by ARP.

ICMPv6 is responsible for many more tasks than ICMP in IPv4. ICMPv6 still performs error reporting and creates echo packets for testing connectivity. However, it is now also responsible for managing multicast groups, and obtaining physical addressing information from remote hosts. A subset of ICMPv6 called **Multicast Listener Discovery (MLD)** replaces the functionality of IGMP from IPv4. Another subset of ICMPv6 called Neighbor Solicitation replaces the functionality of ARP from IPv4.

CHAPTER SUMMARY

- The TCP/IP model is composed of four layers: the application layer, the transport layer, the Internet layer, and the network interface layer.

- There are many application layer protocols, each of which is associated with a client application and service.

- HTTP is the most common protocol used on the Internet today.

- FTP is used for transferring files across the Internet.

- Telnet is used to remotely connect to UNIX and Linux systems.

- SMTP is used to send and receive e-mail messages between e-mail servers.

- POP3 is the most common protocol used for reading e-mail messages. IMAP4 is another protocol used for reading e-mail messages.

- The two transport layer protocols are TCP and UDP.

- TCP is connection-oriented and reliable.

- UDP is connectionless and unreliable.

- Internet layer protocols are responsible for all tasks related to logical addressing and are all very specialized.

- Internet layer protocols include IP, RIP, OSPF, ICMP, IGMP, and ARP.

- Ethernet is the most common network interface layer protocol used in corporate networks today.

- Wireless LANs are one of the fastest growing network types.

- Some of the changes included with IP version 6 are new versions of TCP and UDP, the discontinued use of ARP, and the replacement of IGMP with Multicast Listener Discovery.

KEY TERMS

ACK bit — A bit used in TCP communication to indicate that a packet is an acknowledgement of a previous packet.

Address Resolution Protocol (ARP) — A protocol used by hosts to find the physical MAC address of another host with a particular IP address.

application layer — The layer of the TCP/IP architecture that provides access to network resources.

Bluetooth — A short-range wireless communication protocol.

Common Gateway Interface (CGI) — A vendor-neutral mechanism used to pass information from a Web page to an application running on a Web server.

connection-oriented — A term used to describe a protocol that verifies the existence of a host and agrees on terms of communication before sending data.

connectionless — A term used to describe a protocol that does not establish a communication channel before sending data.

graphical user interface (GUI) — A user interface for an operating system that supports graphics in addition to characters.

Infrared Data Association (IrDA) — A standard for communication using infrared ports in mobile devices. This is also the name of the organization that created the standard.

Institute of Electrical and Electronics Engineers (IEEE) — The organization responsible for maintaining many physical layer protocols used in networks, including Ethernet and Token Ring.

Internet Assigned Numbers Authority (IANA) — The organization that maintains standards for Internet addressing, including well-known port numbers and ICMP packet types.

Internet Control Messaging Protocol (ICMP) — The protocol used by routers and hosts to send Internet protocol error messages.

Internet Group Management Protocol (IGMP) — The protocol used by routers to track the membership in multicast groups.

Internet layer — The layer of the TCP/IP architecture that is responsible for logical addressing and routing.

Internet Message Access Protocol version 4 (IMAP4) — A protocol used to retrieve e-mail messages from an e-mail server. It is more flexible than POP3 for managing message storage.

Internet Server Application Programmer Interface (ISAPI) — A programmer interface defined by Microsoft for passing information from Web pages to programs running on a Web server.

Multicast Listener Discovery (MLD) — An ICMPv6-based protocol used with IPv6 that replaces IGMP used with IPv4.

Neighbor Solicitation — An ICMPv6 packet used with IPv6 in place of ARP used with IPv4. This is a multicast packet.

Netscape Server Application Programmer Interface (NSAPI) — A programmer interface defined by Netscape to pass information from Web pages to applications running on a Web server.

network interface layer — The layer of the TCP/IP architecture that controls placing packets on the physical network media.

Open Shortest Path First (OSPF) — A protocol that is used by routers to share information about known networks and calculate the best path through an internetwork. OSPF calculates routes based on user definable cost values.

Open Systems Interconnection (OSI) reference model — An industry standard that is used as a reference point to compare different networking technologies and protocols.

packet — A single unit of data sent from one computer to another. It contains a source address, destination address, data, and error-checking information.

port — A TCP port or UDP port is used by transport layer protocols to direct network information to the proper service.

Post Office Protocol version 3 (POP3) — A protocol that is used to retrieve e-mail messages from an e-mail server.

Request For Comment (RFC) — A submission to the Internet Engineering Task Force that is evaluated for use as part of the TCP/IP protocol suite.

Routing Information Protocol (RIP) — A protocol used by routers to exchange routing table information and determine the best path through an internetwork based on the number of hops.

sliding window — A process used in the TCP protocol to track which packets have been received by the destination host.

SYN bit — A bit used in TCP communication to indicate a request to start a communication session.

Telnet — A protocol used to remotely access a command-line interface on Unix and Linux servers.

Time to Live (TTL) — A parameter of IP packets used to ensure that if a packet becomes trapped in a router loop, it will expire. Each hop through a router reduces TTL by one.

Token Ring — An older physical layer protocol developed by IBM that operated at either 4 Mbps or 16 Mbps.

Transmission Control Protocol (TCP) — A connection-oriented and reliable transport layer protocol that is part of the TCP/IP protocol suite.

transport layer — The layer of the TCP/IP architecture that breaks messages into smaller packets and tracks their delivery.

User Datagram Protocol (UDP) — A connectionless, unreliable transport layer protocol used in the TCP/IP protocol suite.

wireless LAN — A standard for wireless communication created by the IEEE. The most common variant of wireless LAN is 802.11b.

REVIEW QUESTIONS

1. Which transport protocol establishes a connection with the remote host before sending data?

   a. UDP

   b. TCP

   c. ARP

   d. FTP

2. Which protocol supports the use of multicast groups?

   a. UDP

   b. TCP

   c. ARP

   d. ICMP

   e. IGMP

3. Token Ring operates at which speed(s)? (Choose all that apply.)

   a. 1 Mbps

   b. 4 Mbps

   c. 10 Mbps

   d. 16 Mbps

   e. 1 Gbps

4. Which of the following is not an application layer protocol?

    a. FTP

    b. HTTP

    c. IP

    d. Telnet

    e. SMTP

5. Which network layer protocol is responsible for routing packets on the network?

    a. TCP

    b. UDP

    c. IP

    d. ICMP

    e. IGMP

6. ARP is used to resolve IP addresses to what?

    a. NetBIOS names

    b. MAC addresses

    c. Fully Qualified Domain Names

    d. Internet addresses

7. Bluetooth wireless technology is defined by which IEEE standard?

    a. 802.2

    b. 802.3

    c. 802.5

    d. 802.11

    e. 802.15

8. Which of the following statements regarding Trivial File Transfer Protocol (TFTP) are true?

    a. TFTP uses port 21.

    b. TFTP uses port 23.

    c. TFTP uses TCP for file transfer.

    d. TFTP uses UDP for file transfer.

9. The network card operates at which layer of the IP stack?

    a. application

    b. transport

    c. Internet

    d. network interface

10. Which of the following statements regarding TCP are false?

    a. TCP is a connection-oriented protocol.

    b. TCP uses a three-way handshake to establish a connection to the remote host.

    c. Packets lost during transit are re-sent.

    d. HTTP and POP3 use TCP.

    e. none of the above

3

11. Which of the following are routing protocols? (Choose all that apply.)

    a. RIP

    b. LCR

    c. OSPF

    d. ICMP

12. Which of the following statements regarding e-mail protocols are true? (Choose all that apply.)

    a. SMTP is only used by clients to send e-mail.

    b. POP3 allows user to view multiple folders.

    c. IMAP4 can be configured to download only mail headers.

    d. POP3 stores all e-mail messages on the server.

13. Which port is used by HTTP?

    a. 21

    b. 23

    c. 25

    d. 53

    e. 80

    f. 110

14. Which of the following physical layer protocols uses Carrier Sense Multiple Access/Collision Detection?

    a. Token Ring

    b. ARCnet

    c. Ethernet

    d. FDDI

15. The Time to Live (TTL) of a packet is a combination of what factors? (Choose all that apply.)

    a. router hops

    b. date

    c. Internet connectivity

    d. seconds

    e. destination MAC address

16. What is the maximum distance for infrared data transfer?

    a. two feet

    b. three feet

    c. four feet

    d. 10 feet

    e. 30 feet

17. Which transport layer protocol is most likely to be used for streaming media?

    a. TCP

    b. DNS

    c. UDP

    d. HTTP

    e. ARP

18. When a packet crosses a router, what happens to the packet's TTL?

    a. nothing

    b. It is decremented by one.

    c. It is incremented by one.

    d. It is reset to the default TTL.

19. What happens when a packet's TTL reaches zero?

    a. The packet is returned to the sender.

    b. The packet is discarded.

    c. The packet is forwarded to the recipient by the most direct path.

    d. The router issues a Source Quench Request to slow down the sending of packets.

20. You ping a host that is on a remote subnet. When you view your ARP cache, which MAC address do you see for the remote host?

    a. your own MAC address

    b. the MAC address of the remote host

    c. the MAC address of the router

    d. all of the above

CASE PROJECTS

Internet access has recently been installed by ZAP Internet Services and has been made available to the Arts faculty for testing. The Arts faculty is known for having demanding users and is the perfect place to find user problems.

Case Project 3-1: Slow Internet Access

Bob Jones, an Arts professor, has written an e-mail message to you complaining about the speed of his Internet connection. He regularly downloads large files from a particular Web site. Downloads from this Web site regularly pause for 10 to 15 seconds, then resume. This does not happen when he downloads information from other Web sites. Write an e-mail response to Bob explaining the likely cause of the problem and what you can do to correct it.

Case Project 3-2: Planning Physical Layer Protocols

Your supervisor has been approached by the head of the Arts faculty about redesigning the physical infrastructure for the network. Most of the Arts professors have laptop computers but are unable to use them in the classrooms because there are no LAN hookups. The offices of the Arts professors are wired with twisted-pair (Cat 5e) cabling. Write a short report with your recommendations for the network interface layer protocols that should be implemented to support the professors.

Case Project 3-3: Planning Application Layer Protocols

One firewall that you are evaluating has the ability to control network traffic at the application layer. As part of your own planning process, list the application layer protocols that you would allow through the firewall, those you would block, and your reasons for doing so.

4

SUBNETTING

After reading this chapter and completing the exercises, you will be able to:
♦ Understand why subnetting is necessary
♦ Describe how computers work with binary TCP/IP addresses
♦ Subnet any network
♦ Determine the number of useable hosts on a subnet
♦ Supernet several smaller networks

Subnetting is used to divide a single network into multiple smaller ones, allowing you to use routers to control traffic movement between the networks. When you configure a network, you receive a range of IP addresses from your ISP or you use internal addresses that are not routable on the Internet. If you have multiple physical locations or a large single location, you need to subnet the address range that you are using. Although IP addresses are viewed in dotted decimal notation, to truly understand routing and subnetting you must be familiar with the binary system, because computers work with binary numbers when they route packets from one network to another. In this chapter, you will learn about subnetting and how computers work with binary TCP/IP addresses.

REASONS TO SUBNET

A single network is appropriate for many small and mid-sized companies. However, larger companies with multiple physical locations or a very large single location usually need to use multiple networks. **Subnetting** refers to the process of separating a network into several smaller networks to improve performance. Subnetting is used because it can:

- reduce collisions
- limit broadcasts
- control traffic

After a network has been subnetted, a router is required to move packets from one subnet to another.

Reducing Collisions

When two computers on an Ethernet network using CSMA/CD as an access method attempt to transmit at the same time, a **collision** occurs. All of the computers involved in the collision wait a random period of time after the collision occurs before attempting to send data again.

On a very busy Ethernet network, the actual throughput may be only 30% to 40% of capacity because of lost efficiency due to collisions. A busy 10-Mbps network may only actually carry 3 to 4 Mbps and a busy 100-Mbps network may actually carry only 30 to 40 Mbps. Subnetting reduces the number of hosts on each network, and therefore reduces the amount of traffic on the network. With less traffic on each network, the number of collisions is reduced, and the actual throughput is improved. In a routed network, each network is a separate collision domain. Collisions that occur on one network do not affect another network. In a subnetted network, collisions that do occur affect a lower number of hosts. This increases actual throughput.

Limiting Broadcasts

Broadcast messages are generated by a variety of network services. For example, NetBIOS name resolution, router communication, service advertisements, and other services send broadcast messages when the destination address of hosts is unknown.

A packet addressed to a broadcast address is read and processed by every computer on the network. This is not a problem when there are only a few broadcast packets on the network, but as more computers are added, broadcasts not only can become a drain on the processing resources of workstations and servers, but can also increase network traffic significantly. Subnetting a network creates multiple networks with fewer hosts on each network. The presence of fewer hosts on each network results in fewer broadcast messages, which reduces the processing load on each host.

Routers do not forward packets addressed to the IP address 255.255.255.255. This address is a broadcast on the local network and is processed by every computer on the local network. Depending on configuration, most routers forward directed broadcasts such as 192.168.4.255. Packets addressed to this address are routed to the appropriate network, then processed by all computers on that network.

Controlling Traffic

Introducing routers into a network allows a greater degree of control over network traffic. Most routers have the ability to implement rules about which packets they forward. This lets you control which hosts can talk to each other, as well as which protocols they can use to communicate. On a nonrouted network, the hosts can use any protocol they wish and communicate with any other host on the local network.

BINARY AND TCP/IP

IP addresses are expressed in dotted decimal notation. Most utilities and other software use IP addresses in this format as well. Internally, however, a computer looks at an IP address as a single group of 32 **binary** digits. The subnet mask determines which **bits** are part of the network ID and which bits are part of the host ID.

Decimal Numbering

Decimal is the number system you use on a daily basis. It is a base-ten numbering system, which means that each digit can be one of ten different values. The decimal system uses the values from 0 to 9 for each digit.

When counting in decimal, you start with a single digit. Starting with 0, you increment that digit by 1 until it reaches the maximum value of 9. To further increase the value, you must add a digit to the left one column (or space) with a value of 1 and set the original digit to 0. This gives a value of 10. This pattern repeats as the rightmost digit reaches 9 again. To further increase 19, you increment the left digit by 1 and set the right digit to 0. This gives a value of 20. Similarly, when the value has reached 99, to further increase it you add a digit to the left with a value of 1, and set the other two digits to 0. This gives a value of 100. Table 4-1 shows a counting example in decimal.

Table 4-1   Counting in decimal

7	17	97	197
8	18	98	198
9	19	99	199
10	20	100	200
11	21	101	201

The base of the numbering system determines the overall value of each digit. In the example shown in Table 4-2, each column has a particular value. The value of each column in a numbering system is the base of the numbering system (10 in decimal) to the power of the column number. The numbering of the columns starts with 0. Therefore, the value of the first column in the decimal numbering system is ten to the zero power ($10^0=1$), the value of the second column in the decimal numbering system is ten to the first power ($10^1=10$), and the value of the third column in the decimal numbering system is ten to the second power ($10^2=100$). Table 4-2 shows the values of each column in the decimal number system.

Table 4-2   Decimal column values

Column Number	4	3	2	1	0
Value	10^4	10^3	10^2	10^1	10^0
Expanded Value	10000	1000	100	10	1

 Any number to the power of zero has a value of 1.

Binary Numbering

You don't normally use binary when configuring and working with computers. Values expressed in binary are very long compared to decimal and are difficult to work with. However, subnetting is based on binary. In order to understand subnetting, you must understand binary.

Binary is a base-two numbering system, which means that there are only two potential values for each digit, 0 and 1. Binary counting works on the same principle as counting in decimal. As each column reaches its maximum value, the digit to the left is incremented and the digits to the right are set to 0. However, in binary, the maximum value is reached much faster. Table 4-3 shows an example of binary counting and the equivalent numbers in decimal notation.

Table 4-3   Binary counting

Binary	Decimal Equivalent
0000	0
0001	1
0010	2
0011	3
0100	4
0101	5
0110	6
0111	7
1000	8

In binary, the value of each digit is still determined by the base of the numbering system. As in the previous example, the value of each column is the base of the numbering system to the power of the column number. Table 4-4 shows the values of each column in the binary numbering system.

Table 4-4   Binary column values

Column Number	7	6	5	4	3	2	1	0
Value	2^7	2^6	2^5	2^4	2^3	2^2	2^1	2^0
Value in Decimal	128	64	32	16	8	4	2	1

Conversion Between Binary and Decimal

Since most IP address configuration is done with dotted decimal notation, you need to convert any subnetting work you do from binary back to decimal. Fortunately, the largest number of bits you need to work with at any given time is eight. These are the octets in dotted decimal notation.

To convert a binary octet to a decimal value, you must multiply the digit in each column by the value of each column and then determine the sum of those products. Binary digits are always either 1 or 0, so you multiply the value of each column by 1 or 0. Table 4-5 shows the conversion of the binary number 10011011 to decimal.

Table 4-5   Binary to decimal conversion

Column Number	7	6	5	4	3	2	1	0	Total (in decimal notation)
Value	2^7	2^6	2^5	2^4	2^3	2^2	2^1	2^0	
Value in Decimal	128	64	32	16	8	4	2	1	
Binary Number	1	0	0	1	1	0	1	1	
Value of Column	128	0	0	16	8	0	2	1	155

While you can convert binary to decimal and decimal to binary using charts such as Table 4-5 above, most people use Windows Calculator to do the conversion. Figure 4-1 shows Windows Calculator in scientific mode.

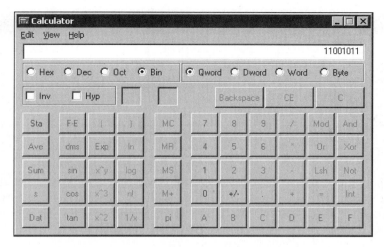

Figure 4-1   Windows Calculator in scientific mode

Activity 4-1: Converting Binary Numbers to Decimal Using Windows Calculator

Time Required: 5 minutes

Objective: Convert numbers between binary and decimal numbering systems.

Description: You will be working on subnetting plans for Arctic University later this week and want to be sure that you understand how to covert binary numbers to decimal and decimal numbers to binary.

1. If necessary, start your server, and log on as Administrator.

2. Click **Start**, point to **All Programs**, point to **Accessories**, and click **Calculator**.

3. Click the **View** menu, and click **Scientific**.

4. Convert the decimal number 177 to binary. To do this, type 177 in the calculator window, and click the **Bin** radio button. The answer should be 10110001. If there are less than eight digits, the leading zeros are not shown.

5. Convert the binary number 11001100 to decimal. To do this, type **11001100** in the calculator, and click the **Dec** radio button. The answer should be 204.

6. For more practice, convert the numbers in the following chart from decimal to binary.

Decimal	Binary
43	
19	
255	
240	
192	

7. For more practice, convert the numbers in the following chart from binary to decimal.

Binary	Decimal
00110011	
11001010	
11111100	
00000011	
01010101	

Binary Subnet Masks

The subnet masks that you have seen are in dotted decimal notation. However, when your computer calculates the host ID and network ID of an IP address, it is working in binary. Where there is a 1 in the subnet mask, that bit is part of the network ID. Where there is a 0 in the subnet mask, that bit is part of the host ID. Table 4-6 shows an example of calculating the host ID and network ID of an IP address using binary.

Table 4-6   Calculating host ID and network ID

	Decimal	Binary
IP Address	192 . 168 . 5 . 20	11000000 . 10101000 . 00000101 . 00010100
Subnet Mask	255 . 255 . 255 . 0	11111111 . 11111111 . 11111111 . 00000000
Network ID	192 . 168 . 5 . 0	11000000 . 10101000 . 00000101 . 00000000
Host ID	0 . 0 . 0 . 20	00000000 . 00000000 . 00000000 . 00010100

The binary process used by your computer to find the network ID is called ANDing. This a mathematical operation that compares two binary digits and gives a result of 1 or 0. If both binary digits being compared have a value of 1, then the result is 1. If one digit is 0 and the other is 1, or if both digits are zero, then the result is 0.

When an IP address is ANDed with a subnet mask, the result is the network ID. Each bit in the IP address is ANDed with the corresponding bit in the subnet mask. For example, in Table 4-6, the rightmost bit of the IP address is 0, and the far right bit of the subnet mask is 0. When 0 is ANDed with 0, the result is 0, and this is shown in the network ID. The far left bit of the IP address is 1, and the far left bit of the subnet mask is 1. When 1 is ANDed with 1, the result is 1, and this is shown in the network ID.

The host ID is the part of the IP address that is not the network ID.

All of the 1s in a subnet mask must be contiguous. There must be no 0s interspersed with the 1s. Table 4-7 shows several examples of invalid subnet masks.

Table 4-7   Invalid subnet masks

Decimal	Binary
255.255.15.0	11111111 . 11111111 . 00001111 . 00000000
255.254.255.0	11111111 . 11111110 . 11111111 . 00000000
254.255.0.0	11111110 . 11111111 . 00000000 . 00000000
255.192.240.0	11111111 . 10101010 . 11110000 . 00000000

Activity 4-2: ANDing

Time Required: 20 minutes

Objective: Find the network ID of several IP addresses based on the given subnet mask.

Description: When you are troubleshooting IP address configuration problems, you may need to find the network ID on which an IP address is located. To practice, complete the chart below. First, convert the decimal numbers to binary, and then calculate the network ID by ANDing the IP address and the subnet mask.

4

	Decimal	Binary
IP Address	130.179.16.67	
Subnet Mask	255.255.255.0	
Network ID		

	Decimal	Binary
IP Address	192.168.32.183	
Subnet Mask	255.255.255.240	
Network ID		

	Decimal	Binary
IP Address	10.155.244.2	
Subnet Mask	255.224.0.0	
Network ID		

SUBNETTING A NETWORK

To subnet a network, you take some bits from the host ID and give them to the network ID. As the manager and designer of a network, you have the freedom to do this.

A Class B address is very large and generally needs to be subnetted to handle routing between different physical locations. To keep subnetting simple, bits are often taken from the host ID in a group of eight. This keeps the entire octet intact. Table 4-8 shows an example of subnetting a Class B address by taking eight bits from the host ID and giving them to the network ID. Originally, the third octet was part of the host ID, but it is now part of the network ID. Using an entire octet for subnetting gives you 256 possible subnets. Traditionally the subnets with all 1s and all 0s are discarded, leaving 254 usable subnets.

Table 4-8 Simple subnetting

	Decimal	Binary
Original Network	172.16.0.0	10101100 . 00010000 . 00000000 . 00000000
Original Subnet Mask	255.255.0.0	11111111 . 11111111 . 00000000 . 00000000
New Subnet Mask	255.255.255.0	11111111 . 11111111 . *11111111* . 00000000
Subnet 1	172.16.0.0	10101100 . 00010000 . *00000000* . 00000000
Subnet 2	172.16.1.0	10101100 . 00010000 . *00000001* . 00000000
Subnet 3	172.16.2.0	10101100 . 00010000 . *00000010* . 00000000
Subnet 4	172.16.3.0	10101100 . 00010000 . *00000011* . 00000000
Subnet 5	172.16.4.0	10101100 . 00010000 . *00000100* . 00000000
Subnet 6	172.16.5.0	10101100 . 00010000 . *00000101* . 00000000
Subnet 7	172.16.6.0	10101100 . 00010000 . *00000110* . 00000000
Subnet 256	172.16.255.0	10101100 . 00010000 . *11111111* . 00000000

When simple subnetting is used, it is still very easy to find the network ID and host ID of an IP address, because each octet is still whole. However, sometimes you need to subdivide an octet to get the number of subnets or hosts that you desire.

Complex subnetting takes less than a full octet from the host ID. Table 4-9 shows an example of subnetting a Class B network by taking three bits from the host ID. Traditionally, subnet 1 and subnet 8 are not used because all the subnet bits are set to 0 and 1, respectively. However, today, with classless routing, both subnet 1 and subnet 8 can be used.

Table 4-9   Complex subnetting

	Decimal	Binary
Original Network	172.16.0.0	10101100 . 00010000 . 00000000 . 00000000
Original Subnet Mask	255.255.0.0	11111111 . 11111111 . 00000000 . 00000000
New Subnet Mask	255.255.224.0	11111111 . 11111111 . *111*00000 . 00000000
Subnet 1	172.16.0.0	10101100 . 00010000 . *000*00000 . 00000000
Subnet 2	172.16.32.0	10101100 . 00010000 . *001*00000 . 00000000
Subnet 3	172.16.64.0	10101100 . 00010000 . *010*00000 . 00000000
Subnet 4	172.16.96.0	10101100 . 00010000 . *011*00000 . 00000000
Subnet 5	172.16.128.0	10101100 . 00010000 . *100*00000 . 00000000
Subnet 6	172.16.160.0	10101100 . 00010000 . *101*00000 . 00000000
Subnet 7	172.16.192.0	10101100 . 00010000 . *110*00000 . 00000000
Subnet 8	172.16.224.0	10101100 . 00010000 . *111*00000 . 00000000

The number of subnets can be calculated using the formula 2^n-2. In this formula n is the number of bits taken from the host ID and used for subnetting. The minus 2 is only used for traditional subnetting where the subnets of all 1s and all 0s are removed.

Activity 4-3: Complex Subnetting

Time Required: 30 minutes

Objective: Subnet a single large network into 10 smaller networks.

Description: A large internal network address such as 172.20.0.0 is too large to be used without subnetting. To practice subnetting, divide the 172.20.0.0 network into 10 subnets using as few bits from the host as possible. List the 10 subnets in the chart below.

	Decimal	Binary
Original Network	172.20.0.0	10101100 . 00010100 . 00000000 . 00000000
Original Subnet Mask	255.255.0.0	11111111 . 11111111 . 00000000 . 00000000
New Subnet Mask		
Subnet 1		
Subnet 2		
Subnet 3		
Subnet 4		
Subnet 5		
Subnet 6		
Subnet 7		
Subnet 8		
Subnet 9		
Subnet 10		

SUBNET HOSTS

The number of hosts available on a subnetted network follows the same pattern as the classful IP networks you have already seen. When the host bits are all set to 0, that address represents the subnet. When the bits are all set to 1, that address is a broadcast on that subnet. Table 4-10 shows the usable hosts for several subnetted networks.

Table 4-10   Usable hosts

	Decimal	Binary
Original Network	172.16.0.0	10101100 . 00010000 . 00000000 . 00000000
Original Subnet Mask	255.255.0.0	11111111 . 11111111 . 00000000 . 00000000
New Subnet Mask	255.255.224.0	11111111 . 11111111 . *111*00000 . 00000000
Subnet 1	172.16.0.0	10101100 . 00010000 . *000*00000 . 00000000
First Host on Subnet 1	172.16.0.1	10101100 . 00010000 . *000*00000 . 00000001
Last Host on Subnet 1	172.16.31.254	10101100 . 00010000 . *000*11111 . 11111110
Broadcast on Subnet 1	172.16.31.255	10101100 . 00010000 . *000*11111 . 11111111
Subnet 2	172.16.32.0	10101100 . 00010000 . *001*00000 . 00000000
First Host on Subnet 2	172.16.32.1	10101100 . 00010000 . *001*00000 . 00000001
Last Host on Subnet 2	172.16.63.254	10101100 . 00010000 . *001*11111 . 11111110
Broadcast on Subnet 2	172.16.63.255	10101100 . 00010000 . *001*11111 . 11111111
Subnet 3	172.16.64.0	10101100 . 00010000 . *010*00000 . 00000000
First Host on Subnet 3	172.16.64.1	10101100 . 00010000 . *010*00000 . 00000001
Last Host on Subnet 3	172.16.95.254	10101100 . 00010000 . *010*11111 . 11111110
Broadcast on Subnet 3	172.16.95.255	10101100 . 00010000 . *010*11111 . 11111111

The formula 2^n-2, which is used to calculate the number of subnets that can be created from a certain number of bits, is also used to calculate the number of usable hosts on a subnet. In both situations, the formula finds the total number of combinations that can be created from n bits. However, when used to calculate the number of usable hosts on a subnet, n is the number of bits in the host ID, and two combinations are removed for the broadcast on the subnet and the subnet itself. Table 4-11 shows the number of usable hosts available for certain numbers of bits.

Activity 4-4: Finding Valid Hosts

Time Required: 30 minutes

Objective: Calculate the number of valid hosts on a subnet.

Description: Once you have calculated the network ID for your subnets, you must find out the number of valid hosts on each subnet. These are the IP addresses you can assign to the hosts on your network. Using three subnets from Activity 4-3, find the first host, last host, and broadcast address for each subnet.

	Decimal	Binary
Subnet Mask	255.255.240.0	11111111.11111111.11110000.00000000
Subnet 1		
First Host on Subnet 1		
Last Host on Subnet 1		
Broadcast on Subnet 1		
Subnet 2		
First Host on Subnet 2		
Last Host on Subnet 2		
Broadcast on Subnet 2		
Subnet 3		
First Host on Subnet 3		
Last Host on Subnet 3		
Broadcast on Subnet 3		

Table 4-11   Usable hosts formula

Host Bits	Formula	Usable Hosts
6	2^6-2	64-2=62
8	2^8-2	256-2=254
10	$2^{10}-2$	1024-2=1022
12	$2^{12}-2$	4096-2=4094

SUPERNETTING

Supernetting is the opposite of subnetting. Subnetting is used to create several smaller networks from a large network, whereas supernetting is used to create one large network from several smaller ones. Subnetting takes bits from the host ID and moves them to the network ID. Supernetting takes bits from the network ID and gives them to the host ID. All of the networks being combined for supernetting must be contiguous. The IP addresses from the first network to the last must be one single range with no breaks. In the first network being supernetted, the bits being taken from the network ID must be zero. In the final network being supernetted, the bits being taken must be one.

Table 4-12 shows an example of supernetting two Class C networks into one larger network.

Table 4-12   Supernetting two Class C networks

	Decimal	Binary
Original Network 1	192.168.10.0	11000000 . 10101000 . 00001010 . 00000000
Original Network 2	192.168.11.0	11000000 . 10101000 . 00001011 . 00000000
Original Subnet Mask	255.255.255.0	11111111 . 11111111 . 11111111 . 00000000
Supernetted Network	192.168.10.0	11000000 . 10101000 . 00001010 . 00000000
New Subnet Mask	255.255.254.0	11111111 . 11111111 . 11111110 . 00000000
First Host	192.168.10.1	11000000 . 10101000 . 00001010 . 00000001
Last Host	192.168.11.254	11000000 . 10101000 . 00001011 . 11111110
Broadcast	192.168.11.255	11000000 . 10101000 . 00001011 . 11111111

Table 4-13 shows an example of supernetting four Class C networks into one larger network.

Table 4-13 Supernetting four Class C networks

	Decimal	Binary
Original Network 1	192.168.76.0	11000000 . 10101000 . 01001100 . 00000000
Original Network 2	192.168.77.0	11000000 . 10101000 . 01001101 . 00000000
Original Network 3	192.168.78.0	11000000 . 10101000 . 01001110 . 00000000
Original Network 4	192.168.79.0	11000000 . 10101000 . 01001111 . 00000000
Original Subnet Mask	255.255.255.0	11111111 . 11111111 . 11111111 . 00000000
Supernetted Network	192.168.76.0	11000000 . 10101000 . 01001100 . 00000000
New Subnet Mask	255.255.252.0	11111111 . 11111111 . 11111100 . 00000000
First Host	192.168.76.1	11000000 . 10101000 . 01001100 . 00000001
Last Host	192.168.79.254	11000000 . 10101000 . 01001111 . 11111110
Broadcast	192.168.79.255	11000000 . 10101000 . 01001111 . 11111111

Reasons for Supernetting

Supernetting is used when a range of IP addresses larger than a Class C network is required, but a full Class B network is not required. For example, a mid-sized company with 300 computers requires IP addresses from their ISP that are usable on the Internet. It would be wasteful to assign an entire Class B address to the company because thousands of IP addresses would go unused. Instead, the ISP can supernet two Class C addresses. This allows the company to have 510 Internet-usable IP addresses.

Supernetting may also be done to reduce routing complexity. For example, an older network running at 10 Mbps may have been configured with multiple Class C networks to reduce packet collisions. With current technology, the routers could be replaced with switches running at 100 Mbps. The switches still reduce packet collisions, and the complexity of the network is reduced. When the routers are removed, the computers on the network need to be reconfigured with supernetted addresses. If DHCP is being used, then this change is very easy to implement.

CHAPTER SUMMARY

- ❏ Subnetting is used to divide a single large network into multiple smaller networks.
- ❏ Subnetting reduces packet collisions on a network, limits broadcasts, and controls network traffic.
- ❏ Binary is a base-two numbering system. Only 0 and 1 are valid binary values.
- ❏ Computers work with IP addresses as 32-digit binary numbers.
- ❏ A 1 in a subnet mask corresponds with a bit that is part of the network ID. A 0 in a subnet mask corresponds with a bit that is part of the host ID.
- ❏ Subnetting takes bits from the host ID and uses them as part of the network ID.
- ❏ The formula 2^n-2, where n is the number of host bits, can be used to calculate the number of useable hosts on a network.
- ❏ Supernetting combines multiple smaller networks into a single larger network.
- ❏ To supernet, the networks being combined must be contiguous.

KEY TERMS

binary — A base-two numbering system. There are only two valid values for each digit: 0 and 1.

bit — A single binary digit.

collision — When two computers attempt to send a packet on the network at the same time, the signals collide and become unreadable.

subnetting — The process of dividing a single IP network into several smaller IP networks. Bits are taken from the host ID and made part of the network ID by adjusting the subnet mask.

supernetting — The process of combining several smaller networks into a single large network by taking bits from the network ID and making them part of the host ID.

REVIEW QUESTIONS

1. An IP address is how many bits in length?

   a. 8

   b. 16

   c. 32

   d. 64

2. What is the default subnet mask for a Class B network?

   a. 255.0.0.0

   b. 255.255.0.0

   c. 255.255.255.0

   d. 255.255.255.255

3. Which of the following is not a reason to subnet a network?

   a. to reduce collisions on the network

   b. to limit the number of collisions on the subnet

   c. to combine smaller networks into a larger network

   d. to control the amount of traffic on the network

   e. to reduce the number of IP addresses in use on the network

4. What is 10101011.11111110.11100111.00011111 in decimal notation?

5. Your computer has an IP address of 172.18.56.17 with a subnet mask of 255.255.248.0. Which of the following IP addresses are on your local subnet? (Choose all that apply.)

   a. 172.18.47.200

   b. 172.18.60.100

   c. 172.18.89.157

   d. 172.18.54.3

   e. 172.18.65.117

   f. 172.18.57.42

6. What is the maximum number of workstations the subnet mask 255.255.240.0 can support on the local subnet?

   a. 2048

   b. 2046

   c. 4096

   d. 4094

   e. 8190

7. You have been assigned the network address 172.32.0.0 to use on your LAN. You need to divide the network into seven subnets. What subnet mask do you use?

    a. 255.240.0.0

    b. 255.224.0.0

    c. 255.255.248.0

    d. 255.255.240.0

8. A packet sent to all workstations on the network is called a _____.

    a. directed packet

    b. unicast

    c. multicast

    d. broadcast

9. Combining smaller subnets into a single, larger subnet is called _____.

    a. subnetting

    b. supernetting

    c. complex subnetting

    d. classful subnetting

10. What is the network ID for the IP address 10.12.56.1 with a subnet mask of 255.255.0.0?

    a. 10.0.0.0

    b. 10.12.0.0

    c. 10.12.56.0

    d. 0.0.0.1

    e. 0.0.56.1

11. When you AND 192.168.12.7 with the subnet mask 255.255.248.0, what is the result in decimal notation?

    a. 192.168.8.0

    b. 192.168.4.0

    c. 192.168.12.0

    d. 192.168.0.0

    e. 192.168.16.0

12. Which of the following subnets is invalid? (Choose all that apply.)

    a. 255.224.0.0

    b. 255.242.255.0

    c. 255.255.255.253

    d. 255.255.127.0

    e. 255.155.155.192

13. You have been assigned the network ID 172.16.5.0 with a subnet mask of 255.255.255.0. What is the maximum number of workstations you can have on the subnet?

    a. 255

    b. 254

    c. 253

    d. 126

14. You need to connect to a computer on your local subnet. Your computer's IP address is 172.28.17.5, and the other computer's IP address is 172.28.30.252. Which subnet mask can you use? (Choose all that apply.)

    a. 255.0.0.0

    b. 255.255.0.0

    c. 255.255.252.0

    d. 255.255.240.0

    e. 255.255.248.0

15. You are using the network ID 10.0.0.0. You need to divide the network into smaller subnets that can support 6,000 workstations on each subnet. Which of the following subnets supports 6,000 workstations? (Choose all that apply.)

    a. 255.192.0.0.0

    b. 255.255.192.0

    c. 255.255.224.0

    d. 255.255.240.0

    e. 255.255.248.0

16. Your computer has been assigned the IP address 192.168.148.72 with a subnet mask of 255.255.252.0. Which of the following IP addresses is on your local subnet? (Choose all that apply.)

    a. 192.168.140.12

    b. 192.168.150.55

    c. 192.158.148.73

    d. 192.168.151.250

    e. 192.168.155.32

17. What is 10.16.8.127 in binary notation?

18. Which of the following formulas is appropriate for finding the number of available hosts on a subnet?

    a. 10^n

    b. $10^n - 2$

    c. 2^n

    d. $2^n - 2$

    e. $2^n - 1$

19. When using classless routing, the formula used to calculate the number of bits required for subnetting is 2^n because the subnets of all 0s and all 1s are allowed. True or False?

20. How many bits are required to supernet seven Class C addresses?

    a. 1

    b. 2

    c. 3

    d. 4

    e. 5

CASE PROJECTS

Now that Arctic University is connecting to the Internet, many existing systems need to be modified so that they are part of a single, well-organized network. The following cases take you through several exercises required as part of the reorganization.

Case Project 4-1: Choosing Subnets for Each Location

There are six different physical locations used by Arctic University to deliver classes. Each of these locations has a minimum of 50 computers and a maximum of 1000 computers. The IP addressing plan needs to be presented at the IT staff meeting this week. Write a short report indicating the range of addresses that should be used for each location and the reasons you chose those address ranges.

Case Project 4-2: Choosing Subnets for Lab Expansion

Because of increased enrollment, Arctic University is expanding its student computer services by adding an additional six computer labs located on the main campus. Each lab will contain 100 new Windows XP-based computers. To reduce the amount of network traffic and increase control, you recommend that each new lab be configured as a separate subnet. The new computer labs can use the network ID 172.16.0.0. What subnet mask will you use to subnet the labs? What range of IP addresses can you assign to each lab? Use a table similar to the one shown below to record your answers.

Subnet Mask:		
	Beginning IP Address	Ending IP Address
Subnet 1		
Subnet 2		
Subnet 3		
Subnet 4		
Subnet 5		
Subnet 6		

Case Project 4-3: Supernetting to Reduce Routing

A router connecting two small test labs has failed and needs to be replaced. The first lab has 10 computers and is assigned the network ID 192.168.21.0 with a subnet mask of 255.255.255.0. The second lab has 25 computers with the network of ID 192.168.23.0 and a subnet mask of 255.255.255.0. Instead of replacing the failed router, you recommend that the two subnets be combined into a single supernet. What subnet mask would you use? What IP addresses are valid for the new supernet?

5

DYNAMIC HOST CONFIGURATION PROTOCOL

After reading this chapter and completing the exercises, you will be able to:

♦ Describe the DHCP lease and renewal process

♦ Understand and describe the purpose of a DHCP relay

♦ Install DHCP

♦ Configure DHCP scopes, superscopes, reservations, vendor classes, and user classes

♦ Manage and monitor DHCP

♦ Troubleshoot DHCP

♦ Install and configure a DHCP relay

Manually going to each workstation to configure IP addresses is a time-consuming task. You can use Dynamic Host Configuration Protocol (DHCP) to reduce the amount of time spent configuring workstations. DHCP automatically configures workstations with an IP address, subnet mask, default gateway, and many other options.

To use DHCP, you must install and authorize the service. Once the service is authorized, you create and configure a scope that defines which IP addresses can be handed out.

THE DHCP PROCESS

Dynamic Host Configuration Protocol (DHCP) is used to automatically deliver IP addressing information to client computers on a network. It can also deliver IP address information to servers and other devices such as printers, although most network administrators prefer to use static IP addresses for network resources such as servers and printers.

Using DHCP reduces the amount of time you spend configuring computers on your network. Imagine that a company with 500 client computers changes the IP address of their router as part of the implementation of a new firewall. If this company is not using DHCP, the network administrator has to visit each client computer and change the default gateway, which might take days. However, if this company is using DHCP, then the new default gateway can be delivered when all the users log in the next morning. In this case, the network administrator does not have to visit any client computers.

Client computers use DHCP by default unless you specify a static IP address during the installation. To confirm that a computer is using DHCP, you can view the properties of TCP/IP. Figure 5-1 shows the TCP/IP properties of a Windows XP client computer.

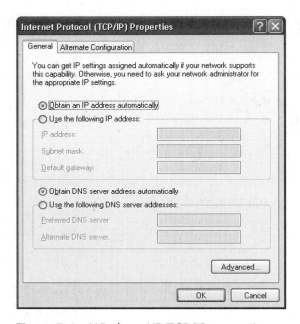

Figure 5-1   Windows XP TCP/IP properties

Leasing an IP Address

A client computer that is configured to use DHCP **leases** an IP address during the boot process when networking is initialized. The overall process to lease an address is composed of four packets:

- DHCPDISCOVER
- DHCPOFFER
- DHCPREQUEST
- DHCPACK

Figure 5-2 shows the four packets transmitted as part of the DHCP process.

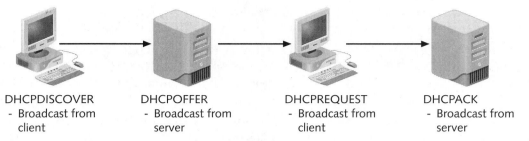

DHCPDISCOVER   DHCPOFFER   DHCPREQUEST   DHCPACK
- Broadcast from   - Broadcast from   - Broadcast from   - Broadcast from
  client   server   client   server

Figure 5-2   The four packets in the DHCP lease process

5

The **DHCPDISCOVER** packet is sent from the client computer to the broadcast IP address 255.255.255.255. A broadcast address must be used because the client is not configured with the address of a DHCP server. The source IP address in the packet is 0.0.0.0 because the client does not have an IP address yet. The MAC address of the client is included in the packet as an identifier.

Any DHCP server that receives the DHCPDISCOVER packet responds with a **DHCPOFFER** packet. The DHCPOFFER packet contains DHCP configuration information such as an IP address, subnet mask, default gateway, and lease length. The destination IP address for the packet is the broadcast address 255.255.255.255. This destination IP address ensures that the client can receive the packet even though it does not yet have an IP address assigned. The MAC address of the client is included in the data portion of the packet as an identifier.

The DHCP client responds to the DHCPOFFER packet it receives with a **DHCPREQUEST** packet. If there are multiple DHCP servers that send DHCPOFFER packets, the client responds only to the first one. The DHCPREQUEST packet contains the lease information that has been chosen by the client. This indicates to the servers that their lease offer to the client has, or has not, been chosen.

The DHCPREQUEST packet is addressed to the broadcast IP address 255.255.255.255. This allows all of the DHCP servers to see the DHCPREQUEST. The servers that were not chosen see this packet and place their offered addresses back into their pool of available addresses.

The chosen DHCP server sends back a **DHCPACK** packet indicating its confirmation that the lease has been chosen and that the client is now allowed to use the lease. This packet is still being sent to the broadcast IP address 255.255.255.255 because the client has not yet initialized IP with the new address. Once DHCPACK is received by the client, the client starts using the IP address and options that were in the lease.

Renewing an IP Address

When an IP address is leased using DHCP, it can be either permanent or timed. When a permanent address is given to a client, the DHCP server never reuses that address for another client. A permanent address is a way to distribute IP address and configuration options to clients if there will never be any changes to the information.

It is very rare to find a computer network that never changes its IP addressing configuration. It is quite common to add additional DNS servers or change the default gateway if a new router is installed. To allow for these changes, **timed leases** are used.

A timed lease allows clients to use an IP address for a specified period of time. Windows clients attempt to renew their lease after 50% of the lease time has expired by sending a DHCPREQUEST message directly to the DHCP server from which it obtained the lease. If a DHCP client cannot renew its lease with the original DHCP server, the client broadcasts a DHCPREQUEST to contact any available DHCP server when 87.5% of the lease period has expired, and again at 100% of the lease time.

Figure 5-3 shows the two packets that are used as part of the DHCP lease renewal process.

The first packet in the renewal process is a DHCPREQUEST packet from the client to the DHCP server. This packet uses the IP address of the client as the source address and the IP address of the DHCP server as the destination address. Broadcast addresses are not required for renewing a DHCP lease because the client already has an IP address, and the client is already aware of the DHCP server's IP address.

The response from the DHCP server is either a DHCPACK packet or a **DHCPNAK** packet. A DHCPACK packet is used to confirm the renewal of the client lease, while a DHCPNAK packet is used to deny the renewal of the client lease. If the renewal is denied, the client can continue to use the current address information until the lease expires.

A client can initiate the release of an IP address before the lease time has expired. Windows NT/2000/XP uses the command **ipconfig /release** to force the release of a DHCP address. In this process, the client sends a **DHCPRELEASE** packet to the DHCP server. The DHCP server then makes the released address available to other clients if required.

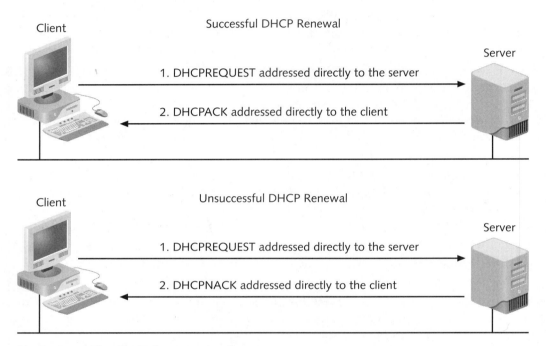

Figure 5-3   The DHCP lease renewal process

 For more information on the packets sent as part of the DHCP process in various situations, view RFC 2131. It can be found at *www.ietf.org/rfc/rfc2131.txt*.

DHCP RELAY

All DHCP packets during the leasing process are broadcast packets, which makes it impossible for these packets to travel across a router. Consequently, a DHCP server must be present on the local network in order to lease IP addresses to clients. DHCP packets cannot travel across a router.

In many larger networks it is desirable to have a single DHCP server handle all leasing even if there are routers. To do this, you must install a **DHCP relay**. This can be either Windows Server 2003 with the DHCP Relay Service installed or a router that is configured as a relay (RFC 1542 compliant).

A DHCP relay receives broadcast DHCP packets from clients and forwards them as unicast packets to a DHCP server. The DHCP relay must be configured with the IP address of the DHCP server to deliver the unicast packets.

The DHCP Relay Service cannot be installed on the same server as the DHCP Service. Both services listen at the same port numbers. If both are installed, the performance is erratic.

INSTALLING **DHCP**

DHCP is a standard service that is included with Windows Server 2003. It is not installed as part of a default installation. Instead, you must add it later through Add or Remove Programs. Figure 5-4 shows the Add or Remove Programs option in Control Panel being used to install DHCP.

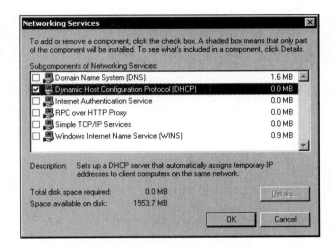

5

Figure 5-4   Installing DHCP

Activity 5-1: Installing DHCP

Time Required: 5 minutes

Objective: Install DHCP on Windows Server 2003.

Description: Most locations in the Arctic University network are using static IP addresses for workstations. To make maintenance of the workstations easier, you are going to configure them to use DHCP. Note that the DHCP server will always have a static IP address. In this activity you will configure your server with a static IP address on the Private connection and install DHCP.

1. If necessary, start your server, and log on as Administrator of the arctic.local domain.

2. Click **Start**, point to **Control Panel**, point to **Network Connections**, right-click **Private**, and click **Properties**.

3. Click **Internet Protocol (TCP/IP)** and click **Properties**.

4. Click **Use the following IP address**.

5. In the IP address box type **192.168.20x.y**, where x is the group number assigned by your instructor, and y is your student number.

6. Press **Tab** to fill in the subnet mask as 255.255.255.0, click **OK**, and click **Close**.

7. Click **Start**, point to **Control Panel**, and then click **Add or Remove Programs**.

8. Click **Add/Remove Windows Components**.

9. Scroll down in the components section, click **Networking Services** to highlight it, and then click **Details**.

10. Click the check box beside **Dynamic Host Configuration Protocol (DHCP)** to select it, and then click **OK**.

11. Click **Next**.

12. Click **Finish**.

13. Close the Add or Remove Programs window.

Authorization

Within a corporation's IT Department, control over network resources is always important. Control over DHCP is very important, as an unauthorized DHCP server can hand out incorrect IP addressing information to hundreds of client computers very quickly. These computers are then unable to access network resources, which can be as serious as a server crashing.

To exercise control over DHCP, Windows Server 2003 must be authorized to start the DHCP Service. When the DHCP Service is starting, it checks to see that the server is authorized. If the server is authorized, then DHCP starts. If the server is not authorized, then the DHCP Service shuts itself down. Figure 5-5 shows the error message that appears in Event Viewer when an unauthorized DHCP server attempts to start.

The authorization of a DHCP server takes place in Active Directory using the DHCP management snap-in. To authorize a DHCP server, you must be a member of the **Enterprise Admins** group, or a member of the Enterprise Admins group must delegate permissions to you using the Active Directory Sites and Services snap-in. Figure 5-6 shows the DHCP management snap-in.

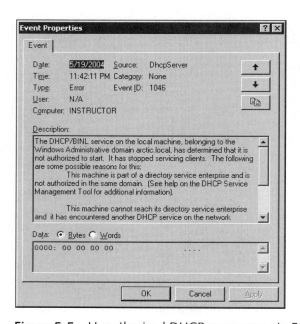

Figure 5-5   Unauthorized DHCP server error in Event Viewer

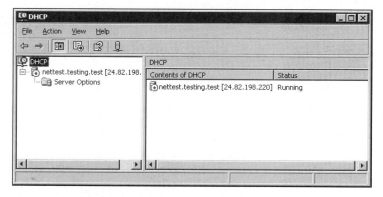

Figure 5-6   The DHCP management snap-in

Figure 5-7 shows the information message in Event Viewer after the DHCP server is authorized and has started.

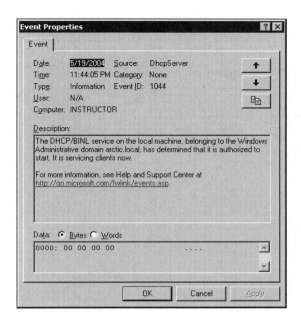

Figure 5-7   Authorized DHCP server information in Event Viewer

Activity 5-2: Starting an Unauthorized DHCP Server

Time Required: 10 minutes

Objective: View the results of starting an unauthorized DHCP server.

Description: You have just installed a new DHCP server on one of your networks. In this exercise, you attempt to start the DHCP Service before the server is authorized. You also view the results in the event log.

1. If necessary, start your server, and log on as Administrator of the arctic.local domain.

2. Click **Start**, point to **Administrative Tools**, and then click **Services**.

3. Scroll to the DHCP Server service, and view the status. Notice that the status is started even though the service is not authorized.

4. Close the Services window.

5. Click **Start**, point to **Administrative Tools**, and then click **Event Viewer**.

6. In the left pane, click the **System** log if it is not already open.

7. Find the error event generated by the DHCP Service. The type is error, the source is DHCPServer, and the event is 1046. Double-click the error event.

8. Read the contents of the error message, and click **OK**.

9. Close Event Viewer.

Activity 5-3: Authorizing a DHCP Server

Time Required: 10 minutes

Objective: Authorize a DHCP server in Active Directory.

Description: You have just installed a new DHCP server in one of your networks. In this activity, you use the DHCP management snap-in to authorize your server as a DHCP server.

1. If necessary, start your server, and log on as Administrator.

2. Click **Start**, point to **Administrative Tools**, and click **DHCP**.

3. In the DHCP snap-in window, right-click **DHCP**, then click **Manage authorized servers**.

4. Click **Authorize**.

5. Type the IP address of your server's Private connection, and click **OK**.

6. Click **OK** again to confirm the authorization.

7. Click **Close** to close the **Manage Authorized Servers** window.

8. Close the DHCP management snap-in.

9. Click **Start**, point to **Administrative Tools**, and click **Event Viewer**.

10. Click the **System** log if it is not already open.

11. Find the information event generated by the DHCP Service. The type is information, the source is DHCPServer, and the event is 1044. Double-click the information event.

12. Read the contents of the information event, and click **OK**.

13. Close Event Viewer.

Configuring DHCP

Once DHCP has been installed and authorized, you must configure it with the IP address information that is to be handed out to client computers. All configuration of DHCP is normally done with the DHCP management snap-in. However, in larger organizations where there is a need to make changes programmatically using batch files, you can also use the **NETSH** command to configure the DHCP Service.

The DHCP elements that can be configured include:

- Scopes
- Superscopes
- Multicast scopes
- Reservations
- Vendor and user classes
- Scope, server, and reservation options

Scopes

A **scope** is used to define a range of IP addresses for the DHCP server to hand out to client computers. Each scope is configured with a name, description, starting IP address, ending IP address, subnet mask, **exclusions**, and lease duration, as shown in Figure 5-8.

The name and description of a scope are what appears in the DHCP management snap-in. These are for your use as an administrator to make it as easy as possible to manage the system. The DHCP Service does not vary its functionality based on scope names or descriptions.

The starting and ending IP addresses define the range of IP addresses that can be handed out by the DHCP server with this scope. These addresses correspond with the different subnets in your network. Each range of addresses must be within a single subnet.

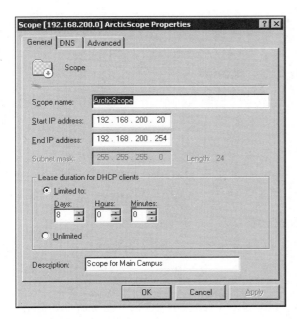

Figure 5-8 Scope settings

There are two different strategies to use when you are defining the starting and ending IP addresses. The first strategy is to configure the scope to use all available addresses on a subnet, and then exclude the static IP addresses being used by hosts such as printers. This strategy is very flexible because additional exclusions can always be added as required. An exclusion is an IP address, or range of IP addresses, within a scope that are not handed out by the DHCP server. The second strategy is to configure the scope to use only addresses that are not already in use. This strategy is used when statically configured hosts use a range of addresses at the beginning or end of a subnet. For example, many administrators place all statically configured hosts in the first few IP addresses on a subnet, and then allocate the remaining IP addresses to DHCP.

The subnet mask for a scope is the subnet mask that is required for hosts on that subnet.

Exclusions are used to prevent some IP addresses in a scope from being handed out dynamically. Choose to use exclusions when any statically configured devices such as servers and network printers have IP addresses that fall between the starting and ending IP address of a scope. If exclusions are not used for statically configured devices, then IP address conflicts can occur if the DHCP server leases out those addresses.

The lease duration for a scope defines how long client computers are allowed to use an IP address. The default lease duration used by Windows Server 2003 is eight days. Windows clients attempt to renew their lease after 50% (or four days, using the default setting) of the lease time has passed, then again at 87.5% (or seven days) if the first attempt failed, and again at the end of the lease time if the second attempt fails. If a lease expires, then the client can no longer use the IP address and cannot communicate on the network.

A DHCP server does not begin using a scope immediately after creation. A scope must be activated before the DHCP Service can begin using the scope. This is useful because it means you get a chance to confirm that the configuration of a scope is correct before addresses are handed out.

Activity 5-4: Creating a Scope

Time Required: 5 minutes

Objective: Create a scope to distribute IP addresses to client computers.

Description: You must create a scope on your newly installed DHCP server so that it can hand out IP addresses to client computers. After the scope is created, you activate the scope. Your instructor assigns you a group number to complete this exercise.

1. If necessary, start your server, and log on as Administrator.
2. Click **Start**, point to **Administrative Tools**, and click **DHCP**.
3. Click your server to select it, right-click your server, and click **New Scope**.
4. Click **Next** to begin configuring the new scope.
5. Type *yourname***Scope** as the name of the scope, and click **Next**.
6. Type **192.168.20x.100** as the Start IP address, where *x* is the group number assigned by your instructor.
7. Type **192.168.20x.200** as the End IP address, where *x* is the group number assigned by your instructor.
8. Confirm that the length of the subnet mask is 24 bits (255.255.255.0), and click **Next**.
9. Exclusions are not required. Click **Next**.
10. Change the lease duration to **1 hour**, and click **Next**.
11. Click **No, I will configure these options later**, and click **Next**.
12. Click **Finish**.
13. Close the DHCP snap-in.

Activity 5-5: Activating and Testing a Scope

Time Required: 20 minutes

Objective: Activate a DHCP scope, and then test it with a partner.

Description: In the previous activity, you created a scope. In this activity, you allow the DHCP Service to use the information by activating the scope. You work with a partner. When your scope is activated, your partner acts as the client computer. When your partner's scope is activated, you act as the client.

1. If necessary, start your server, and log on as Administrator.
2. Partner A: Activate the scope on your server.
   a. Click **Start**, point to **Administrative Tools**, and click **DHCP**.
   b. Click your server to select it, click your scope to select it, right-click your scope, and click **Activate**.
   c. Close the DHCP snap-in.
3. Partner B: Change your Private connection to be a dynamic address.
   a. Click **Start**, point to **Control Panel**, point to **Network Connections**, right-click **Private**, and click **Properties**.
   b. Click **Internet Protocol (TCP/IP)**, and click **Properties**.
   c. Click **Obtain an IP address automatically**, and click **OK**.
   d. Click **Close** to save the changes.

4. Partner B: View the dynamic IP address on the Private connection.

   a. Click **Start** and click **Run**.

   b. Type **cmd** and press **Enter**.

   c. Type **ipconfig /all** and press **Enter**.

   d. If the Private connection is still using an APIPA address then type **ipconfig /renew** and press **Enter**. Then repeat step c to view the new configuration information.

   e. Close the command prompt window.

5. Partner B: Change the Private connection back to a static IP address.

   a. Click **Start**, point to **Control Panel**, point to **Network Connections**, right-click **Private**, and then click **Properties**.

   b. Click **Internet Protocol (TCP/IP)**, and click **Properties**.

   c. Click **Use the following IP address**.

   d. In the **IP address** box type **192.168.20x.y**, where x is the group number assigned by your instructor, and y is your student number.

   e. Press **Tab** to fill in the subnet mask as 255.255.255.0, click **OK**, and click **Close**.

6. Partner A: Deactivate the scope.

   a. Click **Start**, point to **Administrative Tools**, and click **DHCP**.

   b. Click your server to select it, click your scope to select it, right-click your scope, and click **Deactivate**.

   c. Click **Yes** to confirm the deactivation.

   d. Close the DHCP snap-in.

7. Redo this exercise and reverse your roles. If you were partner A, this time become partner B.

Superscopes

A **superscope** is used to combine multiple scopes into a single logical scope. This is used when a single physical part of the network has two subnets on it. Often a network is organized like this because the number of hosts grew too large for a single subnet.

To conceptualize a superscope, consider the following example. A mid-sized company that starts out with 200 workstations has a single Class C network. There are no routers required because the entire network is switched at 100 Mbps. The DHCP server is distributing addresses to the workstations using a single scope.

Over time, the network grows to the point where a single Class C network is not large enough. To increase the number of addresses, another Class C network is added to the same segment of the network. Computers with addresses from both networks are attached to the same segment and a router is added to move packets from one logical network to the other. A second scope is added to the DHCP server.

When a client broadcasts a DHCPREQUEST packet, the DHCP server sees it. However, the DHCP server does not know which logical network the client is from and offers leases from both scopes. Combining two scopes in a superscope indicates to the DHCP Service that both scopes are on the same network segment and should be treated as a single scope. If a superscope is used, then the DHCP server offers only one lease out to computers on a segment with two logical networks.

Figure 5-9 shows a superscope that contains two scopes. The DHCP server treats the superscope as a single unit. Scopes inside a superscope cannot be activated individually. The superscope must be activated and this in turn activates all scopes that are part of the superscope.

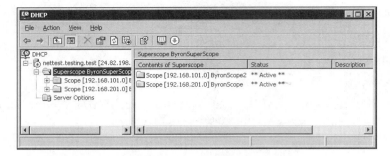

Figure 5-9 A superscope containing two scopes

Activity 5-6: Configuring a Superscope

Time Required: 5 minutes

Objective: Combine two scopes into a single logical unit using a superscope.

Description: One of the sites on your network has grown too large to use a single Class C address. It is already configured with one scope. You add a second scope, and then configure a superscope that combines the two scopes.

1. If necessary, start your server, and log on as Administrator.

2. Click **Start**, point to **Administrative Tools**, and click **DHCP**.

3. Create a second scope.

   a. Click your server to select it, right-click your server, and click **New Scope**.

   b. Click **Next** to begin configuring the new scope.

   c. Type *yourname***Scope2** as the name of the scope, and click **Next**.

   d. Type **192.168.10x.100** as the Start IP address, where *x* is the group number assigned by your instructor.

   e. Type **192.168.10x.200** as the End IP address, where *x* is the group number assigned by your instructor.

   f. Confirm that the length of the subnet mask is 24 bits (255.255.255.0), and click **Next**.

   g. Exclusions are not required. Click **Next**.

   h. Change the lease duration to **1 hour**, and click **Next**.

   i. Click **No, I will configure these options later**, and click **Next**.

   j. Click **Finish**.

4. Create a superscope.

   a. Right-click your server, and click **New Superscope**.

   b. Click **Next** to begin configuring the superscope.

   c. Type *yourname***Superscope** in the Name box, and click **Next**.

   d. Press and hold Ctrl, click *yourname***Scope** and *yourname***Scope2** to select them, and click **Next**.

   e. Click **Finish** to complete the superscope.

5. Click the **+** (plus sign) beside **Superscope** *yourname***Superscope** to see the scopes inside the superscope.

6. Close the DHCP snap-in.

Activity 5-7: Deleting a Superscope

Time Required: 5 minutes

Objective: Delete a superscope, leaving each scope independent.

Description: A location with a superscope enabled has retired some workstations. There is no longer a need for the second scope and the superscope. You remove the superscope, and delete the second scope.

1. If necessary, start your server, and log on as Administrator.
2. Click **Start**, point to **Administrative Tools**, and click **DHCP**.
3. Click your server to select it, right-click **Superscope** *yourname***Superscope**, and click **Delete**.
4. Click **Yes** to delete the superscope without deleting any child scopes.
5. Right-click **Scope [192.168.10x.0]** *yourname***Scope2**, and click **Delete**.
6. Click **Yes** to delete the scope.
7. Close the DHCP snap-in.

Multicast Scopes

A **multicast scope** is used to deliver multicast addresses to applications that require it. A multicast address is used by applications to deliver packets to groups of computers rather than a single computer. Most applications that use multicast addresses are hard-coded with a single address that is used for that application rather than using DHCP to find a multicast address. Thus, using a multicast scope on a DHCP server is rare.

When you create a multicast scope, you configure start and end IP addresses, time to live (TTL), exclusions, a lease duration, and activation. The start and end IP addresses define the range of multicast addresses that the DHCP server can hand out when this multicast scope is activated. The allowable range of addresses is from 224.0.0.0 to 239.255.255.255.

The TTL of the multicast scope defines the number of routers through which a multicast packet can move. If the TTL is set to 5, then the packet is discarded by routers after five hops. This is used to control the movement of multicast packets across wide area networks. The default value for the TTL is 32.

Exclusions define addresses between the start and end IP addresses that are not handed out. Exclusions are used if there are applications using hard-coded multicast addresses within the range of the scope.

The lease duration is the length of time that an application can use a multicast address. The default lease length is 30 days.

Activity 5-8: Creating a Multicast Scope

Time Required: 5 minutes

Objective: Create a multicast scope to deliver multicast addresses to applications.

Description: You have installed a new application that requires a multicast address delivered through DHCP. You must create and activate the multicast scope on your DHCP server.

1. If necessary, start your server, and log on as Administrator.
2. Click **Start**, point to **Administrative Tools**, and click **DHCP**.
3. Click your server to select it, right-click your server, and click **New Multicast Scope**.
4. Click **Next** to begin creating the multicast scope.
5. Type *yourname***MulticastScope** in the **Name** box, and click **Next**.
6. In the Start IP address box, type **224.0.0.0**.

7. In the End IP address box, type **224.0.0.255**.

8. In the TTL box, type **1**, and click **Next**. Setting the TTL to 1 ensures that your server does not start to distribute to other networks.

9. Click **Next**. There are no exclusions that need to be configured.

10. Click **Next** to confirm the default lease time of 30 days.

11. Click **Next** to activate the scope now.

12. Click **Finish** to complete the creation of the multicast scope.

13. Close the DHCP management snap-in.

Reservations

A **reservation** is used to hand out a specific IP address to a particular client computer or device on the network. This can be useful when delivering IP addresses to devices that would normally use static addresses, such as printers and servers. If the IP addresses of these devices ever need to be changed, it is easier to centrally manage the process through DHCP reservations rather than visiting each device that needs to be reconfigured.

Reservations can also be beneficial when firewalls are in place. Some companies use firewalls internally to limit which client computers can communicate with sensitive resources such as accounting and human resources information. Normally, DHCP-delivered addresses have the potential to change, which means that firewall rules based on IP addresses would not be effective. With reservations for secure clients, the firewall rules can be configured to allow packets from the IP address specified in the reservations.

Reservations are created based on the MAC address of the network card. The MAC address is used as the identifier for the client workstation that is matched to a reservation. If the MAC address of the client matches the MAC address defined in the reservation, then the IP address of the reservation is leased to the client. Figure 5-10 shows the creation of a reservation.

Figure 5-10   Creating a reservation

There are software utilities that override the MAC address built into the network card. This makes it possible to falsify the MAC address in a data packet and obtain an improper reservation. Consequently, using DHCP reservations with a firewall offers limited security.

Activity 5-9: Creating and Testing a Reservation

Time Required: 15 minutes

Objective: Create a DHCP reservation, and test it with a client.

Description: In an effort to control access to the Internet, you have configured a firewall to restrict the use of the Telnet protocol. However, internal technical staff need to use Telnet on occasion to manage Linux servers. To allow this, you have created rules on the firewall that allow Telnet traffic from a few internal addresses. You now configure the DHCP server to hand out those addresses to a few specific computers using reservations. You work with a partner to complete this exercise. Partner A is the DHCP client and Partner B is the DHCP server.

1. If necessary, start your server, and log on as Administrator.

2. Partner A: Get the MAC address of the network card on your private connection.

   a. Click **Start** and click **Run**.

   b. Type **cmd** and press **Enter**.

   c. Type **ipconfig /all** and press **Enter**.

   d. Write down the **Physical Address** of the network card listed under **Ethernet adapter Private**. This address is a 12-character hexadecimal number.

   e. Close the command prompt window.

3. Partner B: Create a reservation for student A.

   a. Click **Start**, point to **Administrative Tools**, and click **DHCP**.

   b. Click your server to see the scopes that are configured.

   c. Click your scope to expand the contents.

   d. Click **Reservations** to view the reservations that are configured. There should be none at this time.

   e. Right-click **Reservations**, and click **New Reservation**.

   f. In the Reservation name box, type *yourname***Reservation**.

   g. In the IP address box, type **192.168.20*x*.15**, where *x* is the group number given to you by your instructor.

   h. In the MAC address box, type the physical address of student A.

   i. In the **Description** box, type **Telnet Reservation**, and click **Add**.

   j. Click **Close** to stop adding reservations.

4. Partner B: Right-click your scope, and click **Activate**.

5. Partner A: Test the client reservation.

   a. Click **Start**, point to **Control Panel**, point to **Network Connections**, right-click **Private**, and click **Properties**.

   b. Click **Internet Protocol (TCP/IP)**, and click **Properties**.

   c. Take note of the IP address configuration, because this information is required again at the end of the exercise.

   d. Click **Obtain an IP address automatically**, and click **OK**.

   e. Click **Close** to save the changes.

   f. Click **Start** and click **Run**.

g. Type **cmd** and press **Enter**.

h. Type **ipconfig /all** and press **Enter**.

i. The IP address of the Private connection should be 192.168.20x.15. If it is not, verify that the MAC address was entered correctly in the reservation.

j. Close the command prompt window.

6. Partner A: Change the Private connection back to a static IP address.

a. Click **Start**, point to **Control Panel**, point to **Network Connections**, right-click **Private**, and click **Properties**.

b. Click **Internet Protocol (TCP/IP)**, and click **Properties**.

c. Click **Use the following IP address**.

d. Type in the IP address and subnet mask that were configured before you changed the address to DHCP, and click **OK**.

e. Click **Close**.

7. Partner B: Right-click your scope, click **Deactivate**, and click **Yes** to confirm.

8. Partner B: Close the DHCP snap-in.

9. If time permits, reverse roles and repeat the activity.

Configuring Options

In addition to handing out IP addresses and subnet masks, DHCP can hand out a variety of other IP configuration options such as default gateway, DNS server, WINS server, and many more. These options can be configured for the entire server, a scope, or a single reservation.

It is quite common that all workstations within an entire organization use the same DNS servers. Therefore DNS is often configured at the server level so that it applies to all scopes on that server. The same is true for WINS servers. Figure 5-11 shows the setting of server options.

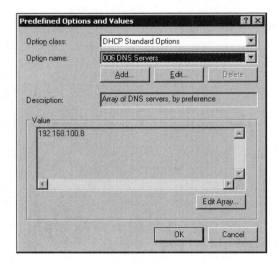

Figure 5-11   Setting server options

The default gateway is different for every subnet and is set in the options for a scope. Figure 5-12 shows the setting of scope options.

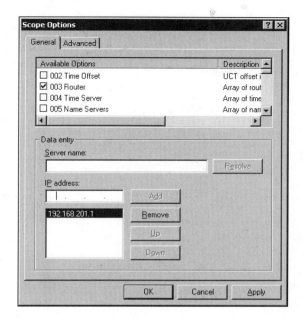

Figure 5-12   Setting scope options

It is unusual to set options in a reservation, but this may be necessary for some users with a special configuration. For example, accounting staff may use a different default gateway than other staff to allow them access to the accounting systems.

Activity 5-10: Setting Server Options

Time Required: 5 minutes

Objective: Set the DNS server option for a DHCP server.

Description: All of the computers serviced by this DHCP server are using the same DNS server. Rather than configuring each scope with a DNS server option, you have decided to configure the DHCP server with the DNS server option.

1. If necessary, start your server, and log on as Administrator.
2. Click **Start**, point to **Administrative Tools**, and click **DHCP**.
3. Click your server to select it, right-click your server, and click **Set Predefined Options**.
4. In the Option name box, click the **down** arrow, and then click **006 DNS Servers**.
5. Click **Edit Array**.
6. In the IP address box, type **192.168.100.8** and click **Add**.
7. Click **OK** to save the changes to the DNS server list.
8. Click **OK** to save the changes to the server level options.
9. Close the DHCP snap-in.

Activity 5-11: Setting Scope Options

Time Required: 5 minutes

Objective: Set the default gateway in the scope options.

Description: You have configured a new scope to lease IP addresses to clients. The server is already configured to include the DNS server option as part of the lease. However, for the clients to access resources outside of their own network, you must configure the default gateway option in the scope.

1. If necessary, start your server, and log on as Administrator.

2. Click **Start**, point to **Administrative Tools**, and click **DHCP**.

3. Click your server to expand it and see the scopes inside.

4. Click your scope to see the options inside the scope.

5. Click **Scope Options** to select it, right-click **Scope Options**, and click **Configure Options**.

6. Click the check box beside **003 Router**.

7. In the **IP address** box, type **192.168.20x.1**, where *x* is the group number given to you by your instructor, and click **Add**.

8. Click **OK** to save the option.

9. Close the DHCP snap-in.

Vendor and User Classes

Vendor and user classes can be used to differentiate between clients within a scope. Each different **vendor class** and **user class** can be configured to get its own set of options.

Vendor classes are based on the operating system being used. The vendor classes predefined within the DHCP server of Windows Server 2003 are:

- *DHCP Standard Options*—Used by all clients regardless of operating system
- *Microsoft Options*—Used by Windows 2000/XP/2003 and Windows 98 clients
- *Microsoft Windows 2000 Options*—Used only by Windows 2000/XP/2003 clients
- *Microsoft Windows 98 Options*—Used only by Windows 98 clients

Figure 5-13 shows the setting of options for vendor classes.

User classes are defined based on how a client is connected to the network or by the network administrator. You can use the ipconfig /setclassid command to set the DHCP user class ID. Figure 5-14 shows the setting of a user class ID on a client.

The DHCP server included with Windows Server 2003 has three predefined user classes:

- *Default User Class*—This is used for all clients, including those that do not specify a user class or if the user class is unknown to the server.
- *Default Routing and Remote Access Class*—This class is used by clients that are assigned an IP address through DHCP when remotely accessing the network through a dial-up or VPN connection. The client computer can be running any operating system because Routing and Remote Access obtains the IP address and options on behalf of the client computer.
- *Default BOOTP Class*—This class is used by clients using the older BOOTP protocol rather than DHCP.

Figure 5-15 shows the setting of user class options.

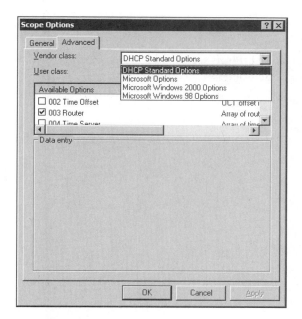

Figure 5-13   Vendor classes

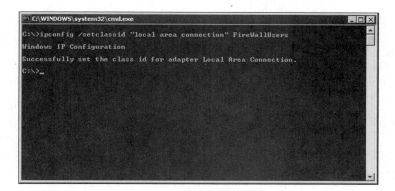

Figure 5-14   Setting a class ID

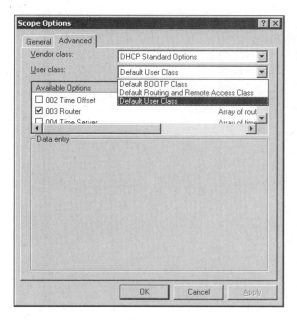

Figure 5-15   User classes

MANAGING AND MONITORING DHCP

It is important to effectively manage and monitor your DHCP server. There are a variety of tasks that can be done and features that can be configured. These include:

- Backing up and restoring DHCP databases
- Reconciling scopes
- Viewing statistics
- Enabling DHCP Audit logging
- Enabling Conflict Detection
- Modifying file paths
- Changing bindings
- Viewing DHCP events in Event Viewer
- Viewing DHCP statistics in the Performance snap-in

Back up and Restore DHCP Databases

The DHCP Service has several files that are stored in C:\WINDOWS\system32\dhcp. The file Dhcp.mdb is the database holding the addressing information that has been assigned to client computers. The file Dhcp.tmp is a temporary database file only present during maintenance operations. The files J50.log and J50#####.log (where ##### is a five-digit code for uniqueness) are transaction logs of changes to the DHCP database. The file J50.chk is a checkpoint file that keeps track of which entries in the log files have been applied to the database. Backing up the database backs up all of these files, as well as DHCP registry entries.

By default, the DHCP database is backed up every 60 minutes. You can back up the DHCP database manually by right-clicking the server in the DHCP snap-in and clicking Backup. You can also modify the automatic backup time by editing the registry key HKEY_LOCAL_MACHINE\SYSTEM\CurrentControlSet\ Services\DHCPServer\Parameters\BackupInterval.

To restore the DHCP database, right-click the server in the DHCP management snap-in, and click Restore. Then select the folder containing the backup, and click OK. Figure 5-16 shows how to access the option to back up or restore the DHCP database.

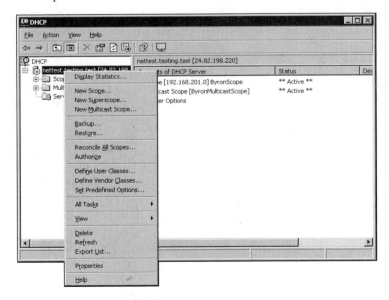

Figure 5-16   DHCP backup option

Reconcile Scopes

The DHCP database holds a summary version and a detailed version of the IP address lease information for a server. If there is a discrepancy between the two versions of information, then you must reconcile the scope to synchronize the information. If information regarding leased addresses is not appearing properly in the DHCP management snap-in, you may need to reconcile the scope. The scope may also need to be reconciled to properly show leased addresses after restoring the DHCP database. To reconcile a scope, right-click it and click Reconcile.

View Statistics

The Windows Server 2003 DHCP Service automatically tracks statistics that you can view. To view these statistics, right-click on the server or scope, and click Display Statistics. By default, to update these statistics, you must manually click the Refresh button while the statistics window is open. You can configure these statistics to automatically update by selecting the Automatically update statistics every option and specifying how often they are updated.

Enable DHCP Audit Logging

DHCP audit logs keep detailed information about DHCP server activity. This logging is enabled by default and keeps up to seven audit logs. The audit logs are named DhcpSrvLog-*XXX*.log, where *XXX* is the day of the week. These logs can be used to troubleshoot why a DHCP server is not functioning as you would expect.

To enable DHCP audit logging, select the option Enable DHCP audit logging in the properties of the DHCP server in the DHCP management snap-in. Audit logs are enabled by default. Figure 5-17 shows the option to turn audit logs off and on.

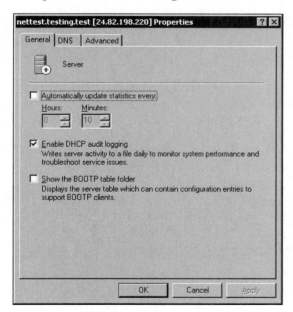

Figure 5-17   Enable audit logs

Conflict Detection

Conflict detection prevents a DHCP server from creating IP address conflicts. When conflict detection is enabled, a DHCP server pings an IP address before it is leased to a client computer. This ensures that even if another device is statically configured with that IP address, it is not leased.

You can configure how many ping attempts are made before an IP address is leased. The default is zero ping attempts. Each ping attempt adds approximately one second to the overall length of the leasing process. The number of pings for conflict detection is configured in the DHCP server properties in the DHCP management snap-in.

File Paths

You can control the location of the audit log file, the DHCP database, and the automatic backup directory. By default, the audit log file and DHCP database are located in C:\WINDOWS\system32\dhcp. The path used for automatic backups of the DHCP database is C:\WINDOWS\system32\dhcp\backup. Generally, these files are left in their default locations.

To modify the paths to where these files are stored, access the properties of the DHCP server in the DHCP management snap-in. Figure 5-18 shows the configuration of the file paths.

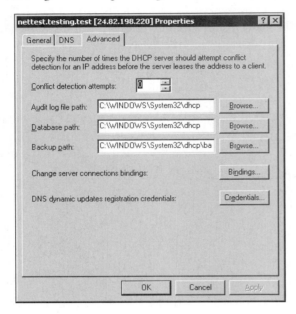

Figure 5-18   File paths

Bindings

If a DHCP server has multiple network cards, then you can choose which network cards the DHCP Service is bound to. The DHCP server only hands out IP addresses through a network card that has the DHCP Service bound. The bindings are controlled in the Advanced tab of the server Properties in the DHCP management snap-in. Figure 5-19 shows the configuration of DHCP bindings.

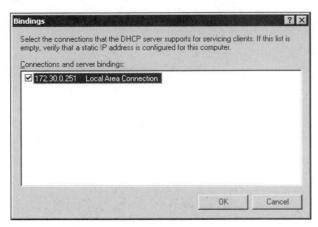

Figure 5-19   DHCP bindings

View DHCP Events in Event Viewer

In addition to audit logging, some summary information generated by the DHCP Service is placed in the system event log. You can view these events using Event Viewer.

Activity 5-12: Viewing DHCP Events in Event Viewer

Time Required: 5 minutes

Objective: See the events placed into the system log by the DHCP Service.

Description: Some of the users on the network have been complaining that they occasionally cannot get an IP address from the DHCP server. As a starting point, you view the system event log to see if the service has been stopped and restarted recently.

1. If necessary, start your server, and log on as Administrator.
2. Click **Start**, point to **Administrative Tools**, and click **Event Viewer**.
3. Click **System** to view the system log.
4. Click **View** and click **Filter**.
5. Click the **down** arrow in the Event source list box, and click **DHCPServer**.
6. Click **OK** to filter the system log.
7. View the DHCPServer events.
8. Click the **View** menu and click **All Records** to remove the filter.
9. Close Event Viewer.

Activity 5-13: Remove DHCP

Time Required: 5 minutes

Objective: Remove the DHCP Server service from your server.

Description: Remove the DHCP Server service to ensure that it does not interfere with activities later in this book.

1. If necessary, start your server, and log on as Administrator.
2. Click **Start**, point to **Control Panel**, and click **Add or Remove Programs**.
3. Click **Add/Remove Windows Components**.
4. Scroll down in the Components box, double-click **Networking Services**, and click the checkbox beside **Dynamic Host Configuration Protocol (DHCP)** to deselect it.
5. Click **OK**, and click **Next**.
6. Click **Finish** to complete removing the DHCP Server service, and close the Add or Remove Programs window.

View DHCP Statistics in the Performance Snap-in

When DHCP is installed on Windows Server 2003, new objects and counters are added to the Performance snap-in. You can monitor these counters to track the performance of DHCP over time. If you establish an initial benchmark of DHCP performance under average conditions, then you can tell if something is functioning abnormally later.

Figure 5-20 shows some of the DHCP performance counters that can be monitored. The number of Discovers/sec indicates how many new clients are being added to the network. If this number is higher than normal it may indicate that the lease length is too short, and computers are not able to renew their lease before it expires. Any number of Declines/sec indicates that some computers are using dynamic IP addresses not assigned by this DHCP server. This may be an indication that someone has installed an unauthorized DHCP server on an operating system such as Linux.

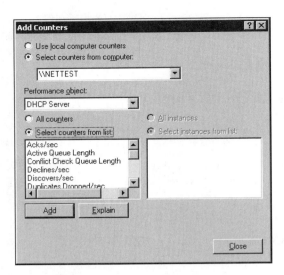

Figure 5-20   DHCP performance counters

DHCP TROUBLESHOOTING

DHCP is a fairly simple broadcast-based protocol that seldom has problems. However, some problems that you may encounter include:

- *All computers are unable to lease addresses*—Confirm that the DHCP Service is running and authorized. If the DHCP Service is authorized, confirm that the proper scope has been activated, and that the DHCP Service is bound to the proper adapter.

- *A single computer is unable to lease an address*—Confirm that the cabling is correct, and the proper network driver is loaded. If the TCP/IP configuration is corrupt, repairing the network connection may also fix the problem.

- *Some computers have incorrect address information*—If the computers have addresses in the range 169.254.X.X, then they were unable to contact the DHCP server. Confirm that the DHCP server is functional. Be aware that Windows XP can also be configured with alternate addresses to use when DHCP is unavailable.

- *A single computer has incorrect address information*—If this computer has a reservation, check the configuration of the reservation. Options set in a reservation override options set in a scope or at the server level.

- *A rogue DHCP server is leasing addresses*—Windows 2000 and Windows Server 2003 must be authorized to function as DHCP servers. However, other operating systems such as Linux, UNIX, and NetWare are not aware of authorization information.

- *Two DHCP servers configured to be redundant on a network segment are leasing the same range of IP addresses and causing conflicts*—DHCP servers are not designed to be redundant. A better solution is to **cluster** your DHCP Service. However, if you cannot cluster the service and still require redundancy, then you should configure the servers to each handle only a portion of the entire subnet. Microsoft recommends that the available addresses be split 25/75 between the two servers.

- *IP address conflicts are created when the DHCP server hands out addresses already used by hosts with static IP addresses*—The ideal solution to this problem is to create exclusions in the scope for the IP addresses used by hosts that are statically configured. However, if this information is not documented, then turning on conflict detection ensures that a DHCP server does not hand out an IP address that is already in use.

- *A client is using an APIPA address*—If a DHCP was down briefly, some clients may be using APIPA addresses. If you would like a client to reattempt leasing an IP address, then use the command ipconfig /renew.

Chapter Summary

- DHCP is used to dynamically assign IP address information to clients on a network. It can also be used to assign multicast IP addresses to applications that request them.

- The DHCP lease process is composed of four packets: DHCPDISCOVER, DHCPOFFER, DHCPREQUEST, and DHCPACK. DHCPNAK packets are used by DHCP servers to decline the renewal of a lease. DHCPRELEASE packets are used by clients to inform a DHCP server that their lease is no longer required.

- A DHCP client attempts to renew its lease at 50%, 87.5%, and 100% of the lease time. If it is unsuccessful in renewing the lease before it expires, then it loses the ability to access network resources.

- The commands ipconfig /release and ipconfig /renew can be used to release and renew DHCP leases.

- A DHCP server must be authorized in Active Directory to lease addresses to clients. To authorize a DHCP in Active Directory you must be a member of Enterprise Admins.

- A scope defines a range of IP addresses that are leased to clients. A scope must be activated before the DHCP server leases addresses in the scope.

- A superscope combines two scopes into a single logical unit to service network segments with two subnets.

- An exclusion in a scope can be used to stop a DHCP server from handing out specific addresses or a range of addresses within a scope.

- A reservation allows you to give a specific workstation a defined IP address by tying the DHCP lease to the MAC address of the client.

- Vendor and user classes can be used to configure some client computers with different options depending on the class to which they belong.

- Audit logging enables you to view detailed information about the operation of the DHCP Service.

- Conflict detection sends a ping packet before leasing an IP address to ensure that it is not in use.

- A DHCP relay is required to communicate with a DHCP server across a router.

Key Terms

cluster — A group of computers that coordinate the provision of services. When one computer in a cluster fails, the others take over its services.

conflict detection — When in use, a DHCP server pings an IP address before attempting to lease it. This ensures that IP address conflicts do not occur.

DHCP relay — A service that accepts DHCP broadcasts on one subnet and forwards them to a DHCP server on another subnet using unicast packets.

DHCPACK — The fourth and final packet in the DHCP lease process. This packet is a broadcast from the DHCP server confirming the lease.

DHCPDISCOVER — The first packet in the DHCP lease process. This packet is broadcast on the local network to find a DHCP server.

DHCPNAK — This packet is sent from a DHCP server to a client when it denies a renewal attempt.

DHCPOFFER — The second packet in the DHCP lease process. This packet is a broadcast from the DHCP server to the client with an offered lease.

DHCPREQUEST — The third packet in the DHCP lease process. This packet is a broadcast from the DHCP client indicating which DHCPOFFER has been chosen.

DHCPRELEASE — This packet is sent from a DHCP client to a DHCP server to indicate it is no longer using a leased IP address.

Enterprise Admins — A default group in Active Directory with administrative rights for the entire forest.

exclusion — An IP address or range of IP addresses within a scope that are not leased to clients.

lease — The length of time a DHCP client computer is allowed to use IP address information from the DHCP server.

multicast scope — A range of multicast IP addresses that are handed out to applications that request them.

NETSH — A command-line utility that can be used to manage many IP configuration settings and IP services.

reservation — A DHCP IP address that is leased only to a computer with a specific MAC address.

scope — A range of addresses that are leased by a DHCP server.

superscope — A logical grouping of scopes that is used to service network segments with more than one subnet in use.

timed lease — An IP address and configuration option given to a client computer from a DHCP server for a limited period of time.

user class — An identifier from the DHCP client that is sent as part of the DHCP lease process. This can be set manually by the administrator on workstations.

vendor class — An identifier from the DHCP client that is sent as part of the DHCP lease process. This is based on the operating system in use.

REVIEW QUESTIONS

1. After installing the DHCP Service, what must be done in Active Directory before it begins delivering leased IP addresses?

    a. Authorize it.

    b. reboot

    c. Activate it.

    d. Modify the firewall rules.

2. After creating a scope, what must be done before the DHCP Service begins servicing the scope?

    a. Authorize it.

    b. reboot

    c. Activate it.

    d. Modify the firewall rules.

3. Which of the following types of packets is used during the DHCP leasing process?

    a. unicast

    b. multicast

    c. broadcast

    d. None—it is all performed internally on the client.

4. How many packets are transmitted as part of the DHCP renewal process?

    a. 1

    b. 2

    c. 3

    d. 4

5. Which type of packet is sent if a request to renew a lease is denied?

    a. DHCPDISCOVER

    b. DHCPACK

    c. DHCPOFFER

    d. DHCPNAK

6. Which command can be used on Windows XP and Windows Server 2003 clients to force the renewal of a DHCP lease?

   a. ipconfig /release

   b. ipconfig /renew

   c. dhcpcon /renew

   d. winipcfg /release

   e. winipcfg /renew

7. Which type of packet is first in the DHCP lease process?

   a. DHCPACK

   b. DHCPOFFER

   c. DHCPDISCOVER

   d. DHCPREQUEST

8. Which utility is used to configure DHCP?

   a. DHCP management snap-in

   b. Active Directory Users and Computers

   c. Active Directory Sites and Services

   d. ipconfig

9. At what levels can you apply different options for leased IP addresses? (Choose all that apply.)

   a. server

   b. scope

   c. exclusion

   d. reservation

10. Exclusions are used to allow certain computers to use a predefined IP address. True or False?

11. Which of the following allow DHCP packets to cross over a router? (Choose all that apply.)

   a. DHCP relay

   b. switch

   c. RFC 1542 compliant router

   d. IPSec

12. What is used to logically combine multiple scopes into a single unit?

   a. megascope

   b. superscope

   c. metascope

   d. It is not possible.

13. What is the default lease length used by a scope created in the Windows Server 2003 DHCP Service?

   a. three hours

   b. three days

   c. seven days

   d. eight days

   e. 30 days

14. Which characteristic of a multicast scope controls how many routers a multicast packet travels through?

    a. lease duration

    b. time to live

    c. hop count

    d. half life

15. Which DHCP feature allows you to distribute a chosen IP address to a particular computer?

    a. exclusion

    b. scope

    c. reservation

    d. user class

    e. vendor class

16. What characteristic of a client computer is used to match a client computer with a reservation?

    a. vendor class

    b. user class

    c. operating system

    d. computer name

    e. MAC address

17. Which file stores the list of IP addresses leased through DHCP?

    a. Dhcp.mdb

    b. Dhcp.tmp

    c. J50.log

    d. J50.chk

    e. J50#####.log

18. Which utility can you use to create a baseline of DHCP functionality?

    a. Active Directory Sites and Services

    b. Event Viewer

    c. Performance

    d. Task Manager

19. Which feature do you enable to ensure that a DHCP server does not hand out IP addresses that are already in use on the network?

    a. audit logging

    b. conflict detection

    c. dynamic DNS

    d. bindings

20. Which of the following are client options that can be set at the scope level? (Choose all that apply.)

    a. DNS

    b. WINS

    c. ROUTER

    d. MAC address

CASE PROJECTS

The planning for new IP address allocations has been done for all of the Arctic University campuses. All campuses will have at least one subnet and some will have several, depending upon the size of the campus. To make the configuration of clients easier, it has been decided that DHCP will be implemented.

Case Project 5-1: Multiple Subnets

You are planning how DHCP will be used to deliver IP addresses to clients on one of your larger campuses with five different subnets. Write a short memo describing the pros and cons of using a single DHCP server versus multiple DHCP servers.

5

Case Project 5-2: Avoiding IP Address Conflicts

One of your newly configured sites is having a problem with IP address conflicts. Some of the addresses being leased by the DHCP server are already configured on servers, printers, and workstations. The DHCP servers are using 192.168.1.10 through 192.168.1.19. The printers are using 192.168.1.20 through 192.168.1.29. What are your options for eliminating these conflicts?

Case Project 5-3: DHCP and Firewalls

As a security measure, you have stopped all of the faculty and students from using instant messaging clients by blocking their ports. However, some of the faculty use an application based on instant messaging. How can you use DHCP to help you allow just these clients access to instant messaging ports?

6

DOMAIN NAME SYSTEM

After reading this chapter and completing the exercises, you will be able to:

♦ Describe the functions of the Domain Name System

♦ Install DNS

♦ Explain the function of DNS zones

♦ Configure a caching-only server to speed hostname resolution

♦ Integrate Active Directory and DNS, including Dynamic DNS

♦ Configure and manage a DNS server

♦ Manage DNS zones

♦ Troubleshoot DNS

This chapter focuses on the Domain Name System, which is used to resolve hostnames to IP addresses. This is an essential function for large networks and for computers accessing the Internet. In this chapter you will learn about the functions of DNS, how to install DNS, the functions of DNS zones, and how to manage DNS servers and zones. You will also learn how to troubleshoot the Domain Name System.

FUNCTIONS OF THE DOMAIN NAME SYSTEM

The **Domain Name System (DNS)** is an essential service for a network that uses Active Directory. Windows 2000/XP client computers use DNS to find domain controllers, which the clients require to log on to Active Directory. DNS is also required if you want resources such as Web servers available on the Internet. Often for Internet resources, your ISP handles the DNS hosting and configuration. The DNS Service on Windows Server 2003 is unique because it has the ability to store DNS information in Active Directory. Once the information is stored in Active Directory it is automatically replicated to all domain controllers providing an easy backup mechanism. In addition, storing DNS data in Active Directory allows security control for Dynamic DNS. While DNS can be used internally to resolve hostnames to IP addresses, it can also be integrated with the worldwide system for resolving hostnames to IP addresses. DNS can do much more than simple hostname conversion. It can also be used as a repository for service information and perform reverse lookups to convert IP addresses to host names.

Hostname Resolution

Windows Sockets (WinSock) and NetBIOS are the two standard methods Windows applications can use to access network resources. Both mechanisms can be used to access IP-based resources. When a name is used to access a resource through WinSock it is referred to as a **hostname**. Hostnames are used because they are easier to remember than IP addresses.

When a program such as a Web browser or e-mail client uses a hostname, the hostname must be converted to an IP address before the resource can be contacted. The steps followed by Windows Server 2003 to resolve hostnames are as follows:

1. Hostname—Windows Server 2003 first checks to see if the hostname being resolved is the same as its own hostname. If it is, then it uses its own IP address and the resolution process stops. If the hostname being resolved is not the hostname of this server, then Step 2 is performed.

2. *HOSTS file is loaded into cache*—Windows Server 2003 loads the HOSTS file into its cache so it can be evaluated in the next step. A HOSTS file is used to list hostnames and IP addresses for resolution. This is a static text file located on the workstation. The contents of the HOSTS file are placed in the DNS cache. Since this step does not actually attempt to resolve the hostname, the resolution process always continues to Step 3.

3. *DNS cache*—After the HOSTS file is loaded into the DNS cache, then Windows Server 2003 evaluates the contents of the DNS cache. If the hostname being resolved is in the DNS cache, then the IP address in the cache is used and no further resolution is performed. The DNS cache also contains the results of previous DNS resolution attempts.

4. *DNS*—If the required hostname is not the hostname of this server and has not been found in DNS cache, then Windows Server 2003 submits a request to a DNS server for resolution. Using DNS as the final hostname resolution method limits the amount of network traffic and speeds the resolution process.

A **HOSTS** file is a simple text file that stores hostname information. This was the original method to convert hostnames to IP addresses. For the HOSTS file to work in Windows Server 2003 it must be located in C:\WINDOWS\system32\drivers\etc.

 A HOSTS file does not have a file extension. If you create or edit this file in Notepad, it often appends the .txt file extension to the file when it is saved. To avoid this, change the Save as type option from Text Documents (*.txt) to All Files.

The contents of a HOSTS file are a list of IP addresses and hostnames. Each hostname entry in the file has the IP address on the left, one or multiple spaces, then the hostname on the right. In addition, comments can be added to the file using the # symbol. Any information after the # symbol is ignored.

Figure 6-1 shows an example of a HOSTS file. Two hosts are defined in the figure. The hostname localhost resolves to the IP address 127.0.0.1. The hostname myserver.mydomain.local resolves to the IP address 10.0.0.5.

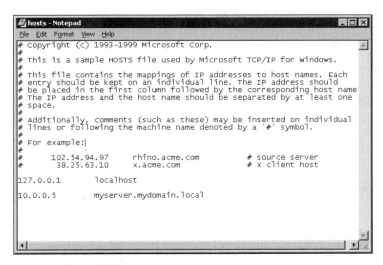

```
# Copyright (c) 1993-1999 Microsoft Corp.
#
# This is a sample HOSTS file used by Microsoft TCP/IP for Windows.
#
# This file contains the mappings of IP addresses to host names. Each
# entry should be kept on an individual line. The IP address should
# be placed in the first column followed by the corresponding host name
# The IP address and the host name should be separated by at least one
# space.
#
# Additionally, comments (such as these) may be inserted on individual
# lines or following the machine name denoted by a '#' symbol.
#
# For example:|
#
#      102.54.94.97     rhino.acme.com          # source server
#      38.25.63.10      x.acme.com              # x client host

127.0.0.1       localhost

10.0.0.5        myserver.mydomain.local
```

Figure 6-1   HOSTS file

Activity 6-1: Configuring a HOSTS File

Time Required: 5 minutes

Objective: Configure and test a HOSTS file.

Description: You are testing the configuration of a new application. This application is hard coded to access the hostname *applicationserver.arctic.local*. When the application is rolled out to all of the users you put this entry in DNS. However, for testing, you use a HOSTS file.

1. If necessary, start your server and log on as Administrator of the arctic.local domain.

2. Right-click **Start,** and click **Explore**.

3. In Windows Explorer go to the **C:\WINDOWS\system32\drivers\etc** directory, and double-click **HOSTS**.

4. At the Open With dialog box, click **Notepad**, and then click **OK**.

5. Place your cursor at the end of the very last line in the HOSTS file, and press **Enter**.

6. Type the IP address of the classroom connection on your server, press **Tab**, and then type **applicationserver.arctic.local**.

7. Exit Notepad, click **Yes** when asked if you want to save changes, and then close Windows Explorer.

8. Click **Start**, click **Run**, type **cmd.exe**, and press **Enter**.

9. In the Command Prompt window, type **ping applicationserver.arctic.local** and press **Enter**.

10. The ping should be successful. The HOSTS file entry you created in this activity is used to resolve the name applicationserver.arctic.local to the IP address of your server.

11. Close the Command Prompt window.

Forward Lookup

The most common task a DNS server performs is resolving a hostname to an IP address. This is called a **forward lookup**.

Resolving hostnames within an organization is a two-packet process. The first packet is a request from the DNS client to the DNS server containing the hostname to be resolved. The second packet is the response from the server to the client containing the IP address of the requested hostname. The DNS Service listens for hostname resolution requests on UDP port 53.

When hostnames are resolved on the Internet, the process is more complex. There are 13 **root servers** that control the overall DNS lookup process for the entire Internet. These servers are located around the world and are maintained by various organizations under the direction of the ICANN DNS Root Server System Advisory Committee. The root servers are responsible for directing requests to DNS servers responsible for top-level domain names such as .com and .net. If these 13 servers were to become unavailable, then much of the Internet would be inaccessible. Resources would have to be accessed via IP address, and not by hostname.

 On October 21, 2002, hackers attempted to perform a denial-of-service attack on the 13 DNS root servers. This attack resulted in degraded performance on 11 of 13 servers. However, because other DNS servers cache much of the root server information, Internet users did not even notice.

Figure 6-2 shows the DNS lookup process that is used when the local DNS server does not hold the requested information. This is called a **recursive lookup** and is a type of forward lookup. In this example, the client computer is attempting to resolve the hostname *www.microsoft.com*. The request is sent from the client computer to the local DNS server. In a corporate environment, the local DNS server is installed and managed by the internal technical staff. In a home or small office environment, the local DNS server is likely to be the DNS server of the ISP.

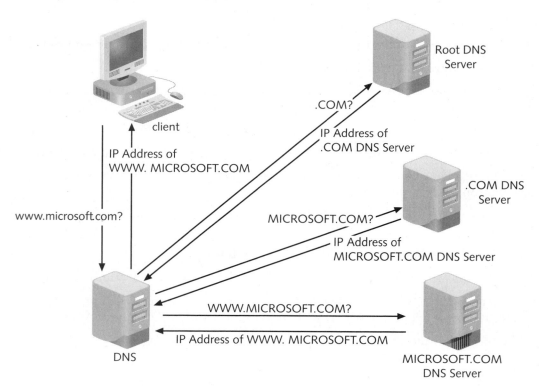

Figure 6-2   DNS lookup process

When the local DNS server receives the request, it looks to see if it has the information that is being requested. Information could be on this server because it is authoritative for the domain or because it has previously looked up the information and has cached it. If the local DNS server does have the information, then it responds to the client with the IP address of the hostname. If the local DNS server does not have information about the hostname, then it starts resolving the name by sending a request to a root server on the Internet.

The request from the local DNS server to the root server asks for the location of a DNS server that can help further resolve the hostname. In this case, the name being resolved is *www.microsoft.com,* and the first step to resolve it is to find a server that knows about the .com domain. The local DNS server asks the root server for the IP address of a DNS server that has information about .com DNS servers. The root server responds with the IP address of a DNS server responsible for the .com domain.

The local DNS server then contacts the .com DNS server and requests the IP address of a DNS server responsible for the microsoft.com domain. The .com DNS server responds with the IP address of the DNS server responsible for the microsoft.com domain.

The local DNS server then contacts the microsoft.com DNS server and requests the IP address of *www.microsoft.com.* The microsoft.com DNS server responds with the IP address of the hostname *www.microsoft.com.* Finally, the local DNS server responds back to the original DNS client with the IP address of the hostname *www.microsoft.com.*

Registering a Domain Name

The **top-level domain** names used by DNS on the Internet are organized by either country or category. The country codes are standard two-character abbreviations for country names. The category names are defined by the Internet Corporation for Assigned Names and Numbers (ICANN). Table 6-1 shows some of the top-level domains that are used on the Internet.

Table 6-1   Top-level domains

Category based		Country Code based	
.com	Commercial	.us	United States
.edu	Educational	.ca	Canada
.org	Nonprofit organization	.uk	United Kingdom
.net	Networking	.de	Germany
.biz	Business	.au	Australia
.name	Personal use	.tw	Taiwan
.pro	Professionals	.ru	Russia

To merge with the worldwide DNS lookup system you must register your domain name with a **registrar**. Registrars have the ability to put domain information into the top-level domain DNS servers. For instance, if you register the domain johndoe.pro, then the registrar would put records into the .pro DNS server that point to the DNS servers for your johndoe.pro domain. You would then be responsible for creating and maintaining the records in the johndoe.pro domain.

Reverse Lookup

In addition to resolving hostnames to IP addresses, DNS can also be used to resolve IP addresses to hostnames. This is called a **reverse lookup**. A reverse lookup allows you to specify an IP address and the DNS server returns the hostname that is defined for it.

Reverse lookups are often performed for the system logs of Internet services. A Web server can be configured to perform a reverse lookup of all clients accessing a Web site. This makes it easier to read the log files because the log files list the hostnames instead of IP addresses.

Reverse lookup DNS information is maintained by the organization that has been assigned an entire class of addresses. Normally this is your ISP. You must contact your ISP to ensure that the addressing information is correct.

DNS Record Types

DNS records are created on a DNS server to resolve queries. Each type of record holds different information about a service, hostname, IP address, or domain. Different queries request information contained in specific DNS records types. For example, to find the server responsible for e-mail in a domain, an MX record is required.

DNS has the ability to hold many different record types. However, there are only a few record types that you use on a regular basis. Table 6-2 shows some of the DNS record types and their purpose.

Table 6-2   DNS records types

Record Type	Purpose
A	Host—Resolves hostnames to IP addresses
MX	Mail Exchange—Points to the mail server for a domain
CNAME	Canonical Name—Resolves one hostname to another hostname
NS	Name Server—Holds the IP address of a DNS server with information about this domain
SOA	Start of Authority—Contains configuration information for the domain on this DNS server
SRV	Service—Used by Active Directory to store the location of domain controllers
AAAA	IPv6 Host—Resolves hostnames to IPv6 addresses
PTR	Pointer—Resolves IP addresses to hostnames

DNS and BIND

Berkeley Internet Name Domain (BIND) is the *de facto* standard for DNS implementation on UNIX and Linux systems. Many other implementations of DNS reference BIND version numbers for feature compatibility. Table 6-3 lists several important BIND versions and the features that make them important. All of these features are discussed later in the chapter.

Table 6-3   BIND versions and features

BIND Version	Feature
4.9.6	SRV records
8.1.2	Dynamic DNS
8.2.1	Incremental zone updates

The Internet Software Consortium is responsible for the maintenance and development of BIND. If you would like more information about BIND, visit *www.isc.org/products/BIND*.

INSTALLING DNS

Windows Server 2003 has the ability to act as a DNS server. In fact, most organizations using Active Directory use Windows for their DNS server.

During the installation of Active Directory, if no DNS server has been configured for the domain, then the **DCPROMO** Wizard asks whether it should install DNS during the installation of Active Directory. This is a very easy way to implement DNS in a small organization with a single server.

In larger organizations, you often install DNS on multiple servers. If this is the case, then you must add DNS individually to each of these servers. It is not automatically added when member servers are promoted to being domain controllers.

Activity 6-2: Installing DNS

Time Required: 10 minutes

Objective: Install DNS on your server and confirm it is running.

Description: You have already installed the main DNS server for Arctic University. To reduce network traffic, you have decided to place a DNS server at each physical campus location. In this activity you will install DNS on your server. In later activities you will configure it to communicate with the instructor's server.

1. If necessary, start your server and log on as Administrator.

2. Click **Start**, point to **Control Panel**, and click **Add or Remove Programs**.

3. Click **Add/Remove Windows Components**.

4. Scroll down in the Components box, click **Networking Services** in the **Components** window, and click **Details**.

5. Click the check box beside **Domain Name System (DNS)** to select it, and click **OK**.

6. Click **Next** to start the installation. If prompted for the Windows Server 2003 CD-ROM, click **OK**. Click the **Browse** button, then select the C:\I386 folder and click **Open**. Click **OK** in the Files Needed dialog box.

7. Click **Finish**.

8. **Close** the Add or Remove Programs window.

9. To verify the installation, click **Start**, point to **Administrative Tools**, and click **Services**.

10. Double-click **DNS Server**.

11. Verify that the Startup type is set to **Automatic** and that the Service status is started.

12. Click **OK** to close the DNS Server Poperties window.

13. Close the Services window.

DNS ZONES

A **DNS zone** (commonly referred to as a zone) is the part of DNS namespace for which a DNS server is responsible. For instance, Arctic University is using the domain arctic.local to store all of the Active Directory information. To store the records for this domain on a DNS server, you first create a zone on the DNS server. Once inside the zone, you can create DNS records and subdomains.

When a zone is created, you designate whether it will hold records for forward lookups or reverse lookups. A zone that holds records for forward lookups is called a **forward lookup zone**. A zone that holds records for reverse lookups is called a **reverse lookup zone**.

Primary and Secondary Zones

For fault tolerance and to reduce network traffic, it is often useful to keep copies of DNS domain information on more than one server. For instance, you might keep a copy of DNS information at each physical location in an organization to limit WAN traffic.

If you store DNS information on multiple servers, it is essential that these servers automatically synchronize information between them. If the information between multiple DNS servers gets out of synchronization, then replication of Active Directory may be affected and clients may be prevented from logging on to the network. From an administrative point of view, it is convenient to automate this process to save time and effort.

Primary and secondary zones are traditionally used to automatically synchronize DNS information between DNS servers. A **primary zone** is the first to be created, and all of the DNS records are created in the primary zone. A **secondary zone** takes copies of primary zone information. You cannot directly edit the records in a secondary zone because they are copied from the primary zone.

The process of moving information from the primary zone to the secondary zone is called a **zone transfer**. Older DNS servers copied the entire zone database every time the secondary zone synchronized with the primary zone. However, new implementations of DNS, including the DNS server included with Windows Server 2003, are capable of performing incremental zone transfers. An **incremental zone transfer** only copies information that has changed from the primary zone.

 There can only be one primary zone in control of a domain. Secondary zones can be created as required.

When primary and secondary zones are created on Windows Server 2003, the contents of the zone are held in a file on the hard drive. The name of the file is the name of the zone with a .dns extension. For example, the zone file for the domain arctic.local is arctic.local.dns. This file is stored in C:\WINDOWS\system32\dns.

Activity 6-3: Creating a Primary Zone

Time Required: 10 minutes

Objective: Create a primary zone to hold resource records.

Description: Arctic University is creating DNS domains for each campus location. Because these servers will be communicating with some non–Windows DNS servers, it has been decided that you will create a primary zone that can communicate with non–Windows secondary zones. You will create the required records for the mail servers in each domain.

1. If necessary, start your server and log on as Administrator

2. Click **Start**, point to **Administrative Tools**, and click **DNS**.

3. Double-click your server to expand it.

4. Click **Forward Lookup Zones** to view the existing zones. No zones are created by default when DNS is installed.

5. Right-click **Forward Lookup Zones**, and click **New Zone**.

6. Click **Next**.

7. Confirm that **Primary zone** is selected, and click **Next**.

8. In the Zone name field, type **locationX.arctic.local**, where *X* is your student number, and click **Next**.

9. Leave the default name for the zone file of **locationX.arctic.local.dns**, and click **Next**.

10. Leave the default of **Do not allow dynamic updates,** and click **Next**.

11. Click **Finish**.

12. Double-click **locationX.arctic.local**. Notice that only the NS and SOA records are created by default.

13. Right-click **locationX.arctic.local**, and click **New Host (A)**.

14. In the Name (uses parent domain name if blank) field, type **mail**. The Fully Qualified Domain Name is modified to be mail.locationX.arctic.local.

15. In the IP address field, type **172.30.0.24**. In the classroom environment no mail server actually exists. This would be the IP address of the mail server if one existed.

16. Click **Add Host**.

17. Click **OK** to confirm the creation of the A record, and click **Done**.

18. Right-click **locationX.arctic.local**, and click **New Mail Exchanger (MX)**.

19. Leave the **Host or child domain** field blank. By leaving this blank you are indicating that this is for the current domain.

20. In the **Fully Qualified Domain Name (FQDN) of mail server** field, type **mail.locationX.arctic.local**, and click **OK**.

21. Close the DNS snap-in window.

Activity 6-4: Creating a Secondary Zone

Time Required: 10 minutes

Objective: Create a local copy of DNS information using a secondary zone.

Description: You have found that users at some locations often need to resolve hostnames in other locations. To reduce the amount of WAN traffic, you have decided to create secondary zones in some of the locations. You will modify your zone to allow zone transfers and create a secondary zone of your partner's primary zone.

1. If necessary, start your server and log on as Administrator.

2. Click **Start**, point to **Administrative Tools**, and click **DNS**.

3. Double-click **locationX.arctic.local**, where X is your student number.

4. Right-click **locationX.arctic.local**, where X is your student number, and click **Properties**.

5. Click the **Zone Transfers** tab.

6. Confirm that **Allow zone transfers** is selected, click **To any server**, and click **OK**.

7. Right-click **Forward Lookup Zones**, and click **New Zone**.

8. Click **Next**.

9. Click **Secondary zone**, and click **Next**.

10. In the Zone name field, type **locationY.arctic.local,** where Y is the student number of your partner, and click **Next**.

11. In the IP address field, type in the IP address of the classroom connection on your partner's server, click **Add**, and click **Next**.

12. Click **Finish**.

13. Double-click **locationY.arctic.local**, where Y is the student number of your partner. The records from your partner's domain are now stored on your server. You may receive the error Zone not loaded by DNS Server. If you receive this error, right-click **locationY.arctic.local**,

and click **Transer from Master**. This will force the secondary zone to update from the primary zone. You may also need to press **F5** to refresh the view.

14. Close the DNS snap-in.

Active Directory Integrated Zones

An **Active Directory integrated zone** stores information in Active Directory rather than in a file on the local hard drive. To store DNS information in an Active Directory integrated zone, the DNS server must also be a domain controller.

Storing DNS information in Active Directory offers the following advantages over traditional primary and secondary zones:

- *Automatic backup of zone information*—When zone information is stored in Active Directory it is automatically replicated to all domain controllers that have been configured to hold the zone information. This means that if a DNS server fails, the zone information is not lost because a copy of the zone information exists in Active Directory on other domain controllers.

- *Multimaster replication*—Active Directory integrated zones offer the advantage of multimaster replication. In traditional DNS zones, changes are made to the primary zone and replicated to the secondary zone. With Active Directory integrated zones, changes can be made on any DNS server servicing the zone. The changes are then replicated through Active Directory to other DNS servers. This is a benefit because when DNS servers are widely dispersed, administrators can more easily make changes to zone information via a local server. In addition, using Active Directory replication reduces complexity because only the Active Directory replication system is maintained.

- *Increased security*—Security is increased when zone information is stored in Active Directory. Traditional primary zones have no security mechanism to control which users are allowed to update DNS records. Active Directory integrated zones use the security mechanisms built into Active Directory to control which users or computers can update DNS records.

DNS Zone Storage in Active Directory

There are two areas DNS zones can be stored in Active Directory:

- The domain directory partition
- The application directory partition

The **domain directory partition** of Active Directory holds information about the objects specific to a particular Active Directory domain, such as users and computers. This partition is replicated to all domain controllers in an Active Directory domain. The information in this partition cannot be replicated to domain controllers in other Active Directory domains.

One drawback to this method of storing a DNS zone is that if a DNS zone is stored in the domain directory partition then all domain controllers in the same domain receive copies of the zone even if they are not configured as DNS servers. This may result in unnecessary network traffic from additional AD synchronization.

If one of the servers holding the Active Directory integrated zone is a Windows 2000 server, then the zone must be stored in the domain directory partition of Active Directory. Figure 6-3 shows a zone being created in the domain directory partition of Active Directory.

Application directory partitions are a new feature of Active Directory in Windows Server 2003. They allow information to be stored in Active Directory but be replicated only among a defined set of domain controllers. The domain controllers that hold an application directory partition must be in the same Active Directory forest but can be in different Active Directory domains.

Using an application directory partition to store a DNS zone in Active Directory offers much more flexibility than storing a DNS zone in a domain directory partition. With a zone stored in a domain directory partition, the zone cannot be replicated to domain controllers outside the Active Directory domain. A zone stored in an application directory partition can be replicated to any domain controller you choose within the same Active Directory forest.

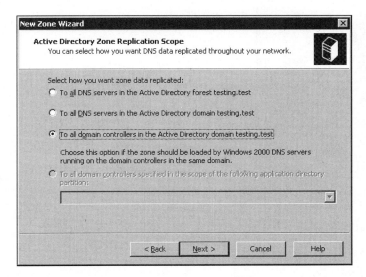

Figure 6-3   Storing a zone in the domain directory partition

There are three options for storing DNS zones in an application directory partition:

- All DNS servers in the Active Directory forest
- All DNS servers in the Active Directory domain
- All servers specified in the scope of an application directory partition

If you choose to store a DNS zone on all DNS servers in the Active Directory forest, then an application directory partition is created to hold this information. This new application directory partition and the zone in it are automatically replicated to all domain controllers in the forest that are configured as DNS servers. In a very large organization with many DNS servers, this may not be acceptable because of the synchronization traffic that would be generated. Figure 6-4 shows a zone being created and stored on DNS servers in the Active Directory forest.

Alternatively, if you choose to store a DNS zone on all DNS servers in the Active Directory domain, then an application directory partition is created to hold this information. The new application directory partition and the zone in it are automatically replicated to all domain controllers in the domain that are configured as DNS servers. This is more efficient than storing the zone in the domain directory partition because synchronization can only happen between servers using the DNS information.

If you would like to be more precise with the replication of zones between domain controllers, you can create your own application directory partition. As part of creating the application directory partition, you must define the domain controllers that will hold a copy of the application directory partition you are creating. Using this option, you can replicate zone information to only a few servers throughout an Active Directory forest or domain rather than all DNS servers.

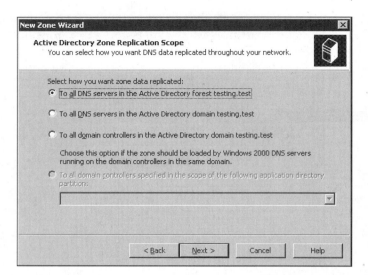

Figure 6-4   Storing a zone on all DNS servers in an Active Directory forest

Activity 6-5: Promoting a Member Server to a Domain Controller

Time Required: 30 minutes

Objective: Promote a member server to a domain controller.

Description: To reduce WAN traffic, you have decided to keep a copy of the arctic.local DNS domain in each location. You have also decided that you would like the zones to be Active Directory integrated. To store an Active Directory integrated zone, you must promote your server to a domain controller using the utility DCPROMO.

1. If necessary, start your server and log on as Administrator.

2. Click **Start**, click **Run**, type **dcpromo**, and press **Enter**.

3. Click **Next** to begin the wizard then click **Next** again after reading the Operating System compatibility information.

4. Click **Additional domain controller for an existing domain**, and click **Next**.

5. In the User name field, type **Administrator**, and in the Password field, type **Password**. Confirm that the domain is **Arctic.local**, and click **Next**.

6. Confirm that **Arctic.local** appears in the **Domain name** field, and click **Next**.

7. Click **Next** to accept the default Active Directory file locations.

8. Click **Next** to accept the default SYSVOL folder location.

9. In the Restore Mode Password field, type **Password**, and in the Confirm password field, type **Password**, and then click **Next**.

10. Click **Next** to continue, and wait for the Active Directory Installation Wizard to complete.

11. Click **Finish** to complete the wizard, and click **Restart Now**.

12. Log on to your server as Administrator.

13. Click **Start**, point to **Administrative Tools**, and click **DNS**.

14. Double-click your server, if necessary.

15. Double-click **Forward Lookup Zones**.

16. The zone Arctic.local is an Active Directory integrated zone that is configured to replicate to all domain controllers within the Arctic.local Active Directory domain. As a result, the DNS Service

on your server will automatically begin servicing the Arctic.local zone when it is replicated to your server in Active Directory. This process may take some time.

Activity 6-6: Creating an Active Directory Integrated Zone

Time Required: 5 minutes

Objective: Create an Active Directory integrated zone.

Description: To reduce network traffic, you have decided to place a copy of the web.arctic.local domain at each location. You will add an Active Directory integrated zone to your server. This zone will be used for Internet services.

1. Log on to your server as Administrator.
2. Click **Start**, point to **Administrative Tools**, and click **DNS**.
3. Right-click **Forward Lookup Zones**, and click **New Zone**.
4. Click **Next** to begin creating the zone.
5. Confirm that the options **Primary zone** and **Store the zone in Active Directory (available only if DNS server is a domain controller)** are selected, and click **Next**.
6. Click **Next** to accept the default replication option **To all domain controllers in the Active Directory domain Arctic.local**.
7. In the **Zone name** field, type **webX.arctic.local**, where X is your student number, and click **Next**.
8. Click **Next** to accept the default dynamic update option of **Allow only secure dynamic updates (recommended for Active Directory)**.
9. Click **Finish**.
10. Close the DNS snap-in.

Merging Active Directory Integrated Zones with Traditional DNS

Active Directory integrated zones replicate information in a fundamentally different way than traditional DNS zones. Consequently, they are limited in how they interact with traditional DNS zones. Active Directory integrated zones interact with traditional zones by acting as a primary zone to traditional secondary zones. This is useful when not all DNS servers are capable of participating in an Active Directory integrated zone.

There are several situations where a DNS server cannot participate in an Active Directory integrated zone:

- The DNS server is pre-Windows 2000.
- The DNS server is Windows 2000 and the Active Directory integrated zone is stored in an application directory partition.
- The DNS server is a non-Windows server.
- The DNS server is a member server, but not a domain controller.
- The DNS server is in a different forest.

Active Directory integrated zones can act only as primary zones when integrating with traditional DNS zones. They cannot act as secondary zones.

Stub Zones

On the Internet, when a DNS server does not have the information to resolve a hostname, it contacts a root server on the Internet to continue the resolution process and find the DNS server that is authoritative for the domain with the requested information. However, this process works only if the domain name is registered on the Internet.

When Active Directory is implemented, many organizations choose to use a domain name that is not registered on the Internet. If a domain name is not registered on the Internet, then an alternative to using root servers must be implemented to ensure the lookup process is functional. In this case, DNS servers can be configured with a **stub zone** to help them resolve DNS requests.

A stub zone is a DNS zone that holds only NS records for a domain. NS records define the name servers that are responsible for a domain. When a client submits a DNS request to a server with a stub zone, then the DNS server continues the lookup process by sending a request to a DNS server specified in the NS records of the stub zone.

For example, in Figure 6-5, Arctic University has a subdomain for student resources called students. arctic.local. This subdomain is created as a separate zone on the server STUDENTDNS. The STUDENTDNS server also has a stub zone for the domain arctic.local. This stub zone has a NS record that points to the server ARCTICDNS which holds the arctic.local zone. When student computers submit DNS requests to STUDENTDNS for arctic.local records, then STUDENTDNS reads the NS record from the arctic.local stub zone. Based on the NS record in the arctic.local stub zone, STUDENTDNS then submits a query to ARCTICDNS. ARCTICDNS responds to STUDENTDNS and STUDENTDNS then responds back to the student client computer.

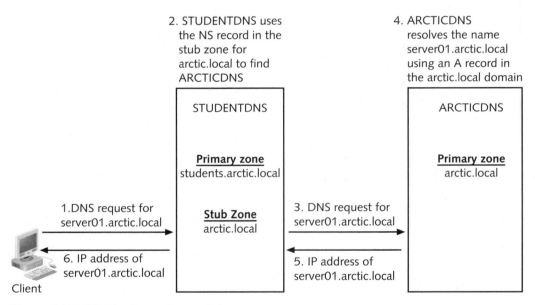

Figure 6-5   DNS lookup using a stub zone

Activity 6-7: Removing Active Directory Integrated Zones

Time Required: 30 minutes

Objective: Remove an Active Directory integrated zone.

Description: After measuring the network traffic caused by Active Directory integrated zones, you have decided to remove them from your network. Most DNS lookups are local and the replication of zones to all domain controllers was excessive. In this activity, you will remove Active Directory from your server, which will also remove Active Directory integrated zones. If more than one server in a domain removes Active Directory at the same time, errors may result. Your instructor will coordinate this activity. Do not start until given permission to do so.

The second student can begin removing Active Directory once all services are stopped and the securing process has begun on the first student's server. The final status window may indicate that errors have occurred, but the demotion will be successful.

1. If necessary, start your server and log on as Administrator.

2. Click **Start**, click **Run**, type **dcpromo**, and press **Enter**.

3. Click **Next** to begin the wizard.

4. Ensure that the option **This server is the last domain controller in the domain** is not selected, and click **Next**.

5. In the New Administrator Password field, type **Password**, and in the Confirm password field, type **Password**, and then click **Next**.

6. Click **Next** to confirm the removal of Active Directory from your server. Your server is no longer required to be a domain controller because Active Directory integrated zones are no longer required on your server. The instructor's server is still configured as a domain controller for the domain to handle logon requests.

7. Click **Finish**, and click **Restart Now**.

Activity 6-8: Creating a Stub Zone

Time Required: 5 minutes

Objective: Create a stub zone to direct recursive queries.

Description: Your DNS server is configured so that it performs a recursive query with root servers on the Internet if it does not have the appropriate information. However, the root servers on the Internet have no information about the arctic.local domain. To help your server resolve domain names in the arctic.local domain, you will create a stub zone.

 The previous activity removed Activity Directory integrated zones from the student servers. However, it takes a significant period of time for the NS records to be removed from the arctic.local zone. The instructor will manually remove these records to avoid errors in the following activity.

1. If necessary, start your server and log on as Administrator.

2. Click **Start**, point to **Administrative Tools**, and click **DNS**.

3. Right-click **Forward Lookup Zones**, and click **New Zone**.

4. Click **Next** to begin creating the stub zone.

5. Click **Stub zone**, and click **Next**.

6. In the **Zone name** field, type **Arctic.local** and then click **Next**.

7. Accept the default file name by clicking **Next**.

8. In the **IP address** field, type **192.168.1.10,** click **Add**, and click **Next**.

9. Click **Finish** to complete creating the stub zone.

10. Double-click **arctic.local**. The name server records for the arctic.local domain have been copied to your server. When a DNS query for a record in the arctic.local domain is submitted to your server it will now submit that query directly to the proper name servers rather than the root servers on the Internet.

11. Close the DNS snap-in.

CACHING-ONLY SERVERS

A **caching-only server** does not have any zones configured on it. It exists only to be a local DNS server for client computers. The first time a caching-only server performs a lookup for a client computer it caches it. Then, if another client computer requires the same information, the caching-only server has a local copy and does not need to use the WAN or Internet to lookup the information.

On very slow WAN links, caching-only servers may create less network traffic than storing Active Directory integrated zones or secondary zones locally. An Active Directory integrated zone can only be created if there is a local domain controller. If WAN links are too slow, then it may not be possible to support Active Directory synchronization. Even the zone transfers between a secondary zone and primary zone may generate more traffic than a caching-only server.

To create a caching-only server, install the DNS Service and do not create any zones. A DNS server installed on Windows Server 2003 automatically caches all lookup requests.

ACTIVE DIRECTORY AND DNS

Active Directory requires DNS to function properly. The most important function that DNS performs for Active Directory is locating services, such as domain controllers. The naming structure for Active Directory domains is exactly the same as DNS domains so that service information about an Active Directory domain can be stored in the corresponding DNS domain. The service information that is stored in DNS helps client computers find domain controllers to log onto, and it also helps domain controllers find each other for replication of Active Directory information.

For example, Arctic University has an Active Directory domain named arctic.local. Domain controllers for arctic.local hold a copy of the Active Directory database for the domain. DNS servers are configured to hold a copy of the arctic.local zone information. In this zone, there are SRV records that describe where to find services such as **Kerberos** and **Lightweight Directory Access Protocol (LDAP)**. Client computers use these SRV records to find the domain controllers that provide these services.

Figure 6-6 shows some of the DNS records created to support the Active Directory domain testing.test.

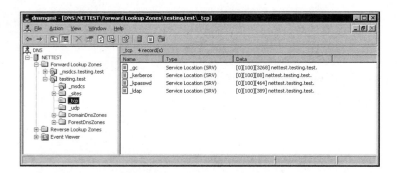

Figure 6-6   DNS records for Active Directory

In addition to the SRV records required by Active Directory it is preferable to have A records for the names and IP addresses of all the servers and client workstations in DNS. Many utilities such as the Microsoft Management Console (MMC) rely on hostname resolution. For example, if you right-click on a client workstation in Active Directory Users and Computers and click Manage, this opens the Computer Management snap-in for that computer. To be able to do this, the MMC must be able to resolve the hostname for the computer to an IP address. If DNS is not configured properly, the attempt to manage the client computer fails.

It is possible to manually add all of the required SRV and A records that an Active Directory domain requires, but this would be very difficult to manage. To simplify management of DNS records for Active Directory, you can implement **Dynamic DNS**.

Dynamic DNS

Dynamic DNS is a system in which records can be updated on a DNS server automatically rather than forcing an administrator to create records manually. It is defined by RFC 2136. Windows 2000/XP/2003 operating systems are compliant with RFC 2136 and have the ability to perform Dynamic DNS updates themselves. Windows 9x/NT are not compliant with RFC 2136 and rely on a DHCP server to perform Dynamic DNS updates for them.

The service records for domain controllers are placed in a DNS zone using Dynamic DNS. When the NETLOGON Service of the domain controller starts, the DNS zone is updated by Windows Server 2003. If the service records for a domain controller become corrupt or are accidentally deleted, you can recreate them by stopping and starting the NETLOGON Service on the domain controller.

Windows 2000/XP clients perform their own Dynamic DNS updates. During the boot process, the clients contact their DNS server to perform a dynamic update, and then they create an A record for their hostname and IP address. Using this mechanism, DNS records for client computers are correct even when using DHCP because the A record is created after the IP address is leased from the DHCP server.

To manually force Windows 2000/XP clients to update their Dynamic DNS information, use the command ipconfig /registerdns.

Activity 6-9: Testing Dynamic DNS

Time Required: 10 minutes

Objective: Verify that a computer is registering a hostname using Dynamic DNS.

Description: You are not sure that a member server is properly registering its IP address and hostname using Dynamic DNS. To confirm that it is working properly you will delete the existing A record from the instructor server and force the reregistration in DNS.

1. If necessary, start your server and log on as Administrator.
2. Click **Start**, point to **Administrative Tools,** and click **DNS**.
3. Right-click **DNS**, and click **Connect to DNS Server**.
4. Click **The following computer,** type **instructor** in the text box, and click **OK**.
5. Double-click **instructor**.
6. Double-click **Forward Lookup Zones**.
7. Double-click **Arctic.local**.
8. Right-click **serverX**, where *X* is your student number, click **Delete**, and click **Yes** to confirm.
9. Click **Start**, click **Run**, type **ipconfig /registerdns**, and press **Enter**.
10. In the DNS snap-in, click **Arctic.local**. If you do not see a new host record for your server, press **F5** to refresh the view.
11. Close the DNS snap-in.

Dynamic DNS and DHCP

The Dynamic DNS information updated by Windows 2000/XP is negotiated with the DHCP server during the lease process. A Windows 2000/XP client will request that the DHCP server update the PTR record for reverse lookups and that the client update its own A record. If the DHCP server does not support Dynamic DNS, then Windows 2000/XP clients can also update the PTR record. Figure 6-7 shows the options that can be configured on the scope of a Windows Server 2003 DHCP server.

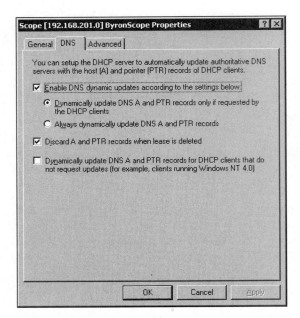

Figure 6-7   Dynamic DNS configuration of a DHCP scope

By default, a DHCP server running on Windows Server 2003 updates DNS records only for Windows 2000/XP clients and only if requested to do so. If you want the DHCP server to always update the A and PTR records for Windows 2000/XP clients, then select the "Always dynamically update DNS A and PTR records" option. If you want the DHCP server to update A and PTR records for clients that are not compliant with RFC 2136, then enable the "Dynamically update DNS A and PTR records for DHCP clients that do not request updates (for example, clients running under Windows NT 4.0)" option.

To specify that the DHCP server delete DNS records it has created when a lease expires, select the "Discard A and PTR records when lease is deleted" option. If this option is not enabled, then A and PTR records created by the DHCP server are never deleted by the DHCP server and out of date information may be left in DNS.

Configuring a Zone for Dynamic DNS

A zone can be configured for Dynamic DNS during creation or by modifying the properties of the zone after configuration. Figure 6-8 shows the Dynamic DNS options that are available during the creation of an Active Directory integrated zone.

The "Allow only secure dynamic updates" option is available only if the zone is Active Directory integrated. This option configures the zone to accept updates as allowed by the security permissions set in Active Directory. The DHCP Service included with Windows Server 2003 allows you to configure a user and password that the DHCP server can use to securely perform Dynamic DNS updates.

If the "Allow any dynamic updates" option is selected, then any client can update records. This option does not have any security and can be vulnerable to hackers placing incorrect information in the zone.

The Do not allow dynamic updates option stops this zone from accepting any dynamic updates. This is not realistic for zones storing records used by Active Directory because of the high volume of record changes. However, this is the best setting to use on a DNS server that is available on the Internet and for zones that do not store records used by Active Directory.

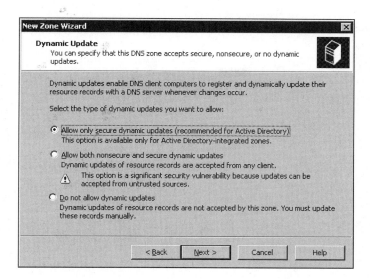

Figure 6-8   Dynamic update options when creating an Active Directory integrated zone

After a zone has been created, you can change the dynamic update option by editing the properties of the zone. Figure 6-9 shows how to change the dynamic update option of a primary zone that is not Active Directory integrated.

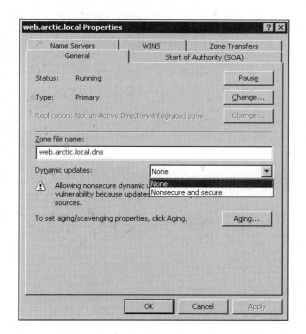

Figure 6-9   Changing the dynamic update option

Notice that the screen shown in Figure 6-9 does not have the option for secure dynamic updates; this is because it is not Active Directory integrated.

MANAGING DNS SERVERS

There are many DNS options that can be configured at the server level. Some of them are:

- Configure aging and scavenging
- Update server data files
- Clear cache
- Configure bindings
- Configure forwarding
- Edit the root hints
- Configure event and debug logging
- Set advanced options
- Configure security

Aging and Scavenging

Aging and scavenging of DNS records is a new feature of DNS in Windows Server 2003. With aging and scavenging, DNS records created by Dynamic DNS can be removed after a certain period of time if they have not been updated. This prevents out-of-date information from being stored in a zone.

For scavenging to occur it must be enabled on the Advanced tab of the DNS server properties. Figure 6-10 shows the aging and scavenging option being enabled. Scavenging is disabled by default. The Scavenging period option specifies how often scavenging is to be performed. By default, the scavenging is performed every seven days.

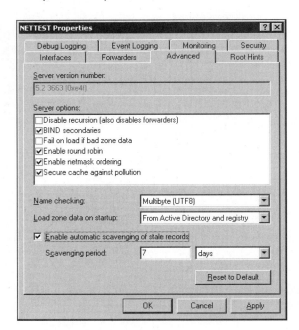

Figure 6-10   Enabling scavenging

After scavenging has been enabled at the server level, you can configure the aging of DNS records for each zone. To configure the **aging/scavenging** properties for all zones on a server, right-click the server, and select "Set Aging/Scavenging for All Zones". Figure 6-11 shows the options available when you right-click on the server.

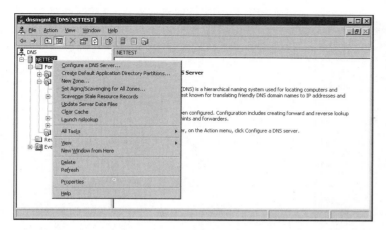

Figure 6-11   Right-clicking on a server

Update Server Data Files

The option to "Update Server Data Files" is available when you right-click on the server. If a zone is Active Directory-integrated, this has no effect. If a primary zone is not Active Directory-integrated, it forces all of the DNS changes in memory to be written to the zone file on disk.

Clear Cache

A DNS server automatically caches all lookups that it performs. Occasionally, you may have outdated information in the cache. To force a DNS server to perform a new lookup before the record in cache times out, you must clear the cache. To clear the cache, right-click the server and select "Clear Cache."

Configure Bindings

By default, the DNS Service listens on all IP addresses that are bound to the server it is running on. However, you can also configure DNS to only respond on certain IP addresses that are bound to the server. This may be useful if you have bound extra addresses to the server for specific purposes such as Web hosting.

The Interfaces tab of the server properties allows you to configure the IP addresses to which the DNS Service listens. Figure 6-12 shows the Interfaces tab of the server properties.

Forwarding

Ordinarily a DNS server that cannot perform a record lookup for a domain follows a process where it queries several servers to find the information. This query process begins with the root servers on the Internet.

Some internal DNS servers are restricted from accessing the Internet for security reasons, so this process is not possible. **Forwarding** allows you to configure a local DNS server to forward queries from clients to another DNS server if the local DNS server does not have the required records.

For example, a company might have several physical locations, each with its own DNS server. All Internet access is routed through corporate headquarters. To ensure that each DNS server is secure from hackers on the Internet, the firewall for this company has been configured to prevent all packets from traveling from the DNS servers to the Internet or from the Internet to the DNS servers. A special Internet-accessible DNS server has been set up at corporate headquarters to perform Internet DNS lookups. The Internet-accessible DNS server does not contain any DNS information for the Active Directory domain. All of the local DNS servers at each physical location are configured to forward queries to the Internet-accessible DNS server.

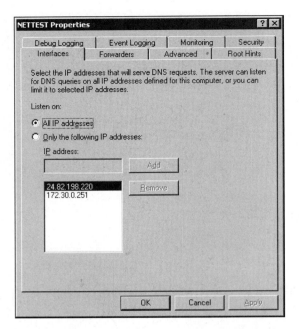

Figure 6-12   The DNS server properties Interfaces tab

In this example, when clients need to resolve a hostname on the Internet the following steps occur:

1. The client sends the query to their local DNS server.

2. The local DNS server forwards the query to the Internet-accessible DNS server.

3. The Internet-accessible DNS server performs the lookup on the Internet.

4. The Internet-accessible DNS server returns a response to the local DNS server.

5. The local DNS server returns a response to the client.

Windows Server 2003 has the ability to forward DNS queries to different DNS servers depending on the DNS domain that is being queried. This allows a very flexible forwarding system where internal DNS lookups can be forwarded to one DNS server and Internet DNS lookups can be forwarded to another DNS server.

Figure 6-13 shows the Forwarders tab for a server that has been configured to forward queries for the domain arctic.local to the IP address 192.168.1.10. If a DNS server attempts to forward a query and it fails, it then attempts to contact the root servers on the Internet. To prevent the DNS server from attempting to further resolve the name, select the "Do not use recursion for this domain" option. You can also configure the number of seconds the DNS server waits for a response before a forwarding attempt is considered a failure. The default is five seconds.

Root Hints

Root hints are servers that are used to perform recursive lookups. The Root Hints tab of the server properties is automatically populated with the names and IP addresses of the DNS root servers on the Internet. The list of root servers is loaded into the root hints from the file cache.dns stored in C:\WINDOWS\system32\dns. Figure 6-14 shows the Internet root DNS servers listed in the Root Hints tab of the server properties.

If your DNS system is completely self-contained and does not need to access the root servers on the Internet, you can configure one of your internal DNS servers to act as a root server. This is done by creating a forward lookup zone named "." (a period). If a DNS server holds a zone named ".", it is considered to be a root server and will not load the list of Internet root DNS servers from cache.dns. You can then edit the list of root hints for other DNS servers to point only at the new root server you have configured.

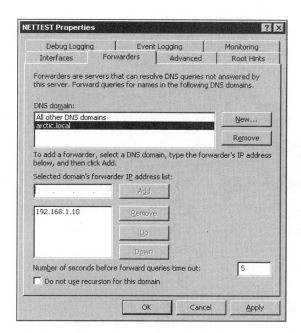

Figure 6-13   The DNS server properties Forwarders tab

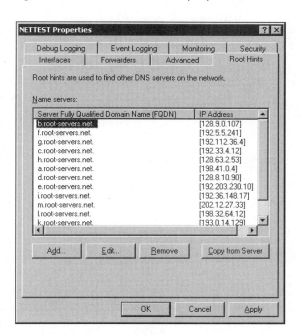

Figure 6-14   The DNS server properties Root Hints tab

Activity 6-10: Creating a Root Server

Time Required: 10 minutes

Objective: Configure your server as a root DNS server.

Description: Some locations on the Artic University network are not allowed access to the Internet. To keep DNS servers in these locations from performing DNS lookups, you configure your server as a DNS root server.

1. If necessary, start your server and log on as Administrator.

2. Click **Start**, point to **Administrative Tools**, and click **DNS**.

3. If necessary, double-click your server to expand it.

4. Click **Forward Lookup Zones**.

5. Right-click **Forward Lookup Zones**, and click **New Zone**.

6. Click **Next**.

7. Ensure that **Primary zone** is selected, and click **Next**.

8. In the Zone name field type "**.**" (a single period), and click **Next**. This indicates that this is to be a root zone.

9. Click **Next** to accept the default file name root.dns.

10. Click **Next** to accept the default of not allowing dynamic updates.

11. Click **Finish**. Your server will now perform DNS lookups only for zones for which it has configuration information.

12. Right-click your server, and click **Properties**.

13. Click **Root Hints**. This tab is empty because your server is configured as a root server. This tab shows the Internet root servers when not configured as a root server.

14. Click **Cancel**.

15. Close the DNS snap-in.

Logging

DNS servers are capable of **event logging** and **debug logging**. Event logging records errors, warnings, and information to the event log. Debug logging records much more detailed information.

Figure 6-15 shows the Event Logging tab of the DNS server properties. You have the option to record:

- No events

- Errors only

- Errors and warnings

- All events

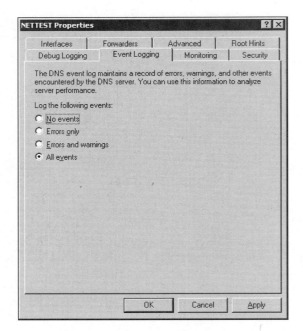

Figure 6-15   DNS server properties Event Logging tab

Debug logging records packet-by-packet information about the queries that the DNS server is receiving. This type of logging is enabled only for troubleshooting because it records a large volume of information. To reduce the amount of information recorded, you can specify what type of information should be logged including:

- Packet direction
- Transport protocol
- Packet contents
- Packet type

Figure 6-16 shows the configuration of debug logging in the DNS server properties.

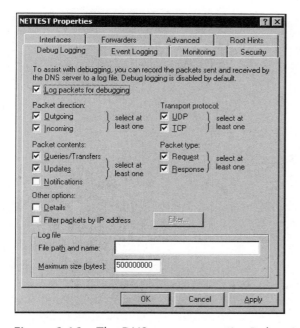

Figure 6-16   The DNS server properties Debug Logging tab

Advanced Options

Several options can be configured on the Advanced tab of the server properties, including:

- Disable recursion (also disables forwarders)
- BIND secondaries
- Fail on load if bad zone data
- Enable round robin
- Enable netmask ordering
- Secure cache against pollution

Figure 6-17 shows the options that can be configured on the advanced tab of the server properties.

The "Disable recursion (also disables forwarders)" option stops this DNS server from contacting any other DNS servers in an attempt to find DNS records. This DNS server recognizes DNS records configured only on this server.

The "BIND secondaries" option disables fast transfers between primary and secondary zones. This is necessary only if the DNS server holding the secondary zone is a non-Windows DNS server and supports a BIND version less than 4.9.4.

By default, if errors are found in a zone file, the DNS server logs the errors and ignores the affected records. You can configure the server to disable the zone when any errors are found by selecting the "Fail on load if bad zone data" option. You may enable this if you wish to ensure that all of the zone data is available.

Round robin DNS occurs when more than one record exists for a DNS query. For example, there may be two A records configured for a single hostname, which allows a single hostname to be tied to multiple IP addresses. This is sometimes done with Internet resources such as a Web server, and it is a simple way to implement "poor man's" load balancing. To enable round robin DNS, select the "Enable round robin" option. This option is enabled by default.

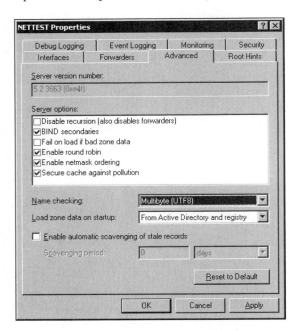

Figure 6-17   The DNS server properties Advanced tab

When a DNS query has multiple matches, a DNS server configured on Windows Server 2003 responds with the IP address that most closely matches the IP address of the client making the request. For instance, if a client with the IP address 192.168.5.100 makes a DNS query with valid responses 10.0.10.98 and 192.168.5.20, then the DNS server responds with IP address 192.168.5.20 because it most closely matches the IP address of the client. In most cases, this results in a response with an IP address that is physically closest to the client. This feature can be disabled by deselecting the "Enable netmask ordering" option.

The "Secure cache against pollution" option controls how the DNS server caches lookups. With this option enabled, the server does not cache lookups that result in a hostname outside of the originally requested domain. For example, if a request is made for the hostname *www.arctic.local,* and it is redirected to *www.testlab.local,* then the DNS server does not cache the response. This option is enabled by default.

The Name checking list box allows you to specify what characters are allowed in the zones. The default setting is "Multibyte UTF-8" which allows non-ASCII characters. The setting "Strict RFC (ANSI)" allows only characters that are defined in RFC 1123. The setting "Non-RFC (ANSI)" allows only ASCII characters to be part of DNS names, but they do not have to conform to RFC 1123. The settings "All names" permits any naming convention.

The Load zone data on startup list box allows you to select from where the DNS Service reads its configuration information. The default option is "From Active Directory and registry". Other options are "From registry" and "From file". If the option to start from file is chosen, then a configuration file named boot is used. This option should be chosen if configuration information has been copied from a BIND-based server.

Security

The Security tab of the server properties allows you to view and modify which users and groups can modify the configuration of the DNS server. The Domain Admins group, Enterprise Admins group, and DnsAdmins group are allowed to manage DNS.

MANAGING ZONES

There are a variety of options that can be configured for a zone. These include:

- Reload zone information
- Create a new delegation
- Change the type of zone and replication
- Configure aging and scavenging
- Modify the Start of Authority (SOA) record
- Name servers
- Enable WINS resolution
- Enable zone transfers
- Configure security

Reload Zone Information

To perform any mass editing of DNS information stored in a non-Active Directory integrated zone, you may find it easier to edit the zone file stored in C:\WINDOWS\system32\dns rather than using the DNS snap-in. To get the DNS server to use the newly edited zone file, you must restart the DNS Service or tell it to reload the zone file. To reload the zone file, right-click on the zone, and click Reload.

Create a New Delegation

In a larger organization, you need more than one zone to hold all of the DNS information. As a zone begins to contain many subdomains you will want to delegate responsibility for some subdomains by creating new zones for them on other servers. This allows you to choose which DNS servers hold what DNS records.

Windows Server 2003 provides a wizard to guide you through the process of delegating the authority for a subdomain to another server. To access the wizard, right-click the original zone, and click New Delegation. When the wizard is complete, DNS servers holding the original zone will redirect requests for the delegated subdomain to the DNS server specified during the delegation process.

Activity 6-11: Delegating Authority for a Subdomain

Time Required: 5 minutes

Objective: Delegate the authority for a subdomain from the instructor computer to your server.

Description: You have created the zone locationX.arctic.local on your DNS server. However, the main instructor server does not know that this exists. The instructor server is authoritative for arctic.local and all subdomains until authority is delegated to your server.

1. If necessary, start your server and log on as Administrator.

2. Click **Start**, point to **Administrative Tools**, and click **DNS**.

3. If necessary, double-click **instructor** to expand it.

4. Inside instructor, double-click **Forward Lookup Zones** to expand it.

5. In the left pane, click **Arctic.local**, right-click **Arctic.local**, and click **New Delegation**.

6. Click **Next** to start the New Delegation Wizard.

7. In the **Delegated domain** field, type **locationX**, where *X* is your student number, and click **Next**.

8. Click **Add**.

9. In the Server Fully Qualified Domain Name (FQDN) field, type **serverX.arctic.local**, where *X* is your student number, click **Resolve**, and click **OK**.

10. Click **Next** to continue, then click **Finish**.

11. Close the DNS snap-in.

Changing the Type of Zone and Replication

When a zone is created you must select whether it is a primary zone, secondary zone, or stub zone. If it is a primary zone you must also choose whether it is stored in Active Directory. If the zone is stored in Active Directory, then you also choose how it is replicated. All of these options can be changed after the zone is created.

The zone type and replication for an existing zone can be modified on the General tab of the zone properties as shown in Figure 6-18.

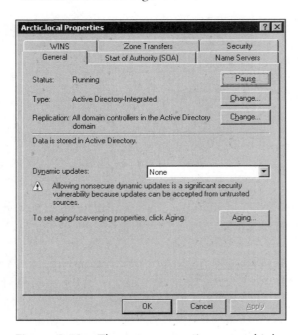

Figure 6-18   The zone properties general tab

The button to change the replication for a zone is only available for Active Directory integrated zones. If the button is grayed out then the zone is not stored in Active Directory.

Configure Aging and Scavenging

Once scavenging has been enabled at the server level, then the aging/scavenging properties must be configured at the zone level. To configure the aging/scavenging properties of a zone, click the Aging button on the General tab of the zone properties. Figure 6-19 shows the aging/scavenging properties of a zone.

To enable the deletion of old DNS records, select the "Scavenge stale resource records" option. Once scavenging is enabled, the "No-refresh interval" option lets you specify how often a DNS record can be refreshed.

By default, there is a no-refresh interval of seven days. This means that Dynamic DNS clients cannot refresh their DNS record more than once every seven days. A refresh is a re-registration of existing DNS information with no changes. DNS updates where there are changes to the DNS record and are always allowed regardless of the no-refresh interval. If a DNS record is updated, then the time stamp on the record is updated and the no-refresh interval begins again for that record.

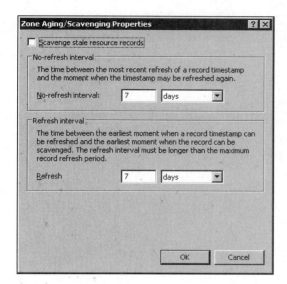

Figure 6-19   Zone aging/scavenging properties

The "Refresh interval" option is the period of time that must pass after the no-refresh interval has expired before DNS records are deleted. During the refresh interval, DNS records can be refreshed by Dynamic DNS clients. If a record is refreshed, a new time stamp is created and the no-refresh interval begins again for that record. If the record is not refreshed during the refresh interval, then the DNS server deletes the record during its next scavenging.

Manually created DNS records are never scavenged. Dynamic DNS records are scavenged only if they have not been updated or refreshed and both the no-refresh interval and refresh interval have expired.

Activity 6-12: Configuring Aging and Scavenging

Time Required: 10 minutes

Objective: Configure a zone to automatically remove old records.

Description: Dynamic DNS is used to create host records in your zone locationX.arctic.local. To ensure that outdated information is not left in the zone you will configure it to automatically remove Dynamic DNS records that have not been updated or refreshed for four weeks.

1. If necessary, start your server and log on as Administrator.

2. Click **Start**, point to **Administrative Tools**, click **DNS**.

3. Right-click your server, and click **Properties**.

4. Click **Advanced**, click **Enable automatic scavenging of stale records**, and click **OK**. This configures the server to look for old records to delete every seven days.

5. Double-click your server.

6. Double-click **Forward Lookup Zones**.

7. Click **locationX.arctic.local**, where *X* is your student number.

8. Right-click **locationX.arctic.local**, where *X* is your student number, and click **Properties**.

9. Click **Aging** on the General tab.

10. Click **Scavenge stale resource records** to select it.

11. Confirm that the **No-refresh interval** is set to **7 days**.

12. In the **Refresh** box, enter **21 days**. Dynamic DNS records are now eligible to be scavenged after the total of 28 days have passed without the record being updated or refreshed.

13. Click **OK**, click **Yes** to confirm the change, and click **OK**.

14. Close the DNS snap-in.

Modify the Start of Authority Record

The **Start of Authority (SOA) record** for a domain defines a number of characteristics for a zone, including serial number and caching instructions. The SOA record is configured in the Start of Authority (SOA) tab of the zone properties, as shown in Figure 6-20.

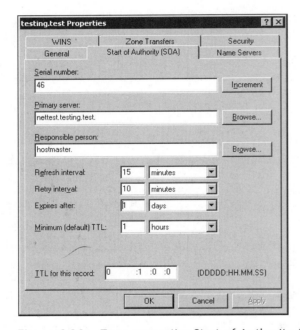

Figure 6-20   Zone properties Start of Authority (SOA) tab

The serial number of a zone is automatically updated when a change is made to the zone. This is used by secondary zones to request changes to the zone. A secondary zone requests a zone transfer if the serial number of the primary zone is higher than the serial number of the secondary zone. You can force all secondary zones to request a zone transfer by manually incrementing the serial number by one.

The "Refresh interval" option specifies how often secondary zones can attempt to update from the primary zone. The "Retry interval" option specifies how long a secondary zone waits before reattempting to contact the primary zone if an initial attempt fails. The "Expires after" option specifies how long a secondary zone can go without contacting the primary zone before it stops functioning because its data is considered unreliable.

The "Minimum (default) TTL" option is used by remote DNS servers that are caching records from this zone. A record that is cached from this zone is not resolved again for the time period specified. This time is also used as the maximum time that a DNS error can be cached.

Name Servers

The name servers configured for a zone are the authoritative DNS servers for the zone. They are used in the recursive lookup process to resolve requests for the domain. In addition, they are used by Dynamic DNS clients for dynamic updates.

 Dynamic DNS cannot be performed on secondary zones. A DNS server holding a secondary zone should never be added as a name server for a zone if Dynamic DNS in being used.

Figure 6-21 shows the Name Servers tab in the properties of a zone.

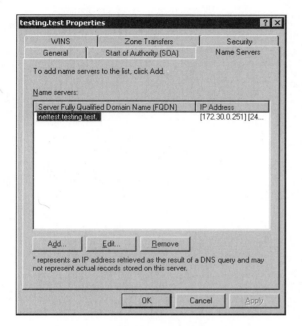

Figure 6-21   Zone properties Name Servers tab

WINS Resolution

A DNS zone can be configured with a WINS server that is used to help resolve names. If a DNS zone receives a query for a hostname for which it has no A record, it forwards the request to a WINS server. For example, if a DNS server with the zone arctic.local receives a hostname resolution request for workstation85.arctic.local and does not have a matching A record, then the DNS server forwards a WINS lookup request for the name workstation85 to the WINS server.

Figure 6-22 shows the WINS tab in the properties of a zone. You can specify that records resolved via WINS are not replicated to other domain controllers by selecting the "Do not replicate this record" option.

Zone Transfers

Zone transfers are used to copy zone information from a primary zone to a secondary zone. You can configure which IP addresses can request zone transfers. Figure 6-23 shows the Zone Transfers tab of the zone properties.

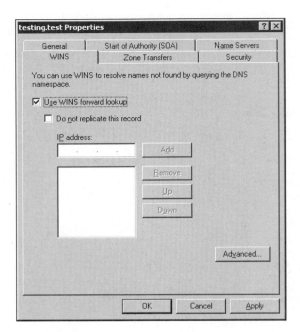

Figure 6-22   Zone properties WINS tab

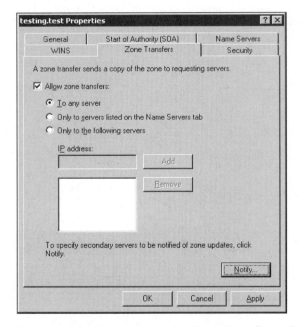

Figure 6-23   Zone properties Zone Transfers tab

By default, zone transfers are allowed. To disable zone transfers, deselect the Allow zone transfers option. If zone transfers are enabled, you can choose whether they are enabled to any server, to only servers listed in the Name Servers tab for the zone, or to specific IP addresses.

You can also specify a list of secondary zones to notify of zone changes by clicking on the Notify button. When a secondary zone is notified of a zone change, it immediately requests a zone transfer. This significantly speeds up the synchronization between primary and secondary zones. Without notification, a secondary zone checks for updates every 15 minutes.

Security

The Security tab in the zone properties allows you to control the permissions to modify the records for this zone. The security tab is only available for Active Directory integrated zones.

TROUBLESHOOTING DNS

Most DNS problems are a result of incorrectly configured DNS records. To test whether a DNS server is functioning correctly, you can use the Monitoring tab of the DNS server properties, as shown in Figure 6-24.

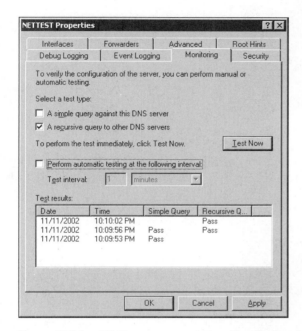

Figure 6-24   DNS server properties Monitoring tab

If a simple query is requested, then the server is tested for iterative query functionality. An iterative query is a query in which the DNS server looks only in the zones for which it is responsible.

If a recursive query is requested, then a NS query is submitted for the root domain ".". If this query is unsuccessful, it may be due to incorrectly configured Internet connectivity or root hints.

You can choose to perform a simple query or recursive query manually or at a scheduled interval. To manually perform a test, select the type of test you want to perform (simple, recursive, or both), then click Test Now. To perform tests at a scheduled interval, select the type of test you would like to perform, then select Perform automatic testing at the following interval. After automatic testing has been enabled, you can choose the interval at which it is repeated.

The results of automatic and manual tests appear only in the Test results box.

NSLOOKUP

The utility **NSLOOKUP** queries DNS records. It is an indispensable tool when troubleshooting DNS problems. With NSLOOKUP you can query any DNS record from a DNS server. This allows you to confirm that each DNS server is configured with the correct information.

NSLOOKUP can be used from a command prompt to resolve hostnames, but is most powerful in interactive mode. To run NSLOOKUP in interactive mode, open a command prompt, type nslookup, and press Enter. Inside NSLOOKUP you can use the help command to get a list of available commands, as shown in Figure 6-25.

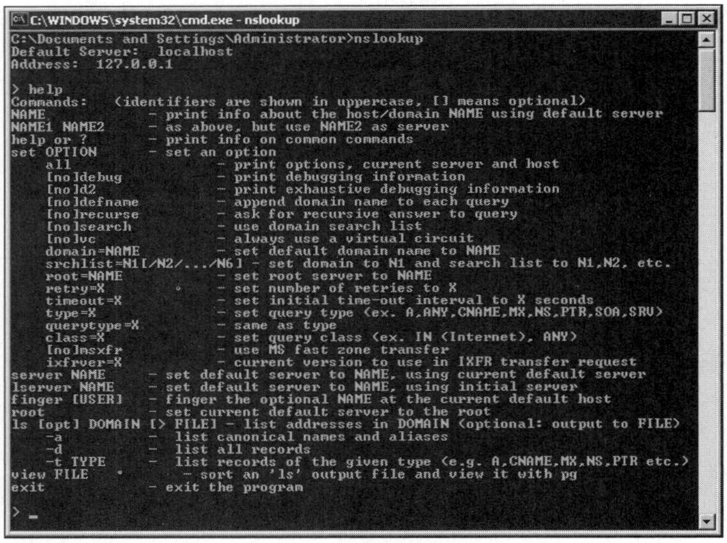

Figure 6-25   NSLOOKUP help

In interactive mode you can use NSLOOKUP to view any DNS records available for a zone. Figure 6-26 shows NSLOOKUP being used to find the MX records for the domain hotmail.com. MX records list the mail servers for a domain.

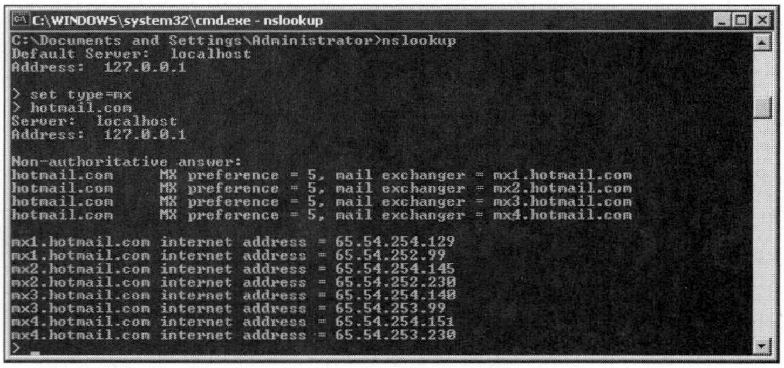

Figure 6-26   Finding MX records for hotmail.com

Activity 6-13: Verifying DNS Records with NSLOOKUP

Time Required: 10 minutes

Objective: Verify proper DNS lookups using the utility NSLOOKUP.

Description: You have configured a stub zone on your server and delegated authority for a domain on the instructor server. To confirm that both of these actions are working properly you will use NSLOOKUP.

1. If necessary, start your server and log on as Administrator.

2. Click **Start**, click **Run**, type **nslookup**, and press **Enter**.

3. If necessary, to change the server that NSLOOKUP queries, type **server 192.168.1.10**, and press **Enter**. Now all the queries NSLOOKUP performs are done by contacting the instructor server.

4. To view MX records, type **set type=mx**, and press **Enter**.

5. To view the MX records for your location zone, type **locationX.arctic.local**, and press **Enter**. This verifies that the delegation from the instructor server to your server is working properly.

6. To view A records, type **set type=a**, and press **Enter**.

7. To have NSLOOKUP query your server, type **server _your ip address_**, where your IP address is the IP address of the classroom connection on your server, and press **Enter**.

8. Type **serverX.arctic.local**, where _X_ is your student number, and press **Enter**. Your server does not hold a copy of the arctic.local domain. This query verifies that the stub zone on your server is functioning and recursive queries are directed to the instructor server.

9. To close NSLOOKUP, type **exit**, and press **Enter**.

CHAPTER SUMMARY

❑ Hostname resolution is performed in four steps. The first step is to check if the hostname being resolved matches the hostname of the local computer. The second step is to load the HOSTS file into DNS cache. DNS cache is checked for the third step. Finally, DNS is used if required.

❑ A forward lookup resolves hostnames to IP addresses. A reverse lookup resolves an IP address to a hostname.

❑ A recursive lookup is performed when a local DNS server queries the root servers on the Internet on behalf of a DNS client.

❑ Common DNS record types include: A, MX, CNAME, NS, SOA, SRV, AAAA, and PTR.

❑ A DNS zone holds records for a portion of DNS namespace.

❑ Traditional primary and secondary zones are stored in a zone file on the hard drive of the DNS server.

❑ Active Directory integrated zones are stored in Active Directory. As a result, Active Directory integrated zones can use the security permissions in Active Directory to control updates.

❑ Active Directory integrated zones can act as primary zones to secondary zones.

❑ A stub zone contains name server records that are used for recursive lookups.

❑ A caching-only server reduces the network traffic generated by DNS queries.

❑ Dynamic DNS allows records to be automatically updated on a DNS server. Client computers create A and PTR records using Dynamic DNS. Older Windows clients are not able to use Dynamic DNS directly, and a DHCP server must perform the updates on their behalf. Domain controllers create SRV records using Dynamic DNS.

❑ Aging and scavenging remove outdated records created by Dynamic DNS.

❑ The root hints are used for recursive lookups. They are loaded from the file cache.dns.

❑ Event logging and debug logging can be used to troubleshoot DNS problems.

❑ A WINS server can be used to help resolve hostnames if a DNS server does not have an A record that matches a query.

❑ The NSLOOKUP utility can be used to verify that a DNS server is configured with the proper records and is answering queries.

KEY TERMS

Active Directory integrated zone — A DNS zone in which DNS information is stored in Active Directory and supports multimaster updates and increased security.

aging/scavenging — The process of removing old records from DNS that have not been updated within a set time period.

application directory partition — A partition that stores information about objects that is replicated to a set of defined domain controllers within the same forest.

Berkeley Internet Name Domain (BIND) — A UNIX-based implementation of the Domain Name System created by the University of California at Berkeley.

caching-only server — A DNS server that does not store any zone information, but caches DNS queries from clients.

DCPROMO — A utility for promoting a member server to a domain controller, or demoting a domain controller to a member server.

debug logging — The processing of logging additional DNS-related events or messages for troubleshooting purposes.

DNS zone — The part of the domain namespace for which a DNS server is authoritative. Commonly referred to as a "zone."

domain directory partition — A partition that stores information about objects in a specific domain that is replicated to all domain controllers in the domain.

Domain Name System (DNS) — The method used to resolve Internet domain names to IP addresses.

Dynamic DNS — A system in which DNS records are automatically updated by the client or a DHCP server.

event logging — The logging of status messages in an event log. This logging is less detailed than debug logging.

forward lookup — The process of resolving a domain name to an IP address.

forward lookup zone — A zone that holds records used for forward lookups. The primary record types contained in these zones are: A records, MX records, and SRV records.

forwarding — The process of sending a DNS lookup request to another DNS server when the local DNS server does not have the requested information.

hostname — The unique name that identifies the computer on the network.

HOSTS — A local text file used to resolve Fully Qualified Domain Names to IP addresses.

incremental zone transfer — The process of updating only modified DNS records from a primary DNS server to a secondary DNS server.

Kerberos — An authentication protocol designed to authenticate both the client and server using secret-key cryptography.

Lightweight Directory Access Protocol (LDAP) — A protocol used to look up directory information from a server.

NSLOOKUP — A command prompt-based utility for troubleshooting DNS.

primary zone — A zone that is authoritative for the specific DNS zone. Updates can only be made in the primary zone. There is only one primary zone per domain name.

recursive lookup — A DNS query that is resolved through other DNS servers until the requested information is located.

registrar — A company accredited by ICANN who has the right to distribute and register domain names.

reverse lookup — The process of resolving an IP address to a domain name.

reverse lookup zone — A zone that contains records used for reverse lookups. The primary record type in these zones is PTR records.

root hints — The list of root servers that is used by DNS servers to perform forward lookups on the Internet.

root servers — A group of 13 DNS servers on the Internet that are authoritative for the top-level domain names such as .com, .edu, and .org.

round robin DNS — The process of creating multiple IP addresses for a specific hostname for fault tolerance and load balancing.

secondary zone — A DNS zone that stores a read-only copy of the DNS information from a primary zone. There can be multiple secondary zones.

Start of Authority (SOA) record — A DNS record that defines which DNS server is authoritative for that particular domain and defines the characteristics for the zone.

stub zone — A DNS zone that stores only the NS records for a particular zone. When a client requests a DNS lookup, the request is then forwarded to the DNS server specified by the NS records.

top-level domain — The broadest category of names in the DNS hierarchy under which all domain names fit. Some top-level domains include .com, .edu, and .gov.

zone transfer — The process of updating DNS records from a primary DNS server to a secondary DNS server.

REVIEW QUESTIONS

1. Which port and transport protocol does the DNS Service use to listen for hostname resolution requests?

   a. TCP port 53

   b. TCP port 25

   c. UDP port 53

   d. UDP port 51

   e. UDP port 389

2. Which DNS record is used to point to a mail server for a specific domain?

   a. MX

   b. A

   c. CNAME

   d. SOA

   e. SRV

3. Resolving an IP address to a hostname is what type of lookup?

   a. forward

   b. cache

   c. reverse

   d. primary

4. Which of the following is not a type of DNS zone in Windows Server 2003? (Choose all that apply.)

   a. Active Directory integrated

   b. primary

   c. secondary

   d. stand-alone

   e. root

5. A stub DNS zone only stores which domain record?

   a. NS

   b. A

   c. CNAME

   d. SOA

   e. MX

6. Which DNS records do clients use to locate domain controllers?

   a. CNAME

   b. MX

   c. SOA

   d. NS

   e. SRV

7. A DHCP server running under Windows Server 2003 updates DNS records for which operating systems by default? (Choose all that apply.)

    a. Windows XP Professional

    b. Windows 2000 Professional

    c. Windows NT 4 Professional

    d. Windows 98

    e. Windows 95

8. Which of the following statements regarding Active Directory integrated zones is false?

    a. Active Directory integrated zones are automatically replicated to all domain controllers.

    b. Active Directory integrated zones support multimaster replication.

    c. Only Active Directory integrated zones support dynamic updates.

    d. Only Active Directory integrated zones support secure dynamic updates.

9. Which of the text files can be used to resolve domain names to IP addresses?

    a. LMHOSTS

    b. HOST

    c. HOSTS

    d. HOSTS.SAM

    e. PROTOCOL.INI

10. Which version of BIND supports incremental zone updates?

    a. BIND 4.9.6

    b. BIND 8.1.2

    c. BIND 8.2.1

    d. all of the above

11. Which of the following zones stores a read-only copy of another zone?

    a. primary

    b. Active Directory integrated

    c. root

    d. secondary

12. What type of zone resolves host names to IP addresses?

    a. forward lookup zone

    b. reverse lookup zone

    c. primary zone

    d. secondary zone

13. Which of the following servers can participate in Active Directory integrated zones? (Choose all that apply.)

    a. Windows 2000 Advanced Server domain controller

    b. Windows NT 4 Server

    c. BIND version 8.2.1 DNS server

    d. Windows Server 2003 member server

    e. all the above

14. A backup network administrator accidentally deleted all the service records in DNS. What is the quickest method to recover the information?

    a. Reinstall DNS server.

    b. Reboot the server.

c. Restore from backup tape.

d. Stop and start the NETLOGON Service.

e. Manually create the deleted records.

15. Which of the following DNS records defines the primary zone?

   a. A

   b. MX

   c. NS

   d. SRV

   e. SOA

16. The process of updating information from the primary zone to a secondary zone is called?

   a. replication

   b. zone transfer

   c. forwarding

   d. scavenging

17. Your company has a remote site containing five workstations connected by a very slow link. Users are complaining of slow DNS lookups. What type of DNS server can you configure in the remote site to speed up DNS resolution without creating more WAN traffic?

   a. Active Directory integrated

   b. primary

   c. secondary

   d. caching-only

18. Which command can be used to manually force a supported client's Dynamic DNS information?

   a. ipconfig /refresh

   b. ipconfig /registerdns

   c. ipconfig /flushdns

   d. ipconfig /displaydns

19. You want to configure a different list of root servers for your DNS server. Which file in \WINDOWS\SYSTEM32\DNS do you edit?

   a. CACHE.DNS

   b. ROOTS.DNS

   c. ZONE.DNS

   d. HINTS.DNS

20. Round robin DNS is the process of?

   a. creating multiple records for a single DNS hostname

   b. creating multiple host names for a single IP address

   c. creating different priorities for an MX record

   d. enabling forwarding to root hint servers

21. An administrator wants to change the replication schedule for a DNS server, but the Replication button is grayed out. What type of zone is it?

   a. primary

   b. secondary

   c. Active Directory integrated

   d. caching-only

CASE PROJECTS

A proper DNS implementation is critical to the success of your Windows Server 2003 rollout. In the following cases you consider how DNS can be implemented for Arctic University.

Case Project 6-1: Integrating Windows Server 2003 DNS with BIND

The university currently has seven UNIX servers providing DNS Services for the whole campus. They are all running BIND version 8.1.2. Another administrator has recommended that the UNIX DNS servers be upgraded to Windows Server 2003 to support the new Windows Server 2003 domain controllers. What options does the university have for DNS? What are the advantages and disadvantages of each option? Which do you recommend?

Case Project 6-2: Creating DNS Zones

It has been decided that the university will not replace the UNIX DNS servers with Windows Server 2003. It has also been discovered that a few small departments also have Windows NT 4 Servers running DNS. In order to reduce replication traffic, not all Windows .NET Server 2000 domain controllers will run as DNS servers. In addition, some Windows Server 2003 member servers will run DNS. The head of the Computer Services Department recommends that only Active Directory integrated zones be created to reduce administrative and management overhead. What are the implications of such a decision? How can all DNS servers be integrated without upgrading the servers to Windows Server 2003?

Case Project 6-3: Securing DNS

The head of the Computer Services Department is very concerned about hackers improperly updating DNS information or getting a list of all the internal computer names and IP addresses. What can be implemented in Active Directory integrated zones to secure DNS from hackers?

7

WINDOWS INTERNET NAMING SERVICE

After reading this chapter and completing the exercises, you will be able to:

♦ Describe the NetBIOS name resolution process

♦ Describe why WINS is used and the tasks it performs

♦ Install WINS

♦ Configure WINS replication

♦ Manage WINS

♦ Understand when to use a WINS proxy

Windows Internet Naming Service (WINS) is required to support older Windows clients. Pre-Windows 2000 clients use WINS to find domain controllers, which are required for the clients to log on to the network. WINS is also used to resolve NetBIOS names to IP addresses. This is critical in an environment with pre-Windows 2000 clients. Windows 9x/NT clients access network resources such as shares and printers using NetBIOS names. The NetBIOS name resolution methods covered in this chapter are only required when using NetBIOS over TCP/IP. If IPX/SPX is used, then the resolution of NetBIOS names is handled automatically, even across routers.

NETBIOS NAME RESOLUTION

As you may recall from the previous chapter, Windows Sockets (WinSock) and NetBIOS are the two standard methods Windows applications can use to access network resources. When NetBIOS is used, the NetBIOS name of the remote resource must be resolved to an IP address.

All of the networking functions in pre-Windows 2000 operating systems, such as UNC paths, use NetBIOS names. In addition, many older applications that access database application servers, such as Microsoft SQL Server, use NetBIOS names. An example of using a NetBIOS name is a Windows NT computer attempting to access a share using the UNC path \\server5\datashare. The name "server5" is a NetBIOS name, and must be resolved to an IP address before the Windows NT client can contact the server. After the name is resolved to an IP address, the share named "datashare" can be accessed.

Microsoft clients use four methods to resolve NetBIOS names. If the first one is not successful, the client proceeds to the next method. These are the methods in order:

1. *NetBIOS name cache*—When a Windows client resolves a NetBIOS name, it keeps a record of the results in the NetBIOS name cache. If the current NetBIOS name being resolved has a record in the cache, then the corresponding IP address in the cache is used and no further resolution is done. To view the content of the NetBIOS name cache, use the command nbtstat −c.

2. *Windows Internet Naming Service (WINS)*—The second method used to resolve NetBIOS names is a WINS server. The client computer sends a NetBIOS name query asking for the resolution of a NetBIOS name. WINS is used early in the name resolution process because it is the resolution method most likely to be successful. By default, client computers do not know the location of a WINS server and must be configured either manually through the properties of TCP/IP or via DHCP.

3. *Broadcast*—If WINS has not been installed on the network or the client has been misconfigured, then WINS is not able to resolve the NetBIOS name. In such a case, a broadcast is sent on the network. The computer using the NetBIOS name being resolved receives the request and then responds with its IP address. For example, if the NetBIOS name being resolved is server5 and the computer named server5 receives a name resolution broadcast, then server5 responds with its IP address. Resolving NetBIOS names via broadcasts is not scalable to large networks because of the amount of network traffic generated and the inability to cross routers.

4. *LMHOSTS*—If no other method is successful, then an LMHOSTS file is parsed to find the NetBIOS name. The LMHOSTS file is a static text file located on the workstation. An LMHOSTS file is to NetBIOS name resolution what a HOSTS file is to hostname resolution. LMHOSTS files are only found on Microsoft operating systems and are not commonly used. They are difficult to maintain because they must be copied to every client.

Activity 7-1: Creating an LMHOSTS File

Time Required: 10 minutes

Objective: Create an LMHOSTS file for NetBIOS name resolution.

Description: You are installing a new accounting application for some of the finance staff. The application uses a NetBIOS name to contact the SQL database server. When you start the application, there are errors indicating that the server cannot be contacted. To ensure that NetBIOS name resolution is not a problem, you are creating an LMHOSTS file to resolve the server name, SQLSERVER, to the IP address 192.168.1.249.

1. If necessary, start your server and log on as Administrator.

2. Click **Start**, right-click **My Computer**, and click **Explore**.

3. In the right pane, double-click **Local Disk (C:)**, double-click **WINDOWS**, double-click **system32**, double-click **drivers**, and then double-click **etc**.

4. If LMHOSTS exists, then skip this step. If there is not already an LMHOSTS file, you must create one based on the lmhosts.sam file.

    a. Right-click **lmhosts.sam**, and click **Copy**.

    b. Right-click the **etc** folder, and click **Paste**.

    c. Right-click **Copy of lmhosts.sam**, and click **Rename**.

    d. Type **lmhosts**, and press **Enter**.

5. Right-click **lmhosts**, click **Open**, click **Notepad**, and click **OK**.

6. On a blank line at the end of the file, type **192.168.1.249 SQLSERVER**.

7. Click **File** and click **Save**.

8. Close Notepad and Windows Explorer.

7

WINS FUNCTIONS

Each NetBIOS name is tied to a service such as file sharing or Windows Messenger. A WINS server is a central repository for NetBIOS name and service information. When WINS is implemented on a network, all of the client computers and servers must be configured to use the WINS server. It is important that all computers use the WINS server, or the database will be incomplete and name resolution will not be possible for some hosts. Even the server running the WINS service must be configured to use itself.

To configure a client or server to use WINS, you must edit the properties of the TCP/IP protocol. Figure 7-1 shows the configuration of a WINS server on a Windows XP client.

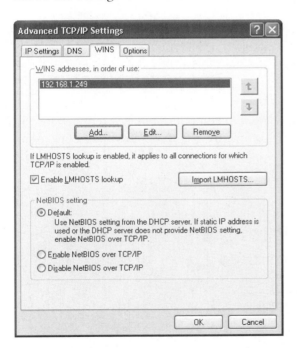

Figure 7-1   WINS configuration in Windows XP

WINS offers several benefits over other NetBIOS name resolution methods because WINS:

- *Functions across routers*—WINS communication is done with unicast packets because all of the clients are configured with the IP address of the WINS server. WINS is required in routed networks because unicast packets are routable.

- *Can be dynamically updated*—The WINS database is dynamically updated as computers are added or removed from the network. Each client computer registers its name during the boot process.

- *Can be automated*—The maintenance of the WINS database contents is automatic. Once the client computers have been configured with the IP address of the WINS servers the process requires no manual updates.

- *Offers client configuration through DHCP*—WINS clients can be configured with the IP address of the WINS server using DHCP. Because this is the only client configuration required, WINS can be implemented without ever visiting the client computers on your network.

- *Offers integration with DNS*—WINS can be integrated with DNS to resolve hostnames. If a DNS server does not have an A record for a hostname, the DNS server submits the hostname to WINS in an attempt to resolve it. This can be useful if there are older Windows clients on your network that use WINS, but do not support dynamic DNS.

There are four common tasks performed with WINS:

- Name registration

- Name renewal

- Name release

- Name query

Name Registration

When a WINS client boots up, it performs a name registration. The name registration places NetBIOS information about the client into the WINS database. This makes the information available to other clients performing name queries. Name registration is a two-packet process.

The first packet is generated by the client and sent directly to the WINS server using a unicast packet. This packet is a **name registration request** and contains the NetBIOS name that the client computer is attempting to register.

If the NetBIOS name is not already registered by another host, then a successful **name registration response** packet is sent from the WINS server to the client computer. This packet contains the NetBIOS name that has been registered and a time to live (TTL). Figure 7-2 shows the communication process for a successful name registration.

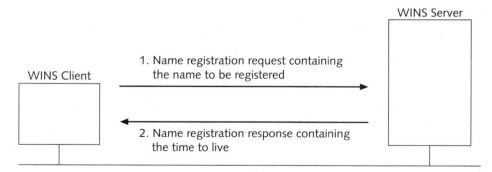

Figure 7-2   Name registration

If the NetBIOS name is already registered by another host, then the WINS server sends a challenge to that host. If the original owner of the name does not respond, then the NetBIOS name is registered to the new client and a successful name registration response packet is sent back to the new client. If the original owner of the name responds to the challenge, then the new client is sent a negative name registration response.

WINS clients can be configured with multiple WINS servers. If a WINS client cannot contact the first WINS server in the list after three attempts, then the second server is contacted. This process continues to the end of the list. However, the second WINS server is not contacted if a negative name registration response is received from the first WINS server.

Name Renewal

Each NetBIOS name registration is assigned a TTL. When the TTL is one half completed, the WINS client attempts to refresh the registration. The default TTL is six days.

Name renewal is a two-packet process. The first packet is a **name refresh request** and is sent from the WINS client to the WINS server. The name refresh request contains the NetBIOS name that is being refreshed. If the WINS client is unable to contact the first WINS server for one hour, then it fails and contacts the second WINS server.

The second packet in the renewal process is a **name refresh response**. This packet is sent from the WINS server to the WINS client and contains the NetBIOS name being renewed, as well as a new TTL. Figure 7-3 shows the name renewal process. If the client is not able to renew its NetBIOS name before the end of the TTL, then the name is released.

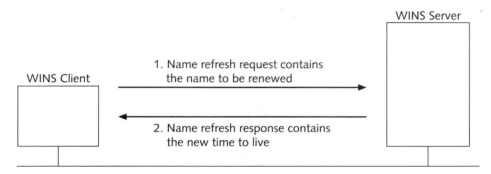

Figure 7-3   Name renewal

Name Release

When a computer is properly shut down, it contacts the WINS server and releases its NetBIOS name. The first packet in this process is a **name release request** sent from the WINS client to the WINS server. This request includes the NetBIOS name being released and the IP address of the WINS client.

The WINS server sends a name release response to the WINS client. The **name release response** contains the NetBIOS name being released and a TTL of zero. Another computer can now register the released name. Figure 7-4 shows the name release process.

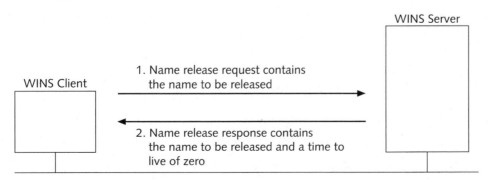

Figure 7-4   Name release

Name Query

A name query is used to resolve a NetBIOS name to an IP address. This is done by a client computer that is accessing resources on a server. A WINS client queries a WINS server if the NetBIOS name being resolved has not been recently resolved and stored in the NetBIOS name cache.

The first packet in the name query process is a **name query request** from the WINS client to the WINS server. This packet contains the NetBIOS name to be resolved. The second packet is a **name query response** from the WINS server to the WINS client. If the WINS server is able to resolve the query, then this packet contains the IP address registered in the WINS database for the NetBIOS name being resolved. If the WINS server is not able to resolve the query, then the packet contains a message indicating the name could not be resolved. Figure 7-5 shows the name query process.

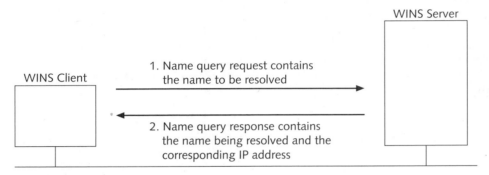

Figure 7-5   Name query

Each WINS client can have a list of multiple WINS servers. If the first WINS server in the list cannot be contacted, then the WINS client queries the second WINS server in the list.

INSTALLING WINS

Windows Server 2003 has the ability to act as a WINS server. It is very unusual to use another operating system as a **NetBIOS name server**. In larger organizations with expansive WANs, there are several WINS servers. If this is the case, then WINS must be installed individually on each server. WINS is never installed automatically.

Activity 7-2: Installing WINS

Time Required: 10 minutes

Objective: Install WINS on your server.

Description: To ensure that all of the client computers on your network can resolve the NetBIOS name servers in a routed network, you have decided to implement WINS. In this activity you will install WINS on your server.

1. If necessary, start your server and log on as Administrator.

2. Click **Start**, point to **Control Panel**, and click **Add or Remove Programs**.

3. Click **Add/Remove Windows Components**.

4. Scroll down in the components window, and double-click **Networking Services**.

5. Click the check box beside **Windows Internet Name Service (WINS)**, and click **OK**.

6. Click **Next** to install WINS. If prompted for the Windows Server 2003 CD-ROM, click **OK**. Click the Browse button, then select the **C:\I386** folder and click **Open**. Click **OK** in the Files Needed dialog box.

7. When the installation is complete, click **Finish**, and close the Add or Remove Programs window.

Activity 7-3: Configuring a WINS Client

Time Required: 5 minutes

Objective: Configure your server to be a WINS client.

Description: It is important to remember that servers must also be configured as WINS clients. If they are not, then the NetBIOS names and IP addresses of the servers are not listed in the WINS database, and client computers cannot use NetBIOS resources on the servers. For these reasons, your server will be configured as a WINS client.

1. If necessary, start your server and log on as Administrator.

2. Click **Start**, point to **Control Panel**, point to **Network Connections**, right-click **Classroom**, and then click **Properties**.

3. Click **Internet Protocol (TCP/IP)**, and then click **Properties**.

4. Click **Advanced**, and then click the **WINS** tab.

5. Click **Add**.

6. Type the IP address of your Classroom connection, and click **Add**.

7. Click **OK**, click **OK** again, and click **Close**.

CONFIGURING WINS REPLICATION

A single WINS server can handle at least 5000 WINS clients. However, you may choose to implement multiple WINS servers in much smaller environments to control network traffic and provide fault tolerance.

In a large network with multiple physical locations, it may reduce network traffic across WAN links if multiple WINS servers are used. If a WINS server is located at each physical location, then WINS clients do all of their registrations and queries with the local server. This creates no WAN traffic. Smaller networks may also benefit from having multiple WINS servers. When two WINS servers are implemented, WINS clients are still able to resolve NetBIOS names if one WINS server fails.

When more than one WINS server is implemented, you must configure replication between them. This allows all the WINS servers to contain the same information. To configure WINS servers as **replication partners**, right-click on the Replication Partners folder, click New Replication Partners, and then enter the IP address of the replication partner.

After a replication partner has been added, you can control how replication occurs. There are three ways replication can be configured:

- Push
- Pull
- Push/Pull

Default replication properties can be configured in the properties of the Replication Partners folder. You can also set the replication properties for a particular partner. To configure replication, right-click on the replication partner, and click Properties. Figure 7-6 shows the replication properties of a replication partner.

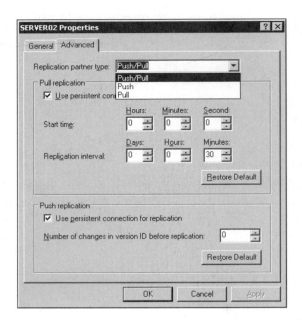

Figure 7-6   WINS server Properties Advanced tab

Push replication occurs based on a certain number of changes occurring in the WINS database. When a defined number of changes occur, the replication partner is notified. The replication partner then requests a copy of the changes. Only changes are replicated between replication partners. Figure 7-7 shows the Push Replication tab in the properties of the Replication Partners folder.

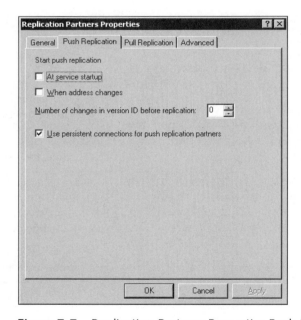

Figure 7-7   Replication Partners Properties Push Replication tab

In a network with few changes, push replication may not be sufficient. If the value is set too high in the "Number of changes in version ID before replication" option, an extended period of time may pass before changes are replicated. Until the changes are replicated, WINS clients resolving queries on the out-of-date server cannot resolve the unreplicated records.

Pull replication occurs based on a set time schedule. You can set a start time for replication and the interval that replication occurs. This type of replication ensures that all changes are replicated between two WINS servers regularly. Figure 7-8 shows the Pull Replication tab in the properties of the Replication Partners folder.

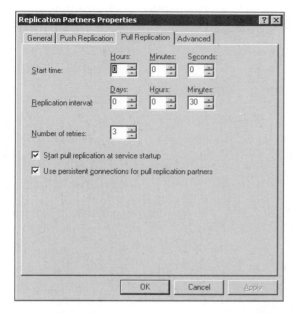

Figure 7-8   Replication Partners Properties Pull Replication tab

Normally, a combination of push and pull replication is used. This is configured by enabling both push and pull replications separately. Push replication ensures that, during periods of high change, records are replicated in a timely way. Pull replication ensures that, during periods of low change, records are replicated even if the criterion for push replication is not met.

Both push and pull replication can be configured to use **persistent connections**. Persistent connections result in faster replication because a new connection does not need to be created for each replication. However, this causes a small amount of additional network traffic that may not be appropriate for slow WAN links.

 You can force replication by right-clicking the Replication Partners folder and clicking Replicate Now.

You can control several replication settings on the General tab of the Replication Partners folder properties. The "Replication only with partners" option forces a server to only replicate its records to servers configured as replication partners. This ensures that replication is two way. The "Overwrite unique static mappings at this server (migrate on)" option allows dynamic WINS registrations from other servers to overwrite static mappings created on this server.

You can enable WINS servers to automatically find replication partners. To do this, a WINS server uses multicast packets to find other replication partners. You can control how often the multicast is sent and the TTL of the packet. A multicast TTL controls the number of routers it can pass through.

A WINS server may hold records for registrations that were not taken by itself or its direct replication partners. In the case of three WINS servers, Server1 replicates to Server2, and Server2 replicates to Server3. You can restrict the records being accepted by a server based on the owner. The owner is the server that originally accepted the registration.

Both automatically finding replication partners and restricting record replication based on the owner can be configured on the Advanced tab of the Replication Partners folder properties, as shown in Figure 7-9.

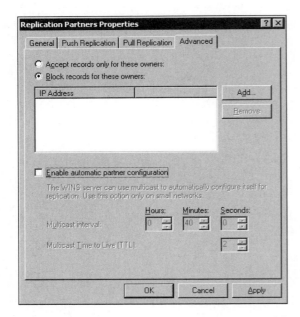

Figure 7-9   Replication Partners Properties Advanced tab

Activity 7-4: Configuring Replication Partners

Time Required: 10 minutes

Objective: Configure your server to replicate WINS information with a partner.

Description: A WINS server has been installed at each physical location on your network to reduce the WAN traffic generated by NetBIOS name resolution. Replication must now be configured so each WINS server can resolve names from other locations. You will configure WINS replication with your partner. For this exercise to be completed, your partner must have successfully completed activities 7-2 and 7-3.

1. If necessary, start your server and log on as Administrator

2. Click **Start**, point to **Administrative Tools**, and click **WINS**.

3. If necessary, double-click your server to expand it.

4. Right-click the **Replication Partners** folder, and click **New Replication Partner**.

5. Type the IP address of your partner's Classroom connection, and click **OK**.

6. Click **Replication Partners** in the left pane to see the configured partner in the right pane of the window. Note that, by default, this replication partner uses both push and pull replication.

7. Right-click **Replication Partners**, and click **Replicate Now**. Click **Yes** to start replication, and click **OK** to close the information dialog box. The event log contains messages regarding the success or failure of replication.

8. Close the WINS snap-in.

MANAGING WINS

In general, the default settings for a WINS server provide adequate service. However there are some settings you can modify if required.

The General tab of the WINS server properties allows you to configure how often statistics are updated for the server, the path for backing up the WINS database, and whether the WINS database should be backed up each time the server is shut down. Figure 7-10 shows the General tab of WINS server properties.

Figure 7-10   WINS server properties General tab

The Intervals tab of the WINS server properties allows you to configure how names are expired and deleted from the WINS database. The **renewal interval** refers to the TTL that is given to WINS clients when a name is registered with the WINS server. The **extinction interval** refers to how long an unused record exists in the WINS database before being marked as extinct. The **extinction timeout** refers to how long an extinct record is kept in the database. When an extinct record has existed in the database for the length of the extinction timeout, it is removed. The **verification interval** refers to how long a WINS server waits before validating a record that is replicated from another WINS server. Figure 7-11 shows the default values on the Intervals tab of the WINS server properties.

The Database Verification tab of the WINS server properties allows you to automate database verification. When database verification occurs, other WINS servers are contacted to confirm that they hold the same WINS information. You can choose whether the records are verified with the original server that took the registration or randomly. Figure 7-12 shows the database verification settings.

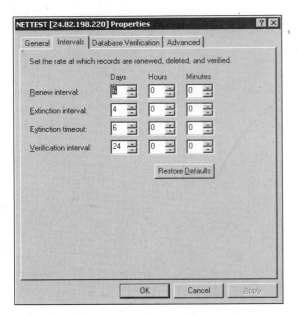

Figure 7-11   WINS server properties Intervals tab

Figure 7-12   WINS server properties Database Verification tab

The Advanced tab of the WINS server properties allows you to set several options. Figure 7-13 shows the Advanced tab of the WINS server properties.

You can enhance the logging of events by selecting the "Log detailed events to Windows event log" option. This should only be used for troubleshooting because the number of events logged can adversely affect server performance.

Burst handling allows a WINS server to handle large volumes of name registration requests in a very short period of time. If the number of name registration requests becomes too large to verify in the WINS database, then the WINS server begins to send successful name registration responses without verifying whether the name is already registered. Later the WINS server registers the name in the WINS database.

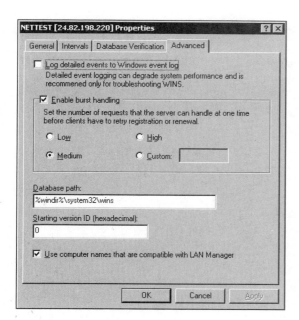

Figure 7-13   WINS server properties Advanced tab

 The database path indicates where the WINS database is stored. The default path is C:\WINDOWS\system32\wins.

The "Starting version ID (hexadecimal)" field is used to force WINS replication. Incrementing this number indicates to replication partners that there is a new version of the WINS database.

The "Use computer names that are compatible with LAN Manager" option restricts registered names to 15 characters. Some non-Microsoft operating systems can use NetBIOS names that are 16 characters long. This option is on by default.

Viewing Database Records

To verify that a client is registered in the WINS database, you may wish to view the contents of the WINS database. To view the records that exist in the WINS database, right-click Active Registrations, and click Display Records. This opens a window that allows you to search the WINS database. You can search for records based on name, IP address, owner, or record type. Figure 7-14 shows the Display Records window used for searching the WINS database.

When viewing records, you have the option to delete them as well. To delete a record, right-click the record, and select Delete. When a record is deleted, you must choose whether to delete it from just the local server or all databases. If you choose to delete it from all servers, then the record is **tombstoned**. The tombstoned status replicates to all servers.

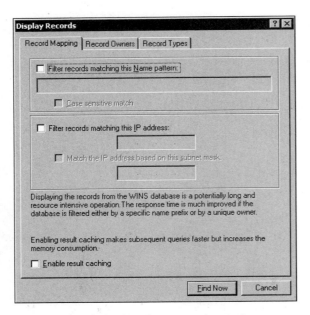

Figure 7-14 The Display Records window

Activity 7-5: Viewing WINS Records

Time Required: 5 minutes

Objective: View WINS records on your server.

Description: A client computer on your network is having problems resolving the NetBIOS name APPSERVER. You have confirmed that the client computer is correctly configured to use the WINS server. You will now verify that the record exists in the WINS database on your server.

1. If necessary, start your server and log on as Administrator.
2. Click **Start**, point to **Administrative Tools**, and click **WINS**.
3. Right-click **Active Registrations**, and click **Display Records**.
4. Leave the fields blank to view all records, and click **Find Now**.
5. You should see WINS records for the ARCTIC workgroup, your server, and your partner's server. There is no record for APPSERVER.
6. Close the WINS snap-in.

Adding Static Records

If non-Microsoft servers provide NetBIOS resources on the network, they may not be able to use a WINS server. If the non-Microsoft server cannot use WINS, then WINS clients cannot resolve their NetBIOS names. To eliminate this problem, you can create a static record in WINS.

To create a static WINS record, right-click Active Registrations, and click New Static Mapping. For each **static mapping**, you enter the computer name, record type, and IP address. Figure 7-15 shows the creation of a static mapping.

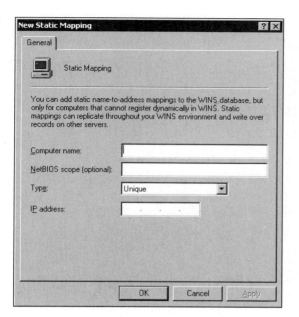

Figure 7-15   Creating a static mapping

Activity 7-6: Adding a Static Mapping

Time Required: 5 minutes

Objective: Add a static mapping to the WINS database.

Description: A UNIX server named APPSERVER runs a database required by an accounting application used by the finance staff. This application uses NetBIOS names, but APPSERVER cannot be configured to use WINS. In this activity you will create a static mapping for APPSERVER so that client computers can use WINS to resolve the name APPSERVER to an IP address.

1. If necessary, start your server and log on as Administrator.

2. Click **Start**, point to **Administrative Tools**, and click **WINS**.

3. Right-click **Active Registrations**, and click **New Static Mapping**.

4. In the **Computer name** text box, type **APPSERVER**.

5. In the **Type** drop-down list, leave the default of Unique. "Unique" is used to identify the name of a single computer and adds records for the Workstation Service, Messenger Service, and File Server Service.

6. In the **IP address** text box, type **192.168.1.202**, and click **OK**.

7. To view the new records, right-click **Active Registrations**, click **Display Records**, and click **Find Now**. Notice that the expiration of the records for APPSERVER is infinite.

8. Close the WINS snap-in.

Backing Up the Database

On a network using NetBIOS-based services, WINS is essential. As a critical resource, the WINS database needs to be backed up in the same way that data needs to be backed up. If the WINS database becomes corrupted, the WINS server stops servicing clients. This results in client computers being unable to access NetBIOS-based resources because NetBIOS names cannot be resolved to IP addresses.

A corrupted WINS database can easily be fixed if you have a backup of the WINS database. Simply stop the WINS Service and restore the database. After the database has been restored, the WINS server receives changes that occurred since the backup from replication partners. The WINS servers determine the changes to replicate based on the version ID of the database records.

Activity 7-7: Backing Up and Restoring the WINS Database

Time Required: 10 minutes

Objective: Backup and restore the WINS database on your server.

Description: To ensure that you can quickly recover your server from a corrupt WINS database, you will configure your server to automatically backup the WINS database. Then you will perform a manual backup and restore to test the process and ensure that it is working properly.

1. If necessary, start your server and log on as Administrator.

2. Create a new folder named **C:\winsbak**:

    a. Click **Start**, click **Run**, type **cmd**, and press **Enter**.

    b. Type **cd ** and press **Enter**.

    c. Type **md winsbak**, and press **Enter**.

    d. Type **exit**, and press **Enter**.

3. Click **Start**, point to **Administrative Tools**, and click **WINS**.

4. Right-click your server, and click **Properties**.

5. On the General tab, in the Default backup path text box, type **C:\winsbak**. After a default backup path has been specified, the database is backed up every three hours.

6. Click the **Back up database during server shutdown** checkbox. This ensures that your server creates a current backup every time it is rebooted.

7. Click **OK**.

8. Right-click your server, and click **Back Up Database**.

9. A window pops up with the folder **C:\winsbak** selected. Click **OK** to confirm that this folder is to be used.

10. Click **OK** to close the backup confirmation window.

11. Right-click your server, point to **All Tasks**, and click **Stop**.

12. Delete the WINS database:

    a. Click **Start**, click **Run**, type **cmd**, and press **Enter**.

    b. Type **cd \windows\system32\wins**, and press **Enter**.

    c. Type **del *.*** and press **Enter**.

    d. Type **Y** and press **Enter** to confirm the deletion.

    e. Type **exit**, and press **Enter**.

13. Right-click your server, and click **Restore Database**.

14. Click **OK** to use the default restore path of **C:\winsbak**.

15. Click **OK** to close the WINS restore confirmation.

16. View the active registrations:

   a. Right-click **Active Registrations**, and click **Display Records**.

   b. Click **Find Now** to accept the default filter and view all records. You may need to click **Active Registrations** to view the records.

   c. The records should be as they were when you backed up the database.

17. Close the WINS snap-in.

Activity 7-8: Removing WINS

Time Required: 5 minutes

Objective: Remove WINS from your server.

Description: You have upgraded all the client computers and services on your network so that NetBIOS is no longer required. In this activity you will remove the WINS Service from your server and configure your server to no longer be a WINS client.

1. If necessary, start your server and log on as Administrator.

2. Click **Start**, point to **Control Panel**, and click **Add or Remove Programs**.

3. Click **Add/Remove Windows Components**.

4. Scroll down in the components window, and double-click **Networking Services**.

5. Click the check box beside **Windows Internet Name Service (WINS)** to remove the checkmark, and click **OK**.

6. Click **Next** to remove WINS.

7. When the removal is complete, click **Finish**, and click **Close**.

8. Click **Start**, point to **Control Panel**, point to **Network Connections**, right-click **Classroom**, and click **Properties**.

9. Click **Internet Protocol (TCP/IP)**, and then click **Properties**.

10. Click **Advanced**, and then click the **WINS** tab.

11. If necessary, click the IP address of your server, and click **Remove**.

12. Click **OK**, click **OK** again, and close the Add or Remove Programs window.

WINS PROXY

A **WINS proxy** is used for computers that need to participate in NetBIOS name resolution but that cannot be configured to use WINS. These computers are often UNIX clients that need to access NetBIOS resources. Using a WINS proxy allows these clients to resolve NetBIOS names to IP addresses using records in a WINS database.

Windows Server 2003 can be used as a WINS proxy. This is enabled by setting the registry key HKEY_LOCAL_MACHINE\SYSTEM\CurrentControlSet\Services\NetBT\Parameters\EnableProxy to a value of 1.

All NetBIOS clients are capable of using broadcasts for name resolution. A WINS proxy receives the NetBIOS broadcasts on a local segment and forwards them to a WINS server. This allows any NetBIOS client to participate in WINS. The WINS proxy must be configured with the IP address of a WINS server.

Take the example of a UNIX client, which is unable to use WINS, accessing NetBIOS-based services on a Windows Server 2003 system. To use these services, it must resolve the name of the Windows Server 2003 system. The UNIX client sends a broadcast-based name resolution request. A WINS proxy on the local subnet sees the broadcast and forwards it to the WINS server as a properly formed WINS name query. The WINS server resolves the request and sends the response back to the WINS proxy. The WINS proxy broadcasts the response back to the UNIX client. Figure 7-16 shows the name query process when using a WINS proxy.

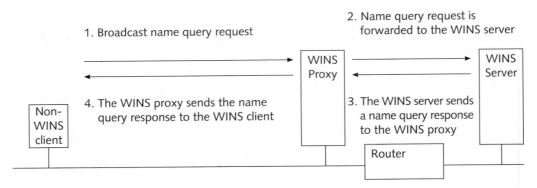

Figure 7-16   Name query process with a WINS proxy

CHAPTER SUMMARY

- The resolution of NetBIOS names to IP addresses is critical for pre-Windows 2000 clients. Pre-Windows 2000 clients use NetBIOS to find domain controllers and use network resources.

- There are four ways a NetBIOS name can be resolved: NetBIOS name cache, WINS, broadcast, and LMHOSTS file.

- Broadcast name resolution is not suitable for large networks because it doesn't work across routers.

- An LMHOSTS file is not suitable for large networks because the file needs to be copied to every server and workstation.

- A WINS server is a central repository for resolving NetBIOS names and offers several benefits over other NetBIOS name resolution methods. A WINS server functions across routers, can be dynamically updated, can be automated, offers client configuration through DHCP, and offers integration with DNS.

- There are four common tasks performed by a WINS server: name registration, name renewal, name release, and name query.

- When a name is registered with a WINS server, the client is assigned a TTL. If the name is not renewed by the end of the TTL, then the client stops using the name.

- When two or more WINS servers exist on a network, replication must be configured between them to synchronize their contents. Only changes to the WINS database are replicated between servers.

- There are two types of WINS replication: push and pull. Push replication is based on a certain number of changes triggering replication. Pull replication is based on a certain period of time passing.

- A static mapping can be configured for resources that are unable to register themselves with WINS.

- You can view the records in a WINS database, as well as delete them.

- The WINS database should be backed up like any other critical resource on a network.

- A WINS Proxy lets non-WINS clients use the WINS Service and verify the validity of NetBIOS names over the network. The WINS Proxy forwards broadcasts from the local segment to the WINS server.

KEY TERMS

broadcast — A packet that is addressed to all computers on a network. A broadcast for the local IP network is addressed to 255.255.255.255.

burst handling — A process used by a WINS server that cannot write name registrations to the WINS database fast enough to keep pace with the number of registrations. The WINS server ceases verifying that the names are not in use before sending out successful name registration requests with a short time to live.

extinction interval — The period of time unused records exist in the WINS database before being marked as extinct.

extinction timeout — The period of time extinct records exist in the WINS database before being removed.

LMHOSTS — A static text file located on the hard drive of NetBIOS clients that is used to resolve NetBIOS names to IP addresses.

name query request — A packet from a WINS client to a WINS server requesting the resolution of a NetBIOS name to an IP address.

name query response — A packet from a WINS server to a WINS client in response to a name query request. If the request is successful, this contains the IP address for the NetBIOS name in the original request.

name refresh request — A packet from a WINS client to a WINS server requesting that the registration for a NetBIOS name be renewed.

name refresh response — A packet from a WINS server to a WINS client in response to a name refresh request. If the response is successful, then the TTL of the client lease is extended.

name registration request — A packet generated by a WINS client and sent to a WINS server requesting to register the NetBIOS name and IP address.

name registration response — A packet generated by a WINS server in response to a name registration request from a WINS client. The response can be successful or negative.

name release request — A packet sent from a WINS client to a WINS server when the WINS client shuts down.

name release response — A packet from a WINS server to a WINS client in response to a name release request. This packet contains the NetBIOS name being released and a TTL of zero.

NetBIOS name cache — The file in which the results of Windows client NetBIOS name resolutions are stored for a short period of time. The storage of these resolutions increases network performance by reducing the number of name resolutions on the network.

NetBIOS name server — A server that holds a centralized repository of NetBIOS name information. The Microsoft implementation of a NetBIOS name server is WINS.

persistent connection — A connection that is created once and maintained over time for data transfer. This reduces communication overhead by reducing the number of packets used to establish connections over time.

pull replication — Replication between two WINS servers triggered by a defined amount of time passing.

push replication — Replication between two WINS servers triggered by a defined number of changes in the WINS database.

renewal interval — The time to live handed out to WINS clients when they register NetBIOS names.

replication partners — Two WINS servers that synchronize information in their databases.

static mapping — An entry manually placed in the WINS database. These are normally created for servers providing NetBIOS services that are unable to use WINS.

tombstoned — The term used to describe a WINS record that has been marked for deletion from all WINS servers. The tombstoned status is replicated among all WINS servers.

verification interval — The period of time a WINS server waits before validating a record that has been replicated from another WINS server.

Windows Internet Naming Service (WINS) — The service in Windows that resolves NetBIOS names to IP addresses as well as stores NetBIOS service information.

WINS proxy — A service that forwards local broadcast NetBIOS requests to a WINS server. This is implemented for NetBIOS clients that are unable to use WINS.

REVIEW QUESTIONS

1. Which of the following client operating systems require WINS to function properly in a routed network? (Choose all that apply.)

   a. Windows 95

   b. Windows 98

   c. Windows NT

   d. Windows 2000

   e. Windows XP

2. WINS is designed to be used with NetBIOS and which protocol?

   a. TCP/IP

   b. IPX/SPX

   c. NetBEUI

   d. AppleTalk

3. Which of the following situations use NetBIOS names? (Choose all that apply.)

   a. resolving a UNC path

   b. accessing the Web page *www.microsoft.com*

   c. opening My Network Places

   d. a Windows NT workstation logging on to the domain

4. Which NetBIOS name resolution method is used to resolve a name if it has recently been resolved?

   a. NetBIOS name cache

   b. WINS

   c. broadcast

   d. LMHOSTS

5. Which NetBIOS name resolution method can be used by all NetBIOS clients including UNIX clients?

   a. NetBIOS name cache

   b. WINS

   c. broadcast

   d. LMHOSTS

6. Which NetBIOS name resolution method dynamically updates a central database?

   a. NetBIOS name cache

   b. WINS

   c. broadcast

   d. LMHOSTS

7. Which NetBIOS name resolution method uses a static text configuration file on the client computers?

   a. NetBIOS name cache

   b. WINS

   c. broadcast

   d. LMHOSTS

8. What file extension is used with an LMHOSTS file?

   a. .txt

   b. .sam

   c. .dat

   d. .nbt

   e. No file extension is used.

9. Which of the following describe WINS? (Choose all that apply.)

   a. functions across routers

   b. uses a static text configuration file

   c. client configuration can be done with DHCP

   d. integrates with DNS

   e. uses broadcast packets

10. Which methods can be used to configure a Windows XP computer with the IP address of a WINS server? (Choose all that apply.)

   a. DNS

   b. DHCP

   c. broadcast

   d. Edit the properties of TCP/IP.

   e. multicast

11. Which WINS process is performed as the WINS client boots up?

   a. name registration

   b. name renewal

   c. name release

   d. name query

12. Which WINS process is used by WINS clients to resolve NetBIOS names to IP addresses?

   a. name registration

   b. name renewal

   c. name release

   d. name query

13. Which WINS process is initiated by WINS clients when one half of the time to live is complete?

   a. name registration

   b. name renewal

   c. name release

   d. name query

14. Which WINS process is initiated by WINS clients during shutdown?

    a. name registration

    b. name renewal

    c. name release

    d. name query

15. What process is implemented between two WINS servers to synchronize the contents of their databases?

    a. synchronization

    b. zone transfer

    c. database transfer

    d. replication

16. Which type of replication is triggered by a defined period of time passing?

    a. push replication

    b. pull replication

17. Records are deleted from the WINS database when the _____ is complete.

    a. renewal interval

    b. extinction interval

    c. extinction timeout

    d. verification interval

18. WINS clients send a name refresh request when one half of the _____ is complete.

    a. renewal interval

    b. extinction interval

    c. extinction timeout

    d. verification interval

19. What status is assigned to a WINS record that is being deleted from all WINS databases, not just a singe server?

    a. extinct

    b. expired

    c. dead

    d. tombstoned

    e. irrelevant

20. What can be done to accommodate NetBIOS servers that are unable to participate in a WINS environment? (Choose all that apply.)

    a. Create a HOSTS file on each client.

    b. Configure a WINS proxy.

    c. Create static mappings in the WINS database for each server.

    d. Configure replication between WINS servers.

CASE PROJECTS

Arctic University has a number of different client operating systems and older applications that require NetBIOS name resolution. These case projects will present you with several situations to consider.

Case Project 7-1: Choosing a Name Resolution Method

The Arctic University network is composed of hundreds of client and server computers. All of them need to be able to resolve NetBIOS names. As part of the network design process, create a document that analyzes the benefits and drawbacks of each name resolution method and decide which you think is most appropriate.

Case Project 7-2: Configuring Replication

Arctic University has eight physical locations connected by WAN links. Each of these WAN links is slow, so you have decided to install a WINS server at each location. Occasionally, clients at each location need to access NetBIOS resources in other locations. To accommodate this you must configure replication. What things need to be taken into consideration when designing the replication topology? What will the replication topology look like?

7

Case Project 7-3: Accommodating Non-Windows Operating Systems

The main campus of Arctic University is routed and has a variety of operating systems in use as both clients and servers. Many of the clients and servers are non-Windows operating systems such as Macintosh OS, Linux, and UNIX. Some of the non-Windows operating systems are not able to participate in WINS. How will you accommodate these operating systems?

8

CERTIFICATE SERVICES

After reading this chapter and completing the exercises, you will be able to:

♦ Describe the types of cryptography

♦ Understand how cryptography is used for encryption and digital signatures

♦ Understand the components of Certificate Services

♦ Install and configure Certificate Services

♦ Manage certificates

Certificates are used to encrypt and decrypt data such as e-mail and files. In addition, certificates are used as part of the Encrypting File System (EFS) built into Windows 2000 and newer versions of Windows. In this chapter you will learn about the different types of cryptography used with Windows Server 2003, and how these types of cryptography are applied. You will also learn how to install, configure, and manage Certificate Services.

CRYPTOGRAPHY

Cryptography is the process of **encrypting** and **decrypting** messages and files to ensure that they are read only by the intended recipient or recipients. When a message is encrypted, it is converted to a format that is unreadable. Decryption is the reverse of encryption, and this process makes the data readable again. The term **"ciphertext"** is used to refer to encrypted information.

To encrypt information, an **algorithm** is used. In computerized cryptography, an algorithm is a mathematical formula that is used to modify the data. Also required for encryption and decryption are keys. A **key** is a large number that is difficult to guess, and is used in combination with an algorithm to encrypt and decrypt data.

There are four main objectives for cryptography. Depending on the method of cryptography used, some or all of these objectives can be achieved. The objectives are:

- *Confidentiality*—Ensure that the data cannot be read by an unauthorized person.
- *Integrity*—Ensure that the data has not been modified.
- *Nonrepudiation*—Guarantee that the sender or creator cannot deny that the process happened.
- *Authentication*—The identity of the sender or creator can be verified.

Depending on goals that need to be accomplished, one or several types of encryption may be used. The three generic types of encryption are:

- Symmetrical
- Asymmetrical
- Hash

Symmetrical Encryption

Symmetrical encryption uses a single key to encrypt and decrypt data. For example, if User A sends a file to User B using symmetrical encryption to encrypt the file, then User B decrypts the file using the same key that is used to encrypt the file.

This type of encryption is relatively simple from a mathematical perspective. A computer can symmetrically encrypt large amounts of data quickly. Consequently, this is this type of encryption used when encrypting files and large amounts of data across network transmissions.

Asymmetrical Encryption

Asymmetrical encryption uses two separate keys, called the **public key** and the **private key**, to encrypt and decrypt data. Anything encrypted by the public key can be decrypted with the private key, and anything encrypted by the private key is decrypted with the public key.

When asymmetrical encryption is used, the public key is made available to anyone that wants it. The private key is held only by the individual, or computer, to which it is assigned. This provides enhanced security when two people or computers need to encrypt communication data because the private key is never transmitted on the network. There is a security risk with symmetrical encryption if the key is moved across the network.

This type of encryption is more mathematically complex than symmetrical encryption. As a result, asymmetrical encryption requires more processing power than symmetrical encryption. Thus, it is not practical or efficient to use asymmetrical encryption for large amounts of data.

Hash Encryption

Hash encryption is unique because it is one-way encryption. A hash algorithm uses a single key to convert data to a **hash value**. The hash value is a summary of the data. For example, a 128-bit hash value might be generated for a 100 KB file. Even if the algorithm is publicly known, the hash value cannot be decrypted because the hash value does not contain enough information. The purpose of a hash value is to be a unique identifier, not to secure data.

This type of encryption is often used to store passwords. This ensures that the database storing the hash values for the passwords can be publicly available, but the actual passwords are unknown. To verify a password, the system applies the hash algorithm to a submitted password and compares the newly generated hash value with the hash value in the password database. If the two hash values match, then the password is correct. If the two hash values do not match, then the password is incorrect.

USES FOR CRYPTOGRAPHY

Cryptography is commonly used for a number of computing tasks where confidentiality is required, the integrity of data must be ensured, or the identity of the sender must be verified. Nonrepudiation can also be attained if a randomized sequence number or time stamp is included in the encrypted data. Depending on the goal, various types of cryptography may be used. Three common tasks that use different types of encryption are:

- Encrypting e-mail
- Ensuring data integrity with digital signatures
- Securing data communication with Secure Sockets Layer (SSL)

Encrypting E-mail

Encrypting e-mail ensures that a message in transit cannot be read by unauthorized people. Sending an encrypted e-mail message between two clients using asymmetrical encryption requires each user to have a public key and a private key. The private key is known only to the person to which it is assigned. The public key is known to all clients, and thus is not inherently secure.

The process for encrypting e-mail uses the public and private keys of the recipient. First, the sender creates an e-mail message. Then the e-mail software used by the sender encrypts the message using the public key of the recipient. The public key of the recipient may be published in a directory or given to the sender via e-mail before the encryption process is performed. The encrypted message is then sent to the recipient. The intended recipient receives the encrypted message and their e-mail software decrypts the message using the recipient's private key. This process is shown in Figure 8-1.

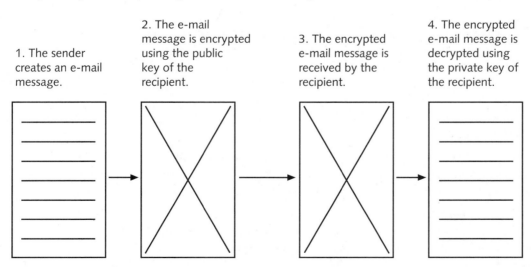

Figure 8-1   Encrypting e-mail

Using this type of encryption, no one is able to read the message while it travels from the sender to the recipient. The message has been encrypted with the public key of the recipient and can only be decrypted by using the private key of the recipient. The private key of the recipient is known only to the recipient.

Digital Signatures

A **digital signature** is used to ensure that a message has not been modified while in transit and that it truly came from the named sender. This is important for electronically delivering information such as contracts and agreements.

 A digital signature does not encrypt the contents of a message.

The public and private keys of the sender are used for a digital signature. First the sender creates the document that will be signed. Then a hash algorithm is used to create a hash value of the document, and the hash value is encrypted with the private key of the sender. Then the sender transmits the original document and the encrypted hash value. This process is shown in Figure 8-2.

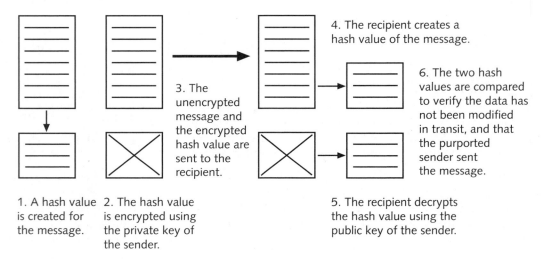

4. The recipient creates a hash value of the message.

3. The unencrypted message and the encrypted hash value are sent to the recipient.

6. The two hash values are compared to verify the data has not been modified in transit, and that the purported sender sent the message.

1. A hash value is created for the message.

2. The hash value is encrypted using the private key of the sender.

5. The recipient decrypts the hash value using the public key of the sender.

Figure 8-2   Digital signature

The recipient takes the original document and creates a hash value using the same hash algorithm as the sender. The recipient then decrypts the encrypted hash value from the sender using the public key of the sender. If the two hash values match, then the document was not modified in transit. This also verifies the message came from the named sender, as only that sender has access to the private key that matches the public key used.

Secure Sockets Layer

Secure Sockets Layer (SSL) is a Transport layer protocol that can be used with any application protocol that is designed to communicate with it. SSL is used to secure communication between Web servers and Web browsers, e-mail clients and e-mail servers, as well as a variety of other services.

Servers are the only participants in SSL that are required to be configured with a public key and a private key. The public key and private key are used to encrypt a symmetrical key and make it secure during transit. The symmetrical key is used to encrypt data transferred between the client and server.

When a Web browser is connecting to a secure Web server, it uses Hypertext Transport Protocol Secure (HTTPS). When the browser connects to the server, the server sends the client the public key of the server.

The browser then generates a key to be used for symmetrical encryption, encrypts it using the public key of the server, and sends the encrypted symmetrical key to the server. This process is shown in Figure 8-3.

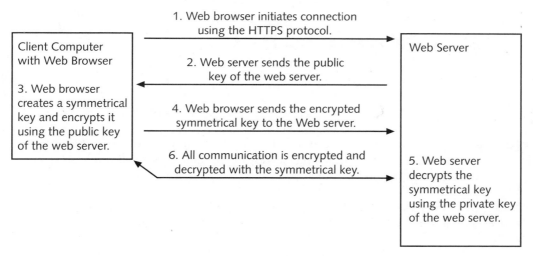

Figure 8-3   Secure Sockets Layer (SSL)

The server decrypts the symmetrical key using the private key of the server. The symmetrical key has been securely transmitted from the browser to the server, and both the browser and the server have a copy of the symmetrical key. The symmetrical key is now used to encrypt and decrypt all data sent between the browser and the server.

CERTIFICATE SERVICES COMPONENTS

Certificate Services is the Microsoft implementation of **public key infrastructure (PKI)**. PKI is a system for creating and managing public keys, private keys, and **certificates**. A certificate contains two things: information about a user or computer, and a public key. There is no standard that defines how PKI overall is supposed to work, but there are several standards for PKI components. One of the standards, **X.509**, was created by the International Telecommunications Union – Telecommunication (ITU-T) and defines how a certificate should be structured.

 The terms "certificate," "digital certificate," and "public key certificate" are often used interchangeably when reading documentation from different vendors.

PKI is composed of several components:

- Certificates
- Certification authority (also known as certificate authority)
- A Certificate Revocation List (CRL)
- Certificate-enabled applications

Certificates

A certificate defined by the X.509 standard has fields such as subject (or user name), serial number, validity period, public key, issuer name, and issuer signature. An X.509 certificate is not private information, and can be used to distribute a public key to validate a digital signature or create encrypted e-mail.

The issuer name and signature are an important part of the certificate because they are used to validate the certificate. The signature of the issuer ensures that the certificate has not been modified; otherwise, anyone could make up a certificate for themselves, and thus the certificate would be rendered useless as a means of identifying the certificate holder.

 The certificates created by Certificate Services are X.509 certificates.

Certification Authority

A **certification authority** is a server that issues certificates to client computers, applications, or users. The certification authority is responsible for taking certificate-signing requests from clients and approving them. As part of the approval process, the identity of the requestor is verified.

 When implementing PKI, you can install your own internal certification authority using Certificate Services, or you can buy certificates from a third-party certification authority, such as VeriSign or Thawte.

When a certificate is presented as proof of identity, it must be validated. This is accomplished using the digital signature of the certification authority. For a client application to trust that this information in the certificate is correct, it must trust the certification authority that issued the certificate.

Every Web browser and many other applications include a list of **trusted root certification authorities**. These are certificate authorities that are trusted by the application. When using Internet Explorer, any Web site using a certificate signed by one of the trusted root certification authorities is accepted without any messages appearing on the screen.

However, if a Web site is using a certificate that is not issued by a trusted root certification authority, then a warning message appears on the screen, as shown in Figure 8-4. This error indicates that Internet Explorer does not trust the source of the certificate. This is not acceptable for most applications as users will be nervous about using the service if there is an error message indicating it is not trusted.

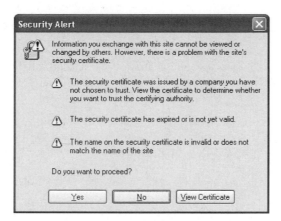

Figure 8-4   Certification authority warning message

Third-party certification authorities are in the list of trusted root certificate authorities used by Internet Explorer. If you implement an internal certification authority using Certificate Services, your certification authority is not automatically included in the list of trusted root certificate authorities. You need to add your internal certification authority to the list of trusted root certificate authorities on each workstation to prevent warning messages from appearing.

In general, internal certification authorities are only used with internal clients because you have control over internal client computers and can add the internal certification authority to the list of trusted root certification authorities. In most cases, you do not have the ability to visit clients outside of your organization to configure them to trust your internal certification authority.

The main benefits of using an internal certification authority are cost and control. With an internal certification authority you can create as many certificates as you like for no cost other than the time spent managing the certification authority and approving certificate requests. You also have complete control over when and how certificates are issued.

Third-party certification authorities are used when an application or server needs to be trusted by clients outside of your organization where you do not have control over their computers and applications. Because a third-party certification authority is already listed as a trusted root certification authority, there is no need to modify the client. The main disadvantage of a third-party certification authority is cost. You must pay for each certificate provided.

Activity 8-1: Viewing Trusted Root Certification Authorities

Time Required: 5 minutes

Objective: View the trusted root certification authorities installed by default on Windows Server 2003.

Description: You are considering using a third-party certification authority to provide certificates for Web servers using SSL. However, the lowest bid on the contract is so low you are concerned about the quality. To verify that this company is in the list of trusted root certification authorities installed by default, you view the list of trusted root certification authorities included with Windows Server 2003.

1. If necessary, start your server and log on as Administrator.
2. Click **Start**, point to **Control Panel**, and click **Internet Options**.
3. Click the **Content** tab, and click **Certificates**.
4. Click **Trusted Root Certification Authorities**, and view the list.
5. Click **Close**.
6. Click **Cancel**.

Certificate Revocation List

The certification authority maintains a **Certificate Revocation List (CRL)**. This is a list of certificates issued by the certification authority that are no longer valid. The administrator adds certificates to this list. It is not created automatically.

Certificates are added to the CRL if you think there has been a security breach or something unexpected has happened. If the private key of a user is stolen, or if a user unexpectedly quits, then you would add his or her certificate to the CRL to prevent it from being used fraudulently.

Each certificate issued by the certification authority has an expiry date. If the certificate is presented after this date, then, depending on the application, a warning message appears, or the application fails. Certificates that have expired are not added to the CRL because the certificate has the expiry date embedded in it.

Certificate-enabled Applications

Not all applications can use certificates for encryption and authentication. An application must be designed by its developer to use certificates. Some of the more common applications for certificates include e-mail clients, Web browsers, and smart cards.

Windows client computers have the ability to store certificates in a store that can be used by multiple applications. Many certificate-enabled applications running on Windows use this central windows store, but other applications store certificates in a private database.

INSTALLING AND MANAGING CERTIFICATE SERVICES

If you have made the decision to implement an internal certification authority, then you will install Certificate Services on Windows Server 2003. There are two classes of certification authorities available:

- Enterprise
- Stand-alone

Enterprise certification authorities integrate with Active Directory. As a result, an enterprise certification authority has an expanded feature set when compared with stand-alone certification authorities.

When issuing certificates, an enterprise certification authority is able to use certificate templates, which define how a particular certificate can be used. Access to these templates is based on the permissions of the user requesting the certificate. This allows the certificate creation process to be entirely automated with no action on the part of an administrator.

A **stand-alone certification authority** does not integrate with Active Directory. As a result, it is unable to automatically issue certificates based on a user object in Active Directory. All certificate requests must be manually approved by an administrator. Certificate templates cannot be used by a stand-alone certification authority because access to the certificate templates is based on user permissions that are not understood by a stand-alone certification authority. A stand-alone certification authority also cannot issue certificates used for smart card authentication.

Both enterprise certification authorities and stand-alone certification authorities do publish CRLs in Active Directory. This ensures that, regardless of which certification authority you choose, the CRL is accessible to client computers. In addition, both classes of certification authority create a CertificationAuthority object in Active Directory to describe themselves.

Only enterprise certification authorities use Active Directory as a publication point for user certificates. A certificate is published as part of the user object. For example, if user Bob is issued a certificate by an enterprise certification authority, then the certificate is added as an attribute of Bob's user object.

If you are issuing certificates internally in an Active Directory-enabled environment, it is wise to use an enterprise certification authority to take advantage of the extra features it affords. If you are issuing certificates externally or in an environment where Active Directory does not exist, then you can use a stand-alone certification authority.

Certificate Hierarchy

A **certificate hierarchy** is a chain of trust through which client computers and applications are assured that a certificate is valid. Within the hierarchy, a certification authority is either a root certification authority or a subordinate certification authority.

A **root certification authority** is a starting point for a certificate hierarchy. This is the certification authority that must be trusted by client computers. Only if the root certification authority is trusted can certificates issued by the root certification authority be accepted by client computers and applications.

A **subordinate certification authority** is certified by another certification authority, usually a root certification authority. After a subordinate certification authority has been certified, it can issue certificates based on the trusted status of the certification authority that certified it. For example, the server SECURE1 has been installed as a root certification authority, and the server SECURE2 has been certified as a subordinate certification authority. If a client trusts the server SECURE1, then it also trusts certificates issued by SECURE2. The entire hierarchy is trusted based on the root certification authority being trusted.

It is very important that root certificate authorities are kept secure. If the security of a root certification authority is compromised, then all certificates issued by it and all its subordinate certificate authorities are considered compromised and must be revoked and reissued. For example, if the private key of the root certification authority were stolen, all certificates issued by the root certification authority would need to be revoked. This includes the certificates that certify the subordinate certification authorities. The certificates issued by the subordinate certification authorities would also need to be revoked. Then the root certification authority must be recreated, the subordinate certificate authorities recertified, and new certificates issued to all users.

Installing Certificate Services

When installing a certification authority, the first step in the installation requires you to choose which type of certification authority you are installing: enterprise root CA, stand-alone root CA, enterprise subordinate CA, or stand-alone subordinate CA, as shown in Figure 8-5. You also have the option to configure custom settings for the key pair and CA certificate.

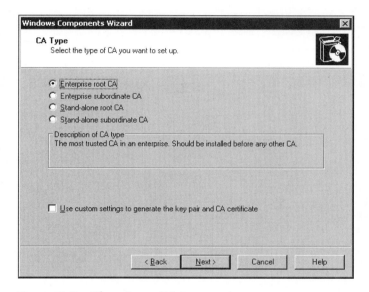

Figure 8-5 Choosing a CA type

The custom settings for the key pair and CA certificate, shown in Figure 8-6, allow you to configure the **cryptographic service provider (CSP)**, hash algorithm, key length, or to use an existing key. The CSP determines the algorithms you can use and the key length that is used. The hash algorithm is the mathematical formula that is used in the creation of the CA certificate. The key length is the number of bits in the key used in the creation of the CA certificate. A longer key is more secure. You are also given the option to use an existing key. An existing key is used when Certificate Services is being reinstalled.

The second step, shown in Figure 8-7, requires you to assign a name to the certification authority. This is the name of the CertificateAuthority object created in Active Directory. If this is a root certification authority then you can choose the lifetime of the certificate. If this is a subordinate certification authority, then the lifetime is specified by the certification authority that authorizes it.

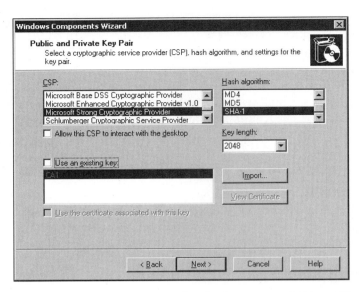

Figure 8-6   Custom settings for the key pair and CA certificate

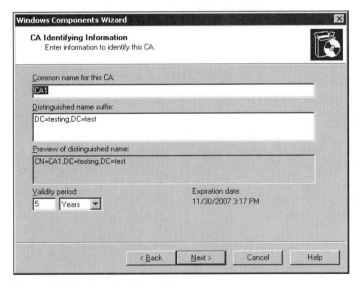

Figure 8-7   Naming the CA

The third step, shown in Figure 8-8, allows you to set the location of a certificate database and certificate database log. The default location for both locations is C:\WINDOWS\system32\certlog. You can also specify a shared folder for storing the CA certificate and information about the certification authority. The information in the shared folder is normally available only through a Web browser. The name of the share created for the folder is CertConfig.

The fourth step, shown in Figure 8-9, is only required when installing a subordinate certification authority. A subordinate certification authority must be certified by another certification authority, and this can be done directly across the network or via a certification request that is saved to file. If the parent certification authority is online, then making the request directly across the network is faster. However, if the parent certification authority is a third-party certification authority outside of your network, then you are required to save the request to file. After the request is saved to file, it must be sent to the parent certification authority. The process for sending the request varies depending on the parent certification authority.

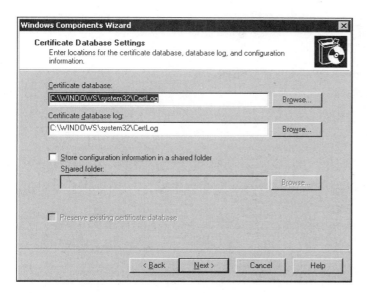

Figure 8-8   Choosing database and log locations

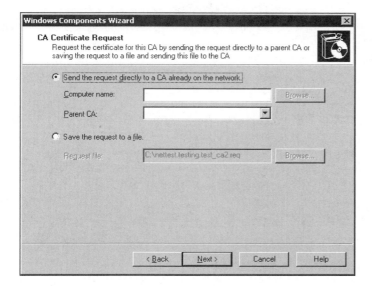

Figure 8-9   Certificate request for subordinate CA

When a subordinate certification authority saves a request to file, the installation is not complete. The response to the request is received as a file, and must be imported to certify the subordinate certification authority. To import the response, open the Certification Authority snap-in, right-click the subordinate certification authority, click Install CA certificate, browse to the response file, click the response file, and click Open.

Activity 8-2: Installing Certificate Services

Time Required: 10 minutes

Objective: Install Certificate Services and configure your server as an enterprise root certification authority.

Description: Arctic University is interested in enhancing the level of security for the workstations in the Payroll Department. To do this, smart cards will be issued to authorized payroll staff, and the workstations will be configured to accept only smart card authentication. You will install Certificate Services to enable your server to create certificates that can be used for smart card authentication.

1. If necessary, start your server and log on as Administrator.

2. Click **Start**, point to **Control Panel**, and click **Add or Remove Programs**.

3. Click **Add/Remove Windows Components**.

4. Double-click **Certificate Services**.

5. Click the check box beside **Certificate Services CA,** and click **Yes**.

6. Click **OK**, and click **Next**.

7. Click **Enterprise root CA** if it is not already selected, and click **Next**.

8. In the Common name for this CA box, type **CA*xx***, where *xx* is your student number, and click **Next**.

9. Click **Next** to accept the default locations for the certificate database and certificate database log. If prompted for the Windows Server 2003 CD-ROM, click **OK**. Click **Browse**, and select the **C:\I386** folder. Click **Open**, then click **OK** in the Files needed dialog box.

10. Click **OK** to acknowledge that Web enrollment for Certificate Services is unavailable until IIS is installed.

11. Click **Finish**, and then close the Add or Remove Programs window.

Backup and Restore Certificate Services

Certificate Services is normally backed up as part of the daily backup process on Windows Server 2003. Certificate Services is included with the backup of system state data, which is the preferred method for backing up Certificate Services.

You also have the option to manually back up and restore just Certificate Services using the Certification Authority snap-in. A manual backup and restore of Certificate Services is necessary if you do not back up the system state data on a server or if you do not wish to restore all of the system state data on a server. For example, if you back up the system state data on a server only once per week and have made many registry changes since the last backup, then you may prefer to restore just the Certificate Services database.

Activity 8-3: Back up Certificate Services

Time Required: 5 minutes

Objective: Perform a manual backup of Certificate Services.

Description: You have installed Certificate Services to issue certificates for Arctic University. Soon after installation, you issue certificates for over 200 staff members. You are concerned that the system state data on this server will not be backed up for another 16 hours during the nightly backup. To be sure that you do not need to reissue the certificates, you decide to backup the Certificate Services database manually.

1. If necessary, start your server and log on as Administrator.

2. Click **Start**, point to **Administrative Tools**, and click **Certification Authority**.

3. Right-click your server, point to **All Tasks**, and click **Back up CA**.

4. Click **Next** to start the Certification Authority Backup Wizard.

5. Click **Private key and CA certificate** to select them for backup.

6. Click **Certificate database and certificate database log** to select them for backup.

7. In the Back up to this location box, type **C:\CERTBAK**, and press **Enter**.

8. Click **OK** to create the C:\CERTBAK directory.

9. In the Password box, type **password**.

10. In the Confirm password box, type **password**.

11. Click **Next** and click **Finish**.

12. Close the Certification Authority snap-in.

Activity 8-4: Restoring the Certificate Services Database

Time Required: 5 minutes

Objective: Perform a manual restore of Certificate Services.

Description: A hard drive in the server running Certificate Services for Arctic University has failed. You have replaced the hard drive and restored the most recent backup from one week ago. However, many certificates have been issued since the most recent backup that includes the system state data. Fortunately, you performed a manual backup of Certificate Services earlier today. To bring Certificate Services to the most recent state possible, you will restore from the manual backup.

1. If necessary, start your server and log on as Administrator.

2. Click **Start**, point to **Administrative Tools**, and click **Certification Authority**.

3. Right-click your server, point to **All Tasks**, and click **Restore CA**.

4. Click **OK** to stop Certificate Services.

5. Click **Next** to start the Certification Authority Restore Wizard.

6. Click **Private key and CA certificate** to select them for restore.

7. Click **Certificate database and certificate database log** to select them for restore.

8. In the Restore from this location box, type **C:\CERTBAK**, and press **Enter**.

9. In the Password box, type **password**, and click **Next**.

10. Click **Finish**.

11. Click **Yes** to restart Certificate Services.

12. Close the Certification Authority snap-in.

MANAGING CERTIFICATES

Implementing Certificate Services first requires you to plan and implement a certification hierarchy. Once the hierarchy is implemented by installing Certificate Services and choosing the class and type of each server, then certificates must be issued and managed.

The tasks related to issuing and managing certificates are:

- Issuing certificates
- Renewing certificates
- Revoking certificates
- Publishing a Certificate Revocation List
- Importing and exporting certificates
- Mapping accounts to certificates

Most certificate management is done using snap-ins. However, there is a command-line utility, CERTUTIL, that can be used to manage both certificates and Certificate Services. This can be useful for scripting maintenance.

Issuing Certificates

Certificates can be requested using the **Certificate Request Wizard**, the Certificate Services Web pages, and autoenrollment. The Certificate Request Wizard and autoenrollment are available only for enterprise certification authorities, while the Certificate Services Web pages can be used by both stand-alone and enterprise certificate authorities.

The Certificate Request Wizard

The Certificate Request Wizard is run by users to create certificates. The types of certificates that can be created are controlled by **certificate templates**. The Administrator can create, configure, and control access to these templates. Users are given the option to create certificates based on the templates to which they have either read or enroll permissions. Table 8-1 lists the default certificate templates available on an enterprise certification authority.

Table 8-1   Default Certificate Templates

Certificate Template	Description
EFS Recovery Agent	Issued to users; it can be used for file recovery for the encrypting file system (EFS)
Basic EFS	Issued to users; it can be used to encrypt files for the encrypting file system (EFS)
Domain Controller	Issued to computers; it can be used for client authentication and server authentication
Web Server	Issued to computers; it can be used for server authentication
Computer	Issued to computers; it can be used for client authentication and server authentication
User	Issued to users; it can be used for the encrypting file system (EFS), secure e-mail, and client authentication
Subordinate Certification Authority	Issued to computers; it can be used for any task
Administrator	Issued to users; it can be used for the encrypting file system (EFS), secure e-mail, client authentication, and Microsoft trust list signing

The modification and creation of templates is accomplished by using the Certificate Templates snap-in. The easiest way to access this snap-in is through the Certification Authority snap-in. In the Certification Authority snap-in, double-click the server, right-click Certificate Templates, and click Manage. Access control for templates is also controlled using this snap-in.

The Certificate Request Wizard is initiated with the Certificates snap-in. This snap-in is not part of Administrative Tools. You need to start an empty MMC console and add the Certificates snap-in.

Certificates requested using the Certificate Request Wizard are automatically issued if the default settings are used. This is done because access to the certificate templates used by the Certificate Request Wizard allows you to control access. However, individual templates can be configured such that manual approval is required.

Activity 8-5: Requesting a Certificate

Time Required: 10 minutes

Objective: Request a user certificate using the Certificate Request Wizard.

Description: Arctic University has completed the installation of Certificate Services, and users now need to be issued certificates. A colleague is going to be helping each user request their certificate, but first you must show him how it is done. You will request a user certificate using the Certificate Request Wizard.

    1. If necessary start your server and log on as Administrator of the Arctic.local domain.

    2. Create a new user using Active Directory Users and Computers

       a. Click **Start**, click **Run**, type **mmc**, and press **Enter**.

    b. Click **File**, click **Add/Remove Snap-in**, click **Add**, double-click **Active Directory Users and Computers**, click **Close**, and click **OK**.

    c. Double-click **Active Directory Users and Computers**, double-click **arctic.local**, right-click **Users**, point to **New**, and click **User**.

    d. In the First name box type **Studentxx**, where xx is your student number.

    e. In the User logon name box type **Studentxx**, where xx is your student number.

    f. Click **Next**.

    g. In the Password box type **Password!**.

    h. In the Confirm password box type **Password!**.

    i. Click **User must change password at next logon** to deselect this option.

    j. Click **Next**, and click **Finish**.

    k. Close the Active Directory Users and Computers snap-in. Click **No,** if prompted to save the console settings.

3. Log off as Administrator

4. Log on as **Studentxx**, where xx is your student number. Use Password! as the password.

5. If necessary, click **Start**, click **Run**, type **mmc**, and press **Enter**.

6. Click **File**, and click **Add/Remove Snap-in**.

7. Click **Add**, and double-click **Certificates**.

8. Click **Close** and click **OK**.

9. In the left pane, double-click **Certificates – Current User**, and click **Personal**.

10. Right-click **Personal**, point to **All Tasks**, and click **Request New Certificate**.

11. Click **Next** to start the Certificate Request Wizard.

12. Click **User**, click the **Advanced** checkbox, and click **Next**.

13. Click **Next** to accept the default cryptographic service provider information.

14. Ensure that the CA selected is your server. If your server is not selected click **Browse** and select your server. Click **Next** to continue**.**

15. In the Friendly name box type **MyUserCertificate**, and click **Next**.

16. Click **Finish**.

17. Click **OK** to close the successful completion message.

18. To view your certificate, double-click **Certificates** in the right pane.

19. Close the Certificates snap-in. If you are asked to save the console settings, click **No**.

20. Log off as Studentxx.

Certificate Services Web Pages

The Certificate Services Web pages can be used by users to request certificates from both enterprise certification authorities and stand-alone certification authorities.

When a stand-alone certification authority is used, the certificate request must be manually approved by an Administrator. After the certificate is approved, it is retrieved through a Web page as well. When an enterprise certification authority is used, the certificate request is automatically generated. However, the user must still retrieve the certificate from a Web page.

Authentication is an important consideration when using an enterprise certification authority and the Certificate Services Web pages. When a user accesses Web pages through Internet Information Services (IIS), there is no authentication by default. IIS automatically logs in as a user named IUSR_*servername*. Whatever permissions are granted to this user, determine the permissions of anonymous Web users. If you do not force Web users to authenticate before requesting a certificate, the subject of the certificate (user) will be IUSR_*servername*.

You can force users to authenticate by restricting the file permissions for the folder storing the Certificate Services Web pages. If IUSR_*servername* does not have permission to read the files in C:\WINDOWS\ system32\certsrv, then IIS will ask for authentication information. The users can then authenticate using their username and password. The user must have permissions for the C:\WINDOWS\system32\certsrv.

The Certificate Services Web pages are accessed through the URL *http://server/certsrv*.

IIS is required for the Certificate Services Web pages. IIS is not installed on Windows Server 2003 during a default installation because of security enhancements. If IIS is installed after the Certificate Services Web pages, then the administrator must create a virtual directory called CERTSRV that points to C:\WINDOWS\system32\certsrv. This is done automatically if IIS is installed first.

Autoenrollment

Autoenrollment issues certificates to users automatically without any intervention on the part of the user. If certificates are required for a task where there is no user intervention, then this can be very useful. Users receive their certificates, and the application works without the user being inconvenienced by being asked questions they may not understand.

Autoenrollment is a new feature of Windows Server 2003, and works only when the domain controller is Windows Server 2003 and the client is Windows XP. To enable autoenrollment, perform the following steps:

1. Duplicate an existing certificate using the Certificate Templates snap-in. Autoenrollment is automatically enabled.

2. Ensure that the option **Publish certificate in Active Directory** is selected.

3. On the security tab of the certificate, add the required users or groups, and assign them the **enroll** and **autoenroll** permissions.

4. Enable the new certificate template in the Certification Authority snap-in.

5. Configure a Group Policy to enable **Enroll certificates automatically**.

For step-by-step instructions on enabling and configuring autoenrollment, search for "autoenrollment" in Help and Support.

Renewing Certificates

All certificates are issued with an expiration date. This ensures that in the case of a certificate being compromised, it is not a security risk for an extended period of time. In the case of an employee unexpectedly leaving, this ensures that the employee does not have access to company resources after the certificate has expired.

To avoid an interruption in service, a user must renew a certificate before it expires. The lifetime of a certificate is defined by the administrator when a certificate template is created. A shorter lifetime is more secure than a longer one. However a shorter lifetime also inconveniences the user by forcing them to renew their certificate more often.

If autoenrollment is used to issue certificates, it can also be used to renew certificates. In this case, the lifetime of the certificate can be kept very short with no inconvenience to the user.

Renewing a certificate is accomplished by the user through the Certificates snap-in.

Revoking Certificates

When a certificate has been compromised or a user has left the company you need to revoke the certificate. This places the certificate on the CRL of the certification authority. Windows 2000 and newer clients automatically download the CRL for Active Directory.

Windows Server 2003 publishes delta CRLs in addition to the entire CRL. The delta CRLs are changes that have occurred since the full CRL was published. A client that downloads the delta CRLs rather than the full CRL helps to reduce network traffic in high-volume environments.

A CRL has a default lifetime of seven days. After a client has downloaded the CRL, it does not download another copy until the local copy expires in seven days. This applies even if a new CRL has been published. The CRL lifetime can be changed in the Certification Authority snap-in by right-clicking Revoked Certificates, and clicking Properties. Figure 8-10 shows the Revoked Certificates properties.

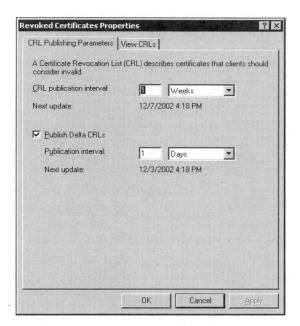

Figure 8-10   Revoked Certificates properties

Activity 8-6: Revoking a Certificate

Time Required: 10 minutes

Objective: Revoke a certificate and publish a new CRL.

Description: A laptop used by one of the professors has been stolen from an office on campus. The laptop has a user certificate stored on it that was used by the professor for digital signatures. To ensure that other users are informed that this certificate is no longer valid for signatures, you will revoke the certificate and publish a new CRL. After the certificate is revoked you remove it from your server.

1. If necessary, start your server and log on as Administrator.

2. Click **Start**, point to **Administrative Tools**, and click **Certification Authority**.

3. Double-click your server.

4. Click **Issued Certificates**.

5. Click the certificate you created in Activity 8-5. This certificate has the Requester Name of **ARCTIC\Student***xx*, where *xx* is your student number.

6. Click **Action**, point to **All Tasks**, and click **Revoke Certificate**.

7. In the Reason code box, click the option **Key Compromise**, and click **Yes**.

8. Click **Revoked Certificates**. Notice that the certificate you revoked is now listed here.

9. Click **Action**, point to **All Tasks**, and click **Publish**.

10. Click **OK** to publish a new CRL.

11. Close the Certification Authority snap-in.

12. Log off as Administrator, and log on as student*xx*, where *xx* is your student number. Use **Password!** as the password.

13. Click **Start**, click **Run**, type **mmc**, and press **Enter**.

14. Click **File**, and click **Add/Remove Snap-in**.

15. Click **Add**, and double-click **Certificates**.

16. Click **Close** and click **OK**.

17. In the left pane, double-click **Certificates – Current User**, double-click **Personal**, and click **Certificates**.

18. Right-click your certificate, click **Delete**, and click **Yes** to confirm the deletion.

19. Close the Certificates snap-in. If prompted to save console settings, click **No**.

20. Log off as Student*xx*.

Importing and Exporting Certificates

There are several times you may want to move or copy certificates from one computer to another. If a user receives a new workstation, you will want to move their certificates to the new workstation. In addition, if a user uses more than one workstation, you will want to create copies of their certificates on each workstation.

When a key is exported, you can choose several standard formats:

- DER encoded binary X.509 (.cer)—This type of file is only available if the private key is not being exported. This is a standard file type used by non-Windows applications and operating systems.

- Base-64 encoded X.509 (.cer)—This type of file is only available if the private key is not being exported. This is a standard file type used by non-Windows applications and operating systems.

- Cryptographic Message Syntax Standard – PKCS #7 Certificates (.p7b)—This type of file is only available if the private key is not being exported. This is a standard file type used by non-Windows applications and operating systems. The advantage of this file format is the ability to export all of the certificates in the certification path.

- Personal Information Exchange – PKCS #12 (.pks)—This is the only option available if the private key is being exported. This type of file uses a password to encrypt the contents of the file. When the file is imported, the password must be entered to decrypt the file.

Activity 8-7: Moving a Certificate

Time Required: 10 minutes

Objective: Move a user certificate from one computer to another.

Description: A professor has received a new laptop computer. He has been using a personal certificate to access a secure Web site. It must be moved to the new laptop. In this activity, you will create the personal certificate, export the certificate, and then import it, all on the same computer. Normally the certificate would be exported on the old computer, and then imported on the new computer.

1. If necessary, start your server and log on as **Studentxx**, where xx is your student number. Use **Password!** as the password.

2. Click **Start**, click **Run**, type **mmc**, and press **Enter**.

3. Click **File**, and click **Add/Remove Snap-in**.

4. Click **Add**, and double-click **Certificates**.

5. Click **Close** and click **OK**.

6. Double-click **Certificates – Current User**, and click **Personal**.

7. Right-click **Personal**, point to **All Tasks**, and click **Request New Certificate**.

8. Click **Next** to start the Certificate Request Wizard.

9. Click **User**, click the **Advanced** checkbox, and click **Next**.

10. Click **Next** to accept the default cryptographic service provider information.

11. Ensure that the CA selected is your server. If your server is not selected click **Browse** and select your server. Click **Next** to continue.

12. In the Friendly name box type **MyUserCertificate2** and click **Next**.

13. Click **Finish**.

14. Click **OK** to close the successful completion message.

15. To view your certificate, double-click **Certificates** in the right pane.

16. Right-click your certificate, point to **All Tasks**, and click **Export**.

17. Click **Next** to start the Certificate Export Wizard.

18. Click **Yes, export the private key**, and click **Next**.

19. To accept the default settings for file format click **Next**.

20. In the Password box type **password**, in the Confirm password box type **password**, and click **Next**.

21. Click **Browse**, click **My Documents** to select it if required, in the File name box type **MyCertificate**, click **Save**, and click **Next**. To make it easier to transfer this file you would normally save it to a network drive or a floppy disk.

22. Click **Finish**, and click **OK**.

23. Right-click your certificate, click **Delete**, and click **Yes**.

24. Right-click **Certificates**, point to **All Tasks**, and click **Import**.

25. Click **Next** to start the Certificate Import Wizard.

26. Click **Browse**, and click **My Documents** to select it, if necessary.

27. In the Files of type list box, click the down arrow, and click **Personal Information Exchange (*.pfx;*.p12)**.

28. Double-click **MyCertificate.pfx**, and click **Next**. If your server is configured to hide known file extensions then the .pfx file extension may not be visible.

29. In the Password box, type **password**, and click **Next**.

30. Confirm that **Place all certificates in the following store** is selected, and click **Next**.

31. Click **Finish**, and click **OK**. The imported certificate can now be used.

32. Close the **Certificates** snap-in. If prompted to save the console settings, click **No**.

33. Log off as **Student*xx***.

Mapping Certificates to User Accounts

If certificates are used to authenticate users for Windows Server 2003 services, then the certificate must be mapped to a user account. If a certificate is mapped to a user account, whenever that certificate is presented, the person presenting it gets the permissions of the account to which it is mapped.

For example, a certificate is created and mapped to the user account WebUser. This certificate is distributed to several people that remotely access a Web site. The users import the certificate into Internet Explorer. Then when the users access the Web site, the certificate is presented to the Web server. The Web server allows the user access to all parts of the Web site to which WebUser has been granted access.

Active Directory Users and Computers is used to map certificates to user accounts. To map a certificate to a user, right-click the user and click Name Mappings. This option is only available if you have enabled Advanced Features in the View menu.

There are three options that can be used when mapping certificates to user accounts:

- One-to-one mapping—A single certificate is mapped to a single user account.
- Many-to-one mapping (subject)—All certificates with the same subject are mapped to a single user account regardless of the issuing CA.
- Many-to-one mapping (CA)—All certificates with the same issuing CA are mapped to a single user account regardless of the subject.

Figure 8-11 shows the options available to you when mapping a certificate to a user account. If the "Use Issuer for alternate security identity" option is chosen alone, then it is a many-to-one mapping based on the issuing CA. If the Use "Subject for alternate security identity" option is chosen alone, then it is a many-to-one mapping based on the subject. If both options are chosen, then it is a one-to-one mapping.

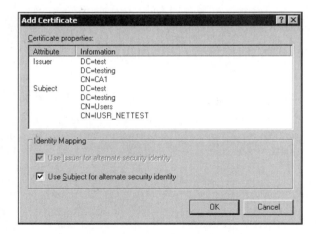

Figure 8-11   Certificate mapping options

CHAPTER SUMMARY

❑ Cryptography uses algorithms and keys to encrypt and decrypt information. Depending on the process used, cryptography can ensure or perform confidentiality, integrity, nonrepudiation, and authentication.

- Symmetrical encryption uses the same key to encrypt and decrypt information.

- Asymmetrical encryption uses a pair of keys. Information that is encrypted by one key is decrypted by the other key. These keys are often referred to as the private key and the public key.

- Hash encryption is a form of one-way encryption. Anything encrypted with hash encryption cannot be decrypted.

- A digital signature does not ensure the confidentiality of the information, only its integrity, nonrepudiation, and authentication.

- Certificate Services is the Microsoft implementation of a certification authority for PKI. A certification authority issues certificates to users, computers, and applications.

- Internal certification authorities are used when supporting only internal clients. They are inexpensive, and you have complete control.

- Third-party certification authorities are used when supporting external clients. The main disadvantage is the cost of certificates.

- Certificates issued by Certificate Services are X.509 certificates.

- Only certificate-enabled applications are able to use certificates. They are designed that way by the developer.

- Enterprise certification authorities integrate with Active Directory and can issue certificates without intervention by an Administrator. A stand-alone certification authority does not integrate with Active Directory, and can only issue certificates after the request is approved by an Administrator.

- Clients trust a certificate because they trust the root certification authority. There is only one root certification authority in a certificate hierarchy. All other certification authorities are subordinate certification authorities.

- The Certificate Request Wizard, the Certificate Services Web pages, and autoenrollment can be used to issue certificates. A stand-alone certification authority can only issue certificates using the Certificate Services Web pages. An enterprise certification authority can use any method to issue certificates.

- Certificates can be revoked if they are compromised or if an employee leaves the company. Revoked certificates are published in a Certificate Revocation List.

- When certificates are used to authenticate to services on Windows Server 2003, the certificates must be mapped to a user account.

KEY TERMS

algorithm — A formula used to process data for encryption or decryption.

asymmetrical encryption — An encryption method that uses two different keys. When one key is used to encrypt, the other key must be used to decrypt.

certificate — A part of public key infrastructure that contains a public key and an expiry date. Certificates are presented for authentication and to share public keys.

Certificate Services — A service installed on Windows Server 2003 that allows it to act as a certification authority.

certification authority (CA) — A server that issues certificates.

certificate hierarchy — The structure of trusted certification authorities consisting of a single root CA and possibly subordinate CAs.

Certificate Request Wizard — A wizard used to request certificates from an enterprise certification authority.

Certificate Revocation List (CRL) — A list of certificates that have been revoked before their expiry date.

certificate template — A template used by enterprise certification authorities to issue certificates with certain characteristics.

ciphertext — Data that has been encrypted.

cryptographic service provider (CSP) — Software or hardware that provides cryptographic services.

cryptography — The process of encrypting and decrypting messages and files using an algorithm.

decryption — The process of making encrypted data readable.

digital signature — A process using both hash encryption and asymmetrical encryption that ensures data integrity and nonrepudiation.

encryption — The process of rendering data unreadable by applying an algorithm.

enterprise certification authority — A certification authority that integrates with Active Directory, and can issue certificates without Administrator intervention.

hash encryption — A type of one-way encryption that cannot be decrypted. It is used to store information such as passwords and to create checksums.

hash value — A summary of the data being encrypted using hash encryption.

key — A number, usually large, to prevent it from being guessed, used in combination with an algorithm to encrypt data.

private key — The key in asymmetrical encryption that is seen only by the user to which it is issued.

public key — The key in asymmetrical encryption that is freely distributed to other users.

public key infrastructure (PKI) — The system that supports the issuance and management of certificates, public keys, and private keys.

root certification authority — The first CA in the certificate hierarchy. Clients trusting this CA trust certificates issued by this CA and all subordinate CAs.

Secure Sockets Layer (SSL) — A Transport layer protocol that encrypts data communication between a client and service. Both the client and service must be written to support SSL.

stand-alone certification authority — A certification authority that does not integrate with Active Directory, and requires an Administrator to approve certificate requests.

subordinate certification authority — A certification authority that has been authorized by a root CA or another subordinate CA.

symmetrical encryption — Encryption that uses the same key to encrypt and decrypt data.

trusted root certification authority — A CA from which a client or application accepts certificates.

X.509 — A standard for certificates that was created by the International Telecommunications Union – Telecommunication (ITU-T).

REVIEW QUESTIONS

1. Verifying that data has not been modified is called _____.

   a. confidentiality

   b. authentication

   c. repudiation

   d. integrity

2. Which of the following encryption methods uses a single key to encrypt and decrypt data?

   a. symmetrical

   b. asymmetrical

   c. hash

   d. Blowfish

3. Darrin wants to encrypt an e-mail message to Tracey. Which key does Tracey use to open the encrypted e-mail?

a. Darrin's public key

b. Darrin's private key

c. Tracey's public key

d. Tracey's private key

4. Erin digitally signs an e-mail message to Jennifer. Which key does Jennifer use to verify the digital signature?

a. Erin's public key

b. Erin's private key

c. Jennifer's public key

d. Jennifer's private key

5. Which of the following statements regarding enterprise certification authorities is false?

a. Enterprise CAs require Active Directory.

b. Enterprise CAs can use templates.

c. Certificate requests to an Enterprise CA must be manually approved by the Administrator.

d. Enterprise CAs cannot issue certificates outside the organization.

6. Users require a certificate for secure remote mail. An Enterprise CA has been installed on a server named Apollo. What Web site does the user access to request a certificate?

a. https://Apollo/certsrv

b. http://apollo/certsrv

c. http:/Apollo/certreq

d. http://apollo/certsvr

7. Third-party CAs are normally used in which of the following scenarios? (Choose all that apply.)

a. The server needs to be trusted by clients outside your organization.

b. You need full control over how and when certificates are issued.

c. You need a low-cost solution.

d. Client computers require no modifications to use the certificate.

8. A list of certificates that are no longer valid is called a _____.

a. certification authority

b. Expired Certificate List

c. Certificate Revocation List

d. Certificate Expiration List

9. Certificates created by a Stand-alone CA follow which format?

a. X.400

b. X.500

c. X.509

d. X.501

10. Which of the following components is not part of a certificate hierarchy?

a. Enterprise root CA

b. Stand-alone subordinate CA

c. Stand-alone root CA

d. Enterprise child CA

11. Which of the following use symmetrical encryption?

    a. digital signature

    b. EFS

    c. encrypting e-mail

    d. password protected files

12. A certification authority is a server that issues certificates to which of the following? (Choose all that apply.)

    a. users

    b. computers

    c. applications

    d. routers

13. Web browsers contain a list of certificate authorities that are trusted by the application. What are these CAs called?

    a. root certification authorities

    b. trusted certification authorities

    c. enterprise certification authorities

    d. stand-alone certification authorities

14. Certificates that have expired are added to the Certificate Revocation List. True or False?

15. A subordinate certification authority can be certified by which certification authorities?

    a. external CA

    b. Enterprise root CA

    c. Stand-alone root CA

    d. all the above

16. Hash encryption is often used for which of the following? (Choose all that apply.)

    a. EFS

    b. e-mail encryption

    c. passwords

    d. digital signatures

17. Certificate Services can be included in the daily backup by selecting what option in the backup application?

    a. certification authority

    b. system state

    c. registry

    d. COM+ Class Registration Database

18. Which of the following certificate templates can be used for EFS, e-mail, and client authentication?

    a. Computer

    b. Basic EFS

    c. Web Server

    d. User

    e. Domain Controller

19. What is the default lifetime of a Certificate Revocation List?

    a. 24 hours

    b. two days

    c. five days

    d. seven days

    e. 14 days

20. What format must be selected when exporting a private key?

    a. DER encoded binary X.509

    b. Base-64 encoded X.509

    c. Cryptographic Message Syntax Standard

    d. Personal Information Exchange

8

CASE PROJECTS

As a research organization, Arctic University has a commitment to be on the cutting edge when it comes to security and technology. Part of this includes evaluating the use of PKI for various university services, specifically Certificate Services.

Case Project 8-1: Deciding on a Certificate Strategy

Because of privacy issues and concerns regarding security, the university IT management wants to encrypt all internal e-mail, and create a secure Web site for ordering books and paying for courses. You have been asked to create a PKI infrastructure that addresses the following:

    ❑ All internal e-mail must be digitally signed and encrypted.

    ❑ All credit card numbers and ordering information must be encrypted between the client and the Web server when ordering materials on the university's Web site.

    ❑ Certificates must be issued without administrative intervention.

    ❑ Internal users must be able to request certificates using an automated process.

    ❑ Web browsers must not display a warning message about not trusting the certificate.

Explain how you would implement PKI given this set of criteria.

Case Project 8-2: Certificate Server Roles

A backup administrator has asked you to explain the difference between an Enterprise root CA and a Stand-alone root CA. She would like to implement a certification authority in an NT domain for remote authentication. Which CA would you recommend and why?

Case Project 8-3: Certificate Services Features

The board of directors has approved your plan for implementing a PKI infrastructure. However they are concerned that staff will be confused about how to renew certificates, and how to install them on their local workstations. What additional functionality does Windows Server 2003 have that addresses the board of director's concerns? What additional upgrades must be performed to support the enhanced functionality?

9

IP SECURITY

After reading this chapter and completing the exercises, you will be able to:
♦ Describe IP security issues and how the IPSec protocol addresses them
♦ Choose the appropriate IPSec mode for a given situation
♦ Implement authentication for IPSec
♦ Enable IPSec
♦ Create IPSec policies
♦ Monitor and troubleshoot IPSec

While TCP/IP is very popular and used worldwide on the Internet, it is not very secure. Each IP packet that is sent on a local area network or the Internet can be read by people other than the intended recipients. Even worse, the potential exists for IP packets to contain false information that permit you or anyone to be impersonated by someone else. IPv6 has new features that allow IP packets to be both digitally signed to prevent impersonation and encrypted to prevent unauthorized people from reading the contents of the packets. IPv4 has no such features built in. IPSec is an enhancement for IPv4 that allows packets to be digitally signed and encrypted. In this chapter you will learn how to implement IPSec.

IPSec Overview

IPv4 has no built-in security mechanisms to protect the communication between two hosts. There are a variety of ways that hackers can corrupt or eavesdrop on IP-based communications. For example:

- Packet sniffing—Using special software called a **packet sniffer**, a hacker can view all of the packets traversing your network. Using these sniffed packets, a hacker can view the contents of files that are being stored on network servers, read e-mail, and possibly even view passwords. It may seem unlikely that a hacker can gain access to your premises to run a packet sniffer, but hacked Internet routers can also be used for packet sniffing.

- **Data replay**—Advanced packet sniffers can capture packets and allow the user to replay them at a later time. For example, a hacker could capture the packets involved in transferring money from one bank account to another and, even without understanding the contents of the packets, could replay the packets from one side of the communication to initiate the transaction again and again.

- **Data modification**—Some packet sniffers allow the user to modify packets before replaying them. For example, an e-mail message with a contract attached could be modified while in transit and the recipient would never know.

- **Address spoofing**—The only way IPv4 can control which users can access resources is via a firewall. Most firewall rules control access to resources based on the source IP address. Clever hackers can falsify the source IP address in a packet and gain unauthorized access to resources.

IP Security (IPSec) is a standards track protocol, supported by the Internet Engineering Task Force (IETF), which is designed to secure IP-based communication. To do this it uses authentication, encryption, and digital signatures.

IPSec authenticates the endpoints of any IP-based conversation using IPSec. This means that each participant must be known and trusted. When the two partners in a conversation using IPSec are authenticated, IP addresses are no longer used to verify the identity of the partners. Authentication stops unauthorized communication that is missed by firewalls, which are vulnerable to spoofed IP addresses. IPSec authentication identifies computers or devices involved in any IP-based communication using IPSec, not individual users.

Encryption can be used by IPSec to hide the contents of data packets. This prevents hackers with a simple packet sniffer from eavesdropping on network communication. Digital signatures on each packet of information ensure that the packet has not been modified while in transit. Time stamps placed in the signatures ensure that the data is not being replayed.

IPSec exists at the Network layer of the TCP/IP architecture. Because applications communicate with the Transport layer of the TCP/IP architecture, and because IPSec operates at the Network layer, applications are unaware of the existence of IPSec. Any TCP/IP-based application can use IPSec without being specially written to do so. This is a significant advantage over other data encryption methods such as SSL, which need to be embedded in the client software.

As a standards track protocol sponsored by the IETF, IPSec is widely used by many vendors. While it is possible that parts of IPSec may be modified in the future, the current specifications ensure at least a minimal level of compatibility between implementations from different vendors. As a result, you should be able to use a Windows Server 2003 router with IPSec to communicate with a Cisco router using IPSec.

Given the advantages of IPSec, you would think that all IP-based communications would use it. However, it is not practical or desired in all situations. Pre-Windows 2000 operating systems from Microsoft do not support the IPSec protocol. This prevents any network with Windows 9x/NT clients from implementing IPSec for all communication. You can use a mix of IPSec protected packets and unprotected packets to increase security for those operating systems that do support IPSec.

IPSec can also significantly slow communication on a network. Authentication, digitally signing each packet, and encrypting the contents of each packet consumes processing resources and time. A busy server may not have enough processing power to support using IPSec for all communication. Fortunately, you can buy network cards with devoted processors to speed IPSec calculations.

Another drawback to using IPSec is that the majority of businesses connected to the Internet use some type of network address translation (NAT) to allow an entire office to share one IP address when accessing the Internet. IPSec is not able to be routed through NAT, and this is a very serious limitation for remote users. However, if NAT and IPSec are implemented on the same router, it functions properly. Figure 9-1 shows implementations of NAT and IPSec.

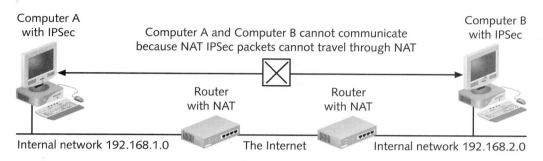

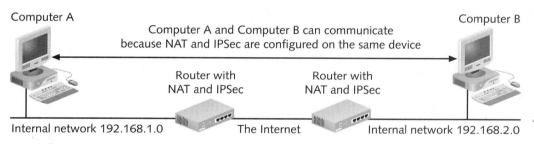

Figure 9-1   Implementing NAT and IPSec

IPSec adds complexity to a network. While the Windows Server 2003 implementation of IPSec is reliable, any service added to a network has the potential to break. In real terms, a broken service translates into lost money via user downtime and additional administrative expense. Without a demonstrated need, IPSec is a waste of time and money.

IPSec can, however, be a valuable addition to a network when data integrity or confidentiality are required. On a LAN, IPSec can be implemented between client computers and specific servers holding confidential data such as financial records or human resources information. On a WAN, IPSec can be used to create a cost-effective virtual private network that allows a company to securely send private data across the Internet without fear of eavesdropping.

IPSec Modes

When configuring IPSec you must choose between different modes of operation. The modes of operation define whether communication is secured between two hosts or two networks, and which IPSec services are used. Attempting to use all modes of operation is not appropriate because the large amount of processing power used on routers and hosts slows down network communications.

IPSec communication between two networks is called **tunnel mode**. IPSec communication between two hosts is called **transport mode**. **Authentication headers (AH) mode** enforces authentication of the two IPSec clients and includes a digital signature on each packet. **Encapsulating security payload (ESP) mode** has all the features of AH mode plus encryption of data in the packet.

When implementing IPSec you must choose tunnel mode or transport mode. In addition you must choose AH mode or ESP mode. For example, you could choose to implement IPSec in tunnel mode and ESP mode if encryption is required. Or, you could choose to implement IPSec in tunnel mode and AH mode if encryption is not required.

AH Mode

The AH mode of IPSec provides authentication of the two endpoints and adds a checksum to the packet. Authentication guarantees that the two endpoints are known. The checksum on the packet guarantees that the packet is not modified in transit, including the IP headers. AH mode does not provide data confidentiality. The payload of the packet is unencrypted.

It would be appropriate to use AH mode in a situation where you are concerned about packets being captured with a packet sniffer and replayed later. The checksum feature ensures that packets cannot be modified to create a new connection. AH mode is less processor-intensive than ESP mode because there is no need for encryption calculations.

ESP Mode

The ESP mode of IPSec provides authentication of the two endpoints, adds a checksum to each packet, and encrypts the data in the packet. Authentication guarantees that the two endpoints are known. The checksum guarantees that the packet was not modified in transit, excluding the IP headers. Encryption ensures that unintended recipients cannot read the data in the packet.

Most implementations of IPSec use ESP mode because data encryption is desired. When implementing IPSec in ESP mode you must ensure that the devices have enough processing power to encrypt and decrypt all of the packets addressed to, or passing through, them. For example, if two routers are using IPSec in ESP mode to encrypt all of the packets transmitted across the Internet between two locations, then the processors in those routers must be able to encrypt and decrypt all the packets moving between the two networks.

Transport Mode

IPSec in transport mode is used between two hosts. Both endpoints in the communication must support IPSec. This limits the implementation of IPSec, because many devices, such as printers, rarely offer IPSec support. Figure 9-2 shows IPSec in transport mode. In this example, packets are encrypted on both internal networks as well as the Internet.

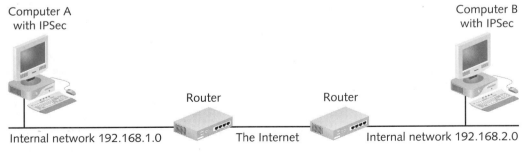

Figure 9-2 IPSec in transport mode

The two endpoints authenticated in this example are the hosts communicating when transport mode is used. Therefore, you are guaranteed to be communicating with a known host. This may be required for some secure communication.

The structure of a packet built using ESP in transport mode is shown in Figure 9-3. This packet is built locally on the host, and therefore includes all of the IPSec information inside the original IP header. There is no need to encapsulate an entire packet.

Original IP packet

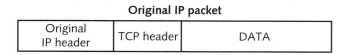

Original IP header	TCP header	DATA

IP Packet Encrypted Using IPSec in Transport Mode

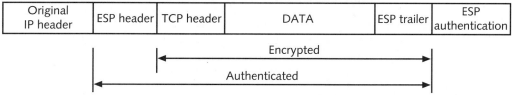

Original IP header	ESP header	TCP header	DATA	ESP trailer	ESP authentication

Encrypted

Authenticated

Figure 9-3   Packet structure for ESP in transport mode

Tunnel Mode

IPSec in tunnel mode is used between two routers. The two hosts communicating through the routers do not need to support IPSec; rather, the routers take the original IP packets and encapsulate them. This means that any IP devices can take advantage of routers running IPSec in tunnel mode.

Figure 9-4 shows IPSec in tunnel mode between two routers. All of the communication between computers on both internal networks is encrypted as it crosses the Internet because the routers encapsulate the original IP packets. However, communication within each internal network is not encrypted. Figure 9-5 shows the structure of a packet built using ESP in tunnel mode.

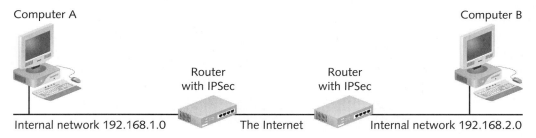

Computer A   Computer B

Router with IPSec   Router with IPSec

Internal network 192.168.1.0   The Internet   Internal network 192.168.2.0

Figure 9-4   IPSec in tunnel mode

Original IP packet

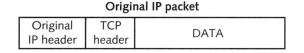

Original IP header	TCP header	DATA

IP Packet Encrypted Using IPSec in Tunnel Mode

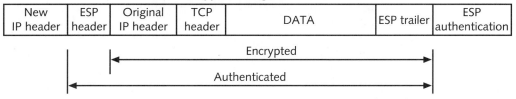

New IP header	ESP header	Original IP header	TCP header	DATA	ESP trailer	ESP authentication

Encrypted

Authenticated

Figure 9-5   Packet structure for ESP in tunnel mode

Authentication takes place between the two routers when using IPSec in tunnel mode. The computers taking part in the conversation are not authenticated. In some situations this may be considered insecure.

IPSEC AUTHENTICATION

Both endpoints of an IPSec communication are authenticated. The authentication is for the actual devices, not the users logged into the devices. When two routers are engaged using IPSec in tunnel mode, both of the routers are authenticated to each other. When two computers are engaged using IPSec in transport mode, both of the computers are authenticated to each other.

Internet Key Exchange (IKE) is the process used by two IPSec hosts to negotiate their security parameters. The security parameters negotiated include the method of authentication, AH or ESP mode, transport or tunnel mode, encryption and hashing algorithms, and parameters for key exchange. When security parameters have been agreed upon, this is referred to as a **security association (SA)**.

There are three methods Windows Server 2003 can use to authenticate IPSec connections:

- **Preshared key**
- **Certificates**
- **Kerberos**

Preshared Key

A preshared key is simply a combination of characters entered at each endpoint of the IPSec connection. Authentication is based on the fact that both endpoints know the same secret, and no one else has been told the secret. Effectively, this is the same as configuring both ends of the IPSec connection with a password. If both ends are using the same password, then the connection is established. The major advantage of this authentication method is its simplicity. Authentication occurs as long as the preshared key is typed in correctly on each device.

The major disadvantage of this authentication method is movement of the preshared key when configuring the two devices. For example, if Bob is configuring a device in New York to use IPSec and authenticate using a key he has generated, then Bob needs to give that key to Susan in Atlanta so she can configure her device before they can communicate using IPSec. When Bob gives the key to Susan using e-mail, postal mail, or over the telephone, there is a risk someone might intercept the message.

Certificates

Certificates may be presented for authentication. If the two certificates used are part of the same certificate hierarchy, then each IPSec device accepts the certificate of the other device.

This type of authentication is very useful when clients are from outside of your organization. The clients can obtain a certificate from a third-party certificate authority so you, as network administrator, are not responsible for maintaining the infrastructure that creates and approves certificates.

The main disadvantage of using third-party certificates is cost. Each client needs to buy a certificate. If there are hundreds or thousands of clients, then this can be expensive. In addition, many clients may not be technically savvy enough to obtain a certificate.

Kerberos

Kerberos is the authentication system used by Windows 2000/XP/2003 for access to network resources. The two devices must be in Kerberos realms that trust each other. In Active Directory, a domain is equivalent to a Kerberos realm.

The main benefit of Kerberos as an authentication method for IPSec is its seamless integration with domain security. The client computers do not need to be configured with any extra information if they have a computer account in the Active Directory forest.

Kerberos is not a commonly supported authentication system for IPSec on non-Microsoft products such as routers, and is not appropriate for Windows computers that are not part of the Active Directory forest.

ENABLING IPSEC

IPSec is enabled on Windows Server 2003 using **IPSec policies**. These policies can be configured manually on each server or distributed through Group Policy. IPSec policies configured on each server can be accessed through the Local Security Policy snap-in found in Administrative Tools. IPSec policies distributed through Group Policy can be configured using the Active Directory Users and Computers snap-in, or the Group Policy Object Editor snap-in.

IPSec policies define the circumstances under which IP traffic is tunneled using IPSec, permitted without using IPSec, or blocked. In addition, the policies define the type of authentication, which network connections are affected, and whether IPSec is to be used in tunnel mode or transport mode. The three policies installed by default are:

- Server (Request Security)
- Client (Respond Only)
- Secure Server (Require Security)

The default policies are configured to use Kerberos for authentication. This allows them to be used internally within an Active Directory forest with no configuration.

All ICMP traffic is permitted by the default policies. This means that network traffic generated by utilities such as ping and tracert is not encapsulated using IPSec. It is assumed that this traffic is public and does not need to be kept secure.

All of the default policies respond to requests to use IPSec. However, they differ in whether they request security. The Client (Respond Only) policy never requests IPSec for IP communication, but uses it if requested. The Server (Request Security) policy always requests IPSec for IP communication, but it can communicate without it if a security association cannot be established using IPSec. The Secure Server (Require Security) policy does not respond to any non-IPSec traffic for IP communication.

An IPSec policy must be in place to use IPSec. If there is no IPSec policy established, IPSec cannot be used.

Assigning IPSec Policies

A single server can be configured with many IPSec policies. However, no policy is used until it is assigned. Only one policy can be assigned at a time per machine. The Local Security Policy snap-in can be used to assign an IPSec policy on a single computer. Group Policy can be used to assign an IPSec policy to a group of computers.

Once a policy has been assigned, it does not take effect immediately. The IPSec Policy Agent must be restarted for the change to take effect. You can restart the IPSec Policy Agent by rebooting the server. However, the preferred method is by using the Services snap-in. In the Services snap-in, the IPSec Policy Agent is named IPSEC Services.

Activity 9-1: Assigning an IPSec Policy

Time Required: 10 minutes

Objective: Assign an IPSec policy to enable encryption of data packets.

Description: Several of your servers hold confidential student information. You want to enable IPSec on these servers to protect the information from packet sniffers. The client computers accessing your confidential servers are a mix of Windows XP/2000 and Windows 9x/NT. You will enable the Server (Request Security) policy to accommodate the older clients that do not support IPSec.

1. If necessary, start your server and log on as Administrator.

2. Click **Start**, point to **Administrative Tools** and click **Local Security Policy**.

3. Under Security Settings, click **IP Security Policies on Local Computer**.

4. In the right pane, right-click **Server (Request Security)**, and click **Assign**. Notice that under the column Policy Assigned, "Yes" now appears next to the description for this policy.

5. Close the Local Security Settings window.

6. Click **Start**, point to **Administrative Tools**, and click **Services**.

7. Scroll down through the list of services, right-click **IPSEC Services,** and click **Restart**.

8. Close the Services window.

Activity 9-2: Verifying an IPSec Security Association

Time Required: 10 minutes

Objective: Verify that the IPSec policy you have enabled is working.

Description: To verify that the IPSec policy you created in the previous exercise is working, you will use the **IPSec Monitor snap-in**. This snap-in shows you the status of IPSec security associations. The test you perform first creates a file share on your server, and then connects to the file share created on your partner's computer.

1. If necessary, start your server and log on as Administrator.

2. Create a new folder in the root of your C: drive named test, and share it by following these steps:

   a. Click **Start**, point to **Administrative Tools,** and click **Computer Management**.

   b. In the left pane, click **Shared Folders**. In the right pane, right-click **Shares**, and click **New Share**.

   c. In the Share a Folder Wizard dialog box, click **Next**.

   d. In the Folder path box, type **c:\test**, click **Next**, and click **Yes** to create the specified path.

   e. Click **Next** to accept the default share name of test.

   f. Click **Administrators have full access; other users have read-only access**, and click **Finish**.

   g. Click **Close**.

   h. Close the Computer Management window.

3. Click **Start**, click **Run**, type **mmc**, and press **Enter**.

4. Click **File,** click **Add/Remove Snap-in**, click **Add**, scroll through the list and double-click **IP Security Monitor**, click **Close**, and click **OK**.

5. Double-click **IP Security Monitor**.

6. Double-click your server.

7. Click **Active Policy**. Notice the information displayed in the details pane.

8. Double-click **Main Mode**, and click **Security Associations**. At the moment, it shows that there are no items to display in this view.

9. Next, you and your partner establish a secure connection between your computers. You can view the status of security associations on your computer during the connection.

   a. Click **Start**, click **Run**, type **\\ServerXX\test**, where *XX* is your partner's student number, and press **Enter**.

   b. A window should open showing the test share on your partner's computer. If the policies have been applied properly on each server, a secure connection should be established.

10. In the IPSecurity Monitor window, click **Action**, and click **Refresh**. Note the details of the security association that has now been established between the two servers.

11. Close all open windows. If asked to save console settings, click **No**.

CREATING AN IPSEC POLICY

In many circumstances the three default policies are sufficient for your needs. However, you can create your own IPSec policies that are tailored to your environment. For example, the default policies encrypt all IP communication between two hosts. You may only wish to encrypt the traffic for one application that handles confidential information.

Each IPSec policy is composed of **IPSec rules**, as shown in Figure 9-6. Each rule is composed of an **IP filter list, IPSec filter action**, authentication methods, **tunnel endpoint**, and connection type.

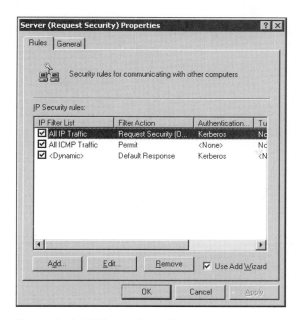

Figure 9-6   IPSec policy rules

IP filter lists and IPSec filter actions are maintained in a central list by Windows Server 2003. This means that any IP filter list or IPSec filter action created can be reused by other rules within a policy or other policies. IP filter lists and IPSec filter actions can be added to this central list when using the Local Security Policy snap-in to create and edit policies, or by right-clicking IP Security Policies on Local Computer and clicking Manage IP filter lists and filter actions, as shown in Figure 9-7.

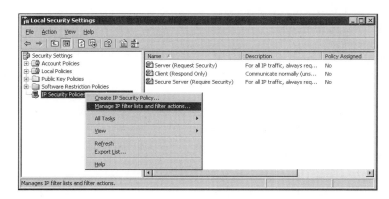

Figure 9-7   Local Security Policy snap-in

To create a new IPSec policy, you use the IP Security Policy Wizard. This wizard helps you create an IPSec policy, but cannot completely define it for you. It asks you for a name, description, whether to activate the default response rule, and authentication type.

The name and description for the policy are shown in IP Security Policies on the Local Computer when you are assigning IPSec policies. These should be descriptive so they can be easily picked from the list.

You are given the choice of activating the default response rule, as shown in Figure 9-8. The default response rule is used when the filters from other rules do not apply. For example, an IPSec policy may have one rule that requires security for a Web application on port 80 and the default response rule. The default response rule is used for all incoming packets not addressed to port 80. If the default response rule is not activated and a rule is not defined for a particular port, then traffic addressed to that port cannot use IPSec.

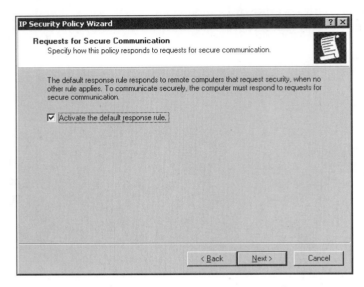

Figure 9-8   Activating the default response rule

If the default response rule is activated, there are three choices for authentication, as shown in Figure 9-9. The "Active Directory default (Kerberos V5 protocol)" option is generally used for internal client computers and servers. The "Use a certificate from this certification authority (CA)" option is generally used to support external clients or in an environment where certificate services are already configured. The "Use this string to protect the key exchange (preshared key)" option requires both devices in an IPSec communication to be configured with the same key.

Activity 9-3: Creating an IPSec Policy

TimeRequired: 5 minutes

Objective: Create a new IPSec policy that is more flexible than the default policies.

Description: All of the faculties have agreed that they will upload final marks for the students using FTP. FTP was chosen because all of the client operating systems throughout Arctic University support it. However, you are concerned that this confidential information may be viewed by unauthorized people using packet sniffers on the network. To secure this traffic, you will be implementing IPSec because FTP has no built-in security.

1. If necessary, start your server and log on as Administrator.

2. Click **Start**, point to **Administrative Tools**, and click **Local Security Policy**.

3. Right-click **IP Security Policies on Local Computer**, and click **Create IP Security Policy**.

4. Click **Next** to start the IP Security Policy Wizard.

5. In the Name box, type **FTP Traffic Policy**. In the description box, type **Secure FTP Traffic**, and click **Next**.

6. Confirm that **Activate the default response rule** is selected, and click **Next**.

7. Confirm that **Active Directory default (Kerberos V5 protocol)** is selected, and click **Next**.

8. Click **Edit properties** to deselect it, and click **Finish**.

9. Note that the FTP Traffic Policy now appears in the right pane as an IP Security Policy.

10. Close the Local Security Settings window.

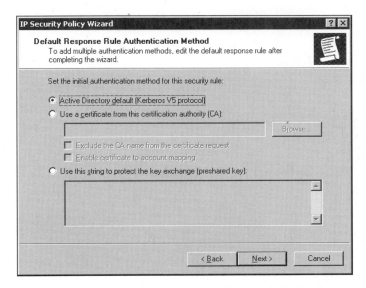

Figure 9-9   Authentication options for the default response rule

Creating Rules

After an IPSec policy is created you must edit it to add the rules that define how different types of IP traffic are handled. The only rule that may exist by default is the Default Response rule, as shown in Figure 9-10. This is present if you chose to add it during the creation process.

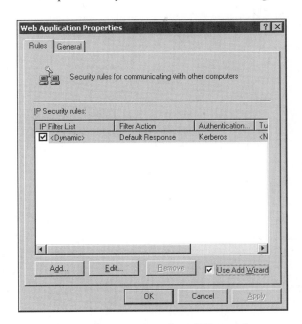

Figure 9-10   Properties of an IPSec policy

When you add a rule, the Create IP Security Rule Wizard is used by default. This wizard allows you to configure the most commonly used options. If you prefer not to use the wizard, deselect the "Use Add Wizard" option before clicking on the Add button.

The first screen in the Create IP Security Rule Wizard, shown in Figure 9-11, prompts you to choose tunnel mode or transport mode. If you choose the "This rule does not specify a tunnel" option, then transport mode will be used. If the "The tunnel endpoint is specified by the following IP address" option is chosen, then tunnel mode is used between this computer and the IP address specified.

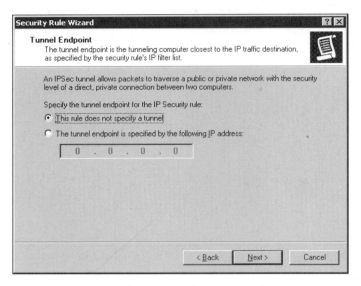

Figure 9-11   Tunnel endpoint for a new rule

The second screen presented by the Create IP Security Rule Wizard concerns the network type, as shown in Figure 9-12. Here you can choose whether this rule applies to all network connections, LAN connections, or remote access connections. If remote access is chosen, this applies to both dial-up and VPN connections.

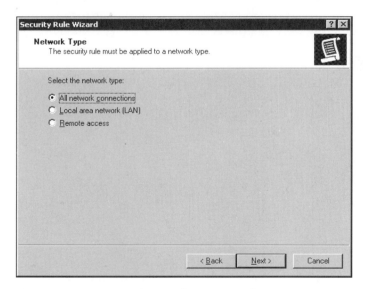

Figure 9-12   Network type for a new rule

Next you are presented with the IP Filter List window, as shown in Figure 9-13. IP filters define packet types to which actions are applied. The two IP filter lists that exist by default are All IP Traffic and All ICMP Traffic. However, you can create new IP filter lists here that suit your needs. The All IP Traffic IP filter list is normally used to specify that all IP packets be encrypted. The All ICMP Traffic IP filter list is normally used to specify that all ICMP packets not be encrypted.

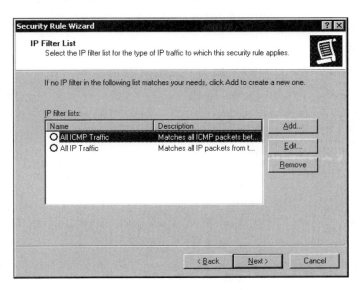

Figure 9-13   IP filter lists

After you have selected an IP filter list, you must select an action to be performed on the packets that match the IP filter list. The Filter Action window, shown in Figure 9-14, allows you to select an existing filter action or create new actions.

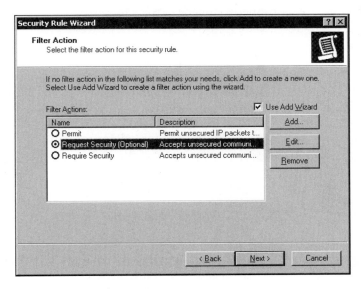

Figure 9-14   Filter actions

The three actions that exist by default are:

- Permit—Allows packets to pass through the IP filter unmodified

- Request Security (Optional)—Attempts to create IPSec connections with all other computers, but uses non-IPSec communication if an SA cannot be established.

- Require Security—Accepts non-IPSec packets, but responds only using IPSec packets. If Require Security is chosen, then this computer is only able to communicate with other computers using IPSec when packets match the IP filter.

The Authentication Method window appears next. Here you can choose to use Active Directory, certificates, or a preshared key for authentication.

Activity 9-4: Creating a New IPSec Filter Rule

Time Required: 10 minutes

Objective: Add a new IPSec filter rule that allows ICMP traffic to pass through unmodified.

Description: ICMP traffic is often used for network troubleshooting. As such, you would like it to never be encrypted by IPSec. You will create a new IPSec filter rule that ensures ICMP packets are not modified by IPSec even if the client computer requests it.

1. If necessary, start your server and log on as Administrator.
2. Click **Start**, point to **Administrative Tools**, and click **Local Security Policy**.
3. Right-click **FTP Traffic Policy**, and click **Properties**.
4. Click **Add** to create a new rule.
5. Click **Next** to start the Create IP Security Rule Wizard.
6. Confirm that **This rule does not specify a tunnel** is selected, and click **Next**.
7. Confirm that **All network connections** is selected, and click **Next**.
8. On the IP Filter List page, click the **All ICMP Traffic** option button, and click **Next**.
9. On the Filter Action page, click the **Permit** option button, and click **Next**.
10. Click **Finish**.
11. Click **OK** to close the FTP Traffic Policy Properties dialog box.
12. Close the Local Security Settings window.

IPSec Filter Lists

The two default IPSec filter lists for all IP traffic and all ICMP traffic do not allow you very much control over which traffic uses IPSec and which does not. If multiple applications are running on a server, it may be unnecessary for all IP traffic to be encrypted. For instance, if a server is running file and print services as well as SQL Server, then it may be necessary to protect the SQL Server traffic, but not the file and print services traffic. If this is the case, only TCP port 1433 needs to be encrypted, and not all IP traffic.

Encrypting only the necessary packets reduces the load on the CPU. Performing encryption and decryption can create a significant load on a busy server.

When a new IP filter list is created, you give it a name and have the option of giving it a description. In addition, you must add IP filters that make up the list and specify the traffic to which this list will apply. By default, when an IP filter is added, the IP Filter Wizard is used. If you prefer not to use the IP Filter Wizard, deselect the Use Add Wizard check box. Figure 9-15 shows the dialog box used for adding an IP filter list.

The IP Filter Wizard first requests a description for the new IP filter you are creating, as shown in Figure 9-16. In addition, this same screen has a Mirrored option. This option automatically applies this IP filter to the opposite source and selected destination ports specified in the IP filter. For example, if an IP filter is created for a source of any IP address, any port, and a destination of the local server and port 80, then the mirrored option automatically applies this IP filter to the return traffic with a source IP address of the local server and port 80 to a destination of any IP address and any port.

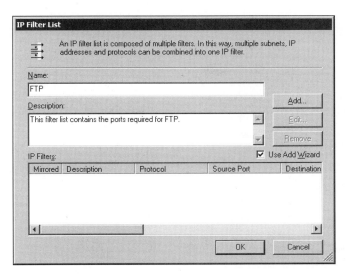

Figure 9-15   Creating an IP filter list

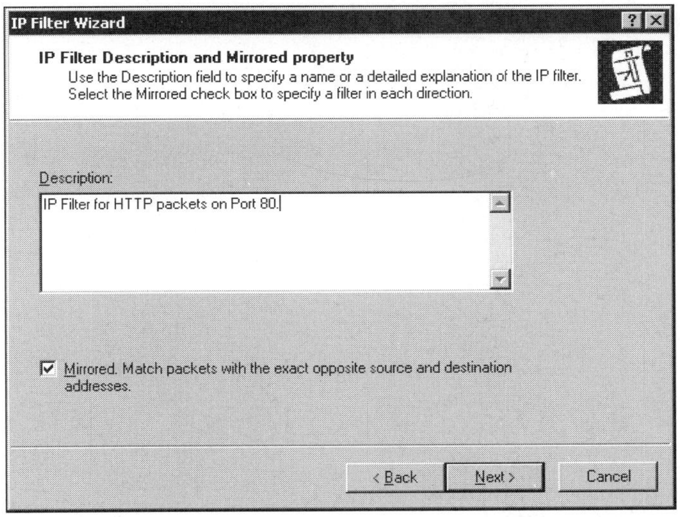

Figure 9-16   The Mirrored option for a new IP filter

The second window of the IP Filter Wizard asks for the source IP address in the filter. As shown in Figure 9-17, this can be statically configured as: My IP Address, Any IP Address, A specific DNS Name, A specific IP Address, or A specific IP Subnet. In addition, there are dynamic source IP addresses that can be configured. These are based on the IP configuration of the computer using the filter and are: DNS Servers, WINS Servers, DHCP Server, and Default Gateway.

The next window in the IP Filter Wizard asks for the destination IP address in the filter. This window provides the same choices as for the source IP address as in the filter.

Within IP packets, there is a field to describe the protocol type. You can set this as part of an IP filter in the next window, as shown in Figure 9-18. The most common protocol types used here are TCP, UDP, and ICMP. Other packet types are relatively rare. If the packet type you wish to define is not in the drop-down list, you can enter in a protocol number directly by choosing Other. An Internet standard list of protocol numbers is maintained by the IETF.

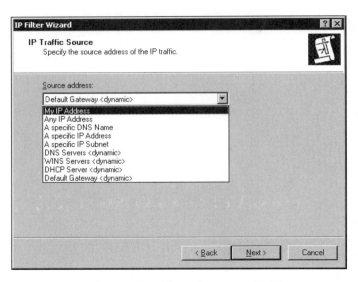

Figure 9-17   Source IP address for a new IP filter

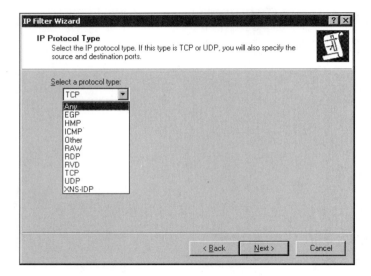

Figure 9-18   Protocol type for a new IP filter

If TCP or UDP is chosen for the packet type, then you must define the source and destination port numbers. Most client applications use a randomized port number above 1023. To affect incoming traffic from client applications, filters configured on servers should use the option "From any port." Most server applications use a defined port number. To affect incoming traffic to server applications, filters configured on servers should use the option "To this port." Figure 9-19 shows the window where this is configured.

Activity 9-5: Creating an IPSec Filter List

Time Required: 15 minutes

Objective: Create a new IPSec filter list for all FTP traffic

Description: The policy you created in the previous activity has only the default response rule enabled. This allows IPSec communication to happen if a client requests it, but does not force the client to use IPSec. You must create a new rule that encrypts all FTP traffic. The TCP port used for control messages is 21, and the TCP port used for data transfer is 20.

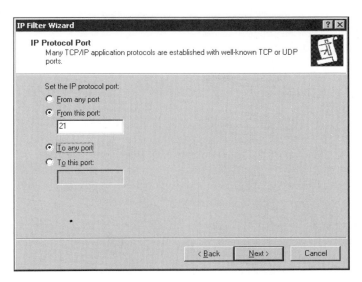

Figure 9-19 TCP or UDP port for a new IP filter

1. If necessary, start your server and log on as Administrator.

2. Click **Start**, point to **Administrative Tools**, click **Local Security Policy**.

3. Right-click **IP Security Policies on Local Computer**, and click **Manage IP filter lists and filter actions**.

4. Click **Add** to create a new IP filter list.

5. In the name box, type **FTP**.

6. Click **Add** to create a new IP filter.

7. Click **Next** to start the IP Filter Wizard.

8. In the Description box, type **FTP Data – TCP Port 20**, confirm that **Mirrored. Match packets with the exact opposite source and destination addresses** is selected, and click **Next**.

9. Confirm that **My IP Address** is selected, and click **Next**.

10. Confirm that **Any IP Address** is selected, and click **Next**.

11. Click the drop-down arrow, click **TCP**, and click **Next**.

12. Click **From this port**, type 20 as the port number, confirm that **To any port** is selected, and click **Next**.

13. Click **Finish**.

14. Click **Add** to create a new IP filter.

15. Click **Next** to start the IP Filter Wizard.

16. In the Description box, type **FTP Control – TCP Port 21**, confirm that **Mirrored. Match packets with the exact opposite source and destination addresses** is selected, and click **Next**.

17. Confirm that **My IP Address** is selected, and click **Next**.

18. Confirm that **Any IP Address** is selected, and click **Next**.

19. Click the drop-down arrow, click **TCP**, and click **Next**.

20. Click **From this port**, type 21 as the port number, confirm that **To any port** is selected, and click **Next**.

21. Click **Finish**.

22. Click **OK** to close the IP Filter List dialog box.

23. Click **Close**.

24. Close the Local Security Settings window.

Filter Actions

Filter actions define what is done to traffic that matches an IP filter list. There are only three default filter actions available: Permit, Request Security (Optional), and Require Security. All the default filter actions define a number of security parameters including the type of encryption that can be negotiated. In highly secure situations, you may wish to modify these or create your own.

To create a new filter action, you can use the IP Security Filter Action Wizard. This is invoked by default when you choose to add a new filter action. To avoid using the wizard, uncheck the Use Add Wizard option box, as shown in Figure 9-20.

Figure 9-20   Creating an IPSec filter action

The first window of the IP Security Filter Action Wizard requests a name and description for the new filter action. The second window, shown in Figure 9-21, asks for an action behavior. Selecting the Permit option allows the traffic to move without being affected by IPSec. The "Block" option discards traffic that matches the IP filter list. The "Negotiate security" option lets you define which encryption options are used.

In the next window, shown in Figure 9-22, you are asked whether to allow unencrypted communication with computers that do not support IPSec. If you choose the "Do not communicate with computers that do not support IPSec" option, then computers using this filter action cannot communicate with Windows clients that do not have an IPSec policy assigned. This is appropriate in high-security situations. If you choose the "Fallback to unsecured communication" option, then communication is possible with any client, whether an IPSec policy is assigned or not. This is not appropriate for high-security environments.

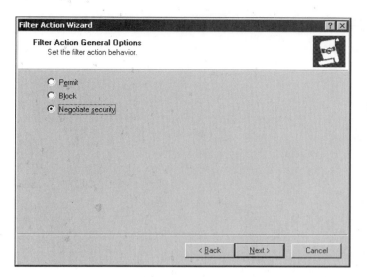

Figure 9-21   Action behavior for a new filter action

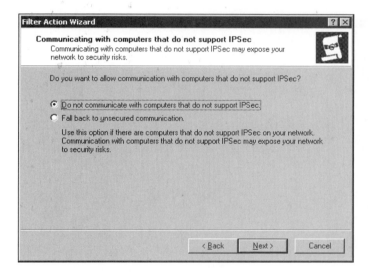

Figure 9-22   Allow unencrypted communication

Each filter action requires at least one security method. The security method defines the algorithms used for encryption and authentication, as well as whether IPSec modes AH or ESP will be used. The IP Security Filter Action Wizard allows you to add only one security method, as shown in Figure 9-23. Additional security methods can be added by editing the filter action after creation. Security methods are prioritized with the first security method listed in a filter action being the highest priority and the first attempted during negotiation.

The "Integrity and encryption" option specifies using IPSec in ESP mode with the SHA1 algorithm for data integrity and the 3DES algorithm for data encryption. The "Integrity only" option specifies using IPSec in ESP mode with the SHA1 algorithm for data integrity, but no encryption is performed. Performing only data integrity is useful when you want to be sure the data has not been modified in transit, you are not concerned about data confidentiality, and would like to conserve processing power by avoiding the CPU time required by encrypting the data portion of the packet.

You can also specify custom settings for the security method, as shown in Figure 9-24. In this window, you can specify that IPSec modes AH and ESP are used. ESP mode ensures integrity and performs encryption on the data portion of the packet. AH mode ensures integrity of the data portion of the packets as well as the IP headers in the packet.

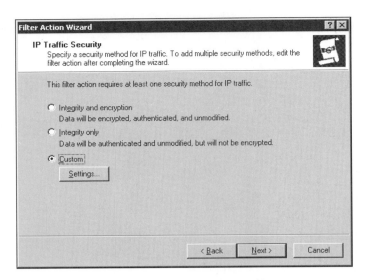

Figure 9-23   Security method for a new filter action

Figure 9-24   Custom Security Method settings

The custom settings for a security method also allow you to define how often the key used for encryption and integrity is changed. You can define that the key is changed based on the amount of data transmitted, time passed, or both. If you do not define this setting, the default values of 100 MB and 1 hour are used. The first parameter reached triggers a key change. For example, if an IPSec communication sends 100 MB of data in 20 minutes, then a key change is triggered. Likewise, if less than 100 MB of data is transmitted in an IPSec communication, then a key change is triggered after one hour.

Cryptography Algorithms

IPSec offers both data integrity and encryption. Each type of cryptography uses different algorithms.

The two algorithms that can be used for AH and ESP data integrity are:

- **Secure Hashing Algorithm (SHA1)**—A widely used hashing algorithm that produces a 160-bit message digest. Federal Information Processing Standards (FIPS) specifies this algorithm for use in U.S. federal government contracts.

- **Message Digest 5 (MD5)**—This is the most commonly used hashing algorithm for commercial applications. It produces a 128-bit message digest. It is less secure than SHA1, but it is faster.

The two algorithms that can be used for ESP data encryption are:

- **Data Encryption Standard (DES)**—This is a common encryption algorithm that uses a 56-bit key. It was first designated for U.S. federal government use in 1977. Because of enhancements in computational power, it is now recommended that 3DES be used instead.

- **Triple Data Encryption Standard (3DES)**—This encryption algorithm performs three rounds of encryption using three different 56-bit keys giving an effective key length of 168-bits. This is significantly stronger than DES and requires significantly more computational power to use. Windows 2000 computers must have installed the High Encryption Pack or have Service Pack 2 to use 3DES.

Activity 9-6: Creating a Filter Action

Time Required: 10 minutes

Objective: Create a new filter action that enforces encryption.

Description: A filter action needs to be defined to describe what will be done when the security matches the filter list for FTP packets. The university policy dictates that secure transmissions use SHA1 for data integrity and 3DES for data encryption.

1. If necessary, start your server and log on as Administrator.
2. Click **Start**, point to **Administrative Tools**, and click **Local Security Policy**.
3. Right-click **IP Security Policies on Local Computer**, and click **Manage IP filter lists and filter actions**.
4. Click the **Manage Filter Actions** tab, and click **Add**.
5. Click **Next** to start the IP Security Filter Action Wizard.
6. In the name box, type **FTP Packet Filter Action**, and click **Next**.
7. Confirm that **Negotiate security** is selected, and click **Next**.
8. Confirm that **Do not communicate with computers that do not support IPSec** is selected, and click **Next**.
9. Click **Custom**, and click **Settings**.
10. Verify that **Data integrity and encryption (ESP)** is selected. Also verify that the Integrity algorithm is set to **SHA1**, and that the Encryption algorithm is set to **3DES**. Click **OK** to close the Custom Security Method Settings dialog box.
11. When the IP Security Policy Management message box appears, indicating that the settings you have selected correspond to an encryption and integrity security level and that your security method's type will be changed to reflect this state, click **OK**.
12. Click **Next**, and click **Finish**.
13. Click **Close**.
14. Close the Local Security Settings window.

Activity 9-7: Adding a Customized Filter List and Filter Action

Time Required: 10 minutes

Objective: Edit your FTP filter, and add a rule using the customized filter list and filter action you have created.

Description: The filter list and action you have created are not yet part of a policy. You must edit your FTP policy and add a new rule using the FTP filter list and filter action you created. Finally, to use the policy you must assign it.

9

1. If necessary, start your server and log on as Administrator.

2. Click **Start**, point to **Administrative Tools**, and click **Local Security Policy**.

3. Right-click **FTP Traffic Policy**, and click **Properties**.

4. Click **Add**.

5. Click **Next** to start the Create IP Security Rule Wizard.

6. Confirm that **This rule does not specify a tunnel** is selected, and click **Next**.

7. Confirm that **All network connections** is selected, and click **Next**.

8. Click the **FTP** option button to select it, and click **Next**.

9. Click the **FTP Packet Filter Action** option button to select it, and click **Next**.

10. Confirm that **Active Directory default (Kerberos V5 protocol)** is selected, and click **Next**.

11. Click **Finish**.

12. Click **OK**.

13. Right-click the **FTP Traffic Policy**, and click **Assign**.

14. Close the Local Security Settings window.

TROUBLESHOOTING IPSEC

IPSec troubleshooting can cover a wide range of possibilities dealing with general network issues, IPSec-specific configuration settings, and Group Policy settings.

 Remember that both participants in an SA must be configured to use the same modes, encryption algorithms, and authentication method.

The most common IPSec troubleshooting tools are:

- Ping
- IPSec Security Monitor
- Event Viewer
- Resultant Set of Policy
- Netsh
- Oakley logs
- Network Monitor

Ping

The ping utility is used to test network connectivity between two hosts. The default IPSec policies permit ICMP packets and do not interfere with the operation of ping. This utility does not test IPSec specifically, but it can be used to confirm that the two hosts can communicate. If they cannot communicate, they are not able to create an IPSec SA.

IPSec Security Monitor

IPSec Security Monitor is an MMC snap-in that allows you to view the status of IPSec SAs. IPSec Security Monitor can be used to confirm that an SA was negotiated between two hosts. In addition, IPSec Security Monitor can be used to view the configuration of the IPSec policy that is applied.

Event Viewer

The IPSec Policy Agent automatically writes events to the security event log. These show the configuration settings that IPSec is using as well as events generated during the creation of SAs. These events are only written to the log if the Audit logon events option has been enabled in the local security policy or Group Policy.

Additional information from the IPSec Policy Agent can be written to the system log. To enable this logging you must modify the registry. Set the key HKEY_LOCAL_MACHINE\SYSTEM\CurrentControlSet\Services\IPSec\EnableDiagnostics to a value of 7.

Resultant Set of Policy

Applying Group policies can be quite complex. If you are attempting to distribute and apply IPSec policies through Group Policy, and they are not functioning as you expect, then you can use the **Resultant Set of Policy (RSoP)** snap-in. The RSoP snap-in allows you to view which policies apply, and to simulate the application of new policies to test their results.

Netsh

The Netsh command allows you to configure a number of network-related settings. This is useful when batch scripts are used to remotely make changes on clients and servers. Configuration categories include: bridging, DHCP, diagnostics, IP configuration, remote access, routing, WINS, and remote procedure calls.

IPSec configuration can also be modified using Netsh, including:

- Viewing policies
- Adding policies
- Deleting policies

Oakley Logs

Oakley logs track the establishment of SAs. This logging is not enabled by default and must be enabled with the command "netsh ipsec dynamic set config ike logging 1". The log file created is C:\WINDOWS\Debug\Oakley.LOG. By default, this registry key does not exist.

Network Monitor

Network Monitor can be used to view packets that are traveling on the network, and to identify IPSec traffic. However, it cannot view encrypted information inside of an IPSec packet.

Network Monitor is useful for determining whether packets are being properly transmitted between computers, but Network Monitor is not useful for troubleshooting application-level problems if the traffic is encrypted. For application troubleshooting purposes, you may need to disable IPSec, or encryption within IPSec.

Activity 9-8: Disabling IPSec

Time Required: 5 minutes

Objective: Disable IPSec policies that have been applied.

Description: In this activity you will unassign all IPSec policies so that they do not interfere with activities later in the course.

1. If necessary, start your server and log on as Administrator.
2. Click **Start**, point to **Administrative Tools**, and click **Local Security Policy**.
3. Right-click **FTP Traffic Policy**, and click **Un-assign**.
4. Close the Local Security Settings window.
5. Click **Start**, point to **Administrative Tools**, and click **Services**.
6. Scroll through the list of services until you see IPSEC Services.
7. Right-click **IPSEC Services**, and click **Restart**.
8. Close the Services window.

CHAPTER SUMMARY

- ❏ IPV4 has no built in security mechanisms and uses IPSec as an add-on protocol to make communication secure from packet sniffing, data replay, data modification, and address spoofing.
- ❏ IPSec operates at the Network layer and can be used by any IP application without the application being modified.
- ❏ Pre-Windows 2000 operating systems do not support IPSec.
- ❏ IPSec cannot be used with NAT.
- ❏ IPSec AH mode does not perform data encryption, but can authenticate and guarantee data integrity for an entire IP packet including the IP headers.
- ❏ IPSec ESP mode has the ability to perform data encryption, authentication, and guarantees data integrity for the data portion of the packet, but not the IP headers.
- ❏ Transport mode is used between two hosts. Tunnel mode is used between two routers.
- ❏ The Windows Server 2003 implementation can perform authentication using a preshared key, certificates, or Kerberos. IKE is used to negotiate the security association.
- ❏ IPSec policies contain rules that control authentication, which traffic is affected, what is done to the affected traffic, the type of connections affected, and whether this computer is a tunnel endpoint.
- ❏ Filter lists are used in IPSec rules to define the packets affected by a rule. Filter actions are used to define what is done to the traffic that matches the filter list.
- ❏ The two algorithms used for data integrity are SHA1 and MD5.
- ❏ The two algorithms used for data encryption are DES and 3DES.
- ❏ Tools that can be used to troubleshoot IPSec include: ping, IPSec Security Monitor snap-in, Event Viewer, Resultant Set of Policy snap-in, Netsh, Oakley logs, and Network Monitor.

KEY TERMS

address spoofing — The act of falsifying the source IP address in an IP packet, usually for malicious purposes.

authentication headers (AH) mode — The IPSec mode that performs authentication and ensures data integrity on the entire IP packet including the headers.

Data Encryption Standard (DES) — An algorithm for data encryption defined by the U.S. government in 1977 that uses a 56-bit key.

data modification — Modifying the contents of packets that have been captured with a packet sniffer before resending them on the network.

data replay — Resending packets that have been previously captured with a packet sniffer.

encapsulating security payload (ESP) mode — The IPSec mode that performs authentication, data integrity, and encryption on the data portion of an IP packet. Integrity of IP headers is not performed.

Internet Key Exchange (IKE) — A protocol used by IPSec to negotiate security parameters, perform authentication, and ensure the secure exchange of encryption keys.

IP filter list — A list of IP protocols that are affected by a rule in an IPSec policy.

IP Security (IPSec) — A protocol that adds security functions to IPv4.

IPSec filter action — Defines what is done to traffic that matches an IP filter list in an IPSec rule.

IPSec Security Monitor snap-in — An MMC snap-in that allows the monitoring of IPSec security associations and configuration.

IPSec policy — A set of rules that defines how packets are treated by IPSec. An IPSec policy must be applied to be in use.

IPSec rule — The combination of an IP filter list and an IPSec filter action.

Kerberos — The preferred authentication method used by Active Directory. It is the simplest authentication method to implement for IPSec if all devices are part of the same Active Directory forest.

Message Digest 5 (MD5) — A hashing algorithm that produces a 128-bit message digest.

Oakley logs — A type of logging that tracks the establishment of security associations.

packet sniffer — Software used to view (capture) all packets that are traveling on a network.

preshared key — An IPSec authentication method where each device is preconfigured with a string of text.

Resultant Set of Policy (RSoP) snap-in — An MMC snap-in that is used to troubleshoot the implementation of Group Policies.

Secure Hashing Algorithm (SHA1) — A hashing algorithm that produces a 160-bit message digest.

security association (SA) — The security terms negotiated between two hosts using IPSec.

transport mode — The IPSec mode used when two hosts create a security association directly between them.

Triple Data Encryption Standard (3DES) — A data encryption algorithm that uses three 56-bit keys in three rounds to give an effective key length of 168 bits.

tunnel endpoint — In tunnel mode, this is the other end of the tunnel with the local host.

tunnel mode — The IPSec mode used when two routers encapsulate all traffic transferred between two or more networks.

REVIEW QUESTIONS

1. IPSec operates at what layer of the OSI model?

a. Application

b. Presentation

c. Session

d. Network

e. Data Link

f. Physical

2. Which operating systems do not support IPSec? (Choose all that apply.)

   a. Windows 95

   b. Windows 98

   c. Windows NT

   d. Windows 2000 Professional

   e. Windows XP Professional

3. Which of the following statements about IPSec is false?

   a. IPSec adds complexity to the network.

   b. IPSec is a standards track protocol.

   c. IPSec can be routed through NAT.

   d. IPSec requires additional processing power.

4. IPSec between two hosts is called _____.

   a. tunnel mode

   b. transport mode

   c. encrypted mode

   d. VPN mode

5. You want to implement IPSec to authenticate two computers and encrypt data. Which mode do you select?

   a. AH mode

   b. ESP mode

   c. tunnel mode

   d. transport mode

6. Which of the following is not encrypted with the default IPSec policy? (Choose all that apply.)

   a. FTP

   b. HTTP

   c. ping

   d. tracert

   e. SMTP

7. Once an IPSec policy has been defined, it takes effect immediately. True or False?

8. Which of the following is not an authentication option when creating an IPSec policy?

   a. password

   b. Kerberos

   c. certificate

   d. preshared key

9. Which of the following cryptography algorithms is used for U.S. government contracts?

   a. MD5

   b. SHA1

   c. DES

   d. 3DES

10. Which of following cryptography algorithms uses three different 56-bit keys for encryption?

    a. MD5

    b. SHA1

    c. DES

    d. 3DES

11. In tunnel mode, what traffic is encrypted?

    a. all workstation-to-router traffic

    b. all workstation-to-workstation traffic

    c. only router-to-router traffic

    d. all traffic

    e. none of the above

12. The default IPSec policy is configured to use what authentication method?

    a. Kerberos

    b. preshared key

    c. certificates

    d. access token

13. You want to enable IPSec encryption on a Windows Server 2003 server and still allow communication with Windows 98 workstations. Which filter action(s) would you implement?

    a. Permit

    b. Request Security (Optional)

    c. Require Security

    d. all of the above

14. Which of the following cryptography algorithms are used for ESP data encryption? (Choose all that apply.)

    a. SHA1

    b. MD5

    c. DES

    d. 3DES

15. Which troubleshooting utility allows you to simulate the application of new IPSec policies?

    a. IPSec Monitor

    b. Resultant Set of Policy

    c. Network Monitor

    d. Oakley logs

    e. Netsh

16. AH mode performs which of the following functions? (Choose all that apply.)

    a. Authenticates two endpoints.

    b. Generates a checksum to verify a packet was not modified in transit.

    c. Encrypts data.

    d. Authenticates applications.

9

17. Which of the following situations can use Kerberos for authentication in IPSec? (Choose all that apply.)

    a. two routers on the Internet

    b. two workstations in the same Active Directory domain

    c. two workstations in the same Active Directory forest

    d. two workstations on the same subnet

18. How many IPSec policies can be assigned to a workstation?

    a. one

    b. two

    c. five

    d. ten

    e. unlimited

19. A combination of characters entered at both endpoints of an IPSec connection is called a _____.

    a. password

    b. certificate

    c. preshared keys

    d. shared secret

20. By default, Oakley logs are stored in which folder?

    a. \WINDOWS\OAKLEY

    b. \WINDOWS\LOGS

    c. WINDOWS\SYSTEM32\OAKLEY

    d. \WINDOWS\DEBUG

CASE PROJECTS

Case Project 9-1: Selecting an IPSec Policy

Because of security concerns, an IPSec security policy is being evaluated for the university. The board of directors wants all communication between staff workstations and all servers encrypted. They would also like to encrypt all communication between students' computers and the servers. Student computers run various operating systems including Windows 95, Unix, Linux, Windows 2000, and Windows XP.

How would you implement IPSec to encrypt as much TCP/IP traffic as possible with minimum overhead?

Case Project 9-2: Encrypting Remote Traffic

Arctic University has three satellite campuses set up in various remote locations. Students can take courses and connect to the university's servers from the remote locations. Each remote campus connects to the main campus using a Cisco router. Your manager would like to encrypt all traffic from the remote sites through the Internet to the main campus. He has recommended implementing IPSec in transport mode using third-party certificates. What are your concerns?

Case Project 9-3: Evaluating IPSec

A junior administrator has commented that implementing IPSec is a waste of time. He used Network Monitor to capture ICMP packets between two systems and was able to view the packet details. He also doesn't believe that IPSec can protect the university computers from hackers. What do you tell him?

10

REMOTE ACCESS

After reading this chapter and completing the exercises, you will be able to:

♦ Describe the purpose and features of Windows Server 2003 remote access capabilities

♦ Enable and configure Routing and Remote Access Service as a dial-up server

♦ Enable and configure Routing and Remote Access Service as a VPN server

♦ Configure a remote access server

♦ Allow remote clients access to network resources

♦ Create and configure remote access policies

♦ Understand and describe the purpose of the RADIUS protocol

♦ Troubleshoot remote access

Remote access, used to provide users outside of an office access to resources on the internal network, is a vital component to many networks today. Without remote access, frequent business travelers, such as salespeople, would not have the use of the basic resources necessary to complete their jobs. In this chapter you will learn about the remote access capabilities of Windows Server 2003. You will learn how to create and configure dial-up and VPN connections, how to grant users access to network resources, how to create remote access policies, and how to configure RADIUS servers and relay agents. Finally, you will learn how to troubleshoot remote access.

REMOTE ACCESS OVERVIEW

Remote access allows remote and **mobile users** access to network resources on the internal network, including files, printers, databases, and e-mail, among others. Traveling salespeople, for instance, often need network access from hotel rooms and client sites to make orders and retrieve updated price lists, and executives often need to access their e-mail from hotels and conferences when they are on the road. Network administrators also need remote access to network resources, as they can save hours of valuable time if they can repair after-hours network problems remotely from home. Windows Server 2003 has the ability to be a remote access server.

Dial-up Remote Access

Remote access using **dial-up** connections is the oldest type of remote access. In the past this type of connection was very slow, and transferring even the smallest files was a tedious process. However, with advances in **modem** technology, current speeds are more reasonable when transferring documents less than 1 MB in size.

A dial-up connection allows two computers to connect and transfer information using modems and a phone line. The modems convert the digital signals of the computer to analog signals that can be transmitted across the phone line. Both the dial-up server and dial-up client must have a modem. When the analog signals reach the computers on each end of the phone line, the modems then convert the signals back to digital format, which can then be interpreted by the computers.

When a connection is created between a dial-up server and a dial-up client, the client can access resources on the network on which the dial-up server is located. From the perspective of the user, the modem acts like a network card to provide access to network resources. Files can be downloaded, and e-mail can be read.

Current modems can download information at 56 Kbps when using modems that are based on the **v.90** or **v.92** standards from the ITU-T. These standards are asymmetrical standards that allow faster download speeds than upload speeds. The v.90 standard allows uploads at 33.6 Kbps, and the v.92 standard allows uploads at 48 Kbps.

Line noise in the phone system can limit connection speeds. Line noise can be introduced by low-quality phones connected to the circuit, poor-quality lines from the phone system provider, or electrical interference. The existence of line noise can likely cause modem connections to be limited to 50 Kbps or less.

The main benefit of dial-up connections is availability. Roaming users almost always have access to a phone line. Most hotels include a data port for dial-up connectivity as a standard feature in rooms.

The main drawback of dial-up connections is their speed. When compared with connectivity options, such as cable modems and DSL modems, a dial-up connection is very slow. In addition, maintenance of a **modem pool** at the office for dial-up users can be expensive and time consuming as new standards are introduced and modems need to be replaced.

VPN Remote Access

A **virtual private network (VPN)** uses a public network to transmit private information. Encryption is used to keep the private information from being read by unauthorized persons as it traverses the public network. This allows a relatively inexpensive public network to be used in the place of a relatively expensive private network.

The public network most commonly used for VPN connections is the Internet. The client computers can be connected to the Internet via dial-up, a company LAN, or broadband such as cable modem, or DSL modem. VPN remote access started to become popular in the mid '90s. As the Internet became popular and more available, so did the popularity of VPN remote access.

Once connected to the Internet, client computers initiate a VPN connection with a VPN server. The VPN client is then able to access the network on which the VPN server is located, in the same way that a dial-up client is able to access the network on which the dial-up server is located.

Maintaining a VPN server is much easier than maintaining a dial-up server. A VPN server generally uses a standard network card to communicate with the Internet; thus, no special hardware, such as a modem pool, is required.

The speed of VPN connections is potentially much higher than those of dial-up connections. When high-speed access to the Internet is available through broadband or a company LAN, then a VPN connection may be as fast as 10 Mbps. However, if Internet access is provided through a dial-up connection, then the VPN connection is limited to the speed of the dial-up connection.

The main advantages of VPN connections are their potentially high speed and the reduced maintenance achieved by eliminating a modem pool. The main drawback to VPN connections is the security risk presented by allowing access to network resources from the Internet.

ENABLING AND CONFIGURING A DIAL-UP SERVER

Windows Server 2003 uses the **Routing and Remote Access Service (RRAS)** to act as a dial-up server. This service is always installed, but is not configured by default. Using the Routing and Remote Access Setup Wizard you can configure RRAS as a dial-up server, a VPN server, or a router.

10

For your server to act as a dial-up server, it must have a modem installed. Modems are installed using Phone and Modem Options in Control Panel. The first time you open Phone and Modem Options you are forced to configure a **location**, as shown in Figure 10-1.

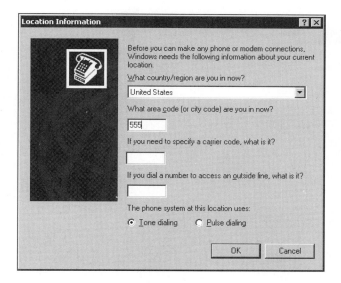

Figure 10-1 Configuring a location

Locations are used to control how Windows Server 2003 creates dial-up connections. For instance, locations allow you to specify whether any special codes need to be dialed from this location. This is useful if the internal phone system in a company requires you to dial "9" to get an outside line.

To add a modem to your server, click the Modems tab, and click Add. This starts the Add Hardware Wizard, as shown in Figure 10-2. By default, Windows Server 2003 attempts to find the modem through plug and play. However, if the modem is not a plug-and-play device, or has known plug-and-play detection problems, you can instead choose to select your modem from a list of known vendors. This can also be used in a test environment when a physical modem is not present, but a modem driver must be configured for other software to be installed or configured.

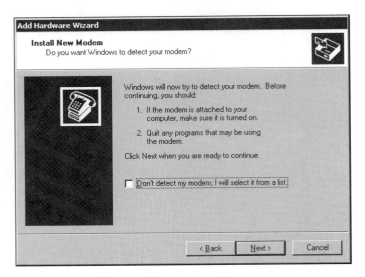

Figure 10-2   Add Hardware Wizard

If plug and play is unable to find a modem, or you have chosen to manually add your modem, then you are prompted to choose a driver from a list, as shown in Figure 10-3. Windows Server 2003 ships with several standard modem drivers, but you can also use drivers from a vendor by clicking the "Have Disk" option, and browsing to the location of the driver.

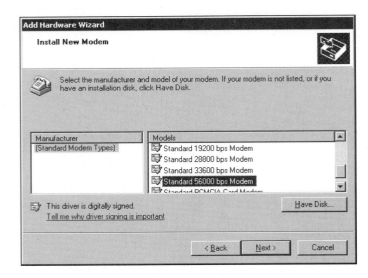

Figure 10-3   Modem drivers

After choosing a driver, you must choose the **COM port** to which the driver is connected, as shown in Figure 10-4. A COM port is a serial port. External modems normally use either COM1 or COM2, as they represent internal serial ports that are built into the computers. Internal modems normally use a COM port numbered from COM3 to COM8 that is chosen by plug and play.

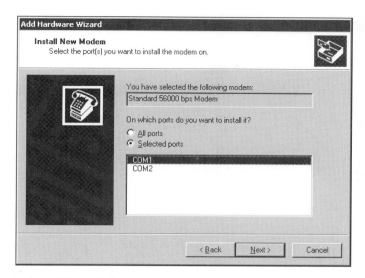

Figure 10-4   Selecting a COM port

Activity 10-1: Installing a Modem

Time Required: 5 minutes

Objective: Install a modem on your server.

Description: You want to configure Windows Server 2003 as a dial-up server. Before configuring RRAS, you must install a modem.

1. If necessary, start your server and log on as Administrator of the Artic.local domain.

2. Click **Start**, point to **Control Panel**, and click **Phone and Modem Options**.

3. In the **What area code (or city code) are you in now** box, type **555**, and click **OK**.

4. Click the **Modems** tab.

5. Click **Add**.

6. Click the **Don't detect my modem; I will select it from a list** checkbox to select this option.

You are selecting this option because your server does not have a modem physically installed. You are installing the software manually to simulate a modem being installed. If a modem were physically installed in this server, then you would allow the wizard to detect the modem.

7. Click **Next**.

8. In the Models box, click **Standard 56000 bps Modem**, and click **Next**.

9. Click **COM1** to select this as the serial port on which the modem is installed, and click **Next**.

10. Click **Finish** to close the Add Hardware Wizard.

11. Click **OK** to close the Phone and Modem Options window.

Enabling RRAS for Dial-up Connections

Management of RRAS is done with the Routing and Remote Access snap-in available in the Administrative Tools menu. When the Routing and Remote Access snap-in is started for the first time, you will notice a red arrow pointing down beside the name of your server, as shown in Figure 10-5. This indicates that RRAS is not started. In this case, it is because RRAS has not yet been configured.

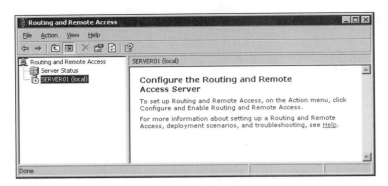

Figure 10-5   RRAS is not configured

The Routing and Remote Access Wizard is used to enable and configure RRAS for the first time. After you have completed the wizard and RRAS is started, the arrow beside your server in the Routing and Remote Access snap-in will point up and be green, as shown in figure 10-6.

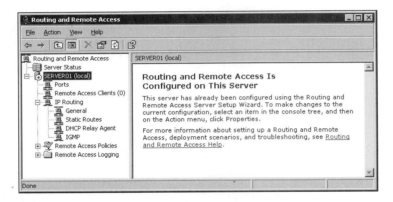

Figure 10-6   RRAS is configured and functional

Activity 10-2: Enabling RRAS as a Dial-up Server

Time Required: 10 minutes

Objective: Configure RRAS on your server to act as a remote access server.

Description: Arctic University needs to provide professors with access to the network file system when they are away on conferences. Most professors will be accessing the remote access server using a laptop computer and hotel phone line. To support this, you will configure your server as a dial-up server.

1. If necessary, start your server and log on as Administrator.

2. Click **Start**, point to **Administrative Tools**, and click **Routing and Remote Access**. Notice that your server has a red down arrow beside it to indicate that RRAS is not functional.

3. Right-click your server, and click **Configure and Enable Routing and Remote Access**.

4. Click **Next** to begin the Routing and Remote Access Server Setup Wizard.

5. Confirm that the **Remote access (dial-up or VPN)** option is selected, as shown in Figure 10-7, and click **Next**.

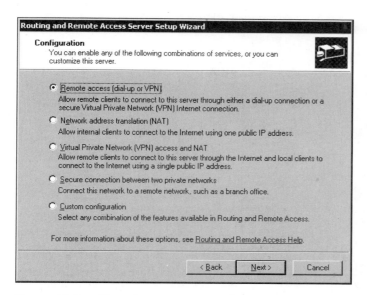

Figure 10-7   Choosing an RRAS configuration

6. Click the **Dial-up** checkbox to allow this server to be a dial-up server, as shown in Figure 10-8, and click **Next**.

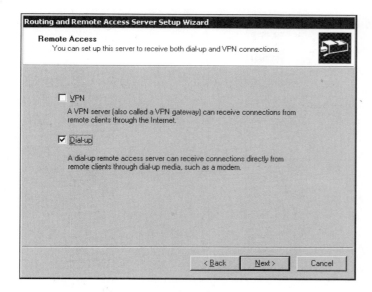

Figure 10-8   Choosing Dial-up as a remote access server type

7. If necessary, click **Classroom** in the Network Interfaces box to select it, as shown in Figure 10-9, and click **Next**. This indicates that dial-up clients receive IP addresses on the Classroom network.

10

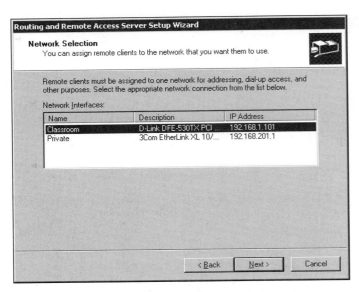

Figure 10-9   Choosing an interface for dial-up clients

8. Confirm that **Automatically** is selected as the method of IP address assignment, as shown in Figure 10-10, and click **Next**.

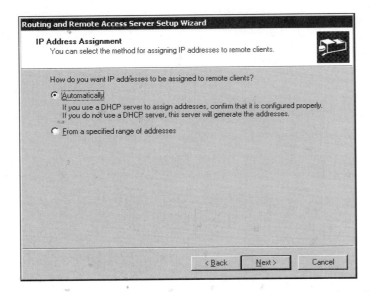

Figure 10-10   Choosing how IP addresses are assigned to dial-up clients

9. Confirm that **No, use Routing and Remote Access to authenticate connection requests** is selected, as shown in Figure 10-11, and click **Next**.

10. Click **Finish** to complete the Routing and Remote Access Server Setup Wizard.

11. Click **OK** to close the warning dialog box about DHCP relay.

12. Notice that the arrow next to your server is now green and pointing up to indicate that RRAS is configured and started.

13. Close the Routing and Remote Access snap-in.

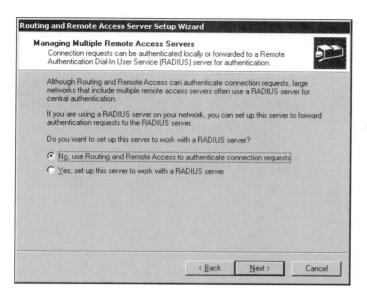

Figure 10-11   Configuring where authentication will happen

Dial-up Protocols

LAN protocols and **remote access protocols** need to be considered when configuring Windows Server 2003 for dial-up networking. LAN protocols supported by RRAS for dial-up networking are TCP/IP, IPX/SPX, and AppleTalk. Remote access protocols supported by RRAS for dial-up networking are **Point-to-Point protocol (PPP)** and **Serial Line Internet Protocol (SLIP)**.

When a dial-up client is connected to the dial-up server, it has access to the resources on the LAN. The same protocols required by client computers to access resources on the LAN are required by dial-up clients to access resources on the LAN through the dial-up server. Most dial-up clients use TCP/IP, but support for IPX/SPX is included to support older applications, and support for AppleTalk is included to support Macintosh clients. These LAN protocols can also be used for VPN connections.

Remote access protocols are used only for dial-up connections, not VPN connections. SLIP is an older, and rarely used, remote access protocol supported only when Windows Server 2003 is acting as a dial-up client. SLIP cannot be used when Windows Server 2003 is a dial-up server. The only time SLIP is used is when dialing up to older UNIX remote access servers, and TCP/IP is the only LAN protocol required.

PPP is a newer remote access protocol that is commonly in use. Windows Server 2003 can use PPP when acting as a dial-up client or server. PPP has a number of advantages over SLIP, including the ability to automatically configure clients with IP configuration information, wide availability, and the ability to use multiple LAN protocols.

Two remote access protocols supported in Windows 2000 Server have been removed in Windows Server 2003. The Microsoft RAS protocol used to support older Microsoft clients using the NetBEUI protocol has been removed. As well, the AppleTalk Remote Access Protocol used to support older Macintosh clients has been removed.

The selection of a remote access protocol when using Windows Server 2003 as a dial-up client is made in the properties of the dial-up connection on the Networking tab, as shown in Figure 10-12.

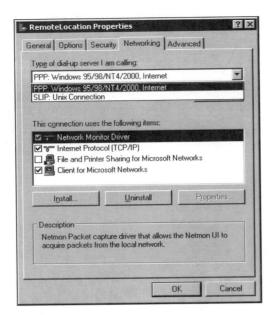

Figure 10-12   Networking tab in the Properties of a dial-up connection

Activity 10-3: Creating a Dial-up Connection

Time required: 5 minutes

Objective: Configure your server with a dial-up connection.

Description: One of the more remote locations for Arctic University is unable to use Internet connectivity to communicate with the other locations. As a short-term solution, you would like to dial-up to the server in the remote location to download data on a daily basis. You have configured an old UNIX server in the remote location to act as a dial-up server. You now need to configure your server to be a dial-up client using the SLIP remote access protocol.

1. If necessary, start your server and log on as Administrator.

2. Click **Start**, point to **Control Panel**, and double-click **Network Connections**.

3. Double-click **Create a new connection** to start the New Connection Wizard.

4. Click **Next** to begin the New Connection Wizard.

5. Click **Connect to the network at my workplace**, and click **Next**.

6. Confirm that **Dial-up connection** is selected, and click **Next**.

7. In the Company Name box, type **RemoteLocation**, and click **Next**. This is the name you see for the connection after it is created. It is best to use a descriptive name here.

8. In the Phone number box, type **555-1212**, and click **Next**.

9. In the next window, confirm that **Anyone's use** is selected, and click **Next**. If the option **My use only** were selected, only the user account that is creating the dial-up connection could initiate the dial-up connection at a later time.

10. Click **Finish**.

11. In the **Connect RemoteLocation** box, click **Properties**, and click the **Networking** tab.

12. Click the **Type of dial-up server I am calling** box, and click **SLIP: Unix Connection**.

13. Click **OK** to save the new settings.

14. Click **Cancel** because you don't want to connect to the remote server right now.

15. Close the Network Connections window.

PPP has several options that can be enabled to enhance performance. These options are enabled using the Routing and Remote Access snap-in on the PPP tab of the server properties, as shown in Figure 10-13.

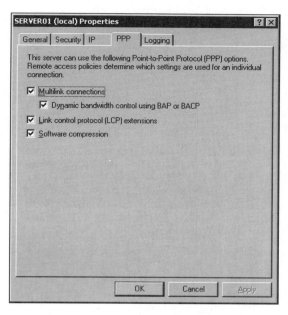

Figure 10-13   PPP tab in the Properties of an RRAS server

Enabling the "Multilink connections" option allows Windows Server 2003 to combine multiple dial-up connections into a single logical connection to speed up data transfer. For example, a client computer with two modems can dial-up to the remote access server and connect to two modems on the remote access server. When data is transferred between the client and the server, the speed of the connection is twice as fast as a single dial-up connection. To use two modems, there must be two phone lines.

If the "Dynamic bandwidth control using BAP or BACP" option is enabled, it allows the **multilink** connection to dynamically add and drop modems from a dial-up connection as the amount of data transferred varies. This is very useful for long-term connections between physical locations, particularly if long distance charges are incurred, as phone line use is minimized. The criteria used for controlling the addition or removal of modems from the multilink connection are set in remote access policies. Remote access policies are covered later in this chapter.

Enabling the "Link control protocol (LCP) extensions" option allows the dial-in server to use enhancements to **Link Control Protocol (LCP)** that control **callbacks** and other options. LCP is a protocol that controls the establishment of PPP sessions. If this option is disabled, then using callback is not possible.

If the "Software compression" option is enabled, then data transferred on this connection is compressed using Microsoft Point-to-Point Compression Protocol.

ENABLING AND CONFIGURING A VPN SERVER

Windows Server 2003 also uses RRAS to act as a VPN server. In many ways, VPN connections behave like dial-up connections. However, when a remote access server is configured to provide VPN connections, no special equipment is required. All connectivity is accomplished through a regular network card.

Enabling a VPN server is accomplished using the Routing and Remote Access Server Setup Wizard. If RRAS has already been configured, then you must disable routing and remote access before you can reconfigure it with the Routing and Remote Access Server Setup Wizard. You can reconfigure the server manually without the wizard, but this often takes longer and is more prone to error.

The first few windows of the Routing and Remote Access Server Setup Wizard are the same when configuring a VPN server and a dial-up server, including choosing to configure the server as a remote access server. However, when asked the type of remote access server, choose VPN instead of Dial-up, as shown in Figure 10-14.

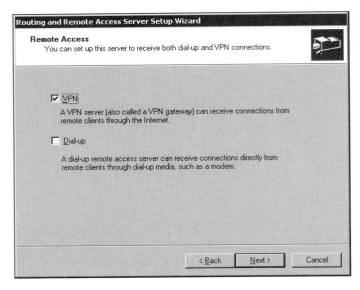

Figure 10-14 Choosing VPN as a remote access server type

The next window, shown in Figure 10-15, asks you to select the network interface that is connected to the Internet. This is the network interface to which VPN clients will be connecting. Checking the "Enable security on the selected interface by setting up static packet filters" option stops all packets going in and out of the selected interface unless they are part of a VPN connection.

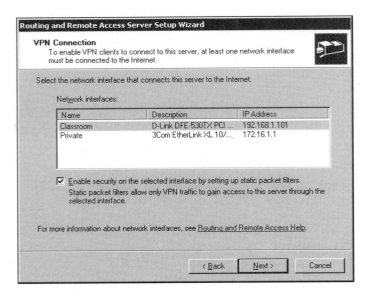

Figure 10-15 Choosing an interface for VPN clients

The option to enable **packet filters** should only be chosen if the server has multiple network cards with the filtered card connected to the Internet and the unfiltered cards connected to the LAN. In this configuration, the interface connected to the Internet only responds to VPN traffic, and the VPN clients can connect to the interface on the Internet. After the VPN connection is created, the VPN clients can access any services on the LAN because the internal interface does not restrict traffic. All requests are tunneled inside VPN packets to the VPN server, then unpacked and delivered to the LAN. Responses are tunneled inside VPN packets by the VPN server and sent to the VPN client.

If a VPN server has multiple network interfaces, then VPN clients receive an IP address from an interface not connected to the Internet.

Just like a dial-up server, the next window asks you to choose how IP addresses are handed out to VPN clients. If you choose the "Automatically" option, then the remote access server leases IP addresses from a DHCP server on the network and passes the IP addresses to the VPN clients. If you choose the "From a specified range of IP addresses" option, then you must configure the remote access server with a static range of IP addresses for it to hand out to VPN clients.

Finally, you must choose how authentication is performed, just like the dial-up server. Your first choice is the "No, use Routing and Remote Access to authenticate connection requests" option, and this means that each remote access server performs its own authentication by querying Active Directory and using policies that exist on that server. Your second choice is the "Yes, set up this server to work with a RADIUS server" option, and this means that all authentication requests are forwarded to a RADIUS server, and the remote access server allows connections based on results from the RADIUS server. The details of how RADIUS functions are covered later in this chapter.

10

Activity 10-4: Enabling RRAS as a VPN Server

Time Required: 5 min

Objective: Enable RRAS as a VPN server.

Description: Several professors have high-speed Internet access at home and would like to use it for remotely accessing files on campus. You will reconfigure your server as a VPN server. The classroom connection will simulate the Internet-connected interface, and the private connection will simulate the LAN interface. The private interface will be configured with a static IP address. For this exercise, your instructor will provide you with your student number and group number.

1. If necessary, start your server and log on as Administrator.

2. Click **Start**, point to **Control Panel**, point to **Network Connections**, right-click **Private**, and click **Properties**.

3. Click **Internet Protocol (TCP/IP)**, and click **Properties**.

4. Click **Use the following IP address**, if necessary.

5. In the IP address box, type **172.16.x.y**, where x is your group number, and y is your student number.

6. In the Subnet mask box, type **255.255.255.0**.

7. In the Preferred DNS server box type **192.168.1.10** and click **OK**.

8. Click **Close**.

9. Click **Start**, point to **Administrative Tools**, click **Routing and Remote Access**.

10. Right-click your server, and click **Disable Routing and Remote Access**.

11. Click **Yes** to confirm you want to continue. When RRAS is disabled, a red arrow appears beside your server.

12. Right-click your server, and click **Configure and Enable Routing and Remote Access**.

13. Click **Next** to begin the Routing and Remote Access Server Setup Wizard.

14. Confirm that **Remote access (dial-up or VPN)** is selected, and click **Next**.

15. Click the **VPN** checkbox to configure the server as a VPN server, and click **Next**.

16. Click **Classroom** to select it as the interface that is connected to the Internet.

17. Click the **Enable security on the selected interface by setting up static packet filters** checkbox to disable this option, and click **Next**. In a real life situation, where this server is connected to the Internet, you would normally leave this option on unless the server were providing services other than VPN remote access.

18. Click **From a specified range of addresses**, and click **Next**. In the classroom, you are not using DHCP, so you are selecting to hand out IP addresses from a static range. Most networks use DHCP to assign the addresses automatically.

19. Click **New** to create a new address range.

20. In the Start IP address box, type **172.16.x.y0**, where x is your group number, and y is your student number.

21. In the Number of addresses box, type **10**, and click **OK**. For the purposes of this exercise, you only need one IP address to hand out. When a VPN server is put into production, it is configured to hand out one IP address for each simultaneous client connection. This may be many more than the 10 you have just configured.

22. Click **Next**.

23. Confirm that **No, use Routing and Remote Access to authenticate connection requests** is selected, and click **Next**.

24. Click **Finish**.

25. Click **OK** to close the warning dialog box about DHCP relay.

26. Notice that the arrow next to your server is now green and pointing up to indicate that RRAS is configured and started.

27. Close the Routing and Remote Access snap-in.

VPN Protocols

Point-to-Point Tunneling Protocol (PPTP) and **Layer Two Tunneling Protocol (L2TP)** are supported for VPN connections by Windows Server 2003 when configured as a VPN server. By default, 128 PPTP ports and 128 L2TP ports are provided, as shown in Figure 10-16.

If your VPN server needs to support more than 128 VPN clients using either protocol, then the number of ports must be increased. If you choose not to allow PPTP because it is less secure than L2TP, then the number of PPTP ports can be reduced to zero. Conversely, if you only want to support PPTP because of its ease of configuration, then the number of L2TP ports can be reduced to zero.

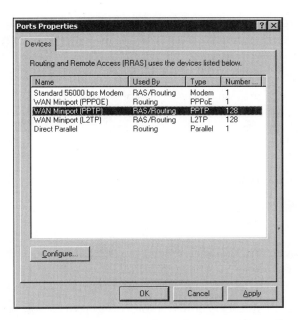

Figure 10-16   PPTP and L2TP port configuration

Activity 10-5: Modifying the Default Number of VPN Ports

Time Required: 5 minutes

Objective: Reduce the number of PPTP and L2TP VPN ports to 10 each.

Description: You have a server with RRAS configured to be a VPN server. By default, 128 PPTP ports and 128 L2TP ports have been created. You are concerned that if this number of connections were ever created on the server, your Internet connection would become congested. You have decided to limit the number of PPTP and L2TP connections to 10 each.

1. If necessary, start your server and log on as Administrator.

2. Click **Start**, point to **Administrative Tools**, and click **Routing and Remote Access**.

3. If necessary, double-click your server to expand it.

4. Right-click **Ports**, and click **Properties** to view the port drivers that are installed.

5. Double-click **WAN Miniport (PPTP)**.

6. In the Maximum ports box, type **10**, and click **OK**.

7. Click **Yes** to close the warning and continue.

8. Double-click **WAN miniport (L2TP)**.

9. In the Maximum ports box, type **10**, and click **OK**.

10. Click **Yes** to close the warning and continue.

11. Click **OK** to close the Ports Properties window.

12. Close the Routing and Remote Access snap-in.

PPTP

PPTP was developed in 1996 by Microsoft, 3Com, U.S. Robotics, and several other companies. As one of the oldest VPN protocols, it is also the most popular and widely supported. It is supported by all versions of Windows starting with Windows 95.

One of the main advantages offered by PPTP is the ability to function properly through NAT. This is very important because many times roaming users are not assigned an Internet-addressable IP address, but are behind NAT implemented at a hotel or client site.

Authentication for PPTP is based on a username and password, and does not authenticate the computers involved in the connection. This means that there is no assurance that the VPN server or VPN client are authorized. For example, a hacker could obtain control of a router and redirect packets destined for a company VPN server to a VPN server controlled by the hacker where passwords are collected. Because the server and client computers are not authenticated, there is no way the client can prevent this or be warned about it.

The encryption used by PPTP is Microsoft Point-to-Point Encryption (MPPE) protocol. This is a part of PPTP, and no extra configuration is required.

L2TP

L2TP alone is not sufficient to provide a VPN connection. It is designed only for tunneling data, not encrypting it. The L2TP implementation used by Microsoft for VPN connections uses IPSec for encryption of data packets. This protocol is only supported by Windows 2000 and newer Microsoft operating systems.

A data packet is first encapsulated in an L2TP packet. This allows non-IP protocols to travel across an IP-based network. Then the L2TP packet is encapsulated in an IPSec packet using ESP for data encryption. The encrypted IPSec packet travels from VPN client to VPN server where the L2TP packet is decrypted and removed from the IPSec packet, and the data packet is removed from the L2TP packet. The structure of an L2TP/IPSec packet is shown in Figure 10-17.

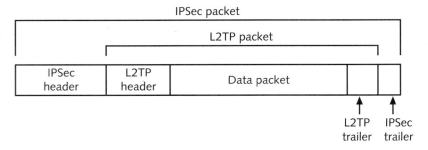

Figure 10-17   Structure of an L2TP/IPSec packet

Until recently L2TP/IPSec connections could not function properly through NAT. However, if the devices implementing IPSec conform to the specifications laid out in the IPSec Protocol Working Group drafts "Negotiation of NAT-Traversal in the IKE" (draft-ietf-ipsec-nat-t-ike-01.txt) and "UDP Encapsulation of IPSec Packets" (draft-ietf-ipsec-udp-encaps-01.txt), then operation over NAT is possible. Windows Server 2003 supports these drafts. The only Microsoft client operating system that supports these drafts is Windows XP with Service Pack 1.

 You can find more information about the latest IPSec drafts at *www.ietf.org/html.charters/ ipsec-charter.html*.

The authentication used by L2TP is based on a username and password, just like PPTP. However, the addition of IPSec adds computer-level authentication as well. This means that IPSec authentication needs to be configured on the VPN clients and VPN server. The options for IPSec authentication include PKI certificates, and preshared keys. Kerberos authentication is not supported for L2TP/IPSec connections.

The main disadvantage of L2TP/IPSec VPN connections is the relative complexity involved in configuring them when compared to PPTP. The second main disadvantage of L2TP/IPSec VPN connections is the limited support for traversing NAT. However, L2TP/IPSec VPN connections are more secure than PPTP connections because in addition to the user authentication performed by L2TP, IPSec performs tunnel authentication which confirms the identity of both the VPN server and VPN client.

CONFIGURING REMOTE ACCESS SERVERS

The default configuration options for a remote access server are generally sufficient for day-to-day operations, but there may be some situations where you need to modify these settings to allow particular types of clients to connect, or to modify the performance of the system.

The General tab in the Properties of the server, as shown in Figure 10-18, allows you to specify whether the server is a remote access server. This is normally configured using the Routing and Remote Access Server Setup Wizard, but you can enable it manually if this server is already functioning and you do not wish to lose the current configuration.

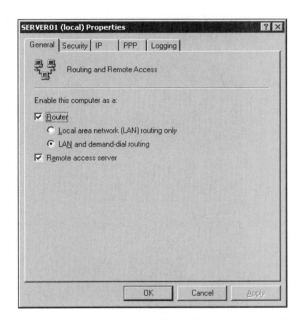

Figure 10-18   General tab in the Properties of an RRAS server

The Security tab in the Properties of the server, as shown in Figure 10-19, allows you to control authentication and logging. The Authentication Methods button allows you to specify which authentication methods this server supports for dial-up, PPTP, and L2TP connections. The Authentication provider box controls whether authentication is performed by Windows or a RADIUS server. The Accounting provider box defines whether logging of connections is disabled, stored on the local server, or passed to a RADIUS server.

The "Allow custom IPSec policy for L2TP connection" option is used when an IPSec policy is already in place for use on the LAN. Using this option you can specify a preshared key used by L2TP/IPSec clients when connecting to the VPN server. This reduces the complexity of configuring IPSec policies for a VPN server.

The IP tab in the properties of the server, as shown in Figure 10-20, allows you to configure whether or not this server is a router for IP, and if it allows IP-based remote access connections. The IP address assignment for the client can be configured here to allow automatic assignment via DHCP or manual assignment via a static pool of addresses. You can also choose the adapter used to obtain DHCP, DNS, and WINS configuration for clients. All of these are normally configured using the Routing and Remote Access Server Setup Wizard.

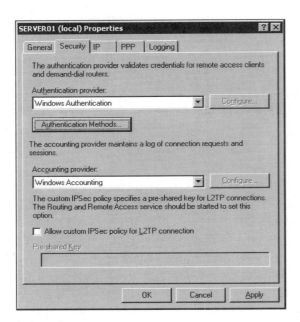

Figure 10-19   Security tab in the Properties of an RRAS server

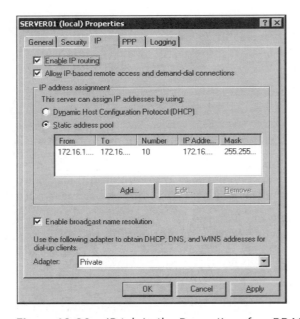

Figure 10-20   IP tab in the Properties of an RRAS server

The "Enable broadcast name resolution" option is new in Windows Server 2003. In the past, because the VPN server acts as a router for VPN clients, NetBIOS name resolution by broadcast was not possible; a WINS server was required. Even with a WINS server, browsing in My Network places was sometimes unreliable. With this option enabled, the VPN server acts as a proxy for NetBIOS broadcasts, and the VPN client does not need to be configured with a WINS server if the network being connected is a single subnet (not routed).

The Logging tab in the Properties of the server, shown in Figure 10–21, allows you to control the events that are written to the event log. In addition, you can enable the Log additional Routing and Remote Access information (used for debugging) option to create C:\WINDOWS\tracing\ppp.log to track detailed information on the establishment of PPP connections.

The logging configured on the Logging tab is not the same as the accounting information configured on the Security tab.

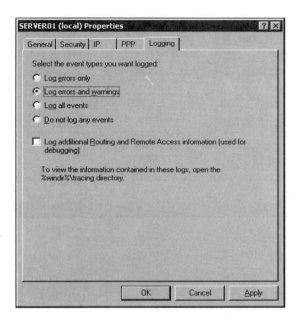

Figure 10-21   Logging tab in the Properties of an RRAS server

Authentication Methods

Windows Server 2003 has the ability to use a number of different authentication methods. These authentication methods can be used for authenticating dial-up, PPTP, and L2TP connections:

- **No Authentication**—If you choose to have no authentication, then all users are permitted access regardless of their username and password.

- **Password Authentication Protocol (PAP)**—PAP transmits passwords across the network in plain text. This makes it unsuitable for use except as a last resort for clients that support no other authentication methods. MPPE cannot be used in conjunction with PAP, which means that a PPTP VPN cannot encrypt the data packets when PAP is used. PAP also cannot change the password during the authentication process. This authentication method is disabled by default.

- **Shiva Password Authentication Protocol (SPAP)**—SPAP uses reversible encryption to transmit passwords. This means that the password can be decrypted if captured with a packet sniffer. It is also vulnerable to replay attacks because the password is encrypted exactly the same each time it is transmitted on the network. MPPE cannot be used in conjunction with SPAP, which means that a PPTP VPN connection cannot encrypt the data packets when SPAP is used. SPAP also cannot change the password during the authentication process. This authentication method is disabled by default.

- **Challenge Handshake Authentication Protocol (CHAP)**—CHAP is a significant enhancement over SPAP because it uses the one-way hashing algorithm MD5 to secure passwords in transit. However, it does require passwords stored in Active Directory to be encrypted in a reversible format, which is a security risk. This authentication method is widely supported by many vendors. MPPE cannot be used in conjunction with CHAP, which means that a PPTP VPN connection cannot encrypt the data packets when CHAP is used. CHAP also cannot change the password during the authentication process. This authentication method is disabled by default.

10

- **Microsoft Challenge Handshake Authentication Protocol (MS-CHAP)**—This is an enhancement to CHAP that allows Active Directory passwords to be stored using nonreversible encryption. MPPE can be used in conjunction with MS-CHAP, which means that a PPTP VPN can encrypt the data packets. In addition MS-CHAP can be used to change the password during the authentication process if the password has expired. Passwords are limited to 14 characters. This authentication method is enabled by default.

- **Microsoft Challenge Handshake Authentication Protocol version 2 (MS-CHAPv2)**—This enhanced version of MS-CHAP corrects several problems. LAN Manager support for older Windows clients is no longer supported because of their weak encryption algorithms. Authentication is performed for both computers in the communication and not just the client, similar to the mutual authentication provided by IPSec. Encryption keys vary with each connection, unlike MS-CHAP which reused the same encryption key for each connection.

- **Extensible Authentication Protocol (EAP)**—This is not an authentication method as much as it is an authentication system. EAP allows multiple authentication mechanisms to be configured. The client and server can negotiate which authentication mechanism to use. The authentication mechanism options included with Windows Server 2003 are MD5-Challenge, Protected EAP (PEAP), and Smart Card or other certificate. In Windows 2000, the Smart Card or other certificate option was known as Transport Layer Security (EAP-TLS). Authentication mechanisms are also known as EAP types.

IP Address Management

When dial-up and VPN clients connect to Windows Server 2003 configured as a remote access server they are assigned an IP address. The IP address can be from a static pool configured on the remote access server or leased from a DHCP server.

Regardless of which IP allocation method is used, the options for the DNS server and the WINS server assigned to the client are taken from the configuration of a specified interface on the remote access server. As you can see below in Figure 10-22, the remote access server is configured to use DHCP for assigning IP addresses to clients. The internal network interface is chosen to provide the DNS option to clients. WINS is not configured. The remote access server leases an IP address from the DHCP server for the client. This is the IP address that is assigned to the remote access client. The DNS option sent to the remote access client is obtained from the internal network interface of the remote access server. The options in the DHCP lease are not used.

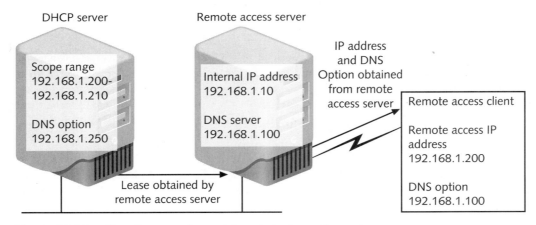

Figure 10-22   IP options configured from interface of remote access server

Windows 2000 and newer clients have the ability to send a **DHCPINFORM** packet after a remote access connection has been established. This allows clients to query a DHCP server for configuration options. If the query is successful, then the options from the DHCP server override the options from the network interface of the remote access server. For this system to work, the **DHCP Relay Agent** on the remote access server must be configured to pass the DHCPINFORM messages on to a DHCP server. The DHCP Relay Agent is also known as a DHCP proxy.

In Figure 10-23, a remote access connection has been established between the remote access client and the remote access server. The remote access client sends a DHCPINFORM message to the remote access server. The DHCP Relay Agent on the remote access server forwards the DHCPINFORM message to the DHCP server. The DHCP Server sends the DNS configuration option back to the DHCP Relay Agent on the remote access server. Finally, the remote access server passes the DNS configuration option to the remote access client where the remote access client overwrites the existing DNS server option with the new configuration.

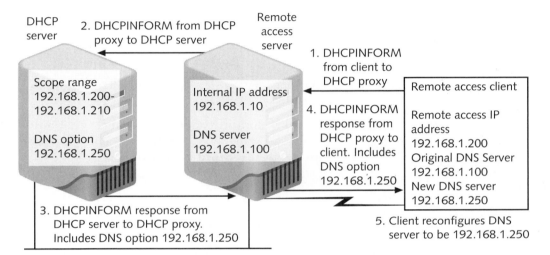

Figure 10-23 IP options configured from DHCP server through DHCP Relay Agent

 If a remote access client attempts to use a DHCPINFORM packet and does not receive a response, then the IP options configured by RRAS continue to be used.

Activity 10-6: Configuring the DHCP Relay Agent

Time Required: 5 minutes

Objective: Configure the DHCP Relay Agent on a remote access server.

Description: All of your servers on your network are configured to use the DNS server 192.168.1.10. However, you would like remote access clients to use a different DNS server that is configured as an option on a DHCP server. You will configure the DHCP Relay Agent on your server to query the DHCP server. Note that there is not a DHCP server actually running on this network. For this activity you are just simulating it.

1. If necessary, start your server and log on as Administrator.

2. Click **Start**, point to **Administrative Tools**, and click **Routing and Remote Access**.

3. If necessary, double-click your server to expand it.

4. Double-click **IP Routing** to expand it.

5. Click **DHCP Relay Agent** to view the interfaces that are connected to this service. The only interface that should be connected is Internal. You must add the interface that is on the same network as the remote access clients.

6. Right-click **DHCP Relay Agent**, and click **New Interface**.

7. Click **Private** and click **OK**. Remember that the Classroom interface is the Internet connection in our scenario.

8. Confirm that the **Relay DHCP packets** option is selected, and click **OK**.

9. Right-click **DHCP Relay Agent**, and click **Properties**.

10. In the Server address box, type **172.16.0.1**, click **Add**, and click **OK**. Communication between the DHCP Relay Agent and the DHCP server uses unicast packets, so this DHCP server can be on any network.

11. Close the Routing and Remote Access snap-in.

ALLOWING CLIENT ACCESS

In most organizations not all users are allowed to access network resources remotely. When remote access is first configured on Windows Server 2003, none of the users are granted remote access permission. Remote access permission allows users to act as dial-up or VPN clients.

In a mixed mode domain with pre-Windows 2000 domain controllers, the dial-in permission is either allowed or denied. When all domain controllers are Windows 2000 or later, and the domain has been switched to at least Windows 2000 **native mode**, then **remote access policies** can be used to control remote access permission.

Remote access permission for users is controlled by their user object in Active Directory. The settings are configured in the properties of the user object on the Dial-in tab, as shown in Figure 10-24. Some of the options on this tab are not available unless the domain is in Windows 2000 native mode.

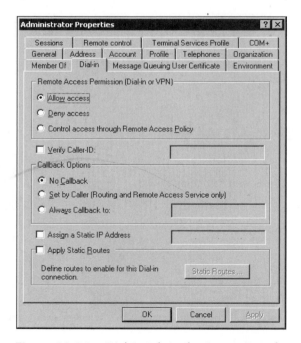

Figure 10-24   Dial-in tab in the Properties of a user object

The Remote Access Permission box on the Dial-in tab allows you to control whether a user has access or not. The "Allow access" option means that a user is allowed to connect remotely. The "Deny access" option means that a user is not allowed to connect remotely. The "Control access through Remote Access Policy" option means that a remote access policy allows or denies the user access. By default, all users are denied access.

The "Verify Caller-ID" option allows the user to connect only if they are calling from a particular phone number. For this option to work, the modems used must be capable of reading caller-ID information, the phone company must provide caller-ID information, and the domain must be in at least Windows 2000 native mode. This option is useful to prevent stolen user accounts and passwords from being used anywhere except from a designated location. Requiring the use of a particular phone line makes remotely hacking into a system much more difficult.

The Callback Options box has settings that allow you to enable or disable callback. If the "No Callback" option is selected, then the user is allowed to connect immediately and stay connected. If the "Set by Caller (Routing and Remote Access Service only)" option is selected, first the client computer gives the remote access server a phone number as part of the connection establishment process, then both client and server will hang up, and then the server calls the client. This is useful to ensure that long distance charges are borne by the main office, and to log where all calls come from. If the "Always Callback to" option is selected, then a phone number must be entered, and when the user dials in, the server always calls the user back at the configured number. This provides the same type of protection for stolen user accounts and passwords as the caller-ID option.

The "Assign a Static IP Address" option ensures that a user gets the same IP address each time they dial in. This overrides the settings configured at the server level for DHCP-based addresses or a static pool. This is useful if firewalls are configured to allow this particular IP address access to network resources not accessible to most users. This option is available only if the domain is in at least Windows 2000 native mode.

The "Apply Static Routes" option is designed for use with demand dial connections configured between routers. The demand dial connection logs in with the user account, then static routes are added to the routing table of the remote access server. These static routes allow the remote access server to route packets back to the network of the demand dial router. This option is available only if the domain is in at least Windows 2000 native mode. Routing and demand dial connections are covered in the next chapter.

Activity 10-7: Allowing a User Remote Access Permission

Time Required: 10 minutes

Objective: Create a new user, and allow it remote access permission.

Description: A new professor that requires VPN access has started working for Arctic University. You must create a new account for him in Active Directory and allow him remote access permission.

1. If necessary, start your server and log on as Administrator.
2. Click **Start** and click **Run**.
3. Type **mmc** and press **Enter**.
4. Click the **File** menu, and click **Add/Remove Snap-in**.
5. Click **Add**, double-click **Active Directory Users and Computers**, click **Close**, and click **OK**. This adds the snap-in that allows you to manage users in Active Directory.
6. Click the **File** menu, and click **Save As**.
7. In the File name box, type **AD Users**, and press **Enter**. This adds the current console to the Administrative Tools menu.
8. Double-click **Active Directory Users and Computers** to expand it.
9. Click **Arctic.local** to select it.
10. Double-click **Arctic.local** to expand it.
11. Right-click **Users**, point to **New**, and click **User**.
12. In the First name box, type **Sherman**.

13. In the Last name box, type **KlumpX**, where *X* is your student number.

14. In the User logon name box, type **SKlumpX**, where *X* is your student number, and click **Next**.

15. In the Password box, type **Password!**, and in the Confirm password box, type **Password!**.

16. Click the **User must change password at next logon** option to deselect it, and click **Next**.

17. Click **Finish**.

18. In the left pane, click **Users**.

19. In the right pane, right-click **Sherman KlumpX**, where *X* is your student number, and click **Properties**.

20. Click the **Dial-in** tab.

21. Click **Allow access**, and click **OK**.

22. Close the MMC. If prompted to save changes, click **No**.

Creating a VPN Client Connection

Most of the time VPN clients are configured on client operating systems such as Windows XP. However, Windows Server 2003 can also be configured as a VPN client. This can be useful when Windows Server 2003 is configured to act as a router between two locations. VPN connections can be used to encrypt traffic sent between the two routers.

VPN client connections are created using the same New Connection Wizard that is used when configuring dial-up connections. If you have a dial-up connection created, you are asked if an initial connection should be dialed before attempting to create the VPN connection. You can select the "Do not dial the initial connection" option if it is not required. This is the appropriate setting if you are connecting via a LAN. You can also choose the "Automatically dial this initial connection" option, and then choose an existing dial-up connection, as shown in Figure 10-25.

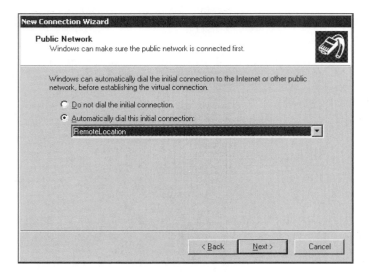

Figure 10-25   Dial initial connection option for a VPN connection

Activity 10-8: Creating a Client VPN Connection

Time Required: 10 minutes

Objective: Create a client VPN connection and then test it.

Description: After installing and configuring a VPN server, you would like to test it using one of the servers in your test lab. In this activity, you will create a VPN client connection on your server and connect to the VPN server configured on your partner's server.

1. If necessary, start your server and log on as Administrator.

2. Click **Start**, point to **Control Panel**, right-click **Network Connections**, and click **Open**.

3. Double-click **Create a new connection**.

4. Click **Next** to begin the New Connection Wizard.

5. Click **Connect to the network at my workplace**, and click **Next**.

6. Click **Virtual Private Network connection**, and click **Next**.

7. In the Company Name box, type **ArcticVPN**, and click **Next**.

8. Click **Do not dial the initial connection**. This feature is not required as you are connecting across the LAN using a network card. Click **Next**.

9. In the Host name or IP address box, type **serverXX.arctic.local**, where *XX* is your partner's student number, as shown in Figure 10-26. For example, server01.arctic.local.

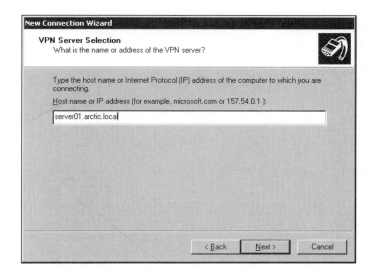

Figure 10-26   Entering the Host name or IP address of the VPN server

10. Click **Next**.

11. Click **Anyone's use**, so that all users can use this connection, and click **Next**.

12. Click **Finish**.

13. In the User name box, type **SKlumpX**, where *X* is your student number. This is the user you created and allowed remote access permission in Activity 10-7.

14. In the Password box, type **Password!**.

15. Click **Connect** to enable the connection. Once the connection is established, you should see an icon of two computers in the system tray.

16. In the Network Connections window, the status of the ArcticVPN should now be connected. Double-click **ArcticVPN**.

17. On the **General** tab you can view how long the VPN connection has been active and the amount of data that has traveled through it.

18. Click the **Details** tab. Here you can view the authentication protocol, encryption protocol, server IP address on the VPN, and the client IP address on the VPN.

19. Click the **General** tab, and click **Disconnect**.

20. Close the Network Connections window.

Configuring a VPN Client Connection

Most configuration of a VPN client connection is done with the New Connection Wizard. However, you can configure all of the same options in the properties of the VPN connection.

The General tab of the VPN connection properties, as shown in Figure 10-27, allows you to configure the IP address of the VPN server to which you are connecting. In addition, you can configure whether an initial connection is created, and control whether or not an icon is placed in the system tray when this connection is active.

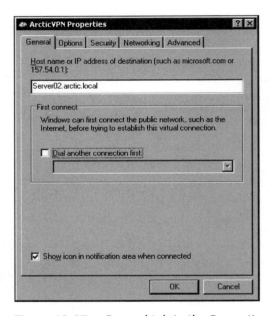

Figure 10-27   General tab in the Properties of a VPN connection

The Options tab of the VPN connection properties, as shown in Figure 10-28, allows you to configure dialing options and redialing options. The redialing options are useful primarily for busy dial-up connections. VPN connections are less likely to be successful with redial attempts.

The Security tab of the VPN connection properties, as shown in Figure 10-29, allows you to set whether or not password encryption and data encryption are required. Based on those settings, only certain authentication methods are allowed. You can also manually choose the authentication methods by clicking Advanced. The "IPSec Settings" option allows you to configure a preshared key that is used for L2TP/IPSec connections.

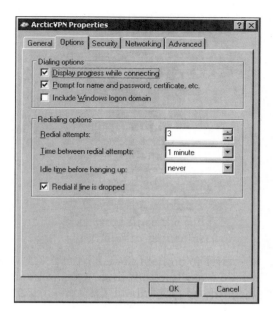

Figure 10-28   Options tab in the Properties of a VPN connection

10

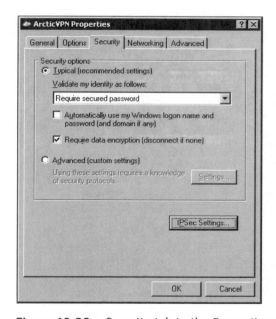

Figure 10-29   Security tab in the Properties of a VPN connection

The Networking tab of the VPN connection properties, as shown in Figure 10–30, allows you to configure the network configuration for the VPN connection. This includes setting a static IP address if required. You can also set the type of VPN connection to PPTP or L2TP. By default, the type of VPN connection is negotiated between the client and server.

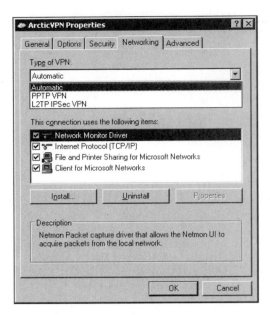

Figure 10-30 Networking tab in the Properties of a VPN connection

The Advanced tab of the VPN connection properties allows you to configure Internet Connection Firewall and Internet Connection Sharing for this connection. Both of these topics are covered in the next chapter on routing.

REMOTE ACCESS POLICIES

Remote access policies are a critical part of controlling and allowing remote access. How remote access policies are applied varies depending on whether the domain is in mixed mode or native mode. Figure 10-31 shows the properties of a default remote access policy.

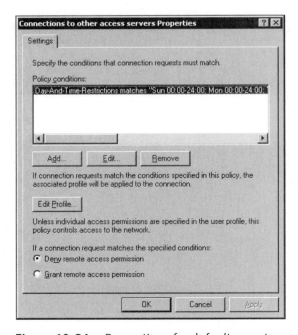

Figure 10-31 Properties of a default remote access policy

These policies are stored on each individual remote access server, not in Active Directory. This means that the policies applied to a user creating a remote access connection will vary depending on the remote access server to which the user connects. As an administrator, this offers you the extra flexibility to provide remote access servers that service only certain types of users. For example, you may configure one remote access server that services all remote users, and another that services only executives. In this way, you can be sure the executives are never blocked out of a busy remote access server. Or you may configure one remote access server that allows connections for an unlimited period, and another that only allows connections for up to 10 minutes. This ensures that all users that need to quickly check e-mail are able to do so, and are not blocked out of a busy remote access server.

 Configuring remote access servers with different policies can be confusing for users. If you do this be sure to provide documentation for your users describing exactly what is different between the remote access servers so they understand which one to use for a given situation.

To effectively use remote access policies you must understand:

- Remote access policy components
- Remote access policy evaluation
- Default remote access policies

Remote Access Policy Components

Remote access policies are composed of **conditions**, **remote access permissions**, and a **profile**. When a domain is in native mode all three of these components are used. When a domain is in mixed mode only the conditions and profile are used.

Conditions

Conditions are criteria that must be met in order for a remote access policy to apply to a connection. A variety of conditions are available to be set. Some of the more common conditions used are listed in table 10-1.

Table 10-1   Common remote access policy conditions

Condition	Description
Authentication type	The authentication method being used by the client; these include CHAP, MS-CHAP, and MS-CHAPv2
Called station ID	This is the phone number phoned by the user; this information is only available if arranged with the phone company
Calling station ID	This is the phone number that the user is calling from; this information is only available if arranged with the phone company
Day and time restrictions	Sets specific days of the week and times of the day. The time is based on the time set on the server providing authorization, which is either the remote access server or RADIUS server.
NAS port type	Identifies the media used to make the connection, including phone lines (async), ISDN, VPN (virtual), IEEE 802.11 wireless, and Ethernet switches
Tunnel type	The VPN protocol being used (either PPTP or L2TP)
Windows group	Group membership for the user attempting the connection. To create a policy with multiple groups you can add this condition several times with different groups, or use nested groups.

Several conditions can be combined in a single remote access policy. All of the conditions in a remote access policy must be matched for a remote access policy to apply.

Remote Access Permission

If the conditions of a remote access policy are met, then the remote access permission is checked. The remote access permission set in a remote access policy has only two options:

- Deny remote access permission
- Grant remote access permission

The permission setting in a remote access policy can only be used for native mode domains. If the domain is in mixed mode, then the permission is always taken from the user object in Active Directory.

Profile

The profile of a remote policy contains settings that are applied to a remote access connection if the conditions have been matched and permission has been allowed. If the settings in a profile, such as the authentication method, cannot be applied, then the connection is denied.

The Dial-in Constraints tab of the profile, as shown in Figure 10-32, allows you to set the number of minutes a connection can be idle before it is disconnected, the maximum number of minutes for a connection, and day and time restrictions. As well, you can configure caller ID settings and port type settings, such as Wireless – IEEE 802.11, ISDN, or Async (modem).

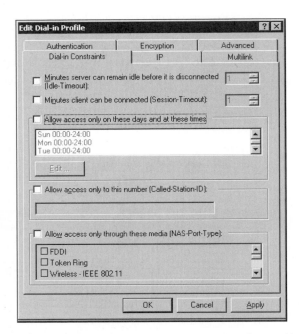

Figure 10-32   Dial-in Constraints tab of a profile

The IP tab of the profile, as shown in figure 10-33, allows you to not only configure how IP addresses are assigned for a connection, but also to set filters to control traffic across the VPN connection. The IP address assignment setting configured in the policy overrides the settings configured on the server and the client. The IP filters can be used to control traffic based on source and destination IP addresses, source and destination port numbers, and packet type. You can use these to control what services are allowed on a connection. For example, to restrict Web-browsing traffic you can configure a profile that denies outgoing packets where the destination TCP port is 80.

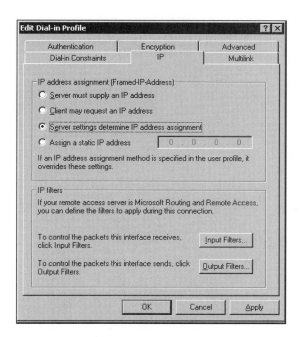

Figure 10-33   IP tab of a profile

10

The Multilink tab of the profile, as shown in Figure 10-34, allows you to control the maximum number of lines used for a multilink connection, and if multilink is allowed at all. In addition, you can set the capacity percentage at which the multilink connection is reduced by a line, and how long it must be at that capacity. If you select the "Require BAP for dynamic Multilink requests" option, then multilink connections are not allowed unless **Bandwidth Allocation Protocol (BAP)** can be used to control the number of phone lines used.

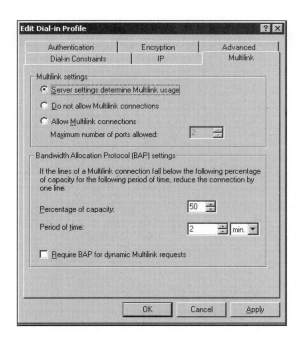

Figure 10-34   Multilink tab of a profile

The Authentication tab of the profile allows you to control the types of authentication that are allowed. These authentication methods must be enabled on the client and on the server in order for them to be used.

The Encryption tab of the profile, as shown in Figure 10-35, allows you to control the types of encryption that are allowed. Table 10-2 lists the types of encryption allowed for each option when PPTP and L2TP/IPSec VPN connections are used.

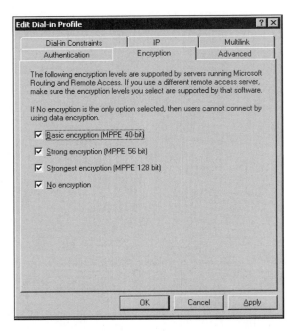

Figure 10-35   Encryption tab of a profile

Table 10-2   Allowed encryption types

Encryption Level	PPTP Encryption	L2TP/IPSec Encryption
Basic encryption	40-bit MPPE	56-bit DES
Strong encryption	56-bit MPPE	56-bit DES
Strongest encryption	128-bit MPPE	Triple DES (3DES)
No encryption	None	None

The Advanced tab of the profile contains settings that are generally intended to be configured when Windows Server 2003 is used as a RADIUS server. The **Ignore-User-Dialin-Properties** attribute can be configured here. If this attribute is false, then remote access policies are processed normally. If this attribute is true then the dial-in settings in the properties of a user account are ignored.

Activity 10-9: Creating a Remote Access Policy

Time Required: 10 minutes

Objective: Create a new remote access policy on your server.

Description: Arctic University has a wide variety of users accessing resources through remote access. You would like to force all of the department heads to use high levels of data encryption and MS-CHAPv2 for authentication when they connect via VPN. The easiest way to implement this is by creating a new policy with a condition for a Windows Group, and a profile with the encryption settings.

1. If necessary, start your server and log on as Administrator.

2. Click **Start**, point to **All Programs**, point to **Administrative Tools**, and click **AD Users.msc**.

3. Double-click **Active Directory Users and Computers** to expand it.

4. Click **Arctic.local** to select it.

5. Double-click **Arctic.local** to expand it.

6. Right-click **Users**, point to **New**, click **Group**.

7. In the Group name box, type **HighSecX**, where *X* is your student number, and click **OK**.

8. Click **Users** in the left pane, and in the right pane double-click **HighSecX**, where *X* is your student number.

9. Click the **Members** tab, and click **Add**.

10. Type **Sherman KlumpX**, where *X* is your student number, and click **OK**.

11. Click **OK** to close the HighSec*X* Properties window.

12. Close MMC. If prompted to save the console settings, click **No**.

13. Click **Start**, point to **Administrative Tools**, and click **Routing and Remote Access**.

14. In the left pane, click **Remote Access Policies**. Notice that there are two policies already created by default.

15. Right-click **Remote Access Policies**, and click **New Remote Access Policy**.

16. Click **Next** to start the New Remote Access Policy Wizard.

17. Confirm that the setting **Use the wizard to set up a typical policy for a common scenario** is selected.

18. In the Policy name box, type **HighSecurity**, and click **Next**.

19. Confirm that the **VPN** option is selected, and click **Next**.

20. Confirm that the **Group** option is selected, click **Add**, type **ARCTIC\HighSecX**, where *X* is your student number, click **OK**, and click **Next**.

21. Verify that the only option selected is **Microsoft Encrypted Authentication version 2 (MS-CHAPv2)**, and click **Next**.

22. Click the **Basic encryption (IPSec 56-bit DES or MPPE 40-bit)** checkbox to deselect it.

23. Click the **Strong encryption (IPSec 56-bit DES or MPPE 56-bit)** checkbox to deselect it.

24. Verify the that **Strongest encryption (IPSec Triple DES or MPPE 128-bit)** checkbox is selected, and click **Next**.

25. Click **Finish**.

26. Notice that your new policy has been placed first in the priority order.

27. If time permits, view the properties of your policy to verify the settings.

28. Close the Routing and Remote Access snap-in.

10

Remote Access Policy Evaluation

To create remote access policies and understand what their results will be, you need to understand not only the contents of remote access policies, but also how they are evaluated by RRAS. If you do not understand this process, you may find users who should be able to create remote access connections unable to do so. The evaluation process varies depending on whether the domain is in mixed mode or native mode.

Evaluate Conditions

Evaluating conditions follows the same process for mixed mode domain and native mode domains, and is shown in Figure 10-36. The first step in the process checks to see if there are any policies at all. If no remote access policies exist, then the connection attempt is rejected. If remote access policies exist, then their conditions are evaluated.

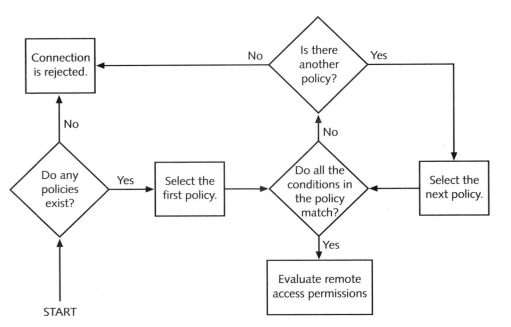

Figure 10-36   Condition evaluation process for remote access policies

The second step is to compare the conditions set in the remote access policies with the actual conditions of the connection being attempted. Remote access policies are assigned an order. The attempt to match conditions of the remote access policies starts with the remote access policy that comes first in order, and continues until a match is found or no remote access policies remain. If no match is found, the connection attempt is rejected.

If multiple remote access policies match the conditions, then only the first one evaluated is used. For example, if a user is attempting to create a VPN connection and the remote access policy that comes second in order and the remote access policy ordered 4 both match, then only the remote access policy ordered 2 is used.

Evaluate Permissions

After a condition match has been found, the permissions of the user attempting the connection must be evaluated, as shown in Figure 10-37. The first step is to check for the Ignore-User-Dialin-Properties attribute in the profile of the remote access policy. This is true for mixed mode and native mode domains.

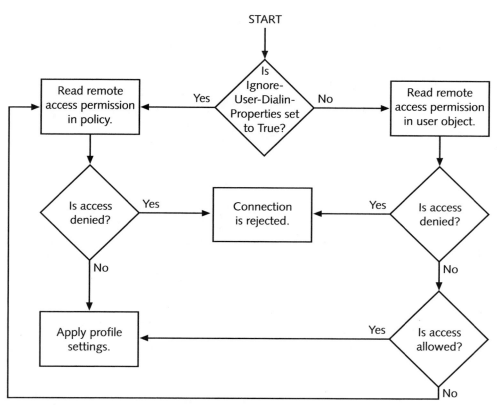

Figure 10-37   Remote access permission evaluation process

In a mixed mode domain, if the Ignore-User-Dialin-Properties attribute is set to False, then the remote access permission from the user object is used to determine whether a user is allowed or denied remote access permission. If the Ignore-User-Dialin-Properties attribute is set to True, then the permission setting of the remote access policy is used to determine whether a user is granted or denied remote access permission.

In a native mode domain, if the Ignore-User-Dialin-Properties attribute is set to False, then the remote access permission from the user object is used to determine whether a user is allowed or denied access, unless the user object is configured with the remote access permission Control Access Through Remote Access policy. If this option is configured, then the remote access policy defines whether the user is granted or denied remote access permission. If the Ignore-User-Dialin-Properties attribute is set to True, then the remote access policy always defines whether the user is granted or denied remote access permission.

 The Ignore-User-Dialin-Properties attribute is new in Windows Server 2003.

 If a Windows NT 4.0 remote access server attempts to read the remote access permissions from a native mode Active Directory domain and the setting is Control Access Through Remote Access policy, then it is read as "Deny access."

If permission is denied based on this remote access policy, no other policies are evaluated. For example, if a user is attempting to create a VPN connection and the remote access policy ordered 2, which denies remote access permission, and the remote access policy ordered 4, which grants remote access permission, both match, then only the remote access policy ordered 2 is used.

Profile Settings

Even if remote access permission is granted, it does not guarantee that a remote access connection will be successful. Some of the profile settings, such as allowed authentication methods and encryption levels, force a connection attempt to be disconnected.

Profile settings are applied in the same way for mixed mode and native mode domains.

Activity 10-10: Testing Remote Policy Evaluation

Time Required: 20 minutes

Objective: Verify the process by which remote access permission is granted.

Description: In this activity you will perform a series of steps to illustrate the process used to evaluate remote access policies and grant remote access permission. These steps are not meant to simulate any real-world situation. You will work with a partner on this activity. One partner will perform configuration tasks on their server; the other will test the changes by initiating a VPN connection from their server.

1. If necessary, start your server and log on as Administrator.

2. Partner A: Verify the existing VPN is functional.

    a. Click **Start**, point to **Control Panel**, point to **Network Connections**, click **ArcticVPN**.

    b. If necessary, type **SKlumpX** in the User name box, where *X* is your partner's student number.

    c. In the Password box, type **Password!**, and click **Connect**.

    d. The VPN connection should now be active and using the settings configured in the HighSecurity policy on the remote access server.

    e. Right-click the VPN icon in the system tray, and click **Status**.

    f. Click the **Details** tab, and verify that Authentication is **MS CHAP V2** and Encryption is **MPPE 128**.

    g. Right-click the VPN icon in the system tray, and click **Disconnect**.

3. Partner B: Create a new low-security policy, and place it first in the order.

    a. Click **Start**, point to **Administrative Tools**, and click **Routing and Remote Access**.

    b. Right-click **Remote Access Policies**, and click **New Remote Access Policy**.

    c. Click **Next** to start the New Remote Access Policy Wizard.

    d. In the Policy name box, type **LowSecurity**, and click **Next**.

    e. Confirm that **VPN** is selected, and click **Next**.

    f. Click **User**, and click **Next**. This policy applies to all users, because "user" was selected.

    g. Verify that the only option selected is **Microsoft Encrypted Authentication version 2 (MS-CHAPv2)**, and click **Next**.

    h. Verify that the **Basic encryption (IPSec 56-bit DES or MPPE 40-bit)** checkbox is selected.

    i. Click the **Strong encryption (IPSec 56-bit DES or MPPE 56-bit)** checkbox to deselect it.

    j. Click the **Strongest encryption (IPSec Triple DES or MPPE 128-bit)** checkbox to deselect it, and click **Next**.

    k. Click **Finish**.

    l. The **LowSecurity** remote access policy is now listed as the first and will be applied before any other policy.

4. Partner A: Verify the policy application.

   a. Click **Start**, point to **Control Panel**, point to **Network Connections**, and click **ArcticVPN**.

   b. In the Password box, type **Password!**, and click **Connect**.

   c. The VPN connection should now be active and using the settings configured in the LowSecurity policy on the remote access server.

   d. Right-click the VPN icon in the system tray, and click **Status**.

   e. Click the **Details** tab, and verify that Authentication is **MS CHAP V2** and Encryption is **MPPE 40**. These settings are from the new **LowSecurity** remote access policy created on your partner's server. The settings are taken from this remote access policy because it has higher priority than the **HighSecurity** remote access policy.

   f. Right-click the VPN icon in the system tray, and click **Disconnect**.

5. Partner B: Verify remote access permission.

   a. Right-click **LowSecurity**, and click **Properties**.

   b. By default, the remote access permission setting in this policy is set to **Deny remote access permission**. However, this setting is not used because the remote access permission for the user SKlumpX is set to **Allow access**. That is why Partner A was able to connect in Step 4.

   c. Click **Cancel**.

6. Partner B: Set the Ignore-User-Dialin-Properties attribute to True.

   a. Right-click **LowSecurity**, and click **Properties**.

   b. Click **Edit Profile**.

   c. Click the **Advanced** tab.

   d. Click **Add**.

   e. Scroll down the list of attributes, and double-click **Ignore-User-Dialin-Properties**. Microsoft is listed as the vendor.

   f. Click **True**, and click **OK**.

   g. Click **Close** to close the Add Attribute window.

   h. Click **OK** to save the profile changes.

   i. Verify that the **Deny remote access permission** option is still selected, and click **OK** to save the remote access policy changes.

7. Partner A: Verify the policy application.

   a. Click **Start**, point to **Control Panel**, point to **Network Connections**, and click **ArcticVPN**.

   b. In the Password box, type **Password!**, and click **Connect**.

   c. You receive this error message: **Error 649: The account does not have permission to dial in.** When the attribute **Ignore-User-Dialin-Properties** is set to True, then the remote access permission setting on the user object is ignored, and the remote access permission from the remote access policy is used instead—even in mixed mode domains.

   d. Click **Close**.

10

8. Partner B: Delete the LowSecurity remote access policy.

   a. Right-click **LowSecurity**, and click **Delete**.

   b. Click **Yes** to confirm you want to delete LowSecurity.

   c. Close the Routing and Remote Access snap-in.

9. If sufficient time exists, trade roles and repeat the exercise.

Default Remote Access Policies

The default remote access policies are created to make managing remote access easier. These default settings reduce the amount of configuration required to have a functional remote access server.

The first default remote access policy listed is named Connections to Microsoft Routing and Remote Access server. This policy has a condition where the attribute MS-RAS-Vendor must contain the characters "311". This applies to all Microsoft remote access servers. This profile for this policy does not allow unencrypted communication.

The second default remote access policy listed is named Connections to other access servers. This policy has a condition where the Day-And-Time-Restrictions attribute matches Sunday to Monday, 24 hours per day. This policy does allow unencrypted communication.

Remote access permission is denied in both of the default policies. For user objects with remote access permission set to Control access through Remote Access policy, this ensures that a new remote access policy must be created that explicitly grants the user remote access permission. This means that users cannot be accidentally granted remote access permission.

For user objects with remote access permission set to Allow access, the Control Access Through Remote Access policy remote access policy ensures that they do obtain access. If no policy exists, the users with remote access permission set to Allow access are rejected. For example, assume all of the default remote access policies have been deleted from a remote access server. When a user attempts to connect, the first part of the remote access policy evaluation process is to find a remote access policy with matching conditions. Because no remote access policy with matching conditions is found, the connection attempt is rejected.

RADIUS

Remote Access Dial-In User Authentication Service (RADIUS) is a protocol designed to centralize the authentication process for large distributed networks. Originally intended for dial-up networks, now RADIUS can be used for many other types of devices including VPN servers, switches, and wireless access points.

When using Windows Server 2003 for remote access, each server performs its own authentication using local remote access policies, and it also keeps a local access log. With RADIUS both of these tasks can be centralized on a single server. This makes it easier to create remote access policies because they do not have to be synchronized between multiple remote access servers. Log analysis is also much easier if the logs are centralized on a single server.

The RADIUS process has two mandatory server roles:

- RADIUS client
- RADIUS server

A **RADIUS client** accepts authentication information from users or devices and forwards the authentication information to a RADIUS server. The RADIUS client is an access point to the network. Traditionally, a RADIUS client is a dial-up remote access server or VPN remote access server. However, in high-security situations, wireless access points and switches can be configured as RADIUS clients to force authentication before allowing network access.

A **RADIUS server** accepts authentication information from a RADIUS client. The RADIUS server then authorizes or denies the request based on the authentication information. The authorization or denial is returned to the RADIUS client, which then allows or denies a connection attempt.

Windows Server 2003 can act as a RADIUS client or a RADIUS server. RRAS can be configured as a RADIUS client when used for remote access. To act as a RADIUS server **Internet Authentication Service (IAS)** must be installed.

A **RADIUS proxy** is an optional component that is used by organizations using multiple RADIUS servers. The job of a RADIUS proxy is to act as an intermediary between RADIUS clients and RADIUS servers.

If a RADIUS proxy is used, it accepts authentication information from RADIUS clients, and passes the authentication information on to the appropriate RADIUS server. The RADIUS server passes the authorization or denial back to the RADIUS proxy, which then passes the authorization or denial back to the appropriate RADIUS client.

IAS can be configured as a RADIUS proxy. This feature is new in Windows Server 2003.

Outsourcing Dial-up Requirements

You can use IAS to outsource your dial-up requirements and allow your roaming users to continue logging on using their Active Directory username and password. To do this you must coordinate configuration with a remote access provider, usually an ISP. Long distance charges can be avoided if you choose an ISP with wide geographical coverage.

The ISP supplies a remote access server that is the RADIUS client. The ISP also supplies a server that acts as the RADIUS proxy. One of your servers with IAS installed is the RADIUS server.

Your users dial in to the ISP, and the dial-up software on the laptop passes the authentication information to the remote access server of the ISP. The remote access server of the ISP does not hold any user or password information for authenticating users. As a RADIUS client, it forwards all authentication requests to the RADIUS proxy.

The RADIUS proxy is configured with information that allows it to determine to which RADIUS server an authentication request should be forwarded. The authentication requests from your users are forwarded to your RADIUS server.

When your server running IAS receives authentication requests, it passes them on to an Active Directory domain controller. If IAS successfully authenticates users to Active Directory and remote access policies permit the connections, then IAS authorizes the connections.

If the connections are authorized, then IAS sends the authorizations to the RADIUS proxy. The RADIUS proxy sends the authorizations to the appropriate remote access servers. The remote access servers then connect the dial-up users and allow them access to the network.

Configuring IAS as a RADIUS Server

IAS is a standard component in Windows Server 2003 and is installed through Add or Remove Programs. After IAS is installed, it must be configured using the Internet Authentication Service snap-in before it can be used.

An IAS server must be registered before it can read the remote access properties of users. To register an IAS server, right-click Internet Authentication Service, as shown in Figure 10-38, and click Register Server in Active Directory. This places the computer account for the server in a domain local group named RAS and IAS Servers. Membership in this group grants the proper rights to read the remote access properties of users.

IAS servers do not respond to requests from RADIUS clients unless the RADIUS clients are listed in the configuration of IAS. If a RADIUS proxy is used, it is listed here instead of the RADIUS client.

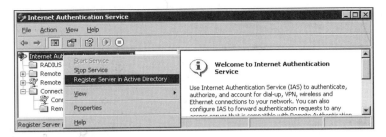

Figure 10-38 Registering an IAS server in Active Directory

When a RADIUS client is added, you are asked for a friendly name, and an IP address or DNS name, as shown in Figure 10-39. Next, you are also asked for the vendor of the RADIUS client, as shown in Figure 10-40. This screen also allows you to set a shared secret that is used to authenticate connections between the RADIUS client and RADIUS server. In addition, the "Request must contain the Message Authenticator attribute" option requires that RADIUS clients include an MD5 hash of their request based on the shared secret. The MD5 hash prevents spoofed requests for authentication.

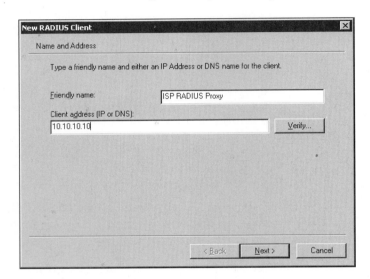

Figure 10-39 Name and Address of a new RADIUS client

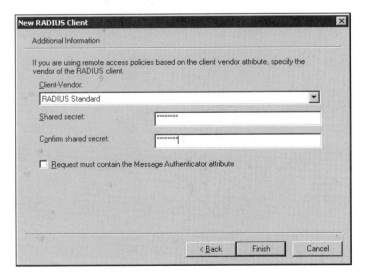

Figure 10-40 Additional Information for a new RADIUS client

Activity 10-11: Configuring IAS as a RADIUS Server

Time Required: 10 minutes

Objective: Install IAS so your server can act as a RADIUS server.

Description: Many of the professors at Arctic University do not have access to high-speed Internet for VPN remote access at home. Until now you have been providing a modem pool for them to dial into. However, this is awkward to maintain, and the cost of phone lines is very expensive. To solve this problem you have struck a deal with a worldwide ISP with 1–800 access. The ISP will configure its RADIUS proxy to forward authentication attempts for your professors back to your RADIUS server. You must now install IAS on your server to act as a RADIUS server.

1. If necessary, start your server and log on as Administrator.
2. Click **Start**, point to **Control Panel**, and click **Add or Remove Programs**.
3. Click **Add/Remove Windows Components**.
4. Scroll down in the Components box, and double-click **Networking Services**.
5. Click the check box beside **Internet Authentication Service** to select it, and click **OK**.
6. Click **Next** to install IAS.
7. Click **Finish**, and close the Add or Remove Programs window.
8. Click **Start**, point to **Administrative Tools**, and click **Internet Authentication Service**.
9. Right-click **Internet Authentication Service**, and click **Register Server in Active Directory**.
10. A message appears indicating the server is already registered in Active Directory because your server was added to the group **RAS and IAS Servers** when RRAS was configured. Click **OK**.
11. Click **RADIUS Clients** to view the list of remote access servers and RADIUS proxy servers that can use this RADIUS server for authentication. None are listed by default.
12. Right-click **RADIUS Clients**, and click **New RADIUS Client**.
13. In the Friendly name box, type **ISP RADIUS Proxy**.
14. In the Client address (IP or DNS) box, type **10.10.10.10**, and click **Next**. This is not a real address on the classroom network. It is used to simulate the IP address of the RADIUS proxy at the ISP.
15. In the Client-Vendor box, confirm that **RADIUS Standard** is selected. This is the option you choose if the actual vendor is not listed.
16. In the Shared secret box, type **password**. For a real implementation you would pick a more secure password than this. Microsoft recommends that a RADIUS shared secret be at least 22 characters long and changed frequently.
17. In the Confirm shared secret box, type **password**, and click **Finish**.
18. Close the Internet Authentication Service snap-in.

Activity 10-12: Centralizing Remote Access Policies

Time Required: 10 minutes

Objective: Configure RRAS and IAS to centralize the management of remote access policies on a single server.

Description: You have several VPN servers at different locations. You would like all of those VPN servers to read their policies from a central location to minimize maintenance on the servers. To do this you will configure your remote access server to use RADIUS for authentication.

1. If necessary, start your server and log on as Administrator.

2. Click **Start**, point to **Administrative Tools**, and click **Routing and Remote Access**.

3. Right-click your server, and click **Properties**.

4. Click the **Security** tab.

5. Click the **Authentication provider** box, and click **RADIUS Authentication**.

6. Click **Configure**.

7. Click **Add** to add a new RADIUS server to the list.

8. In the server name box, type **ServerXX.arctic.local**, where *XX* is your student number. This configures RRAS to pass all authentication requests to IAS on your server.

9. Click **Change** to configure a shared secret for authentication between the remote access server and the RADIUS server.

10. In the New secret box, type **secret**. This shared secret is also configured in IAS.

11. In the Confirm new secret box, type **secret**, and click **OK**.

12. Click **OK** to close the Add RADIUS Server window.

13. Click **OK**, and click **OK**.

14. Read the warning message about restarting RRAS, and click **OK**.

15. Right-click your server, point to **All Tasks**, and click **Restart**.

16. Close the Routing and Remote Access snap-in.

17. Click **Start**, point to **Administrative Tools**, and click **Internet Authentication Service**.

18. Right-click **RADIUS Clients**, and click **New RADIUS Client**.

19. In the Friendly name box, type **MyServer**.

20. In the Client address (IP or DNS) box, type **ServerXX.arctic.local**, where *XX* is your student number, and click **Next**. The remote access server running on your server uses RADIUS to communicate with the IAS server also running on your server. Normally these tasks are performed by separate servers. To centralize authentication and logging, all remote access servers must be RADIUS clients of a single IAS server.

21. Click the **Client-Vendor** box, and click **Microsoft**.

22. In the Shared secret box, type **secret**.

23. In the Confirm shared secret box, type **secret**, and click **Finish**.

24. Close the Internet Authentication Service snap-in.

Configuring IAS as a RADIUS Proxy

A new feature of IAS in Windows Server 2003 is the ability to act as a RADIUS proxy. The previous version of IAS could only function as a RADIUS server.

IAS has the ability to act as both a RADIUS proxy and a RADIUS server at the same time. As a result, a mechanism is required to determine which RADIUS requests received are authenticated locally and which are forwarded to another RADIUS server. Connection request policies are used to determine how a RADIUS request is handled.

Remote RADIUS Server Groups

Remote RADIUS server groups are required for IAS to act as a RADIUS proxy. RADIUS requests and logging information are forwarded to remote RADIUS server groups, not individual RADIUS servers. However, you can create a remote RADIUS server group with a single RADIUS server in it.

Remote RADIUS server groups allow you to perform **load balancing** and **fault tolerance** between RADIUS servers. Each server in a remote RADIUS server group is assigned a priority number and weight, as shown in Figure 10-41. All RADIUS requests are sent to the RADIUS server with the highest priority (1 is the highest possible). If the RADIUS server with the highest priority is unavailable, then the request is forwarded to the RADIUS server with the next highest priority. This system allows fault tolerance between RADIUS servers.

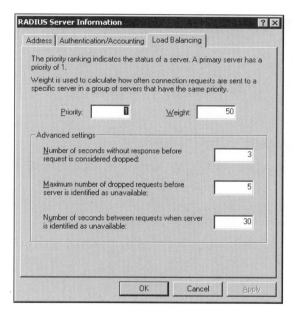

10

Figure 10-41   Load Balancing tab in the Properties of a
                   RADIUS server

To provide load balancing between RADIUS servers, the weight setting is used. If two RADIUS servers are configured with the same priority, then load balancing is performed between them. The weight is used to determine the proportion of requests sent to each RADIUS server. For example, if two RADIUS servers in a remote RADIUS server group are configured with the same priority, but one has a weight of 75 and the other a weight of 25, then the RADIUS server configured with a weight of 75 is sent 75% of RADIUS requests by the RADIUS proxy.

Activity 10-13: Creating a Remote RADIUS Server Group

Time Required: 5 minutes

Objective: Create a remote RADIUS server group that can be used when IAS is configured as a RADIUS proxy.

Description: The engineering college in Arctic University uses a number of UNIX systems for their day-to-day work. All of their user accounts are held on these machines. You would like to configure your remote access system so that engineering users can use your VPN servers to access university resources remotely. To implement this you will configure IAS to act as a RADIUS proxy and forward RADIUS requests for engineering users to the engineering RADIUS servers. The Engineering Department has configured two RADIUS servers to be used for fault tolerance. Load balancing will not be performed.

1. If necessary, start your server and log on as Administrator.

2. Click **Start**, point to **Administrative Tools**, and click **Internet Authentication Service**.

3. Double-click **Connection Request Processing**.

4. Right-click **Remote RADIUS Server Groups**, and click **New Remote RADIUS Server Group**.

5. Click **Next** to start the New Remote RADIUS Server Group Wizard.

6. Confirm that **Typical (one primary server and one backup server)** is selected.

7. In the Group name box, type **Engineering**, and click **Next**.

8. In the Primary server box, type **10.5.5.5**. This is not a real IP address on the classroom network. It is used to simulate one of the engineering RADIUS servers.

9. In the Backup server box, type **10.5.5.6**. This is not a real IP address on the classroom network. It is used to simulate one of the engineering RADIUS servers.

10. In the Shared secret box, type **secret**.

11. In the Confirm shared secret box, type **secret**, and click **Next**.

12. Click the **Start the New Connection Request Policy Wizard when this wizard closes** checkbox to deselect it, and click **Finish**.

13. If necessary, click **Remote RADIUS Server Groups** to view the remote RADIUS server groups that are created. One named "Engineering" should be here.

14. Double-click **Engineering** to view the properties of it. Two RADIUS servers are listed as part of the group. The first is listed with a priority of 1, the second with a priority of two. If the first RADIUS server fails, then the second is used.

15. Click **OK** to close the Engineering Properties window.

16. Close the Internet Authentication Service snap-in.

Connection Request Policies

A **connection request policy** is constructed similarly to a remote access policy. Each connection request policy has conditions. If the conditions match the request, then a profile is applied. It should be noted that there are no permissions in a connection request policy.

The conditions of a connection request policy are a subset of the conditions found in remote access policies. These include Day-And-Time-Restrictions, Client-IP-Address, and Client-Vendor.

The profile in a connection request policy has very different options than a remote access policy. It defines the location for authentication, log settings, rules to modify attributes in requests, and attributes that can be added to requests.

When the location for authentication is defined, as shown in Figure 10-42, you have three choices. The "Authenticate requests on this server" option means that this server acts as the RADIUS server. The "Forward requests to the following remote RADIUS server group for authentication" option means that this server acts as a RADIUS proxy and forwards the request to one of a defined group of RADIUS servers. The "Accept users without validating credentials" option means the users matching the conditions of this policy are authorized regardless of their username and password.

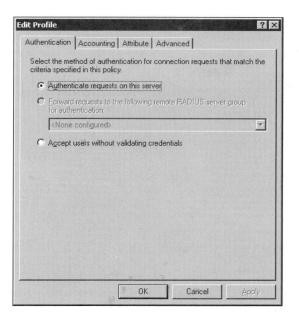

Figure 10-42   Authentication tab in a remote connection
policy profile

The Accounting tab of the profile allows you to pick a RADIUS server group to handle logging for this policy.

The Attribute tab of the profile, as shown in Figure 10-43, allows you to create search and replace rules for values of certain attributes. For example, you could configure this connection request policy so that all forwarded RADIUS requests have a single Calling-Station-ID. This could then be used by the RADIUS server to identify requests from this RADIUS proxy and apply special rules.

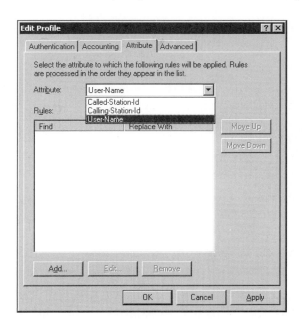

Figure 10-43   Attribute tab in a remote connection
policy profile

The Advanced tab of the profile allows you to specify the value of attributes that are added to the RADIUS request. This is similar to the Advanced tab of the profile in a remote access policy.

Only one connection request policy exists by default. It is named Use Windows authentication for all users. This connection request policy is configured so that all RADIUS requests received by this server are authenticated by this server. This means that this server act as a RADIUS server for all requests it receives.

Connection request policies have an order, just as remote access policies have an order. If you would like your server to act as a RADIUS proxy for some requests, then the policy that defines those conditions must be a higher priority than Use Windows authentication for all users.

Activity 10-14: Creating a Connection Request Policy

Time Required: 5 minutes

Objective: Create a new connection request policy to configure your server as a RADIUS proxy.

Description: In Activity 10-13, you started the configuration process for your server to act as a RADIUS proxy for the Engineering Department. You must now create a new connection request policy that forwards RADIUS requests from engineering users to the engineering remote RADIUS server group.

1. If necessary, start your server and log on as Administrator.

2. Click **Start**, point to **Administrative Tools**, and click **Internet Authentication Service**.

3. Double-click **Connection Request Processing** to expand it.

4. Right-click **Connection Request Policies**, and click **New Connection Request Policy**.

5. Click **Next** to start the New Connection Request Policy Wizard.

6. Click **A custom policy**.

7. In the Policy name box, type **EngineeringProxy**, and click **Next**.

8. Click **Add** to add a condition to the connection request policy.

9. Click **User-Name**, click **Add**, type ***-E**, and click **OK**. This connection request policy now applies to all users with "-E" at the end of the username. All engineering users add this to their regular usernames when they remotely log on.

10. Click **Next**.

11. Click **Edit Profile**.

12. Click **Forward requests to the following remote RADIUS server group for authentication**, and confirm that **Engineering** is selected.

13. Click the **Attribute** tab.

14. Confirm that **User-Name** is selected in the Attribute box.

15. Click **Add** to configure a new rule for the User-Name attribute.

16. In the Find box, type **–E**, leave the Replace with box empty, and click **OK**. This removes the "-E" from the username of engineering users before it is forwarded to the engineering RADIUS server.

17. Click **OK** to finish editing the profile, and click **Next**.

18. Click **Finish** to complete the wizard.

19. Notice that the EngineeringProxy connection request policy has been added as the first in the processing order. This ensures that RADIUS requests for engineering users with "-E" in their username are forwarded to the Engineering remote RADIUS server group. All other RADIUS requests for users without "-E" in their username are handled by the default connection request policy.

20. Close the Internet Authentication Service snap-in.

TROUBLESHOOTING REMOTE ACCESS

Providing remote access for users is a very complex process. The more complex a process, the more difficult it is to troubleshoot. Most of the problems with remote access are due to software configuration errors introduced by users and administrators. Occasionally, however, hardware errors may occur.

Your best troubleshooting tools for remote access are log files and error messages. Other troubleshooting tools include network monitor and ipconfig.

Software Configuration Errors

Users cannot connect remotely if the software on their computers is not configured correctly. The following are some configuration errors to look for:

- Incorrect phone numbers and IP addresses—Users cannot connect if they are attempting to connect to a phone number or IP address that does not exist. To reduce client configuration problems, you can use the **Connection Manager Administration Kit (CMAK)**. CMAK allows you to create remote access connections for dial-up and VPN and distribute them to client computers. For more information on CMAK, search for CMAK in Help and Support.

- Incorrect authentication settings—Ensure that clients, servers, and remote access policies are configured properly to allow authentication to occur. Authentication errors often result in client errors indicating that the user is not authorized. The error messages do not indicate that an authentication method could not be negotiated.

- Incorrectly configured remote access policies—Review your remote access policies to ensure that they really do perform the tasks you think they do. Ensure that the remote access policies are in the proper order. The only remote access policy used is the first one that the conditions match.

- Name resolution is not configured—When a remote access client connects to the remote access server, name resolution must be configured to access resources on the LAN. Ensure that DNS and WINS are configured properly if resources are not accessible when the connection is made.

- Clients receive incorrect IP options—A remote access server gives remote access clients the WINS and DNS configuration from a designated interface on the remote access server. If you want these settings to come from a DHCP server, then you must configure the DHCP proxy on the remote access server.

- The remote access server leases 10 IP addresses from DHCP at startup—This is not an error. RRAS is designed to do this if it is configured to hand out IP addresses from a DHCP server. Leasing 10 addresses at a time is faster and more efficient than leasing IP addresses as required.

- User accounts in Active Directory seem to be locked out at random—When IAS is used as a RADIUS server, it authenticates accounts in Active Directory. The account lockout in your domain can be triggered by hacking attempts on your remote access server when incorrect passwords are attempted.

Hardware Errors

Hardware errors are less common than software configuration errors. If they occur, hardware errors are most common when new hardware is being installed. The following are some considerations for hardware troubleshooting:

- Ideally, new remote access hardware should be on the Hardware Compatibility List (HCL). Many times, hardware that is not on this list works, but hardware on the list has been tested and approved by Microsoft.

- If a VPN connection cannot find the server, use the ping utility to see if the IP address is reachable. You can ping other servers on the Internet to confirm that your Internet connectivity is functional.

10

- If you cannot dial-in using a new modem, see if you can dial-in to a different remote access server. This confirms that the hardware is working properly.

- If you have installed a new network card, ensure that you have reconnected the patch cable and there is a link light on the network card. "Is it plugged in?" and "Is it turned on?" are the two most valuable troubleshooting questions there are. Remember the basics.

- Is the type of hardware you are trying to use supported? When configured as a remote access server, RRAS supports analog modems, ISDN, X.25, frame relay, ATM, cable modems, and DSL modems.

Logging

Logging for remote access can be configured in many places. If RRAS is unable to start or not performing as expected, one of the first places to check is the event log. You can control the events that are placed in the System log from the Logging tab in the properties of the remote access server using the Routing and Remote Access snap-in.

From this same logging tab you can configure detailed connection logs. To enable this, select the "Log additional Routing and Remote Access information (used for debugging)" option. This creates a log file named C:\WINDOWS\tracing \ppp.log to track PPP connections. You can also record a log of modem communications. The log file is named C:\WINDOWS\Modemlog_*modemname*.txt.

IAS can log authentication requests to a file or a SQL server. You can control which events are logged, including accounting requests, authentications requests, and periodic status. You can also choose the format of the log and how often a new log file is created. By default, the file location of this log is C:\WINDOWS\system32\LogFiles\IN*yymm*.log, where *yy* is the year, and *mm* is the month. No events are logged by default.

To configure IAS file logging in the Internet Authentication Service snap-in, click Remote Access Logging, and double-click Local File.

Activity 10-15: Modem Logging

Time Required: 5 minutes

Objective: Enable modem logging.

Description: One particular professor has been complaining that he is often unable to connect to the dial-up server. You have checked all of the configuration settings on his laptop and everything seems correct. As a last attempt to troubleshoot the problem, you are enabling modem logging on the server. Then the next time the professor has problems, you can look in the log to see if there are any clues for further troubleshooting.

1. If necessary, start your server, and log on as Administrator.

2. Click **Start**, point to **Control Panel**, and click **Phone and Modem Options**.

3. Click the **Modems** tab.

4. Click **Properties**.

5. Click the **Diagnostics** tab.

6. Click **Record a Log**, and click **OK**.

7. Click **OK** to close the Phone and Modem Options window.

Troubleshooting Tools

The ping utility can be used to confirm that a host is reachable. If a host responds to ping attempts, then the host is reachable through the network. However, this does not confirm that RRAS is functioning.

The ipconfig utility can be used to confirm that the correct IP settings are being delivered to the remote access client. If incorrect settings are being delivered to the client, the most likely cause is incorrect configuration of the DHCP Relay Agent on the remote access server.

Many of the error messages viewed on the client side of a remote access VPN connection do not give many clues as to what the cause of the actual error is. Network Monitor can be used to perform packet captures, which may give some further clues as to the cause of the error.

CHAPTER SUMMARY

❐ RRAS in Windows Server 2003 can be configured as a remote access server for dial-up and VPN connections. Dial-up connections are slow, but available from almost anywhere. VPN connections are usually faster, but Internet access is required.

❐ The LAN protocols supported by RRAS for dial-up networking are TCP/IP, IPX/SPX, and AppleTalk. The remote access protocols supported are PPP and SLIP. SLIP is only supported when acting as a dial-up client.

❐ A VPN server is easier to maintain than a dial-up server because no specialized hardware such as a modem pool is required.

❐ VPN connections can use PPTP or L2TP/IPSec. PPTP is more common and works properly through NAT. L2TP/IPSec is more difficult to configure and only works through NAT if the latest options are implemented.

❐ L2TP does not perform encryption; IPSec is used to perform encryption.

❐ Many authentication methods are supported by RRAS and include: PAP, SPAP, CHAP, MS-CHAP, MS-CHAPv2, and EAP. PPTP VPNs cannot encrypt data if PAP, SPAP, or CHAP is used. Smart cards can only be used with EAP.

❐ Windows 2000 and newer remote access clients can receive IP configuration options from a DHCP server rather than the interface of a remote access server. To do this they send a DHCPINFORM packet after the remote access connection is created. The DHCP Relay Agent must be configured on the remote access server for this to work.

❐ In a mixed mode domain, remote access permission is controlled using the properties of the user object in Active Directory. In a native mode domain, remote access policies can also be used.

❐ Remote access policies are composed of conditions, remote access permissions, and a profile. All conditions in a remote access policy must be met for the policy to apply. Remote access permissions grant or deny access. The profile contains settings that apply to the connection.

❐ RADIUS is composed of the RADIUS clients, RADIUS servers, and RADIUS proxies. RADIUS clients forward authentication requests to RADIUS servers. RADIUS servers then authenticate the requests and authorize the connections. A RADIUS proxy can be used as an intermediary between RADIUS clients and servers in large environments.

❐ IAS allows Windows Server 2003 to act as a RADIUS server. This allows centralized management of remote access policies and logging. RRAS can act as a RADIUS client when configured as a remote access server.

❐ IAS can also be configured as a RADIUS proxy. Connection request policies are used for each request to determine whether IAS acts as a RADIUS server or a RADIUS proxy. Connection request policies are composed of conditions and a profile.

10

❑ The most common problem with remote access connections is improper software configuration. Hardware configuration problems occur less often, and occur mostly when new hardware is installed.

❑ A variety of logs can be configured to help troubleshoot remote access problems. RRAS logs events to the system log. You can configure PPP logging to obtain detailed information about PPP connections. Logging can be configured for a modem if dial-up remote access is configured. IAS can also log information to a file or SQL server.

❑ The most common troubleshooting tools for remote access are ipconfig, ping, and Network Monitor.

KEY TERMS

Bandwidth Allocation Protocol (BAP) — A protocol used to dynamically control the number of phone lines multilink uses based on bandwidth utilization.

callback — A security enhancement wherein a dial-up user initiates a connection, the connection is dropped, and the server then calls the dial-up client back.

Challenge Handshake Authentication Protocol (CHAP) — An authentication method that encrypts passwords using a one-way hash, but requires that passwords in Active Directory be stored using reversible encryption.

Connection Manager Administration Kit (CMAK) — A utility that can be used to configure dial-up and VPN connections on client computers.

COM port — The Windows term for a serial port in a computer.

conditions — Criteria in a remote access policy, or a connection request policy, that must be met for the policy to be applied.

connection request policy — A policy used by IAS to determine whether a request is authenticated locally or passed on to a RADIUS server. Such policies are composed of conditions and a profile.

DHCP Relay Agent — A service that forwards DHCP broadcasts from a network to a DHCP server on another network. It is required when DHCP broadcasts need to cross a router.

DHCPINFORM — A DHCP packet sent by Windows 2000 and newer remote access clients to retrieve IP configuration options from a DHCP server.

dial-up — Connectivity between two computers using modems and a phone line.

Extensible Authentication Protocol (EAP) — An authentication system that uses EAP types as plug-in authentication modules. This is used for smart cards.

fault tolerance — Configuring a system in such a way that if a single component fails an alternate can be used.

Ignore-User-Dialin-Properties — An attribute that can be configured in the profile of a remote access policy that prevents processing of the dial-in properties of a user object in Active Directory.

Internet Authentication Service (IAS) — A service that allows Windows Server 2003 to act as a RADIUS server and a RADIUS proxy.

LAN protocol — A networking protocol required to communicate over a LAN, or over a remote access connection. The same LAN protocol that is used by clients on the LAN must be used by dial-up and VPN clients to access LAN resources remotely.

Layer Two Tunneling Protocol (L2TP) — A VPN protocol that works with IPSec to provide secure communication. Only the latest versions traverse NAT properly.

Link Control Protocol (LCP) — An extension to PPP that allows the use of enhancements such as callback.

load balancing — Splitting network requests between two or more servers to reduce the load on each server.

location — A dial-up attribute configured in Phone and Modem Options to allow Windows to vary procedures for dialing a connection based on your location.

Microsoft Challenge Handshake Authentication Protocol (MS-CHAP) — An enhancement to CHAP that allows Active Directory passwords to be stored using nonreversible encryption.

Microsoft Challenge Handshake Authentication Protocol version 2 (MS-CHAPv2) — An authentication method that adds computer authentication and several other enhancements to MS-CHAP. This is the preferred authentication protocol for most remote access connections.

mobile users — Users that move from one location to another outside of the local network. They require remote access to use network resources.

modem — A hardware device that enables computers to communicate over a phone line. It converts digital signals from the computer to analog signals that can travel on a phone line, and then back to digital format.

modem pool — A group of modems connected to a remote access dial-up server. In high-volume situations it is implemented as specialized hardware.

multilink — A system for dial-up connections that allows multiple phone lines to be treated as a single logical unit to increase connection speeds.

native mode — A domain that can only have Windows 2000 and Windows Server 2003 domain controllers.

packet filters — Rules that control the forwarding of packets through a firewall based on IP address, port number, and packet type.

Password Authentication Protocol (PAP) — An authentication method that transmits passwords in clear text.

Point-to-Point Protocol (PPP) — The most common remote access protocol used for dial-up connections. It supports the use of TCP/IP, IPX/SPX, and AppleTalk for remote access.

Point-to-Point Tunneling Protocol (PPTP) — A VPN protocol that can be used with multiple LAN protocols and functions properly through NAT.

profile — The part of a remote access policy, or connection request policy, that contains settings that are applied to the connection.

RADIUS client — A server or device that passes authentication requests to a RADIUS proxy or RADIUS server. Most commonly, these are remote access servers.

RADIUS proxy — An intelligent server that acts as an intermediary between RADIUS clients and RADIUS servers. This server decides which RADIUS server should be used to authenticate a request.

RADIUS server — A server in the RADIUS process that accepts and authorizes authentication requests from RADIUS clients and RADIUS proxies.

remote access — Accessing network resources from a location away from the physical network. Connections can be made using a dial-up connection or a VPN.

Remote Access Dial-In User Authentication Service (RADIUS) — A service that allows remote access servers (RADIUS clients) to delegate responsibility for authentication to a central server (RADIUS server).

remote access permissions — The part of a remote access policy that defines whether the policy denies remote access or grants remote access.

remote access protocol — A protocol that is required for dial-up remote access. PPP is the most common remote access protocol.

remote access policies — Policies configured on remote access servers to control how remote access connections are created. They are composed of conditions, remote access permissions, and a profile.

remote RADIUS server group — A grouping of RADIUS servers to which IAS forwards connection requests when acting as a RADIUS proxy. Load balancing and fault tolerance can be configured.

Routing and Remote Access Service (RRAS) — A service that allows Windows Server 2003 to act as a router or remote access server.

Serial Line Internet Protocol (SLIP) — An older remote access protocol that only supports using TCP/IP as a LAN protocol. It is used by Windows Server 2003 only when acting as a client.

Shiva Password Authentication Protocol (SPAP) — An authentication method that uses reversible encryption when transmitting passwords.

v.90 — A standard for modems that allows downloads at 56 Kbps and uploads at 33.6 Kbps.

v.92 — A standard for modems that allows downloads at 56 Kbps and uploads at 48 Kbps.

virtual private network (VPN) — Encrypted communication across a public network such as the Internet. This is cheaper than implementing private lines for connectivity.

REVIEW QUESTIONS

1. Which of the following network resources can be used by remote access clients? (Choose all that apply.)

   a. files

   b. e-mail

   c. applications

   d. databases

2. A VPN connection is often slower than a dial-up connection because of the time required to perform encryption. True or False?

3. How many locations must be configured in Phone and Modem Options?

   a. none

   b. one

   c. two

   d. three

4. What hardware is required for dial-up remote access? (Choose all that apply.)

   a. network card

   b. modem

   c. phone line

   d. cable modem

5. Immediately after enabling remote access in RRAS, without further configuration, from where do remote access clients obtain IP configuration options?

   a. the properties of the remote access server

   b. a DHCP server

   c. a DHCP Relay Agent

   d. a defined interface on the remote access server

6. How many IP addresses does a remote access server lease from a DHCP server at one time?

   a. 1

   b. 3

   c. 5

   d. 10

   e. 20

7. Which remote access protocol can be used by Windows Server 2003 only when acting as a dial-up client?

   a. PPP

   b. TCP/IP

   c. AppleTalk

   d. SLIP

   e. IPX/SPX

8. Which option allows multiple phone lines to be configured into a single logical unit to increase the speed of dial-up connections?

   a. multilink

   b. LCP

   c. TurboDial

   d. PPTP

9. Which VPN protocol uses IPSec to provide data encryption?

   a. PPTP

   b. PPP

   c. SLIP

   d. L2TP

   e. TCP/IP

10. Which VPN protocol functions easily through NAT?

   a. PPTP

   b. PPP

   c. SLIP

   d. L2TP

   e. TCP/IP

11. Which of the following authentication methods can be used when PPTP is required to encrypt data? (Choose all that apply.)

   a. PAP

   b. SPAP

   c. CHAP

   d. MS-CHAP

   e. MS-CHAPv2

12. Which configuration options can be used to ensure that users call from a predefined location? (Choose all that apply.)

   a. Packet filters

   b. Verify-Caller-ID

   c. Callback

   d. Assign a static IP address

13. Which of the following is a component of a remote access policy? (Choose all that apply.)

   a. conditions

   b. profile

   c. encryption protocols

   d. authentication methods

   e. remote access permissions

14. If you require strongest encryption in a remote access policy, what level of encryption must be performed for L2TP/IPSec connections?

   a. 56-bit MPPE

   b. 128-bit MPPE

   c. 56-bit DES

   d. Triple DES (3DES)

10

15. If the Ignore-User-Dialin-Properties attribute is set to true when a domain is in mixed mode, there is no effect. True or False?

16. Which RADIUS component authorizes connections?

    a. RADIUS client

    b. RADIUS server

    c. RADIUS proxy

17. Which Windows service functions as a RADIUS server and RADIUS proxy?

    a. RRAS

    b. Dial-up networking

    c. IAS

    d. Active Directory

    e. IIS

18. Which Windows service functions as a VPN server?

    a. RRAS

    b. Dial-up networking

    c. IAS

    d. Active Directory

    e. IIS

19. In a remote RADIUS server group with two servers, which of the servers handles the incoming requests?

    a. the server with the highest priority

    b. the server with the highest weight

    c. the server with the lowest weight

    d. neither server, they use load balancing

20. If a connection request policy specifies that authentication happens on the local server, then IAS acts as what type of RADIUS component?

    a. RADIUS client

    b. RADIUS server

    c. RADIUS proxy

21. Which utility can be used to configure connections for client computers?

    a. Connection Manager Administration Kit

    b. Active Directory Users and Computers

    c. ipconfig

    d. Network Monitor

CASE PROJECTS

The staff at Arctic University are under increasing pressure to get more work done in less time, and often take work home in an attempt to meet this pressure. You think configuring remote access can help solve many problems that are being experienced.

Case Project 10-1: Traveling Professors

Many of the professors at Arctic University have laptops and are taking them home to finish work on evenings and weekends. However, often when they arrive at home, they find that they are missing a file that they need. Write a short proposal indicating how remote access could help solve this problem.

Case Project 10-2: Protocol Problems

You are about to implement remote access for the arts faculty. As part of the planning process, you need to decide which protocols you will implement. Which LAN protocols, remote access protocols, and VPN protocols do you think should be used and why?

Case Project 10-3: RADIUS configuration

The Engineering Department is using UNIX as its primary operating system. The engineers would like to integrate their system with your VPN server. Is this possible? What services do you need to install for this to work properly, and how are they configured? What services does the Engineering Department need to install?

10

11

ROUTING

After reading this chapter and completing the exercises, you will be able to:

♦ Configure Windows Server 2003 as a router

♦ Create and configure demand-dial connections for routing

♦ Configure Network Address Translation (NAT) for Internet connectivity

♦ Install Internet Connection Sharing (ICS)

♦ Configure Internet Connection Firewall (ICF)

Many technical professionals do not realize that Windows Server 2003 can be used as a very flexible router when required. For instance, in order to decrease network bandwidth requirements and connectivity charges, it can be configured to connect to other offices in your organization only when there is network traffic. It can also act as a router to allow connectivity to the Internet for small and mid-sized organizations. In this chapter, you will learn about the routing capabilities of Windows Server 2003. Its features include Network Address Translation, Internet Connection Sharing, and Internet Connection Firewall.

ROUTER INSTALLATION AND CONFIGURATION

Most large organizations have specialized hardware from Cisco or other vendors to act as routers on their networks. However, Windows Server 2003 can be used as a router for many small and mid-sized organizations. It is able to perform routing for TCP/IP and AppleTalk. IPX/SPX is not supported for routing.

The main benefit of implementing Windows Server 2003 as a router is cost. If you already have a server, to make it a router you only need to add a network card, and then configure Windows. This is useful if the routing requirements for your organization are simple, and a server has unused capacity.

Large organizations are more likely to require the advanced features that a hardware-based router provides. When connecting to the Internet, other advanced features such as a proxy for network requests are also often required. In fact, if advanced Internet connectivity features are required, Microsoft has a product called **Internet Security and Acceleration Server (ISA)** that provides proxy services.

To be a router, the server must be connected to at least two networks. A network interface in the server is connected to each network and has an IP address on that network.

Routing is part of RRAS and can be configured using the same wizard that is used to configure dial-up and VPN servers. If RRAS is already configured on a server, such as a VPN server, then routing can be configured as an additional service without losing the existing configuration.

To add routing as an additional service using the Routing and Remote Access snap-in, open the properties of the server, as shown in Figure 11-1. To enable general routing, click Router. When this option is checked, this server becomes a router. However, to act as an IP router you must also select the Enable IP routing option on the IP tab, as shown in Figure 11-2.

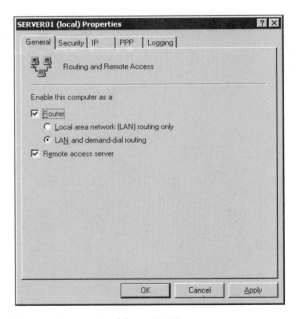

Figure 11-1   Enabling RRAS as a router

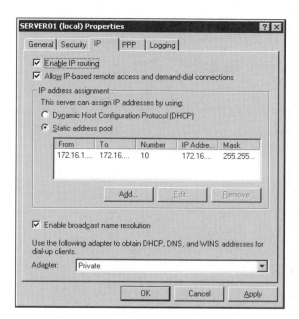

Figure 11-2 Enabling IP routing

Activity 11-1: Configuring RRAS as a Router

Time Required: 10 minutes

Objective: Configure Windows Server 2003 as a router.

Description: You have decided to use Windows Server 2003 as a router in several smaller campus locations where the cost of a specialized hardware router cannot be justified. You will confirm that both network cards in your computer are configured with an appropriate IP address, and then enable routing using the Routing and Remote Access Server Setup Wizard.

1. If necessary, start your server and log on as Administrator of the Arctic.local domain.

2. Confirm that your server has correctly configured IP addresses on both network cards. This was done in Activity 10-4.

   a. Click **Start**, click **Run**, type **cmd**, and press **Enter**.

   b. Type **ipconfig** and press **Enter**.

   c. The adapter **Classroom** should be configured with the IP address **192.168.1.1xx**, where XX is your student number, and a subnet mask of 255.255.255.0. If it is not configured properly, configure it now.

   d. The adapter **Private** should be configured with the IP address **172.16.x.y**, where X is your group number and Y is your student number, and a subnet mask of 255.255.255.0. If it is not configured properly, configure it now.

   e. Close the command prompt.

3. Click **Start**, point to **Administrative Tools**, click **Routing and Remote Access**.

4. Before configuring this server as a router, you remove the existing configuration. The existing configuration was created in Chapter 10. If RRAS is not configured, this step can be skipped.

   a. Right-click your server, and click **Disable Routing and Remote Access**.

   b. Click **Yes** to confirm.

5. Right-click your server, and click **Configure and Enable Routing and Remote Access**.

6. Click **Next** to begin the Routing and Remote Access Server Setup Wizard.

7. Click **Custom configuration** and click **Next**. You want to configure a LAN router, and that is not a standard wizard option.

8. Click the **LAN routing** checkbox, and click **Next**.

9. Click **Finish**.

10. Click **Yes** to start the Routing and Remote Access Service.

11. View the configuration that has been enabled by the Routing and Remote Access Server Setup Wizard.

    a. Right-click your server, and click **Properties**.

    b. On the General tab, the options **Router** and **Local area network (LAN) routing only** are selected.

    c. Click the **IP** tab.

    d. The **Enable IP routing** option is selected.

    e. Click **Cancel**.

12. Close the Routing and Remote Access snap-in.

Routing Tables

Routers are responsible for making intelligent decisions about how to move packets from one network to another in the fastest way possible. To keep track of the different networks that are available, a **routing table** is used.

The routing table is a list of the networks that are known to the router. Each entry in an IP routing table contains the IP address of the network, subnet mask of the network, the gateway that is used to reach the network, the router interface that is used to reach the gateway, and the metric that measures how far away the network is.

 The meaning of the metric value in a routing table varies depending on which routing protocol is being used.

To view the routing table on a server, you can use the **ROUTE PRINT** command, as shown in Figure 11-3. This figure shows the routing table for a router with two network cards, configured with the IP addresses 192.168.101/24 and 172.16.1.1/24, where /24 represents the number of bits in the network ID. The network 0.0.0.0 listed in the routing table is the default gateway. The subnet mask 255.255.255.255 is used to refer to an individual IP address.

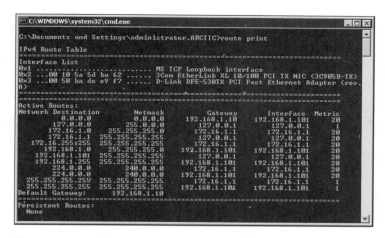

Figure 11-3   The ROUTE PRINT command

By default, the only networks of which a router is aware are the ones it is attached to with a network card. Any other entries in the routing table must be added. If entries are added manually, it is referred to as **static routing**. If entries are added automatically, based on a routing protocol, then it is referred to as **dynamic routing**.

Static routing is generally used when security is required. With static routing tables, you know exactly what is in each routing table and can exactly control how packets move between networks. For example, in a campus environment, to reduce the chances of a packet sniffer being able to capture traffic you may configure only one backbone path on which all network traffic travels.

The maintenance of a static routing table on each router can become cumbersome. Each time a new network is added, the routing table of each server must be changed. Each time a change is made there is also a chance of an error being made in the entry and functionality being lost, even if only for a short period of time.

Dynamic routing is used in most environments. In this system, the routers talk to each other to build their routing tables. By setting the metric on network interfaces, you can still control how packets move through the network without the hassle of configuring each router separately.

Routing Protocols

Routing protocols are responsible for calculating the best path from one network to another, and advertising routes for dynamic routing. When calculating the path, each routing protocol uses a different routing algorithm. When advertising routing, each routing protocol advertises different amounts of information and with a different frequency.

The two routing protocols used in Windows Server 2003 for IP routing are:

- **Routing Information Protocol (RIP)**
- **Open Shortest Path First (OSPF)**

RIP

RIP is the simpler of the two routing protocols and consequently the most popular. No configuration is necessary under most circumstances.

The distance between networks is measured by the number of routers through which the data must pass, or **hops**. For example, if one router must be passed through to reach a network it is one hop away. The best path from one network to another is the path with the least number of hops. This is known as **distance-vector routing**.

The maximum number of hops used by RIP is 15. A network is considered unreachable at 16 hops.

RIP does not differentiate between different link speeds. One hop across an ISDN line is treated the same as one hop across a T-1 line. In larger environments, this is unacceptable and leads to inefficient routing.

Each RIP router sends a broadcast packet every 30 seconds. A complete copy of the routing table is contained in this packet. RIP version 2 is capable of using multicasts instead of broadcast packets for these announcements.

Activity 11-2: Installing and Using RIP

Time Required: 10 minutes

Objective: Configure your server as an RIP router.

Description: The default configuration of the routers you have configured is static routing. You are tired of making manual changes to these routers every time there is a routing change. To implement automatic updating of the routing tables in your routers, you will configure RIP on your server.

1. If necessary, start your server and log on as Administrator.

2. View the existing routing table on your server.

   a. Click **Start**, click **Run**, type **cmd**, and press **Enter**.

   b. Type **route print** and press **Enter**.

   c. There are only two networks in the routing table with the netmask of 255.255.255.0. These are the two networks you are connected to on the Private and Classroom interfaces. Also notice that for each of these two entries, the metric is either 20 or 30.

   d. Close the command prompt.

3. Click **Start**, point to **Administrative Tools**, and click **Routing and Remote Access**.

4. If necessary, double-click your server to expand it.

5. If necessary, double-click **IP Routing** to expand it.

6. Right-click **General**, and click **New Routing Protocol**.

7. In the New Routing Protocol window, click **RIP version 2 for Internet Protocol**, and click **OK**. Notice that RIP is added as an option underneath IP Routing.

8. Click **RIP**. Interfaces using RIP are listed here. By default, there are none.

9. Right-click **RIP**, and click **New Interface**.

10. If necessary, click **Classroom**, and click **OK**.

11. Click **OK** to accept the default configuration

12. Right-click **RIP**, click **New Interface**, click **Private** if necessary, and click **OK**.

13. Click **OK** to accept the default configuration.

14. As your router communicates with other routers in the classroom that have enabled RIP, the routing table grows.

15. View the new routing table.

    a. Right-click **Static Routes**, and click **Show IP Routing Table**.

    b. Expand the window so you can view all of the columns.

    c. The routing table entries with RIP listed in the protocol column are learned through RIP.

    d. Close the IP Routing Table window.

16. Close the Routing and Remote Access snap-in.

OSPF

OSPF is a routing algorithm that determines the best path from one network to another based on a configurable value called **cost**. This makes OSPF more flexible than RIP and better suited to complex routing environments. Since complex routing environments normally use hardware routers, OSPF is not normally implemented on Windows routers.

Each interface on a router using OSPF is assigned a cost. The total cost of a route is calculated by adding the cost value of each router interface that is traveled through. The best path from one network to another is the one with the lowest cost.

Administrators can use the variable cost of router interfaces to differentiate between slower and faster WAN links. For example, a T-1 line may be configured with a cost of 10, while a backup ISDN line can be configured with a cost of 30. Only if the T-1 goes down is the ISDN line used.

When the routing table is built, each router builds a picture of the entire network. This is referred to as **link-state routing**.

When communicating with other routers, an OSPF router sends only changes in its routing table, not the entire routing table. In addition, the changes are sent only when they occur, not every 30 seconds.

 OSPF is not available in the 64-bit versions of Windows Server 2003.

Configuring RIP

Despite the relative simplicity of RIP compared to OSPF, there are still many options that can be configured, if required. A few RIP options can be configured globally for the entire server in the properties of the RIP protocol, but most are configured separately for each interface.

In the properties of the RIP protocol, you can configure the type of events to be logged. In addition, you can configure from which IP addresses this router accepts updates, as shown in Figure 11-4. The default setting is the "Accept announcements from all routers" option. This is a security risk, and should be changed to the "Accept announcements from listed routers only" option.

In the properties of the interfaces listed in the RIP protocol, you can configure settings for each interface. The General tab is shown in Figure 11-5. The Operation mode is set to Periodic update mode, which removes entries from the routing table if the router that originally advertised them is disabled or unreachable. You can also choose Auto static update mode, which adds RIP learned routes to the routing table as static entries, which are never removed. This is useful for routing with dial-up connections to maintain a consistent routing table.

11

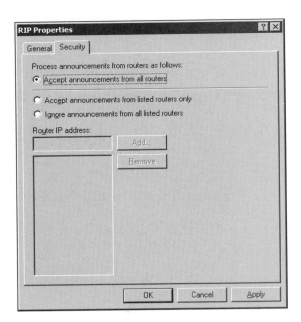

Figure 11-4   RIP security

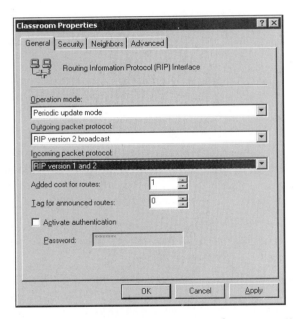

Figure 11-5   General tab, RIP interface properties

The Outgoing packet protocol can be configured as RIP version 1 broadcast, RIP version 2 broadcast, RIP version 2 multicast, and Silent RIP. The default setting is RIP version 2 broadcast. Silent RIP disables outgoing RIP announcements.

The Incoming packet protocol can be configured as Ignore incoming packets, RIP version 1 and 2, RIP version 1 only, and RIP version 2 only. The default is RIP version 1 and 2.

RIP routers advertise the routes they learn from other routers. This allows each router to build a large routing table that lists all networks possible. When a router advertises a route learned from another router, the number of hops is incremented by 1. However, you can change this default by modifying the value in Added cost for routes.

You can also select the "Activate authentication" option to force authentication between routers when announcements are sent. For this to function properly, the feature must be enabled on all routers. The password is sent in plain text and is not an effective form of security.

The Security tab, as shown in Figure 11-6, allows you to configure which incoming and outgoing routes are accepted on this interface. In addition to accepting all routes, you can choose to accept or ignore a range of addresses. If you use only a defined range of network numbers, then it is a good idea to configure the interface to use the "Accept all routes in the ranges listed" option. The options are the same for announcing outgoing routes as for accepting incoming routes.

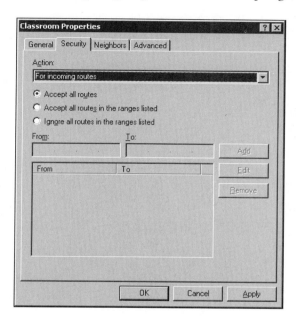

Figure 11-6   Security tab, RIP interface properties

The Neighbors tab, as shown in Figure 11-7, is used only if broadcasts and multicasts are limited on the network. You can configure unicast IP addresses that are neighbors. This interface then communicates with the neighbors instead of, or in addition to, broadcast and multicast announcements.

The Advanced tab, as shown in Figure 11-8, allows you to configure a wide variety of settings. You can adjust how often routing table announcements are sent, how long entries in the routing table last before they expire, and how long after they expire before they are removed from the routing table.

Split-horizon processing and **poison-reverse processing** are used to prevent routing loops in the case of a router failure. Triggered updates are sent when a change is made to the routing table, if this feature is enabled. If the Send clean-up updates when stopping feature is enabled, then a router announcement that expires all of the routes it has been advertising is sent when the router is shut down.

Other options disable the processing or sending of host routes and default routes in router announcements. The "Disable subnet summarization" option stops the router from aggregating multiple subnets as a single router entry.

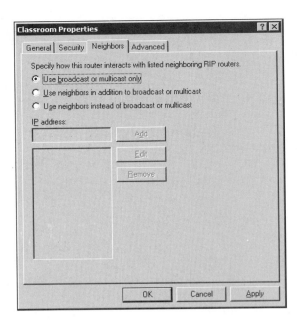

Figure 11-7   Neighbors tab, RIP interface properties

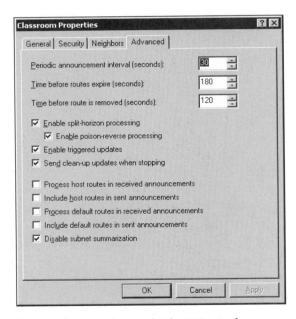

Figure 11-8   Advanced tab, RIP interface properties

DEMAND-DIAL CONNECTIONS

A **demand-dial** connection is used to establish a connection between two routers only when there is data to send. When a router with a demand-dial interface receives packets destined for a remote network, a connection is created so the packets can be sent. The connection can also be configured so that if there are no packets for the remote network, it is disconnected.

Traditionally, demand–dial connections are used to minimize the amount of phone time used on dial-up connection between routers. In this case, the connection is configured to disconnect after a certain period of time if no traffic has crossed the network. Additionally, you can configure the connection to be operational only during a time period when phone rates are minimized.

Demand-dial can also be used to initiate VPN connections between Windows routers. In this situation, the purpose of demand-dial is not to minimize connection time, but to automate the establishment of a connection. This is required when the router is rebooted or when a connection is lost because of a network interruption.

Demand-dial connections can also be created for **Point-to-Point Protocol over Ethernet (PPPoE)** connections. PPPoE is used by many high-speed Internet providers to control access to their network. Just like a dial-up or VPN connection, PPPoE requires a username and password to authenticate the connection. Only after the connection is authenticated does the ISP configure the server with an IP address and allow it on the Internet. Configuring PPPoE for a demand-dial connection ensures the automatic establishment of Internet connectivity when the router is rebooted or connectivity is interrupted.

Creating Demand-dial Connections

For a demand-dial connection to function properly, you must enable the server to perform demand-dial routing, configure a port to allow demand-dial routing, and then create a demand-dial interface. Both of these tasks are completed using the Routing and Remote Access snap-in.

Enabling the server to allow demand dial connections is done in the Properties of the server, as shown in Figure 11-9. Choose the "LAN and demand-dial routing" option to allow demand-dial connections.

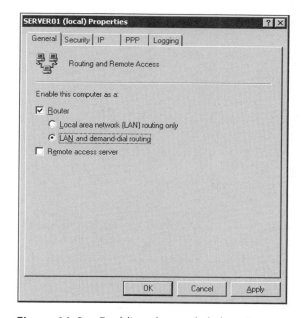

Figure 11-9   Enabling demand-dial routing

After demand-dial routing has been enabled, a Ports option will appear under the server in the Routing and Remote Access snap-in. In the properties of Ports you can configure whether particular port types can be used for demand-dial connections. Port types include modems, PPPoE, PPTP, and L2TP.

Configuring the PPTP port type is shown in Figure 11-10. To enable demand-dial connections, you must select the "Demand-dial routing connections (inbound and outbound)" option or the "Demand-dial routing connections (outbound only)" option.

Demand-dial Interface Wizard

New demand-dial connections are created using the Demand-Dial Interface Wizard. To start this wizard in the Routing and Remote Access snap-in, right-click Network Interfaces, and click New Demand-dial Interface. The first option you are asked to configure is the name for the demand-dial interface, as shown in Figure 11-11.

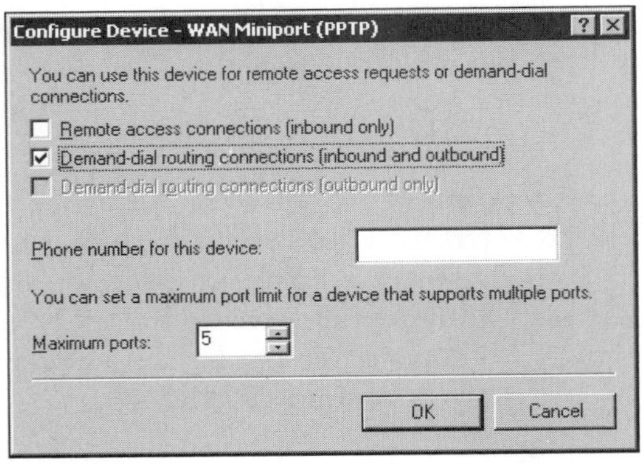

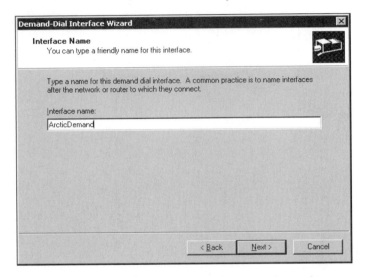

Figure 11-10   Configuring a port for demand-dial routing

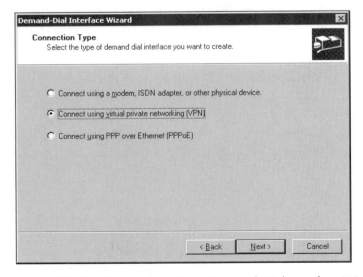

Figure 11-11   Interface Name, Demand-Dial Interface Wizard

The next screen in the wizard asks you what type of demand-dial connection you would like to create, as shown in Figure 11–12. The three options are dial-up, VPN, or PPPoE. Dial-up and VPN are used for connectivity between a remote office and a central office. PPPoE is used to connect to the Internet.

Figure 11-12   Connection Type, Demand-Dial Interface Wizard

If you choose to create a VPN connection, then the next step asks you what type of VPN connection to create, as shown in Figure 11-13. Choosing the Automatic selection option negotiates with the remote VPN server to choose PPTP or L2TP. Otherwise, you can force it to be PPTP only, or L2TP only. After the type of VPN is chosen, you must also configure the IP address of the remote server.

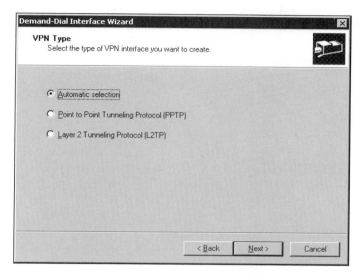

Figure 11-13   VPN Type, Demand-Dial Interface Wizard

The next window asks you about protocol and security options, as shown in Figure 11-14. If the "Route IP packets on this interface" option is selected, then this server routes packets between the networks it is connected to and the remote network. If it is not selected, then only the server running Routing and Remote Access is able to access the remote network. This may be desired if the connection is only used for remote maintenance or data synchronization.

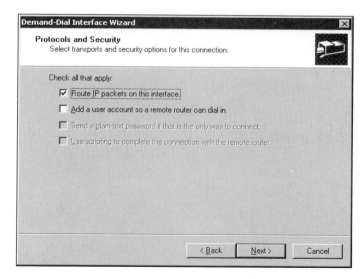

Figure 11-14   Protocols and Security, Demand-Dial Interface Wizard

A user account with remote access permission is required to establish a demand-dial connection. If the "Add a user account so a remote router can dial in" option is chosen, then a user account is automatically created for inbound demand-dial connections. On a member server, the account created is a local user account.

Using the Send a plain-text password if that is the only way to connect option should be avoided if possible. If this option is selected, ensure that the user account is only used for connection establishment and has no rights to the remainder of the system.

Enabling the "Use scripting to complete the connection with the remote router" option allows you to run a script that modifies the connection settings, or adds routing table entries. This is not normally required.

The next window, shown in Figure 11-15, asks you to configure **static routes**. At least one static route is required to trigger the demand-dial interface. Static routes must be added for each network on the other side of the demand-dial connection. The demand-dial connection is activated when a packet addressed to a host on one of the static routes needs to be forwarded.

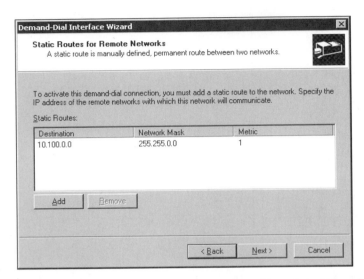

Figure 11-15   Static Routes, Demand-Dial Interface Wizard

When a packet arrives at the demand-dial router, the router looks in its routing table to see where it should be sent. The static route for the remote network specifies the demand-dial interface to reach the remote network. If a packet is addressed to the remote network, then the demand-dial connection is activated. After the demand-dial connection is activated, the packet is forwarded across the demand-dial connection to the remote network.

If you selected the "Add a user account so a remote router can dial in" option on a previous screen, then the next window asks for dial-in credentials, as shown in Figure 11-16. This information is used to create the user account that is used by the remote router to connect to this router. The username is the same as the name for the demand-dial connection.

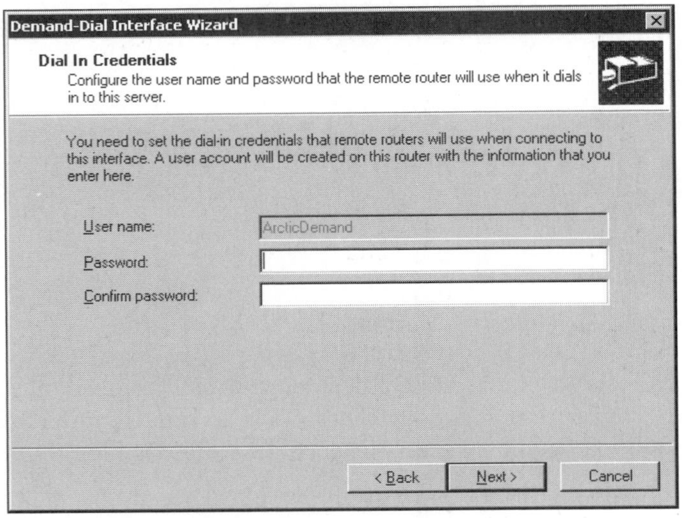

Figure 11-16   Dial In Credentials, Demand-Dial Interface Wizard

Next you are prompted for dial-out credentials, as shown in Figure 11-17. This is the username, domain, and password that are used by the demand-dial connection to login on the remote system. If this information is not correct, the demand-dial connection is unable to connect.

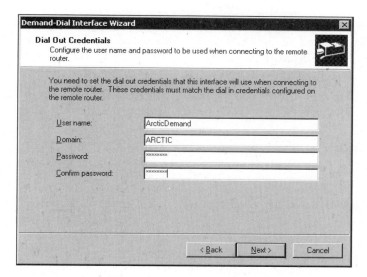

Figure 11-17   Dial Out Credentials, Demand-Dial Interface Wizard

Activity 11-3: Creating a Demand-Dial Connection

Time Required: 15 minutes

Objective: Create a demand-dial VPN connection.

Description: You have configured Windows Server 2003 as a router between sites. To enhance security, you would like to configure a dial-up VPN between the locations. In this activity you will configure a demand-dial VPN interface on your server, and test it by connecting to a VPN server on your partner's server.

1. If necessary, start your server and log on as Administrator.

2. Click **Start**, point to **Administrative Tools**, click **Routing and Remote Access**.

3. Right-click your server, and click **Properties**.

4. Click **LAN and demand-dial routing**, and click **OK**.

5. Click **Yes** to continue and restart RRAS.

6. Right-click **Network Interfaces**, and click **New Demand-dial Interface**.

7. Click **Next** to begin the Demand-Dial Interface Wizard.

8. In the Interface name box, type **ArcticDemand**x, where x is your partner's student number, and click **Next**.

9. Click **Connect using virtual private networking (VPN)**, and click **Next**.

10. Confirm that the VPN type selected is **Automatic selection**, and click **Next**.

11. In the Host name or IP address box, type **192.168.1.10**x, where x is your partner's student number, and click **Next**. This is the IP address of your partner's server.

12. Confirm that the **Route IP packets on this interface** checkbox is selected.

13. Click the **Add a user account so a remote router can dial in** checkbox to select it, and click **Next**.

14. Click **Add** to add a static route.

15. In the Destination box, type **10.100.x.0**, where *x* is your partner's student number. This network does not really exist in the classroom, but is used to trigger the demand-dial interface.

16. In the Network Mask box, type **255.255.255.0**, and click **OK**.

17. Click **Next**.

18. In the Password box of the Dial In Credentials window, type **Password!**, in the Confirm password box, type **Password!**, and click **Next**. This window gathers the password for the user that is created by the wizard for remote routers to log on.

19. In the User name box of the Dial Out Credentials window, type **ArcticDemandy**, where *y* is your student number. This account is created by your partner during the creation of the demand-dial interface.

20. In the Domain box, type **SERVERxx**, where xx is your partner's student number. The account that was automatically created by your partner is a local account. This specifies that the user account is in the local SAM database of your partner's server.

21. In the Password box, type **Password!**. In the Confirm password box, type **Password!**, and click **Next**.

22. Click **Finish**.

23. Configure your server as a VPN server.

  a. Right-click your server, and click **Properties**.

  b. Click the **Remote access server** checkbox to select it, and click **OK**. Even when configured as a router, RRAS creates five PPTP and five L2TP ports automatically. This enables them to be used.

  c. Click **Yes** to restart the router.

24. View the Connection State of your demand-dial connection in Network Interfaces. It should be Disconnected.

25. Wait until your partner has completed Step 19, then test your demand-dial interface.

  a. Click **Start**, click **Run**, type **cmd**, and press **Enter**.

  b. Type **ping 10.100.x.5**, where *x* is your partner's student number and press **Enter**. This IP address does not exist on the network, but triggers the demand-dial connection based on the static route you configured in the Demand-Dial Interface Wizard.

  c. You receive error messages. This is normal. If you receive the error **Destination host unreachable**, then the interface is not connected yet. It takes a few moments for the demand-demand connection to complete. If you receive only this error, then repeat step b. If after two attempts you are still receiving this error then verify your configuration is correct. To verify the authentication credentials right-click your demand-dial connection, and click **Set Credentials**.

  d. After the demand-dial connection is connected the error message will change. If the error changes to **Request timed out**, it indicates that the demand-dial connection connected, but the host is not responding. This is normal since the host does exist on our network. If the host really existed on the remote network, then you would get a positive response. If the error changes to **TTL expired in transit**, then the demand-dial connection is connected and a routing loop has been created.

  e. Close the command prompt.

26. View the Connection State of your demand-dial connection in Network Interfaces. It should be Connected. If the state is not Connected then press **F5** to refresh the screen.

27. Right-click **ArcticDemandx**, where *x* is your partner's student number, and click **Disconnect**. This manually disconnects the demand-dial interface.

28. Close the Routing and Remote Access snap-in.

Demand-dial Interface Properties

Most options for a demand-dial interface can be configured with the Demand-Dial Interface Wizard during creation, but some can only be configured after the interface has been created.

The properties of the demand-dial interface can be used to configure security settings and the idle time-out. The idle timeout is on the Options tab, as shown in Figure 11-18. If the Connection type chosen is the "Persistent connection" option, then the servers are connected whenever RRAS is functional. This is the normal configuration for a VPN demand-dial connection with a permanent Internet connection.

If the Connection type chosen is Demand dial, then you can set an idle timeout. The default setting for the "Idle time before hanging up" option is five minutes. If you are using a dial-up connection, you want to set the idle timeout to be five or 10 minutes. Then, when there is no traffic to be transmitted, the connection is disconnected to reduce phone charges.

The Security tab provides the standard security options available on a VPN connection. You can configure the types of authentication allowed and whether data encryption is used.

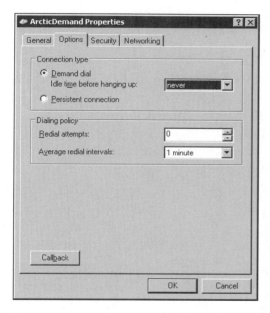

Figure 11-18   Options tab, demand-dial interface properties

Dial-out Hours

A demand-dial connection can be configured with a set of **dial-out hours** that control when it can be active. This is very useful to control dial-up connections which might otherwise result in large long distance charges.

Typically when dial-out hours are configured, they allow a connection every few hours. This results in data being moved from one network to another in batches every few hours. This is useful for Active Directory replication and data synchronization.

If users are expected to access resources using the demand-dial connection at all times, then the dial-out hours should be left at the default of 24 hours per day, seven days per week. To set the dial-out hours, right-click on the demand-dial interface and click Dial-out hours. The window that allows you to set the dial-out hours is shown in Figure 11-19.

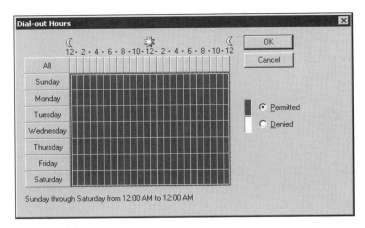

Figure 11-19   Dial-out hours

Demand-dial Filters

With the default configuration, a demand-dial connection is triggered by any IP traffic that needs to be routed. This includes relatively unimportant traffic such as ICMP packets.

To reduce the amount of time a demand-dial connection is active, you can configure **demand-dial filters**. Demand-dial filters control which types of network traffic trigger a demand-dial connection. This reduces the number of connections activated and reduces the amount of long distance charges.

The demand-dial filters are configured the same as a firewall rule. You can set the default option to initiate a demand-dial connection for only specific traffic or for all traffic except that specified by a rule, as shown in Figure 11-20. For each rule you can specify a source and destination network as well as a protocol type, which includes TCP and UDP port numbers, as shown in Figure 11-21.

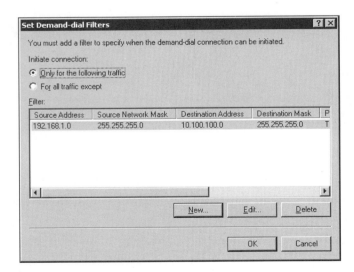

Figure 11-20   Demand-dial filters

Demand-dial filters can be used with a dial-up Internet connection to ensure the connection is not dialed unless it is for allowed traffic. For example, you could configure rules that limit connection establishment to packets that have a source IP address on your internal network and have a destination TCP port of either 80 or 25. Then only communication with Web servers and e-mail servers can cause the Internet connection to be activated. An attempt to ping an Internet server would not activate the Internet connection.

Figure 11-21   Adding a demand-dial filter

Activity 11-4: Configuring Demand-Dial Filters

Time required: 5 minutes

Objective: Configure demand-dial filters to control the activation of demand-dial connections.

Description: Arctic University is charged a fee for bandwidth usage on their Internet connection. You would like to reduce the amount of the fee by stopping ICMP packets from triggering the demand-dial connection.

1. If necessary, start your server and log on as Administrator.

2. Click **Start**, point to **Administrative Tools**, and click **Routing and Remote Access**.

3. Right-click **ArcticDemandx**, where *x* is your partner's student number, and click **Set IP Demand-dial Filters**.

4. Click **New** to create a new demand-dial filter.

5. Confirm that **Source network** is not selected. This acts as a wildcard to match any source address.

6. Confirm that **Destination network** is not selected. This acts as a wildcard to match any destination address.

7. Click the drop-down arrow for the Protocol list box, and click **ICMP**.

8. Leave the ICMP type box and ICMP code box empty. This setting acts as a wildcard to match any ICMP type and code.

9. Click **OK**.

10. Confirm that **For all traffic except** is selected. This means that any traffic can initiate the demand-dial connection except the listed filters, in this case ICMP traffic.

11. Click **OK**.

12. Test the new filter.

    a. Click **Start**, click **Run**, type **cmd**, and press **Enter**.

    b. Type **ping 10.100.x.5**, where *x* is your partner's student number, and press **Enter**. This IP address does not exist on the network, but can trigger the demand-dial connection based on the static route you configured in the Demand-Dial Interface Wizard.

11

   c. You receive an error message. This is normal. The only error is **Destination host unreachable**. This means that the path to the IP address you are pinging is not available because the demand-dial interface is disconnected. This error message does not change because the filter does not allow ICMP packets to trigger the connection.

   d. Close the command prompt.

   e. Click **Start**, point to **All Programs**, and click **Internet Explorer**.

   f. In the Address box, type **http://10.100.*x*.5**, where *x* is your partner's student number, and press **Enter**. Internet Explorer cannot connect to a Web site because there is no Web server at this address, but it triggers the demand-dial interface.

   g. After five to 10 seconds, close Internet Explorer.

13. View the Connection State of your demand-dial connection in Network Interfaces. It should be Connected. If the state is not Connected then press **F5** to refresh the screen.

14. Right-click **ArcticDemand*x***, where *x* is your partner's student number, and click **Disconnect**. This manually disconnects the demand-dial interface.

15. Close the Routing and Remote Access snap-in.

NETWORK ADDRESS TRANSLATION

Most organizations use private internal IP addresses that are not registered for use on the Internet. The address ranges reserved for internal use are:

- 10.0.0.0 through 10.255.255.255
- 172.16.0.0 through 172.31.255.255
- 192.168.0.0 through 192.168.255.255

An organization using these addresses internally must have a mechanism in place to allow client computers to access the Internet. The two most common ways to do this are a proxy server and **Network Address Translation (NAT)**. Both of these allow an organization to use a single Internet IP address to provide Internet access to all client computers.

If a proxy server is implemented, then clients must be configured to use the proxy server. This is a significant administrative drawback. In addition, a proxy server is usually a product that costs extra money. In many cases, a proxy server also provides caching to speed up Internet connectivity.

NAT is included with Windows Server 2003 and is very effective if you are already using your Windows server as a router. Client computers do not need any change in configuration, because all traffic is translated as it is routed through the NAT server.

Some applications do not work properly through NAT. Any application that passes IP address and port information in the data portion of the packet is not properly translated. This includes most remote control software, many authentication algorithms, and FTP. However, most implementations of NAT, including the one on Windows Server 2003, are FTP aware and translate FTP packets properly.

How NAT Works

NAT modifies the IP headers of packets that are forwarded through a router. When a packet is forwarded through the router, NAT removes the original source IP address and source port number. The source IP address is changed to be the IP address of the router. The source port number is changed to a randomly generated port number.

To keep track of the translations that are being performed, NAT builds a table. This table lists the original source IP address, the original source port number, and the new source port number. The new source IP address is always the external interface on the router and does not need to be included in the table.

When a response packet is returned from the Internet, it is addressed to the IP address on the external interface of the router. The destination port in the packet is the randomly generated port number that was used when the original packet was translated. The router looks in its NAT table to find the entry that matches the destination port number.

When the table entry is found, the destination IP address in the packet is changed to be the original source IP address, and the destination port is changed to the original source port. The translated packet is then forwarded to the original host. Using this mechanism allows thousands of computers to access the Internet using a single IP address from an ISP.

Figure 11-22 shows an example of network address translation being performed on a request from a client to a Web server. The IP header is modified when the request reaches the NAT router. The original source IP address (192.168.1.10) is replaced with the IP address of the router's external interface (5.5.5.5). The original source port (2032) is replaced with a randomly generated port number (52333) on the router's external interface. Information about this translation is stored in the NAT table.

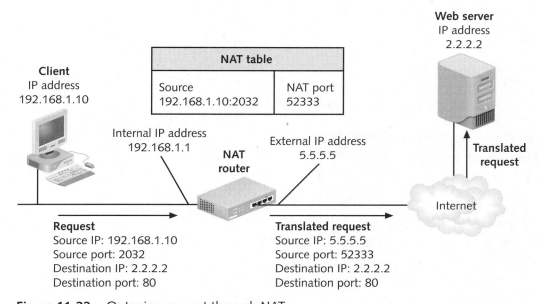

Figure 11-22   Outgoing request through NAT

Figure 11-23 shows an example of a response from a Web server to a client behind a NAT router. The original response packet is addressed to the external interface on the router (5.5.5.5/52333). The response packet is received by the router. The router looks up the port number (52333) in its NAT table. The destination IP address is replaced with the IP address of the client (192.168.1.10), and the destination port is replaced with the port on the client (2032). The packet is then forwarded on to the client.

Installing NAT

The NAT protocol is automatically installed when RRAS is configured to be a router. However, you must add interfaces to it before it is actually used. To add an interface to NAT, right-click NAT/Basic Firewall, and click New Interface.

After adding an interface to NAT, the properties are displayed. The NAT/Basic Firewall tab, as shown in Figure 11-24, allows you to configure whether this interface is a private interface, public interface, or basic firewall. The definition of public and private interfaces is important for proper NAT functionality. Outgoing packets to the Internet use the IP address of the public interface for a source address.

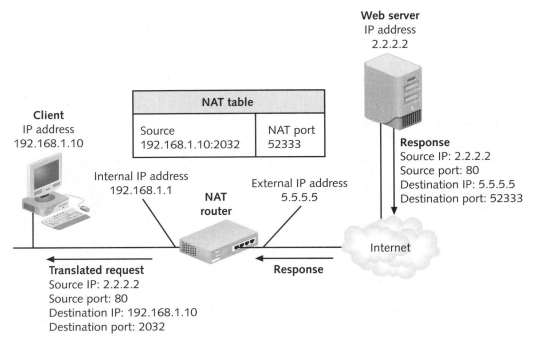

Figure 11-23   Incoming response through NAT

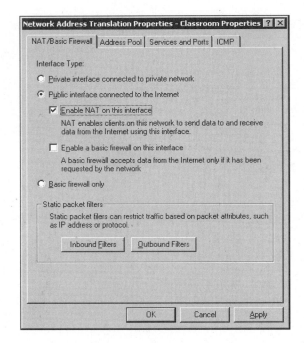

Figure 11-24   NAT/Basic Firewall tab, NAT interface properties

For proper NAT functionality, one interface must be configured as a public interface, and at least one interface must be configured as private. Addresses from the private network are translated when they are routed onto the public network.

A basic firewall allows you to configure static packet filters. When static packet filters are used, a rule must be created to allow network traffic out, and another rule must be created to allow response network traffic in. Custom rules can be added.

Normally, connections through a NAT router must be initiated by a client on the private network. However, the Services and Ports tab allows you to configure special NAT mappings that allow you to host services behind NAT, but still allow access to them from the Internet. For example, if you were hosting an e-mail server behind a NAT router, you could configure a rule that takes all packets addressed to port 25 on the external interface and forwards them to port 25 on an internal SMTP server.

The ICMP tab dictates to which types of ICMP packets the interface responds. Disabling response to ping packets (ICMP echo request) is a standard security precaution.

The Address Pool tab defines a range of IP addresses that are handed out to client computers. If this is configured, then the NAT router is a DHCP server. This option is not normally implemented.

Activity 11-5: Installing and Testing NAT

Time Required: 15 minutes

Objective: Install NAT and confirm it is functioning using a Web page on your instructor's computer.

Description: You are configuring a new server to perform NAT. To be sure it is working, you will use it as a router to access a Web page that echoes back the source IP address and port number. The source IP address and port number will be from the NAT router instead of the client. You will work with a partner. Partner A will be the client computer. Partner B will be the NAT router.

1. If necessary, start your server and log on as Administrator.

2. Both partners view IP connection information.

   a. Click **Start**, point to **All Programs**, and click **Internet Explorer**.

   b. In the Address box type **http://192.168.1.10** and press **Enter**.

   c. A web page will appear in Internet Explorer indicating the source IP address, source TCP port, server IP address, and server port number. Notice that the source IP address is the IP address of the Classroom interface on your server.

   d. Close Internet Explorer.

3. Partner A reconfigure the default gateway and disable the Classroom interface.

   a. Click **Start**, point to **Control Panel**, point to **Network Connections**, right-click **Classroom**, and click **Properties**.

   b. Double-click **Internet Protocol (TCP/IP)**.

   c. Clear the contents of the Default gateway box, click **OK**, and click **OK**.

   d. Click **Start**, point to **Control Panel**, point to **Network Connections**, right-click **Private**, and click **Properties**.

   e. Double-click **Internet Protocol (TCP/IP)**.

   f. In the Default gateway box type **172.16.*x.y***, where x is your group number and y is your partner's student number. This is the IP address of your partner's server on the private interface. For this exercise you will be using your partner's server as a router with NAT enabled.

   g. Click **OK**, and click **OK**.

   h. Click **Start**, point to **Control Panel**, point to **Network Connections**, right-click **Classroom**, click **Disable**.

4. Partner B configure the Classroom interface for NAT.

   a. Click **Start**, point to **Administrative Tools**, and click **Routing and Remote Access**.

   b. Double-click **IP Routing** to expand it.

   c. Right-click **NAT/Basic Firewall**, and click **New Interface**.

   d. Click **Classroom**, and click **OK**.

e. Click **Public interface connected to the Internet**. This indicates that the IP address of this interface will be the source IP address when NAT is performed.

f. Click the **Enable NAT on this interface** checkbox. This tells the system to start performing NAT on this interface.

g. Click **OK**.

5. Partner B configure the Private interface for NAT.

a. Right-click **NAT/Basic Firewall**, and click **New Interface**.

b. Click **Private**, and click **OK**.

c. Confirm that **Private interface connected to private network** is selected and click **OK**.

6. Partner A test NAT by accessing the web page on the Instructor server.

a. Click **Start**, point to **All Programs**, and click **Internet Explorer**.

b. In the Address box type **http://192.168.1.10** and press **Enter**.

c. A web page will appear in Internet Explorer indicating the source IP address, source TCP port, server IP address, and server port number. Notice that the source IP address is the IP address of the Classroom interface on the server of partner B.

d. Close Internet Explorer.

7. Partner B disable NAT.

a. In the NAT/Basic Firewall interfaces, right-click **Classroom**, and click **Delete**.

b. Click **Yes** to confirm the removal.

c. Right-click **Private**, and click **Delete**.

d. Click **Yes** to confirm the removal.

e. Close the Routing and Remote Access snap-in.

8. Partner A reconfigure the default gateway and enable the Classroom interface.

a. Click **Start**, point to **Control Panel**, point to **Network Connections**, right-click **Private**, and click **Properties**.

b. Double-click **Internet Protocol (TCP/IP)**.

c. Clear the contents of the Default gateway box, click **OK**, and click **OK**.

d. Click **Start**, point to **Control Panel**, point to **Network Connections**, right-click **Classroom**, and click **Properties**.

e. Double-click **Internet Protocol (TCP/IP)**.

f. In the Default gateway box type **192.168.1.10**.

g. Click **OK**, and click **OK**.

h. Click **Start**, point to **Control Panel**, point to **Network Connections**, right-click **Classroom**, and click **Enable**.

9. If time permits, reverse roles and repeat the exercise.

Configuring NAT

The NAT protocol is configured by right-clicking NAT/Basic Firewall, and clicking Properties. The General tab controls the level of logging that is performed. The default logging setting is to log errors only.

The Translation tab, shown in Figure 11-25, allows you to configure how long **mappings** are kept in the NAT table. By default, mappings for TCP connections are kept for 1440 minutes, and mappings for UDP are kept for one minute. The Reset Defaults button returns to these defaults.

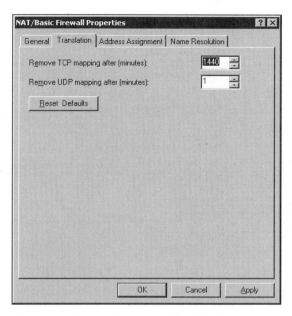

Figure 11-25   Translation tab, NAT/Basic Firewall properties

On the Address Assignment tab, you can configure NAT to act as a DHCP server. To do this you must configure a static range of IP addresses. Exclusions can be configured within the ranges.

The Name Resolution tab, as shown in Figure 11-26, configures the NAT router to act as a **DNS proxy**. Client computers can then query the NAT router as a DNS server. The NAT router then forwards the requests on to the DNS server configured in its own network settings. To enable the DNS proxy, select the "Clients using Domain Name System (DNS)" option. To enable the activation of a demand-dial connection when name resolution requests are received, select the "Connect to the public network when a name needs to be resolved" option. None of the settings on this tab need to be enabled if internal DNS servers exist.

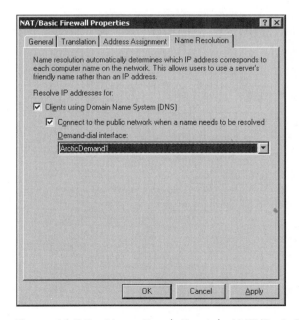

Figure 11-26   Name Resolution tab, NAT/Basic Firewall properties

You can view statistics related to the **DHCP allocator** and DNS proxy to confirm that they are functioning properly. To view DHCP allocator statistics, right-click NAT/Basic Firewall, and click Show DHCP Allocator Information. To view DNS proxy statistics, right-click NAT/Basic Firewall, and click Show DNS Proxy Information.

INTERNET CONNECTION SHARING

Internet Connection Sharing (ICS) is a Windows Server 2003 service that provides an automated way for a small office using Windows Server 2003 as a router to connect to the Internet. It automatically performs NAT and configures network connections. Because NAT is used, the server must have at least two network cards. The configuration used by ICS cannot be changed.

ICS makes the following changes:

- The internal network connection is configured with the IP address 192.168.0.1 and the subnet mask 255.255.255.0.
- Autodial is enabled for dial-up/VPN/PPPOE connections.
- A static route for the default gateway is enabled when the dial-up/VPN/PPPOE connection is activated.
- The ICS service is started.
- The DHCP allocator is configured to distribute IP addresses from 192.168.0.2 to 192.168.0.254.
- The DNS proxy is enabled.

ICS is enabled in the properties of the public network interface on the Advanced tab. To enable it, click the Allow other network users to connect through this computer's Internet connection check box, as shown in Figure 11-27.

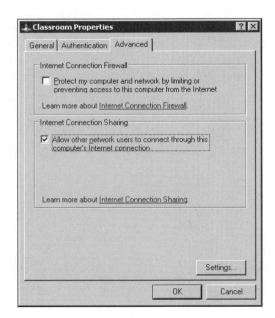

Figure 11-27   Enabling ICS

An ICS server can only have one internal IP address. If an ICS server has multiple internal interfaces, they must be configured to use **network bridging** so that the interfaces can share a single IP address.

 Network bridging is a new feature in Windows Server 2003. It is only available in the 32-bit version.

A bridge controls network traffic based on MAC addresses. It also allows computers on two different physical network segments to be on the same IP network. This is very useful for small networks with multiple media types for wiring. The two media types can be connected into a single logical network without the complexity of routing. When network bridging is enabled, you choose multiple network cards in a server to act as a single IP network.

To enable network bridging, open Network Connections, then control-click at least two connections to select them, right-click the selected connections, and click Bridge Connections.

INTERNET CONNECTION FIREWALL

Internet Connection Firewall (ICF) is a stateful packet filter that can be used to protect any server running Windows Server 2003. In most situations this is only required if the server is connected directly to the Internet. However, you may choose to implement it internally as well to protect systems from internal hackers.

A standard packet filter, such as a basic firewall, requires you to make two rules to allow Internet connectivity. For instance, if you want to allow internal clients access to Web sites on the Internet, you must create one rule that allows traffic addressed to TCP port 80 out, and another that allows return traffic for any TCP port above 1023. Not only is it an administrative hassle to configure the second rule, it is also a large security hole. Ports above 1023 are used by many viruses to transmit information and replicate.

A **stateful firewall**, such as ICF, requires only one rule for the outbound traffic. The firewall keeps track of TCP connections that are created by internal clients and automatically allows response packets to return. This reduces administrative hassle. Security is also increased because no rules allow connections to be created from the Internet to internal clients.

Enabling ICF

ICF is configured per connection. Normally, the only connection that needs to be configured is the one that connects to the Internet. ICF is enabled in the properties of a connection, as shown in Figure 11-28. On the Advanced tab, click the Protect my computer and network by limiting or preventing access to this computer from the Internet option.

If ICF is enabled on a server that is not a router, only that server is protected. If ICF is enabled on a router, then all computers on the internal network are protected.

Configuring ICF

When ICF is enabled, all packets from the network that are addressed to the server are dropped. If this server is running a service, such as a Web server, clients will be unable to communicate with it. However, if the server initiates a request, then the response is allowed to return.

To allow requests from the network to access services on the server running ICF, you need to configure services. The services defined are the firewall rules for ICF. The list of defined services is accessed through the Settings button in the properties of the connection, where ICF is enabled.

11

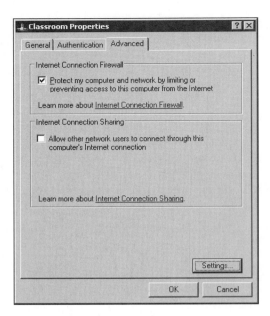

Figure 11-28   Enabling ICF

The Services tab, as shown in Figure 11-29, has a predefined list of services that you can choose to allow. By default, none are selected. You can also define your own services based on IP addresses and port numbers. These services are also used by ICS for static NAT mappings to access services behind the NAT router.

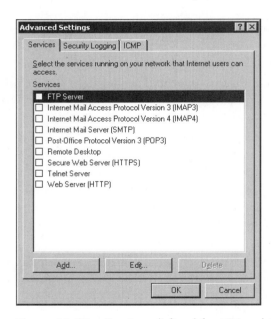

Figure 11-29   Services defined for ICF and ICS

After ICF is enabled, the server does not respond to any ICMP packets on the configured connection. Using the ICMP tab, shown in Figure 11-30, you can allow certain ICMP traffic. For example, to remotely confirm that your server is functional, you may click the Allow incoming echo request check box so that the server responds to the ping utility.

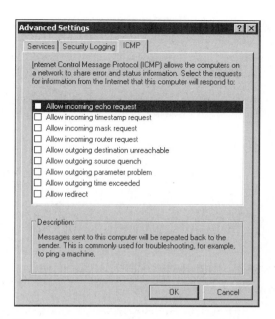

Figure 11-30   ICMP options for ICF

The Security Logging tab, as shown in Figure 11-31, is used to configure the type of information that is logged, the location of the log, and the maximum size of the log. ICF is capable of logging both dropped packets and successful connections. The default location of the log file is C:\WINDOWS\pfirewall.log, and has a maximum size of 4 MB.

11

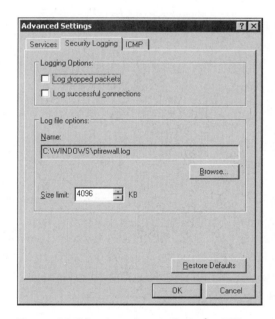

Figure 11-31   Logging options for ICF

 When the ICF log reaches its maximum size it is saved as pfirewall.log.old and a new pfirewall.log.old file is created. If an older pfirewall.log.old already exists, it is overwritten.

In a low-security environment, you may choose not to do any logging at all. In a medium-security environment, you may track dropped packets, although you may be astonished at how many dropped packets there are on an Internet connection. Successful connections are normally logged only in very high-security environments.

Activity 11-6: Installing ICF

Time Required: 10 minutes

Objective: Install and configure ICF on your server.

Description: To enhance security on all of the Arctic University Web servers, you have chosen to implement ICF. In this activity, you will work with a partner to test the functionality of ICF.

1. If necessary, start your server and log on as Administrator.

2. Install Internet Information Server 6.0.

   a. Click **Start**, point to **Control Panel**, and click **Add or Remove Programs**.

   b. Click **Add/Remove Windows Components**.

   c. In the Components window, double-click **Application Server**, and click the **Internet Information Services (IIS)** checkbox. The checkbox will turn grey with a checkmark. This indicates not all components have been installed. The Web server is the only component you require for this activity, and it is installed. Click **OK**.

   d. Click **Next**. If prompted for the Windows Server 2003 CD-ROM, click **OK**. Then click **Browse**, and select the **C:\I386** folder. Click **Open**, and then click **OK** in the Files Needed dialog box.

   e. Click **Finish** to complete the installation.

   f. Close the Add or Remove Programs window.

3. Configure a Web page on your server.

   a. Click **Start**, click **Run**, type **cmd**, and press **Enter**.

   b. Type **copy \\instructor\c$\inetpub\wwwroot\default.asp c:\inetpub\wwwroot** and press **Enter**. This file is now the default page on your Web site.

   c. Close the command prompt.

4. Enable ASP scripts on your Web server.

   a. Click **Start**, point to **Administrative Tools**, and click **Internet Information Services (IIS) Manager**.

   b. If necessary, double-click your server to expand it, and click **Web Service Extensions**. This is where you can control the type of scripts that are allowed to run on the Web server.

   c. In the right pane, click **Active Server Pages**, and click **Allow**. This is required to properly view the default Web page you copied onto your Web server.

   d. Close the Internet Information Services Manager snap-in.

5. Test the Web page on your partner's server. Complete this step only if your partner has finished Step 4.

   a. Click **Start**, point to **All Programs**, and click **Internet Explorer**.

   b. In the Address box, type **http://192.168.1.10x**, where *x* is your partner's student number, and press **Enter**. This accesses the Web site on your partner's server.

    c. You should see a Web page that echoes back the source IP address and port number your computer used to request the Web page. This confirms that your partner's Web server is functioning properly and is accessible.

    d. Close Internet Explorer.

6. Disable Routing and Remote Access on your server. ICF and RRAS cannot run on the same server.

    a. Click **Start**, point to **Administrative Tools**, and click **Routing and Remote Access**.

    b. Right-click your server, and click **Disable Routing and Remote Access**.

    c. Click **Yes** to continue.

    d. Close the Routing and Remote Access snap-in.

7. Configure ICF with default packet filtering options on your server.

    a. Click **Start**, point to **Control Panel**, point to **Network Connections**, right-click **Classroom**, and click **Properties**.

    b. Click the **Advanced** tab.

    c. Click the **Protect my computer and network by limiting or preventing access to this computer from the Internet** checkbox to select it.

    d. Click **OK**.

8. Test your connectivity with Internet Explorer. Do not perform this step until your partner has completed Step 7.

    a. Click **Start**, point to **All Programs**, and click **Internet Explorer**.

    b. In the Address box, type **http://192.168.1.10**, and press **Enter**. This accesses the Web site on the instructor's server.

    c. You should see a Web page that echoes back the source IP address and port number your computer used to request the Web page. This confirms that your server can create Web connections with other hosts after ICF is enabled.

    d. In the Address box, type **http://192.168.1.10*x***, where *x* is your partner's student number, and press **Enter**. This accesses the Web site on your partner's server.

    e. You get an error message indicating the server could not be contacted. This is because ICF on your partner's server is blocking your requests.

    f. Close Internet Explorer.

9. Configure ICF to allow traffic addressed to port 80 on your server. Do not perform this step until your partner has completed Step 8.

    a. Click **Start**, point to **Control Panel**, point to **Network Connections**, right-click **Classroom**, and click **Properties**.

    b. Click the **Advanced** tab, and click **Settings**.

    c. On the Services tab, double-click **Web Server (HTTP)**.

    d. In the Name or IP address of the computer hosting this service on your network box, type **192.168.1.10*y***, where *y* is your student number. This is the IP address of your server, and allows remote clients to access port 80 on your server.

    e. Click **OK** to save the service settings.

    f. Confirm that the check box beside **Web Server (HTTP)** is selected. If it is not, then click the check box beside **Web Server (HTTP)**.

11

g. Click **OK** to close the Advanced Settings window.

h. Click **OK** to close the Classroom Properties window.

10. Test connectivity to your partner's server with Internet Explorer. Do not perform this step until your partner has completed Step 9.

a. Click **Start**, point to **All Programs**, and click **Internet Explorer**.

b. In the Address box, type **http://192.168.1.10x**, where *x* is your partner's student number, and press **Enter**. This accesses the Web site on your partner's server.

c. You should see a Web page that echoes back the source IP address and port number your computer used to request the Web page. This confirms that your server can create a Web connection with your partner's server after the service is configured.

d. Close Internet Explorer.

11. Disable ICF:

a. Click **Start**, point to **Control Panel**, point to **Network Connections**, right-click **Classroom**, and click **Properties**.

b. Click the **Advanced** tab.

c. Click the **Protect my computer and network by limiting or preventing access to this computer from the Internet** checkbox to deselect it.

d. Click **OK**.

e. Click **Yes** to confirm.

CHAPTER SUMMARY

❑ Windows Server 2003 can be configured as a low-cost router for TCP/IP and AppleTalk. IPX/SPX is not supported.

❑ Static routing requires administrators to configure routing tables. Dynamic routing allows routers to communicate and automatically build routing tables.

❑ RIP is a distance-vector routing algorithm that calculates paths based on hops. If a route is 16 hops away it is considered unreachable. RIP advertises its entire routing table every 30 seconds.

❑ OSPF is a link-state routing algorithm that calculates paths based on a configurable metric called cost. Each interface in a router can be assigned a cost. OSPF only advertises changes to a routing table when they happen. The 64-bit versions of Windows Server 2003 do not support OSPF.

❑ Demand-dial connections are activated only when network traffic requires them. They can also be configured to disconnect after a period of time if there is no more traffic to cross the link.

❑ Static routes are required for demand-dial connections.

❑ Demand-dial connections can be configured with dial-out hours to limit the times they are active. They can also be configured with demand-dial filters to limit the types of traffic that can trigger the connection.

❑ NAT allows many computers to access the Internet using a single Internet-addressable IP address.

❑ NAT functions by modifying the IP headers of packets that are routed through the NAT router. The IP address on the external interface of the NAT router is substituted for the original source IP address.

❑ A DHCP allocator and DNS proxy can be configured as part of NAT.

❑ ICS is an automated way to configure a router for NAT. However, the default settings, such as IP address, cannot be changed.

❑ Network bridging is required with ICS if there is more than one internal interface.

❑ ICF is a stateful packet filter. Rules for ICF are configured using services.

KEY TERMS

cost — In routing, a configurable value assigned to a packet being forwarded through a router interface.

demand-dial filters — Rules that limit the types of traffic that can trigger the activation of a demand-dial connection.

demand-dial — A dial-up/VPN/PPPoE connection that is only activated when required to move network traffic.

DHCP allocator — A simplified DHCP service that can be used by NAT and ICS.

dial-out hours — A limit for demand-dial connections that allows connections only during certain time periods.

distance-vector routing — Any routing algorithm based on simple hop calculation. RIP is the most common example.

DNS proxy — A service that accepts DNS requests from clients and forwards them on to a DNS server.

dynamic routing — When routing tables are automatically generated by routers based on communication with other routers.

hop — In routing, a packet being forwarded by a single router.

Internet Connection Firewall (ICF) — A stateful packet filter that can be used to protect servers connected to the Internet.

Internet Connection Sharing (ICS) — An automated way to implement NAT for a small network.

Internet Security and Acceleration (ISA) server — A firewall and proxy server product from Microsoft.

link-state routing — A routing algorithm where routers use a configurable cost metric to build a picture of the entire network. OSPF is the most common example.

mapping — An entry in the NAT table maintained by the NAT router that provides correlation between the original source IP address and port number, and the port number used on the external interface of the NAT router.

Network Address Translation (NAT) — A protocol used by routers to allow multiple clients to share a single Internet-addressable IP address. IP headers are modified to make the packet look as though it came from the NAT router.

network bridging — A feature that combines two network cards in a server as a single logical network. This can be used to combine two different media types such as UTP and coaxial cabling.

Open Shortest Path First (OSPF) — A link-state routing protocol that calculates paths based on a configurable metric called cost. Changes to the routing table are advertised only when they occur.

Point-to-Point Protocol over Ethernet (PPPoE) — A protocol used for authentication and traffic control on high-speed Internet connections such as DSL.

poison-reverse processing — An option for RIP routing where a router advertises a route as unreachable on the interface from which it was learned.

ROUTE PRINT — A command-line utility used to view the contents of a routing table.

Routing Information Protocol (RIP) — A distance-vector routing protocol that calculates paths based on hops. Complete routing tables are advertised every 30 seconds.

routing table — The list of networks and how to reach them that is maintained by a router.

split-horizon processing — An option for RIP routing where a router is not advertised back on the same interface from which it was learned to prevent routing loops.

stateful firewall — A firewall that tracks TCP connections to automatically allow response packets to return without configuring a rule.

static route — An entry in a routing table that is permanently added by an administrator.

static routing — When routing tables are maintained manually by an administrator.

11

REVIEW QUESTIONS

1. The most likely place you will find Windows Server 2003 used as a router is in large corporations with very complex network routing requirements. True or False?

2. Which type of routing allows routers to automatically build their routing tables?

    a. static routing

    b. manual routing

    c. automatic routing

    d. dynamic routing

3. Which routing protocol announces its entire routing table every 30 seconds?

    a. RIP

    b. SAP

    c. OSPF

    d. AppleTalk

4. How often does OSPF send copies of its entire routing table to other routers?

    a. every 30 seconds

    b. every 60 seconds

    c. every 120 seconds

    d. never

5. What number of hops is considered unreachable for RIP routing?

    a. 8

    b. 16

    c. 32

    d. 64

    e. 128

6. Why would you enable Auto static update mode for RIP?

    a. to permanently keep routes learned from a demand-dial connection

    b. for higher security

    c. to limit the packets that can trigger a demand-dial connection

    d. to limit a demand-dial connection to only certain users

7. When authentication is activated for the RIP protocol, which authentication method is used?

    a. plain text

    b. CHAP

    c. MS-CHAP

    d. MS-CHAPv2

    e. PKI certificates on smart cards

8. Which types of connections can demand-dial be used to activate? (Choose all that apply.)

    a. VPN

    b. dial-up

    c. IPX/SPX

    d. PPPoE

    e. FTP

9. If a user account is created when the Demand-Dial Interface Wizard is run on a member server, where does the account exist?

   a. in Active Directory

   b. on all remote access servers

   c. in the local SAM database

   d. on all DNS servers

10. Which criteria can be used to limit how demand-dial connections are activated? (Choose all that apply.)

    a. time of day

    b. month

    c. type of traffic

    d. user

11. Which protocol passes IP address and port information in the data portion of the packets, but can still commonly be used with NAT?

    a. HTTP

    b. FTP

    c. SMTP

    d. NNTP

12. After an outgoing packet has been translated by a NAT router and sent to the Internet, what is the source IP address?

    a. the IP address of the client that generated the request

    b. the IP address of the internal interface of the NAT router

    c. the IP address of the external interface of the NAT router

13. When an incoming packet is received by the NAT router, what part of the packet determines where it is sent?

    a. source IP address

    b. source port

    c. destination IP address

    d. destination port

14. Services hosted by servers behind a NAT router can never be accessed by hosts on the Internet. True or False?

15. Which two additional services can be configured as part of NAT?

    a. DHCP allocator

    b. WINS proxy

    c. DNS proxy

    d. remote access

16. Which service can combine two physical segments using different media types into a single logical network?

    a. NAT

    b. ICS

    c. network bridging

    d. ICF

    e. AppleTalk

11

17. Which service forces the internal interface of the router to use the IP address 192.168.0.1?

    a. RRAS

    b. NAT

    c. ICS

    d. network bridging

    e. ICF

18. Which service provides a stateful packet filter?

    a. RRAS

    b. NAT

    c. ICS

    d. network bridging

    e. ICF

19. What is configured to add a rule to ICF?

    a. rules

    b. firewall table

    c. states

    d. services

20. What is the name of the log file used by ICF?

    a. FIREWALL.TXT

    b. PFIREWALL.LOG

    c. FILTERLOG.TXT

    d. SUCCESS.LOG and DROPPED.LOG

21. What service, not included with Windows Server 2003, provides caching to speed up Internet access?

    a. Web server

    b. FTP server

    c. Streaming media server

    d. Proxy server

CASE PROJECTS

Case Project 11-1: Hardware Routers vs. Software Routers

As a cost-cutting measure for smaller locations, you have decided to use Windows Server 2003 as a router rather than buying hardware routers. This decision has just been announced to the rest of the IT Department. Some of your colleagues with certifications from hardware router vendors are quite upset and have complained to your supervisor.

Write a report justifying your decision. As part of the report include a list of routing services provided with Windows Server 2003 and where they can be used in Arctic University.

Case Project 11-2: Internet Connectivity

You have been approached by one of the professors at Arctic University to help his small business connect to the Internet. He already has Windows Server 2003. Evaluate whether it would be more appropriate to implement ICS or NAT in this situation.

Case Project 11-3: Sharing IP Addresses

One of your colleagues is concerned about implementing NAT on the campus network. He is worried that once NAT is implemented, none of the services on the internal network will be available to Internet users. Explain how NAT can be configured to allow access to internal services.

11

Glossary

ACK bit — A bit used in TCP communication to indicate that a packet is an acknowledgement of a previous packet.

Active Directory — A directory service for Windows 2000/2003 Servers that stores information about network resources.

Active Directory integrated zone — A DNS zone in which DNS information is stored in Active Directory and supports multimaster updates and increased security.

adapter — The networking component that represents the network interface card and driver.

Address Resolution Protocol (ARP) — A protocol used by hosts to find the physical MAC address of another host with a particular IP address.

address spoofing — The act of falsifying the source IP address in an IP packet, usually for malicious purposes.

aggregatable global unicast addresses — The IPv6 equivalent of IPv4 class A, B, and C addresses. They are designed for future use on the Internet.

aging/scavenging — The process of removing old records from DNS that have not been updated within a set time period.

algorithm — A formula used to process data for encryption or decryption.

anycast address — An IPv6 address that can be assigned to multiple hosts. A packet addressed to an anycast address is delivered to the single closest host that is assigned the anycast address.

AppleTalk — A protocol that is used when communicating with Apple Macintosh computers.

application directory partition — A partition that stores information about objects that is replicated to a set of defined domain controllers within the same forest.

application layer — The layer of the TCP/IP architecture that provides access to network resources.

asymmetrical encryption — An encryption method that uses two different keys. When one key is used to encrypt, the other key must be used to decrypt.

attribute — A characteristic of an object in Active Directory.

Authentication Headers (AH) mode — An IPSec operating mode that digitally signs packets but does not encrypt them.

authentication headers (AH) mode — The IPSec mode that performs authentication and ensures data integrity on the entire IP packet including the headers.

Automatic Private IP Addressing (APIPA) — A feature of newer Windows operating systems that automatically generates an IP address on the 169.254.X.X network when a DHCP server cannot be contacted.

Bandwidth Allocation Protocol (BAP) — A protocol used to dynamically control the number of phone lines multilink uses based on bandwidth utilization.

Berkeley Internet Name Domain (BIND) — A UNIX-based implementation of the Domain Name System created by the University of California at Berkeley.

binary — A base-two numbering system. There are only two valid values for each digit: 0 and 1.

binding — Configuring a network protocol to use a network adapter.

bit — A single binary digit.

Bluetooth — A short-range wireless communication protocol.

bridge — A network component that controls the movement of packets between network segments based on MAC addresses.

broadcast — A packet that is addressed to all computers on a network. A broadcast for the local IP network is addressed to 255.255.255.255.

burst handling — A process used by a WINS server that cannot write name registrations to the WINS database fast enough to keep pace with the number of registrations. The WINS server ceases verifying that the names are not in use before sending out successful name registration requests with a short time to live.

caching-only server — A DNS server that does not store any zone information, but caches DNS queries from clients.

callback — A security enhancement wherein a dial-up user initiates a connection, the connection is dropped, and the server then calls the dial-up client back.

certificate — A part of public key infrastructure that contains a public key and an expiry date. Certificates are presented for authentication and to share public keys.

certificate hierarchy — The structure of trusted certification authorities consisting of a single root CA and possibly subordinate CAs.

Certificate Request Wizard — A wizard used to request certificates from an enterprise certification authority.

Certificate Revocation List (CRL) — A list of certificates that have been revoked before their expiry date.

Certificate Services — A service installed on Windows Server 2003 that allows it to act as a certification authority.

certificate template — A template used by enterprise certification authorities to issue certificates with certain characteristics.

certification authority (CA) — A server that issues certificates.

Challenge Handshake Authentication Protocol (CHAP) — An authentication method that encrypts passwords using a one-way hash, but requires that passwords in Active Directory be stored using reversible encryption.

ciphertext — Data that has been encrypted.

class — A type of object in Active Directory. A class is defined by its attributes.

classful routing — An older style of routing in which routing table entries would be based on class A, B, and C networks with default subnet masks.

classless inter-domain routing (CIDR) — An addressing scheme that uses a defined number of bits for the subnet mask rather than relying on default lengths based on address classes. The number of bits in the network ID is defined as $/XX$ after the IP address. XX is the number of bits.

client — A networking component that is installed in computers requesting network services. Client software communicates with a corresponding service.

cluster — A group of computers that coordinate the provision of services. When one computer in a cluster fails, others take over its services.

collision — When two computers attempt to send a packet on the network at the same time, the signals collide and become unreadable.

COM port — The Windows term for a serial port in a computer.

Common Gateway Interface (CGI) — A vendor-neutral mechanism used to pass information from a Web page to an application running on a Web server.

common language runtime (CLR) — A common component that runs code developed for the .NET framework regardless of the language in which it is written.

conditions — Criteria in a remote access policy, or a connection request policy, that must be met for the policy to be applied.

conflict detection — When in use, a DHCP server pings an IP address before attempting to lease it. This ensures that IP address conflicts do not occur.

Connection Manager Administration Kit (CMAK) — A utility that can be used to configure dial-up and VPN connections on client computers.

connection request policy — A policy used by IAS to determine whether a request is authenticated locally or passed on to a RADIUS server. Such policies are composed of conditions and a profile.

connection-oriented — A term used to describe a protocol that verifies the existence of a host and agrees on terms of communication before sending data.

connectionless — A term used to describe a protocol that does not establish a communication channel before sending data.

cost — In routing, a configurable value assigned to a packet being forwarded through a router interface.

cryptographic service provider (CSP) — Software or hardware that provides cryptographic services.

cryptography — The process of encrypting and decrypting messages and files using an algorithm.

Data Encryption Standard (DES) — An algorithm for data encryption defined by the U.S. government in 1977 that uses a 56-bit key.

Data Link Control (DLC) — A nonroutable protocol originally developed for mainframe computers. It is not supported by Windows Server 2003.

data modification — Modifying the contents of packets that have been captured with a packet sniffer before resending them on the network.

data replay — Resending packets that have been previously captured with a packet sniffer.

DCPROMO — A utility for promoting a member server to a domain controller, or demoting a domain controller to a member server.

debug logging — The processing of logging additional DNS-related events or messages for troubleshooting purposes.

decryption — The process of making encrypted data readable.

default gateway — A dedicated hardware device or computer on a network that is responsible for moving packets from one IP network to another. This is another term for IP router.

demand-dial — A dial-up/VPN/PPPoE connection that is only activated when required to move network traffic.

demand-dial filters — Rules that limit the types of traffic that can trigger the activation of a demand-dial connection.

DHCP allocator — A simplified DHCP service that can be used by NAT and ICS.

DHCP relay — A service that accepts DHCP broadcasts on one subnet and forwards them to a DHCP server on another subnet using unicast packets.

DHCP Relay Agent — A service that forwards DHCP broadcasts from a network to a DHCP server on another network. It is required when DHCP broadcasts need to cross a router.

DHCPACK — The fourth and final packet in the DHCP lease process. This packet is a broadcast from the DHCP server confirming the lease.

DHCPDISCOVER — The first packet in the DHCP lease process. This packet is broadcast on the local network to find a DHCP server.

DHCPINFORM — A DHCP packet sent by Windows 2000 and newer remote access clients to retrieve IP configuration options from a DHCP server.

DHCPNAK — This packet is sent from a DHCP server to a client when it denies a renewal attempt.

DHCPOFFER — The second packet in the DHCP lease process. This packet is a broadcast from the DHCP server to the client with an offered lease.

DHCPRELEASE — This packet is sent from a DHCP client to a DHCP server to indicate it is no longer using a leased IP address.

DHCPREQUEST — The third packet in the DHCP lease process. This packet is a broadcast from the DHCP client indicating which DHCPOFFER has been chosen.

dial-out hours — A limit for demand-dial connections that allows connections only during certain time periods.

dial-up — Connectivity between two computers using modems and a phone line.

digital signature — A process using both hash encryption and asymmetrical encryption that ensures data integrity and nonrepudiation.

distance-vector routing — Any routing algorithm based on simple hop calculation. RIP is the most common example.

DNS proxy — A service that accepts DNS requests from clients and forwards them on to a DNS server.

DNS zone — The part of the domain namespace for which a DNS server is authoritative. Commonly referred to as a "zone."

domain controller — A Windows 2000/2003 server that holds a copy of the Active Directory information for a domain.

domain directory partition — A partition that stores information about objects in a specific domain that is replicated to all domain controllers in the domain.

domain name — The portion of DNS namespace that can be registered and controlled by an organization or individual.

Domain Name System (DNS) — A service used by clients running TCP/IP to resolve hostnames to IP addresses. Active Directory uses DNS to store service location information.

Dynamic DNS — A system in which DNS records are automatically updated by the client or a DHCP server.

Dynamic Host Configuration Protocol (DHCP) — A protocol used to automatically assign IP addressing information to clients.

dynamic routing — When routing tables are automatically generated by routers based on communication with other routers.

Encapsulating Security Payload (ESP) mode — An IPSec operating mode that digitally signs packets and encrypts the contents.

encryption — The process of rendering data unreadable by applying an algorithm.

Enterprise Admins — A default group in Active Directory with administrative rights for the entire forest.

enterprise certification authority — A certification authority that integrates with Active Directory, and can issue certificates without Administrator intervention.

Ethernet — The most common networking standard for network cards, hubs, switches, and routers on local area networks. Variations exist for 10 Mbps, 100 Mbps, 1 Gbps, and 10 Gbps.

EUI-64 addresses — A new standard developed by the IEEE to uniquely identify network interfaces. These will eventually replace MAC addresses.

event logging — The logging of status messages in an event log. This logging is less detailed than debug logging.

exclusion — An IP address or range of IP addresses within a scope that are not leased to clients.

Extensible Authentication Protocol (EAP) — An authentication system that uses EAP types as plug-in authentication modules. This is used for smart cards.

Extensible Markup Language (XML) — A simple text-based mechanism to define content. It uses tags similar to HTML, but unlike HTML, developers can define their own tags.

extinction interval — The period of time unused records exist in the WINS database before being marked as extinct.

extinction timeout — The period of time extinct records exist in the WINS database before being removed.

fault tolerance — Configuring a system in such a way that if a single component fails an alternate can be used.

File Transfer Protocol (FTP) — The protocol used by FTP clients and servers to move files. By default, it uses TCP port 21 for control information and TCP port 20 for data transfer.

forward lookup — The process of resolving a domain name to an IP address.

forward lookup zone — A zone that holds records used for forward lookups. The primary record types contained in these zones are: A records, MX records, and SRV records.

forwarding — The process of sending a DNS lookup request to another DNS server when the local DNS server does not have the requested information.

frame — A packet of information that is being transmitted on the network.

frame type — The format of IPX/SPX packets. Multiple frame types are available and two computers must be using the same frame type to communicate.

Fully Qualified Domain Name (FQDN) — The combination of a hostname and domain name that completely describes the name of a computer within the global DNS system.

global catalog — A subset of attributes of every object in an Active Directory forest. A global catalog holds universal group membership information.

graphical user interface (GUI) — A user interface for an operating system that supports graphics in addition to characters.

Group Policy — An Active Directory-based mechanism to apply centrally defined configuration information out to client computers.

hash encryption — A type of one-way encryption that cannot be decrypted. It is used to store information such as passwords and to create checksums.

hash value — A summary of the data being encrypted using hash encryption.

hop — In routing, a packet being forwarded by a single router.

host ID — The portion of an IP address that uniquely identifies a computer on an IP network.

hostname — The name of a computer using the TCP/IP protocol.

HOSTS — A local text file used to resolve Fully Qualified Domain Names to IP addresses.

Hypertext Transfer Protocol (HTTP) — The protocol used by Web browsers and Web servers. By default, it uses TCP port 80.

Ignore-User-Dialin-Properties — An attribute that can be configured in the profile of a remote access policy that prevents processing of the dial-in properties of a user object in Active Directory.

incremental zone transfer — The process of updating only modified DNS records from a primary DNS server to a secondary DNS server.

Infrared Data Association (IrDA) — A standard for communication using infrared ports in mobile devices. This is also the name of the organization that created the standard.

Institute of Electrical and Electronics Engineers (IEEE) — The organization responsible for maintaining many physical layer protocols used in networks, including Ethernet and Token Ring.

interface identifier — The part of an IPv6 address that uniquely identifies the host on a network. It is equivalent to an IPv4 host ID.

internal network address — A unique eight-character hexadecimal identifier used by Windows computers that are providing IPX/SPX-based services. Services are advertised as available on this network.

Internet Assigned Numbers Authority (IANA) — The organization that maintains standards for Internet addressing, including well-known port numbers and ICMP packet types.

Internet Authentication Service (IAS) — The Microsoft implementation of a RADIUS server. It allows distributed authentication for remote access clients.

Internet Connection Firewall (ICF) — A simple firewall suitable for home use or small offices when connecting to the Internet.

Internet Connection Sharing (ICS) — An automated way to configure DHCP, NAT, and DNS proxy to share a single IP address and configuration information from an ISP.

Internet Control Messaging Protocol (ICMP) — The protocol used by routers and hosts to send Internet protocol error messages.

Internet Group Management Protocol (IGMP) — The protocol used by routers to track the membership in multicast groups.

Internet Information Services (IIS) — A popular suite of Internet services that includes a Web server and FTP server.

Internet Key Exchange (IKE) — A protocol used by IPSec to negotiate security parameters, perform authentication, and ensure the secure exchange of encryption keys.

Internet layer — The layer of the TCP/IP architecture that is responsible for logical addressing and routing.

Internet Message Access Protocol version 4 (IMAP4) — A protocol used to retrieve e-mail messages from an e-mail server. It is more flexible than POP3 for managing message storage.

Internet Protocol version 4 (IPv4) — The IP portion of the TCP/IP protocol suite. Version 4 uses 32-bit addresses expressed in dotted decimal notation. This is the version of IP that is currently used on the Internet.

Internet Protocol version 6 (IPv6) — The IP portion of the TCP/IP protocol suite. An update to IPv4, version 6 uses 128-bit addresses expressed in hexadecimal notation and adds many new features.

Internet Security and Acceleration (ISA) server — A firewall and proxy server product from Microsoft.

Internet Server Application Programmer Interface (ISAPI) — A programmer interface defined by Microsoft for passing information from Web pages to programs running on a Web server.

Internet service provider (ISP) — A company that sells Internet access.

Internetwork Packet eXchange/Sequenced Packet eXchange (IPX/SPX) — The protocol required to communicate with servers running Novell NetWare 4 and earlier.

Intersite Topology Generator (ISTG) — The automatic mechanism that decides how domain information is replicated from one domain controller to others.

IP address — A unique address assigned to each computer with the TCP/IP protocol installed. It is 32 bits long and is composed of a network ID and a host ID.

IP filter list — A list of IP protocols that are affected by a rule in an IPSec policy.

IP Security (IPSec) — A service used with IPv4 to prevent eavesdropping on communication and to prevent data from being modified in transit.

IPSec filter action — Defines what is done to traffic that matches an IP filter list in an IPSec rule.

IPSec policy — A set of rules that defines how packets are treated by IPSec. An IPSec policy must be applied to be in use.

IPSec rule — The combination of an IP filter list and an IPSec filter action.

IPSec Security Monitor snap-in — An MMC snap-in that allows the monitoring of IPSec security associations and configuration.

Itanium — A 64-bit processor family manufactured by Intel.

Kerberos — An authentication protocol designed to authenticate both the client and server using secret-key cryptography.

Kerberos — The preferred authentication method used by Active Directory. It is the simplest authentication method to implement for IPSec if all devices are part of the same Active Directory forest.

key — A number, usually large, to prevent it from being guessed, used in combination with an algorithm to encrypt data.

LAN protocol — A networking protocol required to communicate over a LAN, or over a remote access connection. The same LAN protocol that is used by clients on the LAN must be used by dial-up and VPN clients to access LAN resources remotely.

Layer-Two Tunneling Protocol (L2TP) — A protocol that places packets inside an L2TP packet to move them across an IP-based network. This can be used to move IPX or AppleTalk packets through a network that is not configured to support them.

lease — The length of time a DHCP client computer is allowed to use IP address information from the DHCP server.

Lightweight Directory Access Protocol (LDAP) — A protocol used to look up directory information from a server.

Link Control Protocol (LCP) — An extension to PPP that allows the use of enhancements such as callback.

link-local address — The IPv6 equivalent of an IPv4 APIPA address.

link-state routing — A routing algorithm where routers use a configurable cost metric to build a picture of the entire network. OSPF is the most common example.

Linux — An open source operating system that is very similar to UNIX.

LMHOSTS — A static text file located on the hard drive of NetBIOS clients that is used to resolve NetBIOS names to IP addresses.

load balancing — Splitting network requests between two or more servers to reduce the load on each server.

local area network (LAN) — A group of computers and other devices networked together over a relatively short distance.

location — A dial-up attribute configured in Phone and Modem Options to allow Windows to vary procedures for dialing a connection based on your location.

loopback — Any IP address that begins with 127.*X.X.X.* These addresses represent the local host.

MAC address — A number that uniquely identifies a network node. This address is hard-coded onto the NIC.

mapping — An entry in the NAT table maintained by the NAT router that provides correlation between the original source IP address and port number, and the port number used on the external interface of the NAT router.

member server — A Windows server that is part of a domain but not a domain controller.

Message Digest 5 (MD5) — A hashing algorithm that produces a 128-bit message digest.

Metadirectory Services — A service in Windows that synchronizes Active Directory content with other directories and databases.

Microsoft Challenge Handshake Authentication Protocol (MS-CHAP) — An enhancement to CHAP that allows Active Directory passwords to be stored using nonreversible encryption.

Microsoft Challenge Handshake Authentication Protocol version 2 (MS-CHAPv2) — An authentication method that adds computer authentication and several other enhancements to MS-CHAP. This is the preferred authentication protocol for most remote access connections.

Microsoft Management Console (MMC) — The generic utility used to manage most features and components of Windows Server 2003. Snap-ins are required to give MMC the functionality to manage components.

mobile users — Users that move from one location to another outside of the local network. They require remote access to use network resources.

modem — A hardware device that enables computers to communicate over a phone line. It converts digital signals from the computer to analog signals that can travel on a phone line, and then back to digital format.

modem pool — A group of modems connected to a remote access dial-up server. In high-volume situations it is implemented as specialized hardware.

multicast — A packet that is addressed to a specific group of computers rather than a single computer. Multicast addresses range from 224.0.0.0 to 239.255.255.255.

Multicast Listener Discovery (MLD) — An ICMPv6-based protocol used with IPv6 that replaces IGMP used with IPv4.

multicast scope — A range of multicast IP addresses that are handed out to applications that request them.

multilink — A system for dial-up connections that allows multiple phone lines to be treated as a single logical unit to increase connection speeds.

name query request — A packet from a WINS client to a WINS server requesting the resolution of a NetBIOS name to an IP address.

name query response — A packet from a WINS server to a WINS client in response to a name query request. If the request is successful, this contains the IP address for the NetBIOS name in the original request.

name refresh request — A packet from a WINS client to a WINS server requesting that the registration for a NetBIOS name be renewed.

name refresh response — A packet from a WINS server to a WINS client in response to a name refresh request. If the response is successful, then the TTL of the client lease is extended.

name registration request — A packet generated by a WINS client and sent to a WINS server requesting to register the NetBIOS name and IP address.

name release request — A packet sent from a WINS client to a WINS server when the WINS client shuts down.

name release response — A packet from a WINS server to a WINS client in response to a name release request. This packet contains the NetBIOS name being released and a TTL of zero.

native mode — A domain that can only have Windows 2000 and Windows Server 2003 domain controllers.

Neighbor Solicitation — An ICMPv6 packet used with IPv6 in place of ARP used with IPv4. This is a multicast packet.

.NET Framework — A new development system from Microsoft that uses a common language runtime. This makes programming objects language independent.

NetBIOS Enhanced User Interface (NetBEUI) — A nonroutable protocol commonly used in smaller Windows networks. It is not supported by Windows Server 2003.

NetBIOS name cache — The file in which the results of Windows client NetBIOS name resolutions are stored for a short period of time. The storage of these resolutions increases network performance by reducing the number of name resolutions on the network.

NetBIOS name server — A server that holds a centralized repository of NetBIOS name information. The Microsoft implementation of a NetBIOS name server is WINS.

Netscape Server Application Programmer Interface (NSAPI) — A programmer interface defined by Netscape to pass information from Web pages to applications running on a Web server.

NETSH — A command-line utility that can be used to manage many IP configuration settings and IP services.

NetWare — A network operating system from Novell that traditionally uses the IPX/SPX protocol.

network adapter — In Windows networking this represents the network interface card and the driver that goes with it.

Network Address Translation (NAT) — A protocol used by routers to allow multiple clients to share a single Internet-addressable IP address. IP headers are modified to make the packet look as though it came from the NAT router.

network basic input/output system (NetBIOS) — An older interface used by programmers to access network resources.

network bridging — A feature that combines two network cards in a server as a single logical network. This can be used to combine two different media types such as UTP and coaxial cabling.

Network Device Interface Specification (NDIS) — An interface for developers that resides between protocols and adapters. It controls the bindings between protocols and adapters.

network ID — The portion of an IP address that designates the network on which a computer resides. This is defined by the subnet mask.

network interface layer — The layer of the TCP/IP architecture that controls placing packets on the physical network media.

network operating system (NOS) — An operating system that is optimized to act as a server rather than a client.

Non-Uniform Memory Access (NUMA) — A memory architecture for servers with multiple processors. It adds a third level of cache memory on motherboards.

NSLOOKUP — A command prompt-based utility for troubleshooting DNS.

NWLink — An IPX/SPX-compatible protocol created by Microsoft for Windows operating systems.

Oakley logs — A type of logging that tracks the establishment of security associations.

object — An item within Active Directory. An example would be a user or a computer.

octet — A group of eight bits. An IP address is composed of four octets, with each expressed as a decimal number.

Open Shortest Path First (OSPF) — A link-state routing protocol that calculates paths based on a configurable metric called cost. Changes to the routing table are advertised only when they occur.

Open Shortest Path First (OSPF) — A protocol that is used by routers to share information about known networks and calculate the best path through an internetwork. OSPF calculates routes based on user definable cost values.

Open Systems Interconnection (OSI) reference model — An industry standard that is used as a reference point to compare different networking technologies and protocols.

packet — A single unit of data sent from one computer to another. It contains a source address, destination address, data, and error-checking information.

packet filters — Rules that control the forwarding of packets through a firewall based on IP address, port number, and packet type.

packet header — The first few bytes of a packet that contain the source address, destination address, and other information.

packet sniffer — Software used to view (capture) all packets that are traveling on a network.

Password Authentication Protocol (PAP) — An authentication method that transmits passwords in clear text.

persistent connection — A connection that is created once and maintained over time for data transfer. This reduces communication overhead by reducing the number of packets used to establish connections over time.

ping — A utility used to test connectivity by sending an ICMP Reply Request packet.

Point-to-Point Protocol (PPP) — The most common remote access protocol used for dial-up connections. It supports the use of TCP/IP, IPX/SPX, and AppleTalk for remote access.

Point-to-Point Protocol over Ethernet (PPPoE) — A protocol used by some high-speed ISPs to authenticate and control IP traffic on their network.

Point-to-Point Tunneling Protocol (PPTP) — A protocol that can be used to provide VPN connectivity between a Windows client and VPN server. PPTP is supported by Windows 95 and later.

poison-reverse processing — An option for RIP routing where a router advertises a route as unreachable on the interface from which it was learned.

port — A TCP port or UDP port is used by transport layer protocols to direct network information to the proper service.

Post Office Protocol version 3 (POP3) — A protocol that is used to retrieve e-mail messages from an e-mail server.

preshared key — An IPSec authentication method where each device is preconfigured with a string of text.

primary zone — A zone that is authoritative for the specific DNS zone. Updates can only be made in the primary zone. There is only one primary zone per domain name.

private key — The key in asymmetrical encryption that is seen only by the user to which it is issued.

profile — The part of a remote access policy, or connection request policy, that contains settings that are applied to the connection.

protocol — The language that two computers use to communicate on a network. Two computers must use the same protocol to communicate.

proxy server — A server that can be used to control and speed up access to the Internet. It also allows multiple computers to access the Internet through a single IP address.

public key — The key in asymmetrical encryption that is freely distributed to other users.

public key infrastructure (PKI) — The system that supports the issuance and management of certificates, public keys, and private keys.

pull replication — Replication between two WINS servers triggered by a defined amount of time passing.

push replication — Replication between two WINS servers triggered by a defined number of changes in the WINS database.

RADIUS client — A server or device that passes authentication requests to a RADIUS proxy or RADIUS server. Most commonly, these are remote access servers.

RADIUS proxy — An intelligent server that acts as an intermediary between RADIUS clients and RADIUS servers. This server decides which RADIUS server should be used to authenticate a request.

RADIUS server — A server in the RADIUS process that accepts and authorizes authentication requests from RADIUS clients and RADIUS proxies.

recursive lookup — A DNS query that is resolved through other DNS servers until the requested information is located.

registrar — A company accredited by ICANN who has the right to distribute and register domain names.

remote access — Accessing network resources from a location away from the physical network. Connections can be made using a dial-up connection or a VPN.

Remote Access Dial-In User Authentication Service (RADIUS) — A service that allows remote access servers (RADIUS clients) to delegate responsibility for authentication to a central server (RADIUS server).

remote access permissions — The part of a remote access policy that defines whether the policy denies remote access or grants remote access.

remote access policies — Policies configured on remote access servers to control how remote access connections are created. They are composed of conditions, remote access permissions, and a profile.

remote access protocol — A protocol that is required for dial-up remote access. PPP is the most common remote access protocol.

Remote Installation Services (RIS) — A service in Windows that automates the installation of Windows 2000 Professional or Windows XP Professional on client workstations.

remote RADIUS server group — A grouping of RADIUS servers to which IAS forwards connection requests when acting as a RADIUS proxy. Load balancing and fault tolerance can be configured.

renewal interval — The time to live handed out to WINS clients when they register NetBIOS names.

replication partners — Two WINS servers that synchronize information in their databases.

Request For Comment (RFC) — A submission to the Internet Engineering Task Force that is evaluated for use as part of the TCP/IP protocol suite.

reservation — A DHCP IP address that is leased only to a computer with a specific MAC address.

Resultant Set of Policy (RSoP) snap-in — An MMC snap-in that is used to troubleshoot the implementation of Group Policies.

reverse lookup — The process of resolving an IP address to a domain name.

reverse lookup zone — A zone that contains records used for reverse lookups. The primary record type in these zones is PTR records.

root certification authority — The first CA in the certificate hierarchy. Clients trusting this CA trust certificates issued by this CA and all subordinate CAs.

root hints — The list of root servers that is used by DNS servers to perform forward lookups on the Internet.

root servers — A group of 13 DNS servers on the Internet that are authoritative for the top-level domain names such as .com, .edu, and .org.

round robin DNS — The process of creating multiple IP addresses for a specific hostname for fault tolerance and load balancing.

ROUTE PRINT — A command-line utility used to view the contents of a routing table.

router — A network device that forwards packets from one network to another. TCP/IP, IPX/SPX, and AppleTalk can be routed.

Routing and Remote Access Service (RRAS) — A service that allows Windows Server 2003 to act as a router or remote access server.

Routing Information Protocol (RIP) — A protocol used by routers to exchange routing table information and determine the best path through an internetwork based on the number of hops.

routing table — The list of networks and how to reach them that is maintained by a router.

schema — The list of definitions that defines classes and attributes supported by Active Directory.

scope — A range of addresses that are leased by a DHCP server.

secondary zone — A DNS zone that stores a read-only copy of the DNS information from a primary zone. There can be multiple secondary zones.

Secure Hashing Algorithm (SHA1) — A hashing algorithm that produces a 160-bit message digest.

Secure Sockets Layer (SSL) — A Transport layer protocol that encrypts data communication between a client and service. Both the client and service must be written to support SSL.

security association (SA) — The security terms negotiated between two hosts using IPSec.

Serial Line Internet Protocol (SLIP) — An older remote access protocol that only supports using TCP/IP as a LAN protocol. It is used by Windows Server 2003 only when acting as a client.

service — A networking component that provides resources to network clients. Each service communicates with corresponding client software.

Service Advertising Protocol (SAP) — A protocol used by IPX/SPX to advertise the availability of services by sending out a broadcast message every 60 seconds.

Services for Macintosh — A service that allows Macintosh clients to access file and print services on Windows servers.

Shiva Password Authentication Protocol (SPAP) — An authentication method that uses reversible encryption when transmitting passwords.

Simple Mail Transfer Protocol (SMTP) — A protocol used by e-mail clients to send messages to e-mail servers. It uses TCP port 25.

Simple Object Access Protocol (SOAP) — A standardized mechanism to access Web services using HTTP.

site-local address — The IPv6 equivalent of an IPv4 internal network address such as 10.0.0.0/8.

sliding window — A process used in the TCP protocol to track which packets have been received by the destination host.

snap-in — A software component that is used with MMC to manage features and components of Windows Server 2003. Each snap-in manages a single component such as DHCP or DNS.

split-horizon processing — An option for RIP routing where a router is not advertised back on the same interface from which it was learned to prevent routing loops.

stand-alone certification authority — A certification authority that does not integrate with Active Directory, and requires an Administrator to approve certificate requests.

stand-alone server — A Windows server that is not a member of a domain.

Start of Authority (SOA) record — A DNS record that defines which DNS server is authoritative for that particular domain and defines the characteristics for the zone.

stateful firewall — A firewall that tracks TCP connections to automatically allow response packets to return without configuring a rule.

static mapping — An entry manually placed in the WINS database. These are normally created for servers providing NetBIOS services that are unable to use WINS.

static route — An entry in a routing table that is permanently added by an administrator.

static routing — When routing tables are maintained manually by an administrator.

stub zone — A DNS zone that stores only the NS records for a particular zone. When a client requests a DNS lookup, the request is then forwarded to the DNS server specified by the NS records.

subnet mask — A string of 32 bits that is used to define which portion of an IP address is the host ID and which part is the network ID.

subnetting — The process of dividing a single IP network into several smaller IP networks. Bits are taken from the host ID and made part of the network ID by adjusting the subnet mask.

subordinate certification authority — A certification authority that has been authorized by a root CA or another subordinate CA.

supernetting — The process of combining several smaller networks into a single large network by taking bits from the network ID and making them part of the host ID.

superscope — A logical grouping of scopes that is used to service network segments with more than one subnet in use.

symmetrical encryption — Encryption that uses the same key to encrypt and decrypt data.

SYN bit — A bit used in TCP communication to indicate a request to start a communication session.

Telnet — A protocol used to remotely access a command-line interface on Unix and Linux servers.

Terminal Services — A service that lets users access Windows applications running on a remote server. The client software appears as a remote desktop.

Time to Live (TTL) — A parameter of IP packets used to ensure that if a packet becomes trapped in a router loop, it will expire. Each hop through a router reduces TTL by one.

timed lease — An IP address and configuration option given to a client computer from a DHCP server for a limited period of time.

Token Ring — An older physical layer protocol developed by IBM that operated at either 4 Mbps or 16 Mbps.

tombstoned — The term used to describe a WINS record that has been marked for deletion from all WINS servers. The tombstoned status is replicated among all WINS servers.

top-level domain — The broadest category of names in the DNS hierarchy under which all domain names fit. Some top-level domains include .com, .edu, and .gov.

Transmission Control Protocol (TCP) — A connection-oriented and reliable transport layer protocol that is part of the TCP/IP protocol suite.

Transmission Control Protocol/Internet Protocol (TCP/IP) — A suite of protocols that allows interconnected networks to communicate with one another. It is the most common protocol in Windows networking and must be used to access the Internet.

Transport Device Interface (TDI) — A software layer that exists between client or service software and protocols. Clients and services use this layer to access network resources.

transport layer — The layer of the TCP/IP architecture that breaks messages into smaller packets and tracks their delivery.

transport mode — The IPSec mode used when two hosts create a security association directly between them.

Triple Data Encryption Standard (3DES) — A data encryption algorithm that uses three 56-bit keys in three rounds to give an effective key length of 168 bits.

trust — The configuration of a domain to allow access to resources by users from a trusted domain.

trusted root certification authority — A CA from which a client or application accepts certificates.

tunnel endpoint — In tunnel mode, this is the other end of the tunnel with the local host.

tunnel mode — The IPSec mode used when two routers encapsulate all traffic transferred between two or more networks.

unicast addresses — IP addresses that are assigned to a single host.

Universal Description, Discovery, and Integration (UDDI) — A worldwide database of businesses and the Web services that they offer.

user class — An identifier from the DHCP client that is sent as part of the DHCP lease process. This can be set manually by the administrator on workstations.

User Datagram Protocol (UDP) — A connectionless, unreliable transport layer protocol used in the TCP/IP protocol suite.

v.90 — A standard for modems that allows downloads at 56 Kbps and uploads at 33.6 Kbps.

v.92 — A standard for modems that allows downloads at 56 Kbps and uploads at 48 Kbps.

vendor class — An identifier from the DHCP client that is sent as part of the DHCP lease process. This is based on the operating system in use.

verification interval — The period of time a WINS server waits before validating a record that has been replicated from another WINS server.

Virtual Private Network (VPN) — Encrypted communication across a public network.

Web Digital Authoring and Versioning (WebDAV) — A protocol that allows documents to be shared using HTTP.

Web service — A platform-independent service that is available across the Internet or an IP network.

Web Services Description Language (WSDL) — A standardized, XML-formatted mechanism to describe Web services. WSDL is used by UDDI to describe available services.

wide area network (WAN) — Geographically dispersed networks with more than one physical location. The links between each location are relatively slow compared to local area networks.

Windows Internet Naming Service (WINS) — A Windows service used to resolve NetBIOS names to IP addresses as well as store NetBIOS service information.

Windows Media Services — A service that provides streaming audio and video to clients.

Windows Sockets (WinSock) — A programming interface used by developers to access TCP/IP based services.

Windows Sockets Direct (WinSock Direct) — An extension of the WinSock programming interface that allows developers to access resources on a system area network.

WINS proxy — A service that forwards local broadcast NetBIOS requests to a WINS server. This is implemented for NetBIOS clients that are unable to use WINS.

wireless LAN — A standard for wireless communication created by the IEEE. The most common variant of wireless LAN is 802.11b.

X.509 — A standard for certificates that was created by the International Telecommunications Union – Telecommunication (ITU-T).

zone transfer — The process of updating DNS records from a primary DNS server to a secondary DNS server.

Index

IPSec policy rules and, 216
overview, 209
security parameters using, 210
summary, 228
twisted-pair (Cat 5e) Ethernet cable, 62

U

UDDI (Universal Description, Discovery, and IntegrationI), 2, 14
UDP (User Datagram Protocol)
capturing UDP packets in Network Monitor, 55–56
comparison with TCP, 57
defined, 63, 64
IP Filter Lists and, 219
IP filter lists and, 220
location in TCP/IP model, 48
using UDP port numbers, 52
unauthorized servers, 90, 91, 107
UNC paths and NetBIOS, 156
unencrypted communications, allowing, 222–223
unicast
defined, 42
global, 40
global addresses, 31
IPv6 and IPv4 address equivalency, 31
name registration request packets, 158
network number for routing unicast addresses, 32
packets and WINS communication, 157
Universal Description, Discovery, and Integration (UDDI), 2
UNIX
clients and WINS proxy, 171
remote access servers, 241
remote connecting with Telnet, 50
standard for DNS implementation on, 120
upgrade problems, 45
uploading/downloading files, 49
user accounts
anonymity, 32
authentication, 198
certificate templates, 192
classes, 102, 103, 109, 110
configurations for demand-dial connections, 301, 302
User Datagram Protocol (UDP). see UDP (User Datagram Protocol)
utilities
CERTUTIL utility, 191
CHECKV4.EXE, 63
CHECKV4.EXE utility, 63
DCPROMO utility, 121, 150

IPCONFIG utility, 28–29, 281
MMC (Microsoft Management Console) utility, 2, 12, 130
NETSH command-line utility, 2, 63, 92, 110, 227
NSLOOKUP utility, 147–149, 150
ping utility. see ping utility
tracert utility, 211
utility servers, WS 2003 Web Edition and, 3

V

v.90 standard (ITU-T) for modems, 234, 283
v.92 standard (ITU-T) for modems, 234, 284
vendor classes
client computers and, 109
configuration with NETSH, 227
defined, 110
networking devices, identification of, 32
operating systems and, 102
setting options for, 102–103
vendors
popularity of IPSec with, 206
support of TCP/IP by, 20
verification interval (WINS), 173
VeriSign certification authority, 184
Virtual Private Network (VPN). see VPN (Virtual Private Network)
Visual Basic language, 2
Volume Shadow Copy, backup and, 3
VPN (Virtual Private Network). see also remote access
authentication for, 245
broadcast name resolution and, 250
client access permission, 254–256
compared to dial-up, 235, 243
configuration of client connection, 258–260
configuration of IP address of server, 258
connectivity with L2TP/IPSec, 259, 281
connectivity with PPTP, 12, 281
creating client connections, 256–258
defined, 14, 284
demand-dial connections for, 300, 301, 303–304, 305
encryption and, 14, 234
firewall protection for, 3
hackers and, 248
ICF (Internet Connection Firewall) for client connections, 260

icon placed in system tray, 258
initiating VPN connections with demand-dial, 299
Internet Connection Firewall (ICF) for client connections, 260
Internet used as, 234
IP address assignments for, 249
IP address leasing from a DCHP server, 245
IPSec and, 207, 248, 258
IPSec policies and, 249
L2TP and, 246–248, 259
logging control, 250, 251
NAT and, 248
network configuration for client connections, 259–260
New Connection Wizard and, 256, 258
overview, 234–235
packet filters, 245
ports, 246–247
PPP connections tracking, 250
PPTP and, 246–248, 259
preshared key configuration for L2TP/IPSec connections, 258
protocols for, 241, 246–249
RADIUS and, 270
Routing and Remote Access Server Setup Wizard, 243–244
RRAS and, 12
security options for client connections, 258
server, configuring RRAS as a, 235
server, enabling and configuring, 243–249
server, enabling RRAS as a, 245–246
server used as router for IP, 249
server, WS 2003 acting as, 9
servers, RADIUS server option for, 245
servers with multiple network cards and, 245
static IP addresses for clients, 245
traffic control configurations for remote access profile, 262
WINS server and name resolution, 250
WS 2003 Standard Edition and, 4
WS 2003 Web Edition and, 4

W

W3C (World Wide Web consortium), 49
WANs (wide area networks), 34, 42, 161
Web
browsers, 182, 184, 185
pages accessed through IIS, 194
servers, 49, 182, 192, 194
site security, 10